LIBRARY/NEW ENGLAND INST. OF TECHNOLOGY

3 0147 1002 4556 5

BR 1641 .J83 W43 2004

Weber,

P9-ARY-476

New England Institute
of Technology
Library

ON THE ROAD TO ARMAGEDDON

ON THE **ROAD**
TO **ARMAGEDDON**

HOW EVANGELICALS
BECAME ISRAEL'S BEST FRIEND

TIMOTHY P. WEBER

NEW ENGLAND INSTITUTE OF TECHNOLOGY
LIBRARY

Baker Academic
Grand Rapids, Michigan

8/04

54073671

© 2004 by Timothy P. Weber

Published by Baker Academic
a division of Baker Publishing Group
P.O. Box 6287, Grand Rapids, MI 49516-6287
www.bakeracademic.com

Printed in the United States of America

All rights reserved. No part of this publication may be reproduced, stored in a retrieval system, or transmitted in any form or by any means—for example, electronic, photocopy, recording—without the prior written permission of the publisher. The only exception is brief quotations in printed reviews.

Library of Congress Cataloging-in-Publication Data
Weber, Timothy P.
    On the road to Armageddon : how evangelicals became Israel's best friend / Timothy P. Weber.
        p.   cm.
    Includes bibliographical references and index.
    ISBN 0-8010-2577-X (cloth)
    1. Evangelicalism—Relations—Judaism. 2. Judaism—Relations—Evangelicalism. I. Title.
    BR1641.J83W43 2004
    277.3′0825—dc22   2004001041

Unless otherwise indicated, Scripture quotations are from the King James Version of the Bible.

Contents

Preface

This book took a long time to write and a long time to stop writing. The story of the important friendship between dispensationalists and Israel is far from finished. As I wrote, it seemed that every day brought a new idea and a new example of what I was trying to prove. The tragedy of the Middle East will be with us for a long time to come. But every book must end sometime, including this one. Most of this book was written during a sabbatical from my duties as dean at Northern Baptist Theological Seminary in Lombard, Illinois. I am grateful to the trustees at Northern for approving my time off and to my colleagues, who carried on while their dean was nowhere to be found. The book was finished in my first few weeks as president of Memphis Theological Seminary, where new colleagues and responsibilities other than book writing now beckon. As always I have my family to thank for the time and encouragement they gave me to finish this project: Jonathan and Michael, who had their own college papers to write, and Linda, who remains the best thing that has ever happened to me.

Introduction

Millions of Americans believe that the Bible predicts the future and that we are living in the last days. With the Bible in one hand and the newspaper in the other, they look for signs of the times that point to the second coming of Jesus Christ and the end of the world. Their beliefs are rooted in dispensationalism, a particular way of understanding the Bible's prophetic passages, especially those in Daniel and Ezekiel in the Old Testament and the Book of Revelation in the New Testament. Dispensationalists interpret Bible prophecy more or less literally and put prophetic texts together in complex ways. They make up about one-third of America's forty or fifty million evangelical Christians and believe firmly that the nation of Israel will play a central role in the unfolding of end-times events. This book tells the story of how dispensationalist evangelicals became Israel's best friends in the last part of the twentieth century and what difference that friendship has made in recent times.

Entering the World of Christian Millennialism

Dispensationalism is one version of Christian eschatology, the study of last things. In the broadest sense of the term, eschatology includes what happens after death, how the world will end, the inevitability of divine judgment, and the ultimate destination of humanity in either heaven or hell. Throughout Christian history, many believers have been especially interested in the end of human history and whether there will be a golden age of peace connected to the second coming of Christ. Such speculation is rooted in a prophetic passage in the last book of

9

the Bible (Revelation 20) that predicts a time when Christ will return to earth, defeat Satan and his minions, and establish a kingdom on the earth that will last for a thousand years—a millennium (from the Latin for "one thousand," *mille*).

Given the passage's abundant use of apocalyptic and what many believe is figurative language, Christians have interpreted it in vastly different ways. Most early Christians interpreted the passage quite literally and believed that the millennial age would follow Christ's return. Accordingly, they are called *pre*millennialists, since they place the second coming *before* the millennium. Thanks especially to Augustine's *City of God* in the fifth century, most Christians have understood Revelation 20 in more figurative terms. They believe that the "millennium" actually began with Christ's resurrection and can be seen in the church (or in heaven), where it will expand until the end of time and Christ's return. Because they deny that a distinct millennial age will encompass the entire world, they are known as *a*millennialists (in Greek, placing an alpha ["a"] in front of a word negates it). Still other Christians conclude that Jesus' second coming will follow the world's conversion to Christ and its transformation into a Christian golden age. Because they place Christ's return *after* the millennium, they are called *post*millennialists.

Even within these categories there are differences. Most modern scholars and even some millennialists read Revelation in *preterist* terms, that is, they believe the book was written to reflect late first- or early second-century conditions and to bring hope and resolve to people undergoing persecution. Most millennialists, on the other hand, divide into two major camps. *Historicists* believe that Revelation presents a prophetic overview of the entire sweep of church history, while *futurists* believe that its prophecies refer to events that will occur at the very end of the present age, just before Christ's return. A core sample of convictions from almost anywhere in Christian history reveals millennialist teachings in one form or another and in varying degrees of intensity and detail.[1] Of all the groups mentioned above, futurist premillennialists have been most interested in developing elaborate end-times scenarios that contain the following: a crescendo of natural disasters, an increase in persecution of and apostasy among God's people, the rise of the Antichrist and the accompanying great tribulation, wars and rumors of wars that culminate in the battle of Armageddon, and the dramatic return of Jesus to defeat Satan and establish his millennial kingdom. Such notions are the mainstays of countless preachers, teachers, and televangelists. Even people outside the dispensationalist subculture have an inkling of what they are and how they might impact the future.

According to historian Paul Boyer,[2] dispensationalists are not the only people in contemporary America influenced by what he calls "prophecy belief." During times of turmoil and world crisis, many people who ordinarily do not pay the Bible any mind are attentive to Bible teachers who use "signs of the times" to explain where history is headed. In a recent *Time*/CNN poll, more than one-third of Americans said that since the terrorist attacks of 9/11, they have been thinking more about how current events might be leading to the end of the world. While only 36 percent of all Americans believe that the Bible is God's Word and should be taken literally, 59 percent say they believe that events predicted in the Book of Revelation will come to pass. Almost one out of four Americans believes that 9/11 was predicted in the Bible, and nearly one in five believes that he or she will live long enough to see the end of the world. Even more significant for this study, over one-third of those Americans who support Israel report that they do so because they believe the Bible teaches that the Jews must possess their own country in the Holy Land before Jesus can return.[3] This book is about them.

Millennialist Groups in America

The dispensationalists who are the subject of this book are in a long line of Americans who have used Bible prophecy to make sense of the times in which they lived. In the colonial period, Puritan leaders such as John Cotton and Increase and Cotton Mather called the Roman papacy the Antichrist and believed that their own "errand into the wilderness" in the New World had prophetic significance. In the 1740s, Jonathan Edwards viewed the First Great Awakening as the first step in the world's complete Christianization and taught a postmillennial second coming. During the American Revolution, many Christian preachers and patriots identified King George III as the biblical Antichrist and the rebellious colonies as the persecuted "woman in the wilderness" of Revelation 12. Shortly thereafter, many worried Americans, such as Timothy Dwight of Yale College, understood the French Revolution in apocalyptic terms and feared that its excesses would eventually drag the rest of the world to its prophesied destruction. In the years between the American Revolution and the Civil War, most evangelical Protestants adopted postmillennialism's more optimistic view of the future. Revivalists such as Lyman Beecher and Charles Finney viewed the Second Great Awakening and the social reforms that the revivals produced as harbingers of the millennium.[4]

Other nineteenth-century Christians used millennialist ideas to establish their own rather distinctive movements. Mother Ann Lee founded the United Society of Believers in Christ's Second Coming, whose members were better known as the Shakers because of their worship practices. The Shakers believed that Mother Ann Lee was the female incarnation of Christ's second coming and that they needed to prepare for the coming millennium by setting up their own communities in which men and women lived mostly apart and never had sex.[5]

Taking a somewhat different approach was John Humphrey Noyes, a Finney convert who believed that Christ had actually returned to earth in A.D. 70 but had decided not to set up his millennial kingdom because his followers lacked sufficient levels of Christian love. To correct the deficit, Noyes started his own commune in Putney, Vermont, where he and his followers could perfect Noyes's idea of "complex marriage," according to which members of the community could have sex with one another's spouses under Noyes's approval and direction. Of course, such unorthodox expressions of Christian love scandalized the group's neighbors, who forced the commune to move to Oneida, New York. Eventually, the burdensome complications of Noyes's sexual politics led the community to put more energy into commercial development than sexual expression or millennialist speculation.[6]

A more successful millennialist group was the Church of Jesus Christ of Latter-day Saints. After a series of divine revelations, which included the translation of the Book of Mormon, Joseph Smith declared the imminent return of Christ and ordered the relocation of the saints to Jackson County, Missouri, where the New Jerusalem would be built. The Mormons' neighbors were not eager to have them, however, and after a period of violent opposition, in the late 1830s, the Mormons left Missouri for Nauvoo, Illinois. There the prophet had less to say about the second coming than he did his new teachings on the plurality of wives and gods. After the murder of the prophet in the mid-1840s, the Mormons followed their new leader, Brigham Young, to a temporary Zion in Utah, where they still await a new prophet's order to return to Jackson County in anticipation of Jesus' return.[7]

About the same time the Mormons were organizing, William Miller, a Baptist preacher from Vermont, began teaching his brand of historicist premillennialism. Using what he called "millennial arithmetic" on prophetic passages in Daniel, Miller calculated Christ's return in 1843 or 1844. Because time was short, the Millerites turned their backs on all postmillennialist projects for Christianizing the world and began their own intense campaign to advertise what they called the "advent near" and to evangelize their neighbors. Miller eventually pinpointed October 22, 1844, as the date for the second coming. When Christ did not appear, the Millerites experienced their "Great Disappointment." Many Millerites accepted Ellen G. White's explanation: Jesus did not return to earth because believers were not worshiping on Saturday, the Sabbath. In response, they formed the Seventh-day Adventist Church, in which the faithful worshiped on Saturday, promoted vegetarianism, and practiced pacifism.[8]

Following the Civil War, most evangelicals maintained their post-millennial perspective,[9] but new premillennialist groups challenged the majority view. In the 1870s, Charles Taze Russell organized his "Bible Students" into a new prophetic movement that became known as the Jehovah's Witnesses. In 1879, he began publishing his *Watchtower* magazine, which in time evolved into the Watchtower Bible and Tract Society. In his book *Millennial Dawn* (1886), Russell taught that Christ had returned invisibly to earth in 1874 and that the kingdom of God would be established on earth in 1914. As everyone eventually learned, however, 1914 brought a world war, not a new millennium. Russell's successor, Joseph F. Rutherford, later argued that Christ had in fact made another invisible return to earth in 1914 in anticipation of an imminent destruction of the present world order and the creation of a new earthly paradise. In light of the coming judgment, Rutherford ordered his followers to separate themselves from evil "Babylon," which included the world's politics, commerce, and religion. He called them to enter a "theocracy" characterized by, among other things, fervent door-to-door evangelism, a refusal to salute the American flag or have blood transfusions, and a theology that denied the Trinity and taught conditional immortality. Despite occasional fierce opposition, the Jehovah's Witnesses held firm to their belief that the world's judgment was imminent and that they would live forever in an earthly paradise.[10]

Another premillennialist movement that emerged in the 1870s was dispensationalism, which actually originated four decades earlier in Great Britain in the teachings of John Nelson Darby, a disgruntled priest from the Anglican Church of Ireland. For the most part, Darby followed the futurist premillennialism that was popular in the newly organized Plymouth Brethren, but he added some new features, including the belief that the church will be "raptured" before the arrival of the Antichrist and the start of the tribulation. Darby made a number of preaching tours of the United States during the 1870s and won over some leading evangelical pastors and teachers. The new premillennialism spread through Bible conferences, Bible institutes, an elaborate publishing network, and *The Scofield Reference Bible* (1909). By World War I, dispensationalism had become nearly synonymous with fundamentalism and Pentecostalism. At the center of the dispensational system was the belief that before any of the prophesied end-times events could take place, Jews would have to reestablish their own state in the Holy Land. Without a restored Jewish state, there could be no Antichrist, no great tribulation, no battle of Armageddon, and no second coming. In short, everything was riding on the Jews.

Millennialist groups made headlines in the twentieth century when, in 1993, a confrontation between federal agents and the Branch Davidians near Waco, Texas, turned deadly. In 1929, after he became convinced that the Seventh-day Adventist Church had compromised its commitment to holiness, Victor Houteff founded the Davidians, who settled near Waco in 1935 and established a thriving religious commune called Mount Carmel. When Houteff died in 1955, his wife, Florence, succeeded him, but she lost credibility when she predicted Christ's return in 1959. By then Ben Roden had established a new group called the Branch Davidians. Roden saw great prophetic significance in the founding of Israel in 1948 and its expansion in the Six-Day War of 1967. Roden's group managed to get control of Mount Carmel, but he died before he could rebuild the temple in Jerusalem as he had predicted. Lois Roden succeeded her husband as the leader of the Branch Davidians and befriended a new convert named Vernon Howell. After only a few years in the movement, he assumed control in 1987, then changed his name to David Koresh. He was able to gain and then hold leadership through his marathon Bible studies, in which he demonstrated how to systematize all Bible prophecy. Even more important to his followers was his assertion that God had given him the ability to unlock the seven seals of the scroll described in Revelation 5. He also claimed to be one of many Christs, insisted that females at Mount Carmel have sex only with him so that the children of the coming kingdom would be his literal offspring, and warned that the kingdom would come only through violence. It was the latter emphasis that led federal agents to seek his arrest on illegal weapons charges. The ensuing standoff lasted for months and ended with the death of roughly eighty Branch Davidians, including Koresh, when a fire started during the federal assault burned Mount Carmel to the ground.[11]

In 1997, thirty-nine members of Heaven's Gate, a San Diego–based New Age millennialist movement, committed suicide. Their leader, Marshall Applewhite, combined elements from New Age philosophy, astrology, and Christian millennialism to teach that an imminent judgment was coming and that escape to another, better world was possible. He said that the "Harvest Time—the Last Days—the Second Coming" were just around the corner. To attain the coming millennium, people needed to evacuate this terrestrial plane, leaving behind everything, including their "containers," or bodies. In this way, they could rise to the "Evolutionary Level Above Human." Applewhite convinced his followers that the approaching Hale-Bopp Comet would bring spaceships to take their spirits to this heavenly kingdom of God. To expedite their travel to the next level of existence, people in the Heaven's Gate community voluntarily took a lethal mixture of drugs and alcohol.[12]

This Book in a Nutshell

Unlike some of the people named above, dispensationalists never established religious communes, followed a distinctive diet, experimented with sex, or deviated far from the canons of Christian orthodoxy. Though they fine-tuned their prophetic interpretations as needed over time, they retained their core belief about the role of Jews in the last days. For over one hundred years, their insistence on the restoration of the Jewish state in the Holy Land seemed far-fetched and extremely unlikely. But in the middle of the twentieth century, history seemed to follow their prophetic script. After the founding of Israel in 1948 and its expansion after the Six-Day War, dispensationalists aggressively promoted their ideas with the confidence that Bible prophecy was being fulfilled for all to see. Starting in the 1970s, dispensationalists broke into the popular culture with runaway best-sellers, plenty of media visibility, and a well-networked political campaign to promote and protect the interests of Israel. Since the mid-1990s, tens of millions of people who have never seen a prophetic chart or listened to a sermon on the second coming have read one or more novels in the Left Behind series, which has become the most effective disseminator of dispensationalist ideas ever. How did all this happen? This book seeks to answer that question.

The book's thesis is easily stated: Before the founding and expansion of Israel, dispensationalists were more or less content to teach their doctrine, look for signs of the times, and predict in sometimes great detail what was going to happen in the future. They were history's great spectators and explainers: They had the "sure word of Bible prophecy" to help them interpret world events and show how such events were leading to Christ's return. As futurist premillennialists, they believed that they would be raptured before most end-times events actually took place, but they expected to be here long enough to see history moving decisively in a predetermined direction. In essence, they sat high in the bleachers on history's fifty-yard line, watching as various teams took their positions on the playing field below and explaining to everyone who would listen how the game was going to end. For the first one hundred years of their movement, then, they were observers, not shapers, of events.

But all that changed after Israel reclaimed its place in Palestine and expanded its borders. For the first time, dispensationalists believed that it was necessary to leave the bleachers and get onto the playing field to make sure the game ended according to the divine script. As the world edged closer and closer to the end, dispensationalists became important players in their own game plan. When they shifted from observers to participants, they ran the risk of turning their predictions into self-fulfilling prophecies.

The first chapter explains what dispensationalism is, how it came to America, and why some evangelicals found it so appealing. It also reveals how dispensationalists, who never doubted their own orthodoxy, had to struggle to be accepted by other evangelical Protestants. They succeeded because they were able to show important continuities with other parts of evangelical theology and tradition. In the early stages of the counterattack against theological and social liberals, conservative evangelicals needed all the help they could get, and with a world in crisis, dispensationalism looked like a more realistic way of understanding what was happening than did other alternatives.

Chapter 2 discusses why dispensationalists never acted quite like their critics said they should. While outsiders saw only pessimism and fatalism in their prophetic views, dispensationalists developed a logic that enabled them to be passive in the face of civilization's inevitable decline and yet work hard to make things better in the time that remained. Critics said that dispensationalists did not care about social problems, but some of them found ways to "give the devil as much trouble as possible before Jesus comes." Likewise, though they denied that the world would be converted to Christ, as postmillennialists had been predicting for decades, dispensationalists developed their own missionary force, which was enthusiastic about evangelizing as many people as possible before the end. The dispensational worldview could help revivalists save souls and the Christian rank and file stay on the straight and narrow during social changes that made holy living more difficult.

Chapter 3 examines how well dispensationalists did at interpreting the signs of the times. They believed that they had the "sure word of prophecy" to understand both present and future, but there were times when they struggled with their interpretations. Sometimes history took an unexpected turn. For example, while dispensationalists had a remarkably good record at predicting the coming and the results of World War I, they had a difficult time making sense of the decades between World Wars I and II. At no time between the wars, however, did dispensationalists think of leaving the bleachers for the playing field below.

Chapter 4 gets us to the central part of the story. Even before organized Zionism, dispensationalists advocated a Jewish state in the Middle East. For some time, they were more eager to see a restored Israel than most Jews. A few dispensationalists actually tried to help the process along, but they were the exception, not the rule. While dispensationalists carefully kept track of every step toward Jewish statehood, such as the issuance of the Balfour Declaration during World War I, they also targeted Jews for evangelism. Over the years, dispensationalists founded dozens of specialized missions to the Jews. The going was always tough, there were occasionally embarrassing scandals, and the results were usually meager. But dispensationalists maintained that there was no contradiction between supporting the Jews' nationalist aspirations and trying to convert them to Christ.

Chapter 5 discusses another paradox: While dispensationalists believed that Jews in the future would play an essential role in end-times events, their relationship with Jews in the present was always complicated and even controversial. Though they denounced anti-Semitism as an awful sin, in the 1930s, dispensationalists were especially susceptible to anti-Semitic conspiracy theories and actually used many similar arguments themselves, including the infamous *Protocols of the Elders of Zion*. As a result, dispensationalists could condemn anti-Semites such as Adolf Hitler yet still argue that they fit into God's plan for Israel as punishment for their past sins and a catalyst for their desire for a home of their own. While they sympathized with Jews over the Holocaust, dispensationalists warned that a worse horror lay ahead—when the Antichrist would try to destroy Israel and all Jews during the great tribulation. In the end, when Jesus comes, surviving Jews will welcome him as their Savior and Messiah. But before "all Israel is saved," most Jews will have to be destroyed.

Chapter 6 traces dispensationalists' reactions to the emergence of a new Jewish state and its expansion two decades later. While dispensationalists had always been sure that Jews would eventually have their own state, they were often perplexed by the difficulties and apparently insurmountable problems that were found on the road to statehood. Believers in Bible prophecy often struggled to make developments in the Middle East fit into their prophetic plans. But when Israel was finally declared an independent nation, dispensationalists were ecstatic. For the most part they ignored the ethical issues involved in Israeli statehood and showed little interest in the claims of the Palestinians, whom they saw as the enemies of God's purposes. Because dispensationalists expected a much larger Israel than was established in 1948, they approved Israeli efforts to expand their territory. Thus, they supported with great enthusiasm Israel's occupation of Palestinian territory following the Six-Day War and resisted the return of occupied land, especially the city of Jerusalem.

Chapter 7 tells the story of dispensationalism's breakthrough into new markets after 1970. Buoyed by what they considered undeniable successes in interpreting the signs of the times, dispensationalists found ways to take their message to the popular culture. They became masters of mass media and scored with best-sellers such as *The Late Great Planet Earth* in the 1970s and the Left Behind novel series in the 1990s. Even more indicative of their willingness to go beyond their spectator status was their involvement in the New Christian Right. As in the past, dispensationalists had to deal with some unexpected developments, such as the demise of the Soviet Union and the Eastern Bloc, which had played a central role in their end-times scenario. While some Bible teachers struggled to account for these changes within their old system, others preferred to shift their attention to the rise of a one world order and militant Islam. Few of the faithful seemed to notice or care.

Chapter 8 reveals how dispensationalists joined hands with American and Israeli Jews in providing political and practical support for the state of Israel. Beginning in the 1970s, they traveled to Israel in great numbers, then founded dozens of groups at home to lobby for Israel in Congress, the State Department, and the news media. They also provided humanitarian aid to Israel and assisted Jews from the former Soviet Union and other places who wanted to immigrate to the Holy Land. As a result, dispensationalists became Israel's best friends. Some Jews had reservations about teaming up with dispensationalists: They suspected their motives and resented their prophetic teachings that after most Jews are destroyed by the Antichrist, the survivors will accept Jesus. As it turned out, the Jews had cause to worry because at the same time dispensationalists were lending strong political support for Israel, they were renewing their efforts to evangelize Jews through new groups such as Jews for Jesus and Messianic Judaism.

Chapter 9 uncovers how American dispensationalists have been lending support to some of the most extreme and dangerous elements in Israeli society. There is no more explosive issue in Israel today than the plans of some Israelis to construct a third temple on the site of the previous two—the Temple Mount in the Old City of Jerusalem where the Dome of the Rock and the Al-Aqsa Mosque are located. In recent years, a variety of groups have pushed hard for a new temple. This so-called Temple Movement is strongly opposed by both Muslims and most Israelis, including the government. Because dispensationalists believe that a new temple will play a crucial role in the end times, they are extremely interested in the Temple Movement and have provided spiritual, political, and financial support to some of the movement's most controversial leaders. In addition, to help prophecy come true, some dispensationalists have used their cattle breeding skills to produce a "perfect red heifer," which is necessary for purifying the temple site so that construction can begin. Dispensationalists' views of Bible prophecy also make them skeptical about and sometimes even opposed to efforts to bring peace to the Middle East. Such behavior helps to create the kind of world that dispensationalists have been predicting, a world in which they do not expect they will have to live.

1

Dispensationalism Comes to America

Most of the evangelicals who read and believe the basic outline of the Left Behind series assume that its plotline is taken more or less right out of the Bible. But as already mentioned, the prophetic sections of the Bible can be read in a variety of ways. What Tim LaHaye and Jerry Jenkins present in their novels is a fictionalized version of dispensationalism, which is a particular approach to interpreting the Bible that first appeared in Great Britain in the 1830s. How this new approach developed, differed from other biblical interpretations, came to America, and eventually caught on in certain circles is the story of this chapter.

The Origins of Dispensationalism

Dispensationalism came to the United States in the 1870s, but it originated four decades earlier in Great Britain among the Plymouth Brethren, a reform movement that had broken with the Church of England over a lost list of grievances. As an alternative to the established church, the Brethren met together informally to share the Lord's Supper, pray, sing, and engage in intense study of the Bible. Along with other British evangelicals of that period, the Brethren were deeply interested in biblical prophecy. In contrast with many of them, however, the Brethren were futurists who believed that Bible prophecy pointed to future events, those scheduled to take place just before Christ's return. They did not believe that Bible prophecy provided an overview of the entire sweep of church history, as the historicist Millerites and other Adventists in America had taught.[1]

One of the Brethren's most gifted Bible teachers was John Nelson Darby, a former priest in the Anglican Church of Ireland. Like most Plymouth Brethren, Darby was a futurist in his approach to prophetic passages, but he was also an innovator who introduced new elements into the more or less accepted futurist system used by his colleagues. He called his version of futurism "dispensationalism" because he divided all of history into eras or dispensations. According to C. I. Scofield, Darby's most important American popularizer, a dispensation was a distinct period of time in which God tested humanity in relation to a specific revelation of the divine will.[2] In each era, humankind failed to fulfill the responsibility laid on it by God, which in turn led to the beginning of a new dispensation with new opportunities and eventual human failure. "Each of the dispensations may be regarded as a new test of the natural man, and each ends in judgment—making his utter failure in every dispensation."[3] Darby's followers quibbled over the number and names of the dispensations, but most settled on seven. Darby's list included paradise (to the flood), Noah, Abraham, Israel, Gentiles, the Spirit, and the millennium. Eventually, most American dispensationalists followed Scofield's sevenfold scheme: innocency (before the fall), conscience (fall to the flood), human government, promise (Abraham to Moses), law (Moses to Christ), grace (the church age), and kingdom (the millennium).[4]

Thus, dispensationalists viewed the Bible as "progressive revelation" through which people could understand the flow and development of God's ways in the world over time. As an exercise in biblical interpretation, dispensationalism sought to present the complexities and apparent contradictions of biblical revelation as a coherent and consistent system. By dividing history into distinctive eras, dispensationalists hoped to understand why the divine-human encounter kept moving in new directions. In short, dispensationalism was an intricate system that tried to explain the stages in God's redemptive plan for the universe.

THE DISPENSATIONAL SYSTEM UNRAVELED

The Plymouth Brethren who first heard Darby's teachings found them quite controversial and unsettling. The problem was neither his dividing of human history into eras nor his claim that one could arrive at the Bible's meaning only by taking a strictly literalistic approach to the text. Others had made similar claims before. What rattled even fellow futurists was Darby's insistence that the Bible contained two stories, not just one.

To Darby, the Bible revealed two divine plans operating in history, one for an earthly people, Israel, and the other for a heavenly people, the church.[5] Thus, "rightly dividing the word of truth" (2 Tim. 2:15) meant maintaining the distinction between the two peoples of God and never applying biblical passages to one that rightly belonged to the other.

This basic insight into the two peoples of God led Darby to a number of surprising and, according to his detractors, forced conclusions. Darby's system promised to simplify and organize the Bible's message, but dispensationalism turned out to be anything but simple. There are a few keys to understanding Darby's approach: his view of covenants; the failure of the Jews to keep them; the promised coming of the Messiah, then the postponement of his return; and the two phases of the second coming.

Darby believed that the plan for God's earthly people had unfolded through a number of solemn agreements or covenants between Israel and God. The plan originated in the Abrahamic covenant (Gen. 12:2–3), in which God pledged to make Abraham the father of a great nation and to bless the rest of the world through it. The Abrahamic covenant was unconditional, a covenant of grace, which meant that there was nothing Israel could do to nullify it. That was not the case with the Mosaic covenant (Exodus 19–20), in which God's blessing on Israel was conditional on Israel's keeping the law of Moses. Darby taught that Israelites lived to regret ever making such an agreement, since they experienced over and over the dire consequences of their disobedience. Fortunately, for them, the Abrahamic covenant was still in effect. Through the sacrificial system, God provided the mechanism for repairing the damage done by the people's sin.

The next agreement was the Davidic covenant (2 Sam. 7:4–11), in which God promised to preserve King David's royal line forever, even though God might have to punish the Israelites occasionally for their disobedience. Thus, even as the Jews were being carried off into Babylonian exile, God reaffirmed the covenant to David by promising a future restoration of David's throne by an Anointed One, the Messiah, through whom a new and final covenant would be established. This covenant would replace the external law of Moses with a new, inward law capable of producing true righteousness (Jer. 31:31–34; 33:15–16).[6]

Before the glories of the messianic age could be enjoyed, however, the nation would have to experience rough times. Darby found in the Book of Daniel a clear outline of the history of Israel leading to the arrival of the Anointed One (Daniel 7–9). On account of its continuing unfaithfulness, Israel would suffer at the hands of four successive Gentile powers. These "times of the Gentiles" would remain in force until the coming of the Messiah, which Daniel prophesied would occur seventy weeks after one of the Gentile rulers published a decree that permitted exiled Jews to return to Jerusalem to repair its broken walls (Dan. 9:24–27).

The seventy weeks of Daniel's prophecy played a central role in dispensationalists' prophetic system. According to the prophecy, during the first seven weeks following the decree, the city would be rebuilt. Sixty-two weeks later, the Messiah would return but be repudiated ("cut off") by the people. In the seventieth week, an evil ruler would gain power and try to destroy those who oppose him. At the end of the seventieth week, the Messiah would return to rescue God's people from persecution and restore David's throne.

Darby and the dispensationalists believed that these prophetic visions pointed to the first and second comings of Jesus Christ. Because the Hebrew word translated "week" actually meant "a seven," dispensationalists concluded that the prophecy referred to seventy "sevens," 490 years.[7] Therefore, if one could determine the date of the royal decree to rebuild Jerusalem, one could count ahead to the "cutting off" of the Messiah and the establishment of the kingdom seven years later.

Dispensationalists had a lot riding on this interpretation, so they worked hard to show that Jesus was put to death 483 years (sixty-nine "weeks") after Artaxerxes' decision to allow Nehemiah and a small contingent of Jews to return to Israel to work on Jerusalem's fallen walls (Neh. 2:1–8). The problem was that the generally accepted date of Artaxerxes' decree was 444 B.C. Thus, adding sixty-nine "weeks" (483 years) to 444 B.C. placed the Messiah's rejection at A.D. 39, too late for the generally accepted date for the crucifixion of Jesus. Scofield saw the problem and hedged on the dating of the decree, saying that it probably occurred sometime between 454 and 444 B.C. and concluding that "in either case we are brought to the time of Christ."[8] James H. Brookes solved this problem by accepting Bishop Ussher's dating of the decree (454 B.C.), then putting Christ's birth in 4 B.C. Because Jesus died in his thirty-third year, the crucifixion occurred in A.D. 29.[9] Other dispensationalists made the traditional date of 444 B.C. work by insisting that "prophetic years" contained 360 days, not the normal 365. Using that method, they showed that the sixty-ninth week ended on Palm Sunday, right on schedule.[10]

After all that careful calculating, one had a right to expect the Messiah's second coming seven years later, following Daniel's seventieth week. So what had happened? To resolve this obvious difficulty, Darby suggested a "postponement theory." When the Jews rejected ("cut off") Jesus as their Messiah, just as Daniel had said they would, God postponed Christ's scheduled return seven years later and turned to the Gentiles. God suspended the prophetic timetable for Israel at the end of Daniel's sixty-ninth week and set to work building up a new and heavenly people—the church.[11]

C. H. Mackintosh, one of Darby's faithful interpreters, explained the theory:

> The Messiah, instead of being received, is cut off. In place of ascending the throne of David, He goes to the cross. . . . God signified His sense of this act by suspending for a time His dispensational dealings with Israel. The course of time is interrupted. There is a great gap. Four hundred and eighty-three years are fulfilled, seven yet remain—a cancelled week, and all the time since the death of Messiah has been an unnoticed interval—a break or parenthesis, during which Christ has been hidden in the heavens, and the Holy Ghost has been working on earth in forming the body of Christ, the church, the heavenly bride.[12]

In essence, this meant that the Christian church existed outside the Bible's prophetic timetable and had no prophecies of its own. It occupied a prophetic time warp, what dispensationalists called a "great parenthesis" of prophetic time. As Mackintosh explained, "It is vain to look into the prophetic page in order to find the church's position, her calling, her hope. They are not there. It is entirely out of place for the church to be occupied with dates and historic events. . . . The Christian must never lose sight of the fact that he belongs to heaven."[13]

In short, by combining their notion of the complete separation of Israel and the church into two plans of God with the postponement theory, dispensationalists developed a unique understanding of the future. If Bible prophecies describing future earthly events could not refer to God's heavenly people, then to whom did they refer? There was only one alternative: Israel, God's earthly people. Daniel's seventieth week, postponed for the time being by Israel's rejection of Jesus as the Messiah, must be fulfilled sometime. This time of trouble, called the great tribulation by all premillennialists, was described in great detail in Revelation and mentioned in other places (e.g., Matthew 24; 2 Thessalonians 2). But dispensationalists were convinced that the seventieth week could not begin as long as the church remained on earth. They believed that God would not deal with the two peoples or operate the two plans concurrently. Consequently, God had to remove the church before proceeding with the final plans for Israel.

THE RAPTURE: DISPENSATIONALISM'S MOST DISTINCTIVE DOCTRINE

This set of convictions led to dispensationalism's most controversial and distinctive doctrine—the secret, any-moment, pretribulational rapture of the church. In standard premillennialist jargon, the rapture was the "catching away" of the church at the second coming of Christ. According to the apostle Paul, "For the Lord himself shall descend from heaven with a shout, with the voice of the archangel, and with the trump of God; and the dead in Christ shall rise first. Then we which are alive and remain shall be caught up together with them in the clouds, to meet the Lord in the air: and so shall we ever be with the Lord" (1 Thess. 4:16–17). Before Darby, all premillennialists, futurists included, believed that the rapture would occur at the end of the tribulation, at Christ's second advent. But Darby understood the rapture and the second coming as two separate events. At the rapture, Christ will come *for* his saints, and at the second coming, he will come *with* his saints. Between these two events the great tribulation would occur. With the church removed, God could resume dealing with Israel, and Daniel's seventieth week could take place as predicted.[14]

This pretribulation rapture made Darby's version of futurist premillennialism unique. No one knows for sure where this doctrine came from, but there are a number of theories. Samuel P. Tregelles, a respectable biblical scholar in Darby's day and one of the Plymouth Brethren, denied that a pretribulation rapture was taught in the Bible and argued that the idea originated in 1832 during an ecstatic utterance in the London congregation of Edward Irving, where the charismatic gifts of the Spirit were alleged to have been poured out.[15] Since the Plymouth Brethren, and most other English evangelicals for that matter, were scandalized by the goings-on at Irving's church and rejected them out of hand, such a charge was clearly intended to discredit Darby's theory among people who might be otherwise inclined to accept it.

A more recent historical explanation contends that the doctrine originated with Margaret Macdonald, a teenager from Glasgow, Scotland, who began having charismatic experiences in the early part of 1830. According to some recently discovered (but highly confusing) manuscripts, Macdonald claimed to have special insights into the second coming of Christ and may have even advocated a pretribulation rapture of the church.

Along with her various visions, Margaret became famous for speaking in tongues. She and other members of the Macdonald family became the main attractions in a charismatic-type revival in western Scotland. Rattled by the reports of a new Pentecost in the north, the Plymouth Brethren commissioned Darby to go to Scotland and investigate. He arrived in the middle of 1830 and, according to his own testimony twenty-three years later, actually met Macdonald and heard her prophesy. According to the recent theory, Darby returned home totally against the so-called outpouring of the Spirit but convinced that Margaret Macdonald's view of the rapture was true. He subsequently fit it into his system but never acknowledged his debt to her, for obvious reasons.[16]

Without conclusive evidence, we may have to settle for Darby's own explanation. He claimed that the doctrine of the pretribulation rapture virtually jumped out of the pages of the Bible once he understood and consistently maintained the absolute distinction between Israel and the church in the prophetic plans of God. According to his own testimony:

> It is this conviction, that the Church is properly heavenly in its calling and relationship with Christ, forming no part of the course of events of the earth, which makes its rapture so simple and clear; and on the other hand, it shows how the denial of its rapture brings down the Church to an earthly position, and destroys its whole spiritual character and position. Prophecy does not relate to heaven. The Christian's hope is not a prophetic subject at all.[17]

Once the heavenly people of God have been raptured, the divine script can be played out to the end. Shortly after the church's removal, the Antichrist will be revealed. Promising peace in a time of world chaos, the Antichrist will make a covenant with the newly restored state of Israel, pledging to protect it from hostile neighbors. Treacherously, he will break this covenant, outlaw all religious practices of the Jews, and then brazenly demand to be worshiped as God. To solidify his political power, the Antichrist will begin a reign of terror against all who refuse to accept his pretensions, in this case, Jews who have turned to Christ since the church's rapture. In retaliation for the attacks against his people, God will pour out terrible plagues on the earth, which will throw most of humanity into agony and despair.[18]

Finally, things will mount to a crescendo. Forces from north, south, east, and west will converge on Israel in a last attempt to destroy God's people and seize power over the whole world. As the world's armies gather in Armageddon, which is a valley in northern Israel, Christ and his previously raptured saints will break through the clouds and destroy them in the gory battle of Armageddon. After this awesome display of Christ's power, the Antichrist and his followers will be cast alive into a lake of fire, the nations of the world will be judged, and Satan will be bound and thrown into a bottomless pit so that he can no longer deceive the nations. Then, with the conclusion of Daniel's seventieth week, the victorious Messiah will restore the throne of David, and the millennial kingdom will begin. Since all ancient prophecies concerning Israel must be fulfilled literally, the millennium will be a Jewish kingdom, complete with a restored Jerusalem temple, daily animal sacrifices, and a powerful King Jesus reigning from Jerusalem and extending Jewish hegemony over the rest of the world. Thus, all the prophecies originally intended for Christ's first advent, when the Jews' rejection forced their postponement, will be fulfilled at the second.

After a thousand years of Christ's kingly rule, Satan will be freed to foment one last rebellion. After it is quickly squelched, the resurrection of the dead and the last judgment will occur. Once everyone who has ever lived is assigned to his or her proper place in heaven or hell, God will create a new heaven and earth as an eternal dwelling place for the redeemed. The seven dispensations now over, time shall be no more.

In barest outline, that was the dispensationalism that originated in Great Britain in the 1830s and made its way to America after the Civil War. Other premillennial movements contained similar elements and had their faithful adherents, but none achieved the popularity or had the staying power of dispensationalism within American evangelical Protestantism.

The Coming of Dispensationalism to America

Darby visited America a number of times during the 1870s to share his dispensational teachings, but his reception was cautious at best. Since the debacle of the Millerites in the 1840s, most people dismissed premillennialism as silly and discredited. Others considered it a novelty and therefore unworthy of their consideration. The educational and ecclesiastical elite tended to reject dispensationalism as a doctrine, but the conservatives among them usually found a way to welcome dispensationalists into their mounting opposition to theological liberalism and higher criticism. Among the first adopters of the new premillennialism was an impressive group of evangelical movers and shakers, mostly "second-tier" pastors, Bible teachers, and revivalists with large constituencies. This group contained evangelical entrepreneurs who knew how to promote dispensationalism, establish strong supporting institutions, and popularize it among evangelicals in the pew. In this way, dispensationalism often flew under the radar of scholars and church leaders who were out of touch with rank-and-file believers. By the time the elites noticed, dispensationalism was already well established among conservative evangelicals, with vibrant networks of its own. What was the key to their success? During a time of mounting crisis over the Bible's reliability and accessibility to laypeople, dispensationalists were able to "out-Bible" everybody else in sight.

THE STRUGGLE TO GET A HEARING

In America, as in Great Britain earlier, dispensationalism at first got mixed reviews. Among the most outspoken against it were Reformed theologians, for whom dispensationalism was a serious departure from their historic creeds. In the 1880s, A. A. Hodge, the Princeton Seminary professor whose doctrine of biblical inerrancy most premillennialists espoused, called the pretribulational rapture of the church "an unscriptural and unprofitable theory." Francis Patton, the president of Princeton University and another defender of Reformed orthodoxy, often associated with premillennialists but confidentially confessed that he was "not foolish enough to be one of them."[19]

For people like James H. Brookes, such comments hurt badly. In the 1880s, Brookes championed the dispensationalist cause in the Presbyterian Church. Though he was a highly respected pastor among Presbyterian conservatives, his eschatology made him feel like an outsider. On one occasion he tried unsuccessfully to get the General Assembly to take a stand on the status of premillennialism within the church: Either declare it heretical or give it the open hearing and respect that it deserves. In the end, most conservative Presbyterians loved Brookes but remained skeptical about his eschatology. Speaking from personal experience, Brookes warned other dispensationalists to be ready "to be gored and tossed on their way to meet Him in the air."[20]

Decades later, dispensationalism still had few advocates in American Protestant theological schools. In 1919, James H. Snowden, a postmillennial theologian at Western Theological Seminary, a Presbyterian school in Pittsburgh, surveyed 236 theological professors from 28 seminaries sponsored by 8 Protestant denominations. Among them he could locate only 7 premillennialists. "This fact may be allowed to speak for itself. . . . It is hard to kick against the pricks of such scholarship, and in the long run it has its way."[21] In high places, dispensationalism did not amount to much.

J. Gresham Machen, the leader of fundamentalist Presbyterians during the 1920s, demonstrated the ambivalent attitude that even conservative Reformed scholars had toward dispensationalists:

> The recrudescence of "Chiliasm" or "premillennialism" in the modern church causes us serious concern; it is coupled, we think, with a false method in interpreting Scripture which in the long run will be productive of harm. Yet how great is our agreement with those who hold the premillennial view: They share to the full our reverence for the authority of the Bible, and differ from us only in the interpretation of the Bible; they share our ascription of deity to the Lord Jesus, and our supernaturalistic conception both of the entrance of Jesus into the world and of the consummation when He shall come again. CERTAINLY, then, from our point of view, their error, serious though it may be, is not deadly error; and Christian fellowship, with loyalty not only to the Bible but to the great creeds of the church, can still unite us with them.[22]

This amounted to throwing crumbs to a movement that was desperate for acceptance and influence. It was not easy to stand against the Christian consensus and still claim to be orthodox, but that was precisely what dispensationalists were forced to do. If dispensationalism was so clearly taught in the Bible, why had it not been noticed until recently? Why did not all Bible-believing, conservative theologians believe it? Though a British subject, C. H. Mackintosh nonetheless spoke for his American friends when he described the burden that all dispensationalists had to bear during this period:

> There is something peculiarly painful in the thought of having so frequently to come in collision with generally received opinions of the professing church. It looks presumptuous to contradict, on so many subjects, all the great standards and creeds of Christendom. But what is one to do? . . . But we would impress upon our readers the fact that it is not at all a question of human opinion or of a difference of judgment amongst even the best of men. It is entirely a question as to the teaching of Scripture. There have been, and there are, and there will be, schools of doctrine, varieties of opinion, and shades of thought; but it is the obvious duty of every child of God and every student of Christ to bow down in holy reverence, and hearken to the voice of God in Scripture. If it is merely a matter of human authority, it must simply go for what it is worth; but on the other hand, if it be a matter of divine authority, then all discussion is closed, and our place—the place of all—is to bow and believe.[23]

Dispensationalists worked hard to overcome such liabilities by claiming that they had more past and present supporters than their opponents said they did. In 1891, James H. Brookes, the dogged Presbyterian apologist for dispensationalism, published a list of adherents from the United States, Great Britain, and Germany.[24] In 1913, the editors of Moody Bible Institute's *Christian Workers Magazine* printed another list with 245 "eminent exponents of premillennialism." The list included mainly contemporary believers, but it also contained past luminaries such as Martin Luther, John Calvin, Philip Melanchthon, John Knox, Richard Baxter, and John and Charles Wesley. Their inclusion came as a big surprise to followers of the Lutheran, Reformed, and Wesleyan traditions who had never even heard of premillennialism before the dispensationalists came along. When the same editors published an even longer list two years later, a backlash brought a retraction, or at least a further clarification. The editors admitted that while some people on the list were not premillennialists per se, they were included because they were not *post*millennialists. The criteria for making the list, the editors confessed, were a belief that Jesus will come back to earth and a belief that there will be no millennium before his coming. That explained why the editors could put some amillennialists on the list who denied that there would ever be an earthly millennium.

> This is all we are contending for. In other words, it is not a millennium for which we are looking, but for Him. If our brethren differ with us as to the first, but agree as to the second, we are still happy. It is only when they admit a millennium and postpone His coming until the close of it, that we are unhappy. We had rather they were anti-millennialists [i.e., amillennialists] than postmillennialists.[25]

With such expansive criteria, the editors insisted that the list should stand as is, with only one exception. Once Cornelius Woelfkin had believed in the premillennial second coming, but he had changed his mind in order to become a liberal leader within the Northern Baptist Convention.[26] As a result, the authors of the list were glad to remove his name.

Such list making was an obvious attempt to encourage dispensationalists who were suffering from low self-esteem and to demonstrate that premillennialism was an honorable tradition with respectable supporters.[27] Dispensationalists also argued that their doctrine was compatible with other versions of evangelical faith and actually supported and protected them. Reuben A. Torrey, a successor to D. L. Moody on the revival circuit and a leader of Bible institutes in Chicago and Los Angeles, claimed that the premillennial belief in the second coming was the ultimate cure for theological infidelity and an impregnable bulwark against liberalism and false cults:

> In the truth concerning our Lord's return is the safeguard against all current heresies, errors, and falsehoods. . . . One who knows the truth concerning the Second Coming of Christ has proof against them all. For example, no one who knows the truth concerning the Second Coming of Christ could possibly be misled by Christian Science, Millennial Dawnism [Jehovah's Witnesses], Occultism, Theosophy, or Bahaism. It is remarkable how all forms of error touch the doctrine of Christ's Second Coming, and are shattered by the truth revealed about it in the Scriptures.[28]

William Bell Riley, who eventually presided over a fundamentalist empire in Minnesota, called premillennialism "the sufficient if not solitary antidote to the present apostasy."[29] To arrive at a dispensational position, one had to interpret the Bible literally, thus ensuring that one grasped the other essential doctrines of the faith as well.

Building an Evangelical Constituency

Historians of American religion have characterized the five or six decades after the Civil War in terms of conflict and creativity, realignment and reorganization, activity and aimlessness. They speak of "ordeals of transition," the dissolution of the "evangelical empire," the "spiritual crisis of the Gilded Age," the "ordeal of faith" in churchgoing America, and an age filled with divided minds and religious ironies.[30] Once appearing invincible and unflappable, American evangelical religion was shaken by immense and unprecedented social and intellectual crises after the Civil War. The rise of the city, the almost overwhelming influx of immigrants, and the unsettling problems arising from rapid industrialization called into question some of the more traditional evangelical approaches to society and economics and forced the churches onto new and unfamiliar terrain in their attempts to deal with the changes.[31]

Similarly, the churches were threatened by new, revolutionary ways of thinking. The rise of the theory of evolution called into question traditional ways of understanding the universe and the nature of humanity. Biblical higher criticism, comparative religion, and the new social sciences caused many evangelicals to doubt traditional views of biblical inspiration and authority and the uniqueness and superiority of the Christian faith.[32]

As might be expected, evangelicals dealt with these challenges in various ways. As early as 1872, Henry Ward Beecher, for forty years the pastor of the Plymouth Congregational Church in Brooklyn and one of America's most influential preachers, told divinity students at Yale that unless ministers reevaluated the traditional faith in light of modern thought, they would be left behind by "the intelligent part of society." "If ministers do not make their theological systems conform to the facts as they are; if they do not recognize what men are studying, the time will not be far distant when the pulpit will be like a voice crying in the wilderness. And it will not be 'Prepare the way of the Lord,' either."[33]

Consequently, many evangelicals tried to redefine the traditional faith in terms more compatible with modern thinking. There was no single way of adjusting. On the moderate side were the so-called evangelical liberals, who kept close to the tradition by affirming, even as they redefined the finality of the Christian religion, the uniqueness of Jesus, the special nature of the Bible as divine revelation, and the centrality of personal religious experience. On the more radical side were the modernists, who showed less concern about retaining historic Christian categories. Their approach, though at first not that different from the approach of evangelical liberals, eventually led to more extreme conclusions. Whereas evangelical liberals affirmed the outlines of the tradition and tried to bring them into line with modern thought, modernists affirmed the methods of modern science and then examined the tradition to see what could stand up to scientific scrutiny. In short, though all liberals and modernists were responding to the same "modernist impulse," they adjusted to the new intellectual challenges in different ways.[34]

Without question, the liberals' adjustments enabled many people to maintain their religious allegiances, but more conservative evangelicals thought they had accommodated too much to the spirit of the age. By redefining the old gospel in terms that modern people could understand, the liberals had abandoned the faith's historic content. According to conservatives, by making the message of Christ more palatable, liberals had stripped it of its spiritual power.

During the 1880s and 1890s, it was not always easy to find clear dividing lines between liberals and conservatives. There seemed to be ample middle ground where the two sides mingled and cooperated. D. L. Moody, for example, had good friends in both camps. Using the force of his personality and his extensive contacts, he tried to hold the two sides together by emphasizing evangelism over complete doctrinal agreement. In a few seminaries, conservatives put more liberal faculty on trial for heresy, but most people in the pew probably detected few changes in the way their pastors preached. Nevertheless, conservatives with a good nose for doctrinal deviation noticed what was going on and began sounding the alarm. In time, some conservatives openly wondered whether liberalism was even Christianity at all and were ready to organize to put a stop to its spread.

Other conservatives such as E. Y. Mullins and A. H. Strong, leading "mediating" Baptist theologians in the South and the North respectively, interacted (sometimes quite positively) with modern thought, while retaining more or less traditional conclusions. Some orthodox Calvinist theologians, B. B. Warfield most notably, even managed to accept parts of the new evolutionary theory.[35] Even those conservatives who were willing to make some adjustments to new ways of thinking were certain that other people's concessions had gone too far and that like-minded conservatives were going to have to stand up and be counted in their defense of the traditional faith.

To do battle against a common enemy, many did what evangelicals had often done before: They formed an amazingly diverse transdenominational coalition—which was big enough to include dispensationalists. Though premillennialists were few in number and deviated from prevailing eschatological views, most conservatives had to admit that they were well within the evangelical tradition on other points. On that basis, dispensationalists were allowed to join the battle against liberalism.

No better example of such conservative cooperation can be found than the Bible conference movement. At the same time that Darby was planting his seeds in American soil, a group of conservatives, including premillennialists such as James Inglis and George Needham, founded the Believers' Meeting for Bible Study. At first conducted for a select group of insiders, by the mid-1870s, the Bible conference was open to the public. After trying out a number of locations, organizers settled on a permanent site at Niagara-on-the-Lake, Ontario, and changed the conference's name to the Niagara Bible Conference. For over two decades, the Niagara conferences, which met for two weeks each summer, provided an interdenominational gathering place where conservative evangelicals heard the old doctrines confirmed and preached. Though they could have made much of their denominational differences, they "gathered by one Spirit unto the name of the Lord, to worship in perfect sympathy and fellowship, and in utter forgetfulness of all differences, before one Father."[36] Underlying everything that happened at Niagara was the awareness that the people there were standing firm for beliefs that others were starting to deny.

Dispensationalists were at the Niagara conferences from the beginning and quickly became the dominant force in their leadership. Most important was James H. Brookes, who presided over the Niagara Bible Conference for over twenty years and was primarily responsible for drawing up the "Niagara Creed" in 1878, which served to locate the conference within the increasingly complex world of North American religion. The statement was one that the vast majority of conservatives in the evangelical tradition could support. In addition to its plank on premillennialism, which gave many Niagara supporters pause, the creed affirmed the inspiration and authority of the Bible, the Trinity, the fall and sinfulness of humanity, the absolute necessity of personal conversion to Christ, justification by faith alone, the centering of the whole Bible in Christ, the importance of the work of the Holy Spirit in the life of the church and the individual believer, the inclusion of all true believers in the one true church of Christ, and the final separation of all people for eternal life or damnation.[37]

When they participated in the Niagara conferences or in the many other Bible conferences organized later, dispensationalists worked hard at keeping their ties with other conservative evangelicals strong. Though their views on eschatology set them apart, dispensationalists otherwise believed the same things as everybody else. William L. Pettingill, for example, who helped C. I. Scofield start the dispensationalist Philadelphia College of Bible in 1914, denied the charge that dispensational premillennialists were consumed with end-of-the-world concerns. A premillennialist, he said, is not someone who "thinks, sings, prays, and dreams about nothing else but the second coming of Christ." His or her beliefs about the Lord's return are compatible with other evangelical beliefs about Christ's divinity, virgin birth, substitutionary atonement, physical resurrection, and current intercession in heaven for believers.[38] Another premillennialist claimed that "if you accept the second coming, you are under bonds logically to accept the doctrines with which it is so indissolubly bound up. The second coming is so woven into these basic doctrines of the Christian faith . . . that you cannot deny the one without denying the others."[39]

Though they could get along with other conservative evangelicals, dispensationalists sometimes felt they had to go their own way. Shortly after the founding of the Niagara Bible Conference, some dispensationalists wanted to pay more attention to prophetic themes than the other participants were willing to tolerate. So they issued a call for the First American Bible and Prophetic Conference, which was held in New York City at the Holy Trinity Episcopal Church in late October of 1878.[40] Those convening the conference noted that "when from any cause some vital doctrine of God's Word has fallen into neglect or suffered contradiction and reproach, it becomes the serious duty of those who hold it . . . to bring back the Lord's people to its apprehension and acceptance."[41] These dispensationalists were on a mission: They wanted to convince other evangelicals that they had neglected the doctrine of Christ's second coming long enough.

This first prophetic conference went so well that in time six more were held: Chicago in 1886; Allegheny, Pennsylvania, in 1895; Boston in 1901; Chicago again in 1914; and Philadelphia and New York in 1918.[42] As years passed, dispensationalism came to dominate more and more of the proceedings, clearly edging out other varieties of futurism. By stressing this form of premillennialism to the exclusion of all others, dispensationalists were presenting a kind of united front that they hoped would rally other conservative evangelicals to their cause.

Dispensationalism may have started small, but it grew rapidly, thanks primarily to the kinds of people who championed it. One must be careful not to press the argument too far, but the success of dispensationalism seems to have followed the same story line developed by Nathan O. Hatch in his *Democratization of American Christianity*.[43] Between the American Revolution and the 1840s, the American religious scene was revolutionized by the emergence of new popular religious movements that were led by charismatic leaders who knew how to "storm heaven by the back door." Capitalizing on the democratic ethos of the time and the desire common people had to make up their own minds about religion (as well as everything else), these leaders were masters of mass communication who appealed directly to people's hopes, fears, and resentments. By making their audiences sovereign, they were able to bypass the religious and educational establishments of their time and create new religious empires.

Like the subjects of Hatch's study, the leaders of dispensationalism knew how to bypass elites in order to fashion a popular religious movement of their own. But unlike Hatch's cast of often eccentric characters, the leaders of dispensationalism wanted the respect of the evangelical establishment and were for the most part the models of propriety.

DISPENSATIONALISM'S APPEAL

Why did dispensationalism eventually find so much acceptance among American evangelicals? Premillennialists may not have had a majority of seminary professors on their side, but they could point to a number of respected and prominent evangelical leaders within their movement. Revivalist D. L. Moody, "Mr. Evangelical" to nearly everyone at the end of the century, was an early convert to premillennialism, though not a very doctrinaire dispensationalist.[44] Nearly every major revivalist from his time to World War I adopted this eschatology: George Needham, William J. Erdman, Major D. W. Whittle, J. Wilbur Chapman, Leander Munhall, Reuben A. Torrey, and Billy Sunday.

There were also dispensationalist leaders in the evangelical world missions movement. Robert Speer, longtime secretary of the Presbyterian Board of Foreign Missions; A. T. Pierson, editor of the prestigious *Missionary Review of the World;* and A. B. Simpson, at one time a prominent Presbyterian minister in New York City who founded the Christian and Missionary Alliance, all identified themselves with the premillennial movement.

But by far the most important symbols of dispensationalist respectability were the pastors who gave their congregations steady doses of the new premillennialism. James H. Brookes served as pastor of the Walnut Street Presbyterian Church in St. Louis from 1858 to 1897. Adoniram Judson Gordon was pastor of the Clarendon Street Baptist Church in Boston from 1869 to 1906, while George Bishop served with equal distinction at the First Reformed Church of Orange, New Jersey, from 1875 to 1906. In addition to his evangelistic work, Erdman filled Presbyterian pulpits in Chicago; Jamestown, New York; Boston; and Asheville, North Carolina, between 1875 and 1895. Before turning exclusively to writing and conference speaking, A. T. Pierson was a minister in Detroit, Indianapolis, and Philadelphia (at Wannamaker's Bethany Tabernacle). C. I. Scofield served at the First Congregational Church in Dallas from 1882 to 1895. These men, and scores like them, initiated thousands into the premillennial understanding of the Bible and provided evidence that dispensationalism did not undermine evangelical church ministry.

Early on, dispensationalists devised a way to produce a steady stream of new leadership through the Bible institute movement, which they helped to establish at the end of the nineteenth century.[45] Starting in the 1880s, conservatives founded these specialized schools as a hedge against liberal theology and higher criticism of the Bible. The Bible institutes were not liberal arts colleges or theological seminaries; they were training schools for Christian lay workers. Seeing no need to burden students with the laborious study of Greek and Hebrew, D. L. Moody wanted the Bible institute that eventually bore his name to produce "gapmen," people who could "go into the shops and meet these bareheaded infidels and skeptics" and appeal to them "in the name of Jesus Christ."[46] Moody wanted graduates of his school to know their Bibles through and through, but he was more interested in evangelism than in technical exegesis.

Almost without exception, the scores of Bible institutes that were founded between 1880 and 1940 taught dispensationalism. The reason that James H. Snowden could find so few premillennialists on seminary faculties in 1919 was because they were all teaching in the Bible institutes. Every year these schools produced an enthusiastic corps of men and women for church agencies, home and foreign missionary societies, and even the pastoral ministry, though the latter did not become a major goal of the Bible institutes until the third decade of the twentieth century.[47]

It was through the ministries of such people—pastors, evangelists, Bible teachers, missionaries, youth workers, and the like—that dispensationalism spread. These leaders were "doers," admired and successful in the work they felt called to do. Henry Ostrom was an evangelist who claimed that his turning to premillennialism was due partly to the successful image of its leaders:

> I do not mean to say that the apparent outstanding success of these godly men became conclusive. . . . But it did do this for me—it started me again to [study] my Bible . . . and I have been led almost to the conclusion that where men do not accept this teaching of the truth of God, they are usually possessed of such an element of uncertainty about the reliability of the whole Bible that their approach to Christian work is not quite as sure-footed as it would be if they accepted this truth.[48]

Even though most evangelicals after the Civil War had no premillennial background, many were willing to examine the issue after hearing a dispensationalist with impeccable conservative credentials expound it. James M. Gray, dean and later president of Moody Bible Institute

(1904–34), told how he became a dispensationalist after attending the first prophetic conference in New York in 1878. Though he had already completed his theological education, he was highly impressed by such an array of Bible teachers who were convinced that Jesus might be coming soon. Arno C. Gaebelein, a pioneer in Jewish missions and editor of the premillennial *Our Hope,* resisted the teaching until he met the likes of Brookes, Erdman, Gordon, and Pierson at one of the Niagara Bible Conferences. William L. Pettingill was first drawn to premillennialism through a Bible study group of devout dispensationalists at the Rochester, New York, YMCA. Robert McQuilkin, president of Columbia Bible College in South Carolina, learned his premillennialism from Erdman in the Philadelphia YMCA. Others claimed that they turned to dispensationalism after reading the writings of such teachers.[49]

Probably the most important reason for dispensationalism's growing acceptance among evangelicals was dispensationalists' unwavering loyalty to and defense of the Bible. In the religiously fractious decades before and after World War I, when popular notions of the Bible were changing, nobody could out-Bible the dispensationalists.

The new premillennialism spread during a time of revolution in the study of the Bible. The rise of historical-critical biblical scholarship created a crisis among most conservative evangelicals. Biblical scholars called into question the rather straightforward reading of the Bible that most people were used to. The higher critics, as they were quickly called, questioned the authorship and dating of biblical books. Moses did not write the Pentateuch; there were at least two authors of Isaiah; the Book of Daniel was actually written *after* the events it prophesied; and much of the Gospels—especially the stories of miracles—was merely fabricated. The scholars compared the Bible to other ancient texts and often concluded that elements of the Bible had been adapted. All of a sudden, many Christians felt they could no longer look at the Bible the way they used to. It was a much more complicated book than they had imagined. Instead of being a bulwark of comfort and security, the Bible was becoming a problem.

At a time when conservatives were increasingly concerned about the impact of higher criticism on the status of the Bible in the churches, premillennialists stood firmly for inerrancy and biblical authority. Premillennialists opposed higher criticism on a number of grounds. Moody believed that it was "ruining revival work and emptying the churches." People do not spend time and energy in practical Christian work, Moody believed, unless they are certain of their message. Higher criticism robbed believers of their religious certainty.[50]

Higher criticism also took away from ordinary believers the ability—and sometimes the courage—to interpret the Bible for themselves. The understandability of the Bible was one of evangelicalism's most cherished ideas. Most Protestants during the nineteenth century believed that laypeople could understand the Bible completely on their own. But the findings of the higher critics made many laypeople doubt their ability to understand much of anything. Suddenly, many believers were shocked to discover that nothing could be taken for granted. Questions of authenticity, authorship, dating, literary genre, and the impact of surrounding Semitic cultures weighed heavily on anyone trying to read the Bible and come to his or her own conclusions. A. T. Pierson expressed the frustration of many Protestant evangelicals when he complained that higher criticism, "like Romanism, practically removes the Word of God from the common people by assuming that only scholars can interpret it. While Rome puts a priest between a man and the Word, criticism puts an educated expositor between the believer and his Bible."[51]

Dispensationalists still maintained that anyone with an open mind and basic intelligence could read the Bible and understand it.[52] One premillennialist went a bit overboard but made his point: "[T]he Scriptures were not for the erudite, but for the simpleminded. . . . All the material needed for our understanding of the matter are contained in the Bible itself." Another claimed that all one needed to understand the Bible was "a bit of spare time daily, some simple, comprehensive plan of reading, a reverent spirit and daily practice with the Book's spirit and teaching."[53]

Conservative evangelicals tried to keep their traditional hold on interpreting Scripture by developing new techniques of Bible study. One such method was "Bible readings," which was featured in the Bible conference movement. A Bible reading was nothing more than the collection of numerous Bible passages that illustrated a particular point or doctrine. James H. Brookes explained how it was done: "Have your leader select some word, as faith, repentance, love, hope, justification, sanctification, and with the aide of a good Concordance, mark down before the time of meeting the references to the subject under discussion. These can be read as called for, thus presenting all the Holy Ghost has been pleased to reveal on the topic."[54] In this way, Bible readers assured their audiences, the only voice to be heard was God's. According to one practitioner, "[L]ittle that is human is introduced save the expository" comments of the speaker before each new subject, which "form the connecting links whereby the harmony and fullness of the Word . . . will be more readily appreciated."[55]

Such an appraisal obviously ignored the important role of the Bible reader in selecting which passages were read or the limits of "proof texting" to arrive at theological conclusions. But Bible readings did seem to have a powerful effect on those who heard them. Conservatives who wanted their beliefs based on the Bible alone were understandably impressed when passage was piled upon passage. The nice thing about

Bible readings was that anyone could do them. One did not have to be a scholar or a master of biblical content. Anyone could obtain a biblical concordance and make one's own selections. This method was tailor-made for those who refused to rely on the so-called experts. As one pastor sarcastically put it, "Have we to await a communication from Tubingen or a telegram from Oxford before we can read the Bible?"[56]

Dispensationalists insisted that common Christians could still read and understand the Bible on their own, but sometimes even they needed help interpreting the Scriptures. The Bible was understandable, they insisted, but its meaning was not always obvious. Dispensationalist teachers agreed that the biblical text was best studied inductively and developed a rather distinctive approach to Bible study. James M. Gray of Moody Bible Institute taught what he called "the synthetic method," which in time became extremely popular among premillennialists.[57] Gray believed that to avoid getting confused or lost in the Bible's details, one first had to see the big picture. To achieve this panoramic view of the Bible, one needed to read the Bible all the way through, from Genesis to Revelation, each book being read at a single sitting. After this formidable task was completed, the student could undertake the study of particular books. Gray recommended a five-step synthetic study of individual books: (1) read the book at one sitting, (2) ignore its chapter and verse divisions, (3) read it as many times as it takes to feel the flow of the book's argument or content, (4) do not consult any outside help such as commentaries or Bible study helps, and (5) read it prayerfully, being open to the Spirit's guidance. After the sweep of the whole book was understood, one could return to individual passages, themes, or words for further study.

Gray's synthetic method caught on. Other premillennialist Bible teachers such as W. H. Griffith Thomas, I. M. Haldeman, A. C. Dixon, A. T. Pierson, and William Evans developed and promoted their own versions of Gray's approach. By World War I, this type of Bible study was being taught in Bible institute classes and through correspondence courses and demonstrated in countless Bible conferences and local congregations. Those who used such methods were convinced that they provided them with ready and reliable access to the Bible's teachings. By proceeding inductively, Bible students could eliminate personal bias and avoid the pitfalls of subjective interpretations of the text, of which liberals were guilty. According to Gray, "The facts must come first and interpretation afterwards. To a great extent, if we get the facts, the interpretation will take care of itself."[58]

Of course, it was not quite that easy. Gray and the rest of the dispensationalist Bible teachers insisted that one could not do justice to either the Bible's big picture or its smaller parts without a firm grasp of dispensational truth. Ironically, over their inductive method they placed an enormously complex dispensational system and forced the Bible's content to pass through its interpretive grids, which made their method deductive through and through. But the teachers insisted that they were saving the Bible from the higher critics and keeping it in the hands of laypeople, where it belonged. Many conservative evangelicals seemed to agree: When all was said and done, dispensationalists defended the Bible against all its detractors.

For many evangelicals, there was no better example of dispensationalists' committed biblicism than *The Scofield Reference Bible,*[59] which became the most significant premillennialist publication in the twentieth century. Many people were first introduced to premillennialism through its notes, and for many others, Scofield became the ultimate authority, the final court of appeals for biblical interpretation. In many ways, C. I. Scofield was one of the most colorful figures in early dispensationalism. He was born in Michigan, but not much is known about his early years. In the early 1860s, he lived with his sister and her husband in Lebanon, Tennessee, and served for a while in the Confederate army. After the war he moved to St. Louis, where he married and became an attorney. Scofield then moved to Kansas, where he served as a representative in the Kansas legislature and a U.S. attorney, under appointment of President Grant. Shortly thereafter, he resigned his office, under suspicion of using it for personal financial gain. When his marriage then failed, he moved back to St. Louis, where he got involved in some petty criminal activity. After Scofield experienced an evangelical conversion in 1879, his life took a dramatic turn. James H. Brookes, who was pastoring the Walnut Street Presbyterian Church, became his spiritual mentor, leading him into both dispensationalism and a life of evangelical activism.

Scofield became a Congregationalist pastor, serving churches in St. Louis and Dallas. He remarried and developed a reputation as an effective church planter and Bible conference speaker. In 1888, he published *Rightly Dividing the Word of Truth,* which became a popular explanation of the dispensational system of biblical interpretation. In addition, Scofield founded the Central American Mission in 1890, directed the Southwestern School of the Bible in Dallas, and developed the Scofield Bible Correspondence Course, which gained wide popularity. He also became closely involved in Moody's work in Northfield, Massachusetts, and moved there to pastor a church nearby. In short order, Scofield became a major player in the Bible conference movement as a speaker, organizer, and dispensationalist networker. In 1902, Scofield, Arno C. Gaebelein, and others began discussing the idea of publishing a reference Bible to help readers understand Scripture from a dispensational perspective. Scofield began working on the project immediately, using materials he had earlier developed for his correspondence course. He finished the work in 1908, and in the following year Oxford University Press published *The Scofield Reference Bible.* In 1917, Oxford published a revised edition.

Scofield's Bible attempted to guide readers through the intricacies of the dispensationalist system. At the bottom of nearly every page of the biblical text, Scofield placed notes that carefully explained the dispensationalist perspective. In many ways, the Scofield Bible was useful to all kinds of readers, from novices to well-indoctrinated students of the dispensationalist system. The notes referred readers to other passages and notes so that one could go into as much depth as desired. Scofield became the most accessible tutor that dispensationalism had ever produced, and his Bible helped to develop and maintain the movement over time.[60]

A second feature of the evangelical tradition that carried over into dispensationalism was loyalty to apostolic doctrine. When formulating their theology, most evangelicals believed that they took their cues from the first century. The modern discipline of church history took shape after the Civil War, which meant that growing numbers of church historians were beginning to recognize the development of doctrine over time.[61] But for the evangelical rank and file, the faith was "once for all delivered to the saints" during the times of the apostles. Thus, the church's task in every age was simply to restate what the apostles taught—and, of course, their words were found in the Bible alone.

Evangelical liberals were calling these ideas into question. They spoke of development, change, and transformation. Often using an evolutionary model, they were even willing to admit that though first-century Christians had believed in the premillennial return of Christ, modern people were under no obligation to maintain such beliefs. George P. Eckman, a strong opponent of premillennialism, admitted its popularity in the early church, then added that

> the lapse of centuries, the record of history, the development of Christianity, and the deepening of Christian experience have put the Christian student of the Bible in a position to place a sounder evaluation upon the doctrine of Christ's second coming than was possible in a previous era. Ancient prophecy is clearer, the words of Jesus are plainer, the writings of the apostles are more intelligible than ever. If we are deceived to-day by false teachers respecting the second coming of Christ, our fault will be greater than that of any who have gone before.[62]

Harris Franklin Rall, a Methodist theologian from the Garrett Biblical Institute, characterized the apocalypticism of the Book of Revelation as "something taken over from the Jewish church of which Christianity was ridding itself. More and more the church saw that the world was to be changed and the kingdom was to come by gradual moral and spiritual development."[63]

To conservative evangelicals, such reasoning sounded arrogant and naive. How could the nineteenth or twentieth centuries pass judgment on the beliefs of the apostles? How could modern historians or biblical scholars cast aside something clearly taught in the Bible simply because they believed they had a better vantage point from which to judge? At the Chicago prophecy conference in 1886, one participant expressed total bewilderment at such thinking:

> I well remember the shock of surprise . . . with which I read in one of the prominent so-called religious papers of New York City that . . . the doctrine of our Lord's premillennial advent which the writer admitted was undoubtedly held by the early church, did well enough in times of persecution, and sustained the faith of God's people when the church was yet weak and struggling against mighty foes; but now, when the church has become strong and is on its world-conquering way, such a doctrine is no longer of any use, being unadapted to a triumphant church, and therefore, whatever in the Scriptures seems to inculcate this doctrine must be interpreted in the light of modern history: With such a principle of interpretation, the devil could drive a coach and four through any biblical doctrine whatsoever.[64]

Dispensationalists appealed to this sense of loyalty to apostolic doctrine: The Bible clearly contained passages on the apocalyptic return of Jesus Christ at the end of the age. If premillennialism was good enough for Peter, Paul, and the Lord Jesus Christ, then it should be good enough for Christians in modern times. Those who denied the doctrine were following the liberal lead, whether they knew it or not.

Premillennialism also followed the overt supernaturalism of the earlier tradition. American evangelicals historically had believed in an active God who was not only revealed in the Bible but also intervened in the lives of believers, and even in the course of history. The frontier people who writhed in spiritual ecstasy at camp meetings, the more sedate students who found Christ in one of the college revivals, the urbanites who came to Jesus in a big city evangelistic crusade, or the "disinherited" who received the fiery baptism of the Holy Spirit in the just-getting-off-the-ground Pentecostal movement all experienced firsthand a bit of the supernatural. The Bible was full of miracles, and though some conservatives were skeptical about miraculous claims in their own time, they felt it was necessary to affirm them in the Bible—and at the end of history.

Many other Christians seemed to be backing away from the miraculous and the supernatural basis on which the faith had been built. Liberalism's

God was characterized more by immanence than by transcendence. God was present in all of life and had decided to work within nature and the historical process. Liberal evangelicals expected to hear God's still, small voice in their souls or see God's powerful hand at work in human progress and improvement. They often sought other explanations for biblical miracles, and the last thing they expected to see was the parting of the clouds and the coming of Christ. Such images were meant to be understood figuratively.

In contrast, dispensationalists insisted on a literalistic supernaturalism. Their worldview still had room for angels, demons, lakes of fire that burned forever, and a Savior whose personal return would put an end to evil and establish the perfect world order. While liberals were uneasy about the miraculous worldview found in the Bible, dispensationalists still embraced it, even in an age with telephones, telegraphs, motor cars, and flying machines. Dispensationalism's affirmation of the supernatural was just the thing many Protestants were looking for. Instead of placing God within the historical or evolutionary process, instead of playing down God's transcendence for the sake of his immanence, they still believed in a God who stood outside history and intended to intervene in it shortly to bring the redemptive process to a close.[65]

Furthermore, dispensationalism provided a way for many evangelicals to maintain some form of millennialism under changing conditions. Postmillennialism lost credibility after the Civil War because in the eyes of most people things were getting worse, not better. As the evangelical empire began to crumble, the promises of postmillennialism seemed empty and highly improbable. The disillusionment with postmillennialism was a recurring theme in the testimonials of dispensational "converts." In 1914, for example, Howard Pope, the superintendent of men at Moody Bible Institute, admitted that although he had been trained as a postmillennialist at Yale, his study of missions and world population growth convinced him that the world was not being converted to Christ, as he had been taught to expect. When he finally came to terms with such undeniable facts, he "was converted to the premillennial view as quickly as Saul was converted to Christ."[66]

Other former postmillennialists said the same thing. It was becoming harder and harder to read the morning newspaper and believe that the millennium was right around the corner. Times were bad and getting worse. What looked inevitable in the 1830s—the Christianization of the nation and the world through the success of revivals and reform—no longer seemed possible, short of a miraculous intervention of Jesus himself. By the end of the century, premillennialism looked much more believable than postmillennialism.

Despite its rather successful attempt at gaining respectability within conservative evangelical circles, dispensationalism remained a movement set apart. It endured because it was able to create a new subculture, not because it won over the broader mainstream or adapted to it. In time, dispensationalism possessed all the resources it needed to survive and even prosper. Its explanation of the Bible and world events made sense to increasing numbers of people. Its approach to the Bible proved to be enormously flexible over time: While never deviating from their basic expectations, dispensationalists were able to make adjustments when they had to in order to keep their interpretation of history moving in the right direction.

2

The Practical Logic of Dispensationalism

From their beginning, dispensationalists demonstrated a strange blend of passivity and activism. Critics charged that dispensationalism inoculated its advocates with a kind of do-nothing passivity, mainly because of its pessimistic and fatalistic worldview: Human civilization is doomed to decline, the forces of evil will inevitably overwhelm the forces of good, and there is nothing that anyone can do about it. In other words, dispensationalism destroys Christian activism by making its followers detached observers of the world's predestined decline. Dispensationalists, content to leave everything to Jesus at his second coming, sit back and do nothing while the world spirals out of control.

To anyone familiar with dispensationalists' expectations of the future, such accusations have a certain ring of truth to them. Dispensationalists do believe the world is on a steep slide into oblivion, despite all efforts to make it better. They deny that the heroic efforts of Christian reformers, evangelists, and missionaries will succeed in solving the world's problems or altering its downward trajectory. But such stereotypes failed miserably in the 1980s, when dispensationalists discovered their political voice and became a force to be reckoned with. With the rise of the New Christian Right, then, dispensationalists demonstrated both a strong fatalism about civilization's decline *and* a fierce resolve to reform it. Where did this strange blend of passivity and activism come from?

This chapter shows that dispensationalists always demonstrated this sometimes contradictory mixture of outlooks. Understanding the course of history in dispensational terms had a profound impact on the way dispensationalists lived. It is impossible to understand how dispensationalists became such a powerful force in national and international politics at the end of the twentieth century without first seeing how prophecy belief shaped personal beliefs and behaviors. Dispensationalists developed a logic of their own that allowed them both to give up on the world and to engage it simultaneously.

Dispensational Urgency and Its Impact on Personal Life

In dispensationalism's early days, outsiders often expected dispensationalists to behave in distinctive ways. It was only natural for people to compare them to the Millerites, who used "millennial arithmetic" to determine that Jesus was coming back on October 22, 1844. With such information, the Millerites took decisive action. Some quit their jobs, closed down their businesses, left their crops unharvested in the field, or sold everything they had to pay off debts. With time running out, they focused all their energies on spreading the news of what they called the "advent near." On the eve of Christ's coming, they gathered together to await his arrival, as one might expect them to do.[1] The "Great Disappointment" notwithstanding, they acted on what they believed, and other people noticed.

In comparison to the Millerites, dispensationalists looked inconsistent and even hypocritical. James H. Snowden, one of dispensationalism's early critics, claimed that dispensationalists did not seem to take their own beliefs seriously. As far as he could tell, believing in Bible prophecy had little direct impact on their religious behavior:

> What do they do that is different from what other Christians . . . do on this subject? If their theory is true, it must lead them to do something that is distinctive of them, that corresponds with and grows out of and fulfills their doctrine, something that other Christians, such as postmillennialists, do not do. As far as we can make out, they do not differ in their practice from other Christians, unless it be that they hold "prophetic conferences" and carry on a propaganda to convert other Christians to their view. They do not engage in any distinctive or special kind of Christian service that fulfills their doctrine. . . .

On pragmatic principles, if this doctrine is true, it should "make a difference."[2]

Certainly, dispensationalists never developed distinctive behaviors such as those of the Millerites. In fact, their prophetic system made it impossible for them to do so. They were living in the "great parenthesis," the suspension of prophetic time, which meant that millennial arithmetic was useless. Unlike the Millerites and other historicist premillennialists, they could neither take chronological bearings nor make any calculations concerning Christ's return. Before the prophetic clock resumed, the rapture had to occur, and that could happen any day or decades into the future. There was just no way to know. Dispensationalists had strong views about the future, but their uncertainty about the timing of future events made it impossible for them to do anything distinctive.

Snowden did not understand the dispensationalists' dilemma, but they did. With no way of calculating Christ's coming, dispensationalists had to be ready at all times for the rapture. Arno C. Gaebelein put it succinctly:

> The Lord Jesus Christ is coming back! He may be here at any moment! He may come today! . . . Now this is not a foolish assertion that He will come today. Nor is it the setting of a specific time for Him to come, which would be equally foolish and wrong. . . . It is the sober statement of a fact, to arouse souls from their carelessness and indifference, and point them to the clear testimony of God's only Word that the Lord Jesus is coming again, and may be here today.[3]

Believing that Jesus could come at any time was not the same as believing that he would arrive on a particular day. Instead of grappling with the ramifications of a definite date for Jesus' return, dispensationalists learned to live with a new sense of urgency about present tasks. Because there was the possibility that not much time was left, believers needed to get serious about their Christian responsibilities.

Do You Want to Be Left Behind?

By definition, evangelicals were interested in saving souls, and dispensationalism gave them a new sense of urgency for evangelism. If Christ could come to rapture his church at any moment, then sinners—and those who intended to save them—simply had no time to lose. Many of the leading evangelists in the late nineteenth century felt especially motivated by the doctrine of the any-moment rapture. D. L. Moody claimed that "I have felt like working three times as hard ever since I came to understand that my

Lord was coming back again."[4] J. Wilbur Chapman, a leading Presbyterian evangelist of a slightly later period, said that premillennialism was "one of the never-failing inspirations in my ministry. It has constantly stirred me on to increased activity in connection with my evangelistic work, and but for this blessed hope, I think that many times I would have grown discouraged and felt like giving everything up."[5]

Moody expressed this sense of urgency in a now-famous lifeboat metaphor that summarizes how the shortening of time for evangelism spurred dispensationalists on to greater effort:

> I look on this world as a wrecked vessel. God has given me a life-boat, and said to me, "Moody, save all you can." God will come in judgment and burn up this world, but the children of God don't belong to this world; they are in it, but not of it, like a ship in the water. This world is getting darker and darker; its ruin is coming nearer and nearer. If you have friends on this wreck unsaved, you had better lose no time in getting them off.[6]

Dispensationalism provided its followers with not only a new sense of urgency to do evangelism but also a new tool for shaking sinners from their spiritual malaise: the possibility of being surprised by the any-moment rapture. In his often-delivered sermon "The Lord's Return," Moody warned that "the trump of God may be sounded, for anything we know, before I finish this sermon—at any rate, we are told that He will come as a thief in the night, and at an hour when many look not for Him."[7]

Revival preachers were used to warning procrastinating sinners about the prospect of sudden, unexpected death and being ushered into the divine presence unprepared. But people had a way of rationalizing their delay in making a decision for Christ. The rapture presented a new challenge: If Jesus could return at any moment to rapture the church, then sudden death was not the only thing to worry about. Now every unrepentant sinner had to face the possibility of being "left behind."

This left-behind theme is everywhere in dispensationalist preaching and teaching. In 1918, Arthur W. Pink must have made his hearers squirm with this harrowing description of the plight of those not taken by the rapture:

> Multitudes of men and women will, for the first time in their lives, call upon the name of the Lord and cry unto Him for Mercy. But their cry will not be heard. . . . Often had these left-behind ones been warned, but in vain. Servants of God had faithfully set before them their imperative need of fleeing from the wrath to come . . . only to be

laughed at for their pains. And now the tables will be turned. God will laugh at them, laugh at their calamity and mock at their fear.[8]

Reuben A. Torrey omitted the image of God laughing at those left behind, but he knew how to drive home the same point:

> Ah, but for you who are out of Christ, unbelievers—When the Lord comes, it means you are to be left behind, left behind when God takes away the restraining power that holds back the manifestation of the Antichrist. Do you want to live in this world when the salt of the earth is gone? . . . I don't. And then darker and darker and darker and darker until it is the midnight of eternal despair. The common argument today for immediate repentance and acceptance of Jesus Christ is that you may die at any moment. That is not the Bible argument. The Bible argument is, "Be ye ready, for in such an hour as you think not the Son of Man cometh." Are you ready?[9]

Preachers and teachers returned to this theme over and over. They tried to get people to imagine what it would be like to be separated from friends and loved ones to face the horrors of the last days alone. Adoniram Judson Gordon, the late-nineteenth-century Baptist pastor from Boston, told the story of two sisters who heard a sermon on Matthew 24:40: "One shall be taken, and the other left." Before going to bed that night, one sister unsuccessfully invited her unconverted sister to accept Christ. In the middle of the night, the Christian sister left their bedroom to pray for her sister's soul. While she was in the next room praying, the unsaved sister woke up to find herself alone: "Has the Lord really come, and has she been taken and I left?" The thought scared her, and she began to cry. Thoroughly unsettled by the prospect of being left behind, the woman knew what she had to do. "Together they wept and knelt and prayed, and before they closed their eyes again they knew that if He should come, they would part no more."[10]

Along similar lines was a story told by William Evans, a popular Bible teacher affiliated with the Bible institutes in Chicago and Los Angeles in the first two decades of the twentieth century. After reading Paul's account of the rapture in 1 Thessalonians 4, a man went to bed and dreamed that when he woke up the next morning his wife and children were nowhere to be found. The house was locked tight, and the clothes of the missing were right where they had left them the night before. He went to his sister-in-law's house for help and discovered that her maid was missing too. Over time the list grew longer: The milkman had not made his usual delivery. During his normal walk to work, the man discovered similar tales of missing persons. When he finally arrived at the office, he found that a number of his own employees had never arrived. That evening, the churches were filled to capacity with angry and frightened people. By then many of those left behind had put two and two together. Among them were clergy who were now fielding hostile questions about why they had not pressed the truth of the coming rapture on their congregations.

At that point in the dream, the man woke up, greatly relieved to find his wife and children close at hand. "Oh, how glad I was to see her, and to realize that the terrible experience was only a dream! But the more I thought about it, the more solemn seemed the Scripture truths which it contained, and the more I was impressed with the importance of being ready for the coming of the Lord."[11]

Throughout history, dispensationalism's best-selling books, *Jesus Is Coming* (1878) and *The Late Great Planet Earth* (1970), were thinly veiled exercises in evangelism that pressed readers with the question, Are you ready if Christ should come today? The enormously popular Left Behind novel series (1995+) similarly tells in spectacular ways what life will be like for those who miss the rapture because of their unbelief. This doctrine is a powerful tool that dispensationalists show no signs of abandoning.

DO YOU WANT TO BE DOING *THAT* WHEN JESUS COMES?

Dispensationalism was not only an incentive for evangelists and the evangelized; it also left its mark on personal behavior. American evangelicals were deeply committed to holy living during the nineteenth century. Conservative Wesleyans fashioned a "holiness movement" that stressed not only conversion, at which time one's sins were forgiven, but also sanctification, when the power of sin was broken. Thus, Wesleyans talked about a "second blessing" or a "second work of grace" that was as discernible as the first. Charles Finney and his colleagues at Oberlin College created their own Reformed version of holiness teaching ("perfectionism"). It stressed a similar second experience after conversion through which a believer received spiritual power for Christian service. At the end of the century, Pentecostals combined elements of both Wesleyan sanctification and Oberlin perfectionism to shape their own doctrine of the "baptism of the Holy Spirit."[12]

Especially popular among American dispensationalists was a third kind of holiness teaching, the Keswick movement's "victorious Christian life." Like so many other middle-class evangelicals of the late nineteenth century, dispensationalists worried about their spiritual failures. After the initial joy of salvation, many evangelicals found themselves on a spiritual treadmill going nowhere fast. Hannah Whitall Smith, whose book *The Christian's Secret of a Happy Life* (1875) was a catalyst for the Keswick movement, described the common experience of many Christians: "You have been forced to settle down to the conviction that the best you can expect from your religion is a life of alternate failure and victory, one hour sinning, and the next repenting, and then beginning again, only to fail again, and again to repent."[13]

The solution to this problem was not more effort or spiritual discipline but "a moment-by-moment surrender of the self to Jesus, and a moment-by-moment appropriation by faith of the cleansing and strengthening power of Christ. So long as the self is surrendered and Christ appropriated by faith, the Christian can be free of any known sin."[14] To gain the victory, one had to "let go and let God." Since only Christ could live the Christian life perfectly, believers had to subjugate their own will to his so that Christ could live through them.

Starting in 1875, advocates of this holiness doctrine organized a series of yearly conferences in Keswick, England. By the 1890s, teachings about the victorious Christian life had permeated American dispensationalism.[15] Moody welcomed Keswick teachers to his Northfield conferences, and American advocates of the "higher life" sponsored their own conferences at Keswick Grove, New Jersey. Soon leading dispensationalist Bible teachers such as Reuben A. Torrey, A. T. Pierson, Adoniram Judson Gordon, A. B. Simpson, Harry A. Ironside, W. H. Griffith Thomas, and Robert McQuilken were teaching the doctrine. Charles Trumbull devoted his *Sunday School Times* to Keswick holiness teaching, and C. I. Scofield included its perspective in his *Reference Bible.* The Bible institutes endorsed it as well, which meant that generations of students worried about whether they were sufficiently "surrendered" to Christ or whether Jesus was Lord as well as Savior of their lives.[16]

It is not difficult to see the compatibility between dispensationalism and Keswick's views of the higher life. Just as the new premillennialists did not have to work to bring in the millennium, they were also not directly responsible for living the Christian life. Their job was to deny themselves and let Christ live through them.[17] Hannah Whitall Smith's favorite analogy was the potter and the clay: "In order for a lump of clay to be made into a beautiful vessel, it must be entirely abandoned to the potter, and must lie passive in his hands."[18]

It never quite worked that way, however. Maintaining passivity was hard work, and moment-by-moment surrender could be grueling. Unlike the Wesleyan second blessing, which was supposed to happen only once in a believer's life, Keswick surrender was ongoing. As soon as victorious Christian lifers reappropriated the self and exercised their own wills, the Lord Jesus slipped off the "throne of their lives" and they were "out of fellowship" with God. Thus, seekers after the higher life had to be on guard constantly, doing what more recent advocates of this approach call "throne checks" and "spiritual breathing," referring to the cycle of confession of sin and reappropriation of Jesus' lordship in one's life.[19] In short, seekers of the higher life continued to experience the up-and-down, in-and-out spiritual whiplash that Smith promised they could avoid by "letting go and letting God." Keswick holiness was not easy. Lying passive in the potter's hands was hard work. Though higher life advocates talked a great deal about spiritual rest, they seemed to find it rarely. As a popular gospel song put it, one had to "Take Time to Be Holy."[20]

As it turned out, then, Keswick passivity required a lot of energy. The victorious Christian life meant strenuously avoiding worldliness in all its forms and remaining separated from the world as much as possible. Thus, there was no drinking, smoking (this worked best outside the tobacco-growing South), card playing, and theater and later movie going, which was a rather typical list of don'ts for evangelicals in the Victorian era. Underlying much of these and other concerns were worries about illicit sexuality.

To be sure, the late nineteenth and early twentieth centuries were hard on such values. New temptations in the cities, a fierce materialism fed by mass marketing, the "new woman" and the resulting pressures on family life and personal morality, changing dress styles, various unsavory amusements, and intellectual novelties such as behaviorism and Freud's views on human sexuality made traditional evangelical mores seem archaic and irrelevant. Yet while other evangelicals complained about moral slippage in their ranks, dispensationalists claimed that nothing inspired people to holy living more than belief in the imminent coming of Jesus. They used their rapture doctrine as a deterrent to questionable behavior: Would you want to be doing *that* when Jesus comes? Robert Speer, the Presbyterian missionary administrator, once explained how he used the possibility of Christ's return to help him overcome temptation.

> I want to speak this word to the man who would be free from unclean personal sin: the next time the temptation comes, fix your mind on the hope of His coming. No man can easily do an unclean and unholy thing expecting at that moment that Jesus Christ might come. Can I cross the threshold of the questionable place? Can I read the questionable book? Can I be found with that questionable story on my lips? Can I be caught on the verge of that sin, if I am expecting that at that very moment Jesus Christ may come?[21]

Reuben A. Torrey derived the following guideline from the doctrine of the imminent rapture: "Do not do anything that you would not be glad to have your Lord find you doing if He should come. . . . Never go anywhere that you would not like to have the Lord find you if He should come." Torrey testified that "it is simply wonderful how that clears things up."[22]

That method evidently worked for others too. Premillennialists told stories about how their belief in the rapture had kept them from all manner of sinning. Evangelist Leander Munhall told of two members of the same church who were walking through the theater district in New York City one evening. When one remarked that a certain play had received rave reviews and asked if the other would like to attend, he replied, "No, I don't want to. The Lord might come while I was in such a place."[23] If one got used to looking at things that way, there was no end to the deviance that the possibility of the returning Christ might prevent. Another dispensationalist observed that "the modern easy-living, card-playing, theater-going, dancing type of Christian is very rarely found to be one who has learned to look for his Lord's premillennial advent."[24] James M. Gray claimed that during his years in pastoral ministry, his best parishioners had always been premillennialists. "The members of my church on whose hearts the coming of Christ had made any sensible impression were separated from that whole system of worldliness. They were the working force of my church along spiritual lines, and the most intelligent Bible students. They manifested the greatest power in prayer. They were the most self-denying givers. They lived the most even and consistent lives."[25]

The new premillennialists had in their possession a powerful and effective tool for guiding and regulating personal life. The possible arrival of the Son of Man provided all would-be disciples of Jesus with a new motivation to live holy lives, separated from every appearance of evil, for "every man that hath this hope in him purifieth himself" (1 John 3:3).

The Dispensational Approach to Politics and Missions: Activism within Limits

Just as dispensationalism motivated its adherents to holy living and evangelism, it also pushed them into politics and foreign missions. The opponents of dispensationalism claimed that prophecy belief destroyed evangelical commitments to both. But there were always exceptions to the rule. Some dispensationalists became political activists in their own way and the leading promoters of a new kind of foreign missions. The logic of dispensationalism produced a blend of passivity and activism in these areas too.

GIVING THE DEVIL AS MUCH TROUBLE AS WE CAN

While dispensationalism may have encouraged evangelicals to live holy lives, its critics were sure that it decimated the earlier evangelical commitment to social action and reform. Shirley Jackson Case, dean of the University of Chicago Divinity School, condemned dispensationalism's "inherent pessimism," which made its followers impotent and uninterested in making the world a better place:

> The story of man's career upon earth is viewed [by premillennialists] as one long process of deterioration from the days of Adam until the day of final gloom. Life's ills seem altogether too gigantic to be overcome by mere human endeavor, and even with such divine aid as mankind has experienced no gradual process of reform can issue successfully. . . . [Dispensationalism] scorns all efforts made in the name of religion to correct the ills of society. Society must not be redeemed; it must be damned. . . . To inaugurate any program of social betterment or to set the church as a whole upon an upward course would be to thwart the divine purpose and to delay the advent of Christ. Both the world and the church must grow constantly worse in order to meet premillennial ideals. Viewed from this standpoint, the essential function of religion is to insure for a few selected individuals a way of escape from the ultimate wrack and ruin to which the world is destined.[26]

It is easy to find dispensationalists who fit this description, for a logical application of premillennial doctrine left little room for attempts at social betterment. Premillennialists believed they were living in the "times of the Gentiles," which started with ancient Babylon's conquest of the Jews and would remain until Jesus returned to break Gentile power and establish his millennial kingdom. Current evil conditions were prophesied centuries ago, the natural outgrowth of Satan's control over the present age. The church's job was not to try to change the inexorable flow of history but to ride it out until these evil times had run their course. In 1914, one dispensationalist spelled out this widespread perspective:

> Our God . . . keeps His covenants. He gave the government of this world into the hand of the Gentile nations at the time of Nebuchadnezzar. Therefore, the New Testament says, "The powers that be are ordained of God," and the King of Kings Himself could consistently advise Israel to pay tribute to Rome. The function of government includes police authority and the maintenance of law and order. . . . If those to whom God has committed this duty are negligent or corrupt in administering it, the Church, as such, must not interfere. It must not try to help the

Christ-rejecting world make a success of its job. It must wait until the world's "inning" is over, when the Church's time will come.[27]

This passive approach to social and political problems was evident from the beginning of dispensationalism in America. In 1880, the venerable James H. Brookes said he was saddened whenever a Christian got involved in politics. "Well would it be," he said, "if the children of God were to keep aloof from the whole defiling scene. . . . [We] can do more for the country . . . by prayer and godly walk [i.e., behavior] than by being 'unequally yoked together with unbelievers.'" He also urged those who were "dead to the world and alive to Christ" to avoid casting ballots because "dead men do not vote."[28]

Sometime later, such an attitude would mean a repudiation of the social gospel movement, the attempt to apply the "social teachings" of Jesus to society. By the early twentieth century, many Christians had concluded that sin had both personal and social dimensions and that Christians should try to save society as well as souls. In the years before World War I, the most important social gospeler was Walter Rauschenbusch, a Baptist pastor-turned-seminary-professor whose books *Christianity and the Social Crisis* (1907) and *Christianizing the Social Order* (1912) had sensitized large numbers of Christians to their social responsibilities. He censured premillennialism's "historical pessimism" and called it a "dead weight against any effort to mobilize the moral forces of Christianity to share in the modern social movement."[29]

Thanks largely to his evangelical upbringing in a pietistic German Baptist home in Rochester, New York, Rauschenbusch never stopped believing that conversion was absolutely necessary. At the same time, however, he was open to elements of the so-called new theology, whose perspective on the coming kingdom of God was unacceptable to dispensationalists. Instead of expecting an apocalyptic kingdom to be ushered in by the returning Jesus, the social gospel envisioned a gradually realized kingdom, built on the accumulation of ethical behavior and the application of gospel principles to social and political life. Dispensationalists believed there was nothing they could do about the demise of civilization, but social gospelers taught that the kingdom would never come unless they did their duty to redress the ills of society. By World War I, dispensationalists and many other conservative evangelicals had decided to leave society-saving to liberals and social gospelers, while they concentrated on saving souls.[30]

The split between the two perspectives was deep. Some dispensationalists renounced all social reform as Satan-inspired. Arno C. Gaebelein believed that the real power behind reform was demonic: "The world, to which we do not belong, can do its own reforming without our help. Satan, I doubt not, wants to reform his world a little, to help on the deception that men do not need to be born again."[31] Another premillennialist was even more to the point:

> Sociology, or social service as generally emphasized is, in its final outworking, a black winged angel of the pit. . . . Satan would have a reformed world, a beautiful world, a moral world, a world of great achievements. . . . He would have a universal brotherhood of man; he would eliminate by scientific method every human ill, and expel by human effort every unkindness; he would make all men good by law, education and social uplift; he would have a world without war. . . . But a premillennialist cannot cooperate with the plans of modern social service for these contemplate many years with gradual improvement through education as its main avenue for cooperation, rather than the second coming of Christ.[32]

Such thinking amounted to turning the earlier evangelical tradition on its head. One of the distinguishing marks of the Second Great Awakening in the early nineteenth century was the close connection between converting the lost and Christianizing society. In fact, before the Civil War, revivalism and social reform seemed natural allies, not competing alternatives. That was especially true in the North, where revival and radical reform politics often went together, as the history of abolitionism and women's rights demonstrates.[33] For most evangelicals in most of the 1800s, there was no need to choose between revivals and reforms. They went together. Therefore, it is not surprising that even the rise of dispensationalism did not completely eradicate the robust reform tradition out of which most dispensationalist converts had come.

Despite the logic of their eschatology, then, some dispensationalists found ways to continue addressing certain social ills. Because they believed that time was short, dispensationalists never engaged in what they considered long-term solutions to problems or in a program to which they could not join their priority of evangelism. In other words, premillennialists were willing to fight social evil if it was rooted in individual behavior and could be remedied primarily through personal transformation. For example, Henry P. Crowell, CEO of the Quaker Oats Company and longtime president of Moody Bible Institute's board of trustees, was a leader of the Chicago Committee of Fifteen, which successfully agitated for laws against the city's robust sex industry. Even though the Committee of Fifteen came up with a legal remedy, its approach concentrated on individual behavior and paid no attention to the social or economic factors that may have contributed to the vice. Thus, if social service included opposing prostitution, gambling, and the liquor traffic, then many turn-of-the-century premillennial revivalists such as Sam P. Jones, J. Wilbur Chapman, "Gypsy" Smith, William E. Biederwolf, and Billy Sunday qualified as social reformers.[34] Still, even that limited list of reforms made some dispensationalists uncomfortable.

Prohibition was probably the favorite project of evangelical social reformers. Temperance reform had been part of the "Christian America" agenda since the 1820s and 1830s. Most evangelicals considered drinking alcohol a personal vice that had disastrous consequences for family and society. Countless local congregations sponsored their own temperance groups and were willing to exercise church discipline on the buyers, sellers, and users of alcohol. Rescuing people from the ravages and results of drink was a common evangelical preoccupation before the rise of dispensationalism. Thus, it came as a big surprise to evangelical anti-alcohol activists when some dispensationalists condemned their cause as trumped up by the devil "to hinder Christ's return and extend his own probation."[35] Since drunkenness was a prophesied sign of the times (Matt. 24:37–38), some dispensationalists thought that reformers were actually postponing Christ's second coming by trying to alleviate the problem.

Complete separation from the world and its corruptions might seem like the ideal strategy while awaiting Christ's return, but many dispensationalists knew that such a thing was impossible. According to James M. Gray, "We cannot absolutely separate ourselves from its society, its literature, its politics, its commerce, but we can separate ourselves from its methods, its spirit, and its aims."[36] He was typical of other dispensationalists who believed that even if Prohibition were only a stopgap measure, it was still worth pursuing:

> It is said that we carry our heads so high in the air, that we are so absorbed in our heavenly citizenship as to have no interest in the citizenship of earth. But this is not so. We love God, but we love our brother also; and while we believe that the highest expression of love to our brother is to seek the salvation of his soul, yet we would not keep back from him the good, if he will not have the best. We will preach the gospel first, last, and all the time, but we will work and vote against the saloon, and urge others to do the same, on every opportunity.[37]

Therefore, while he was serving as a pastor in Massachusetts, Gray was actively involved in the Prohibition Party. He traveled throughout the state on behalf of the cause, edited the party's magazine, and faithfully attended its conventions. When he moved to Moody Bible Institute, he remained an outspoken enemy of the liquor industry and led students in a Prohibition parade through Chicago streets in 1908.[38]

There were other acceptable ways to attack the liquor problem. Reuben A. Torrey frequently included a special service for drunkards in his evangelistic crusades. After the regular revival service was over, Torrey sent his associates into the saloons and alleys to round up those who needed to hear a sermon on the evils of alcohol. At one such midnight service in Birmingham, Alabama, Torrey addressed three thousand people, the majority of whom were obviously inebriated. Most preachers would freeze up at the thought of preaching to such a crowd, but evidently Torrey was quite good at it. Roughly 180 people had sufficient presence of mind to make decisions for Christ that night, which evangelicals considered the first step toward permanent rehabilitation.[39] For some dispensationalists, then, such reform efforts were certainly doable and appropriate in the short time remaining before Christ's return.

Dispensationalists also engaged in what historian Norris Magnuson has called "evangelical social welfare" work. A. B. Simpson's Christian and Missionary Alliance was both premillennial in theology and heavily engaged in urban ministry. While other Christians evacuated the crime-ridden inner cities, dispensationalists with plenty of spiritual stamina stayed behind and did the hard ministries that others avoided. Melvin Trotter, who was converted in Chicago's Pacific Garden Mission in 1897, strongly believed in the imminent second coming and founded sixty-seven rescue missions to meet the physical and spiritual needs of urban derelicts.[40] Rescue mission work was another example of addressing, in mostly individualistic terms, issues that had complicated social and economic components.

Clearly, then, dispensationalists were not totally passive in the face of social problems. Within careful limits, they too could be involved, despite their conviction that no reform would be lasting or would succeed in changing the downward course of history. Their selective activism was an important rear guard, harassing action against Satan and the Gentile powers before Christ's return. Regardless of civilization's inevitable decline, God still expected the church to stand up for truth and righteousness. James M. Gray made the point as well as anyone: "The Church does not expect to conquer this world in the present dispensation or with present methods, but it expects to remain on earth as its saving light and its preserving salt until Jesus comes to take it away and substitute other agencies for the execution of His will. In the meantime, let us continue to shine and to hold corruption in check." Just because the ultimate solution was in Christ's return, there was "no reason why we should let the rogues in some city hall steal our money, or the rum-seller or procurer debauch our youth. It is admitted that we are not undoing the works of Satan very fast, but we are giving him all the trouble we can till Jesus comes, and that is something."[41]

Throughout their history and under certain circumstances, dispensationalists were willing to fight the good fight of reform, even when they knew that their efforts could not ultimately succeed. The willingness to give the devil all the trouble they could till Jesus came would be seen again in the rise of the New Christian Right in the 1980s.

A New Approach to Foreign Missions

In the early decades of dispensationalism's rise within American evangelicalism, critics often claimed that it cut the nerve of foreign missions. In his rather negative study of premillennialism and its effects, James H. Snowden quoted a St. Louis minister who condemned it as "the rankest type of pessimism" and concluded that "it discredits the church, belittles the power of the gospel, and dishonors the Holy Spirit. It makes his work a failure and confesses him to be unequal to the task for which he was sent into the world."[42] W. O. Carver, professor of missions at Southern Baptist Theological Seminary, blamed premillennialism for the church's "missionary indifference" and called it "unworthy of God" and "utterly at variance with God's declared desire that all might come to repentance and salvation."[43] Such criticism was largely baseless. Just as evangelist D. L. Moody "felt like working three times as hard" after he became a premillennialist, other converts to dispensationalism felt a similar urgency to bring the gospel to a dying world in its final slide toward doom—but in a way consistent with their worldview.

The nineteenth century was the great century of Christian missions. Starting with the American Board of Commissioners for Foreign Missions in 1810, evangelicals founded dozens of denominational and interdenominational mission agencies during the 1800s. Given the prevailing postmillennial perspective of the time, most evangelicals saw missions as one of the God-ordained means by which the world would be Christianized before Christ's return. Revivals and reforms had transformed America into an "evangelical empire" by the middle of the nineteenth century, and therefore evangelicals expected their efforts overseas to produce a similar turning to Christ.

Fueling much of this missionary drive was the conviction that their efforts could not fail. Though the going was tough and the costs enormously high, evangelical postmillennialists never doubted that they would ultimately succeed. Premillennialists, on the other hand, denied that the missionary enterprise would transform the world into Christ's kingdom. They agreed that someday soon Jesus would reign over the entire earth, but not until after the second coming and the establishment of his millennial throne. Given those convictions, how could dispensationalists stay actively involved in an enterprise that they expected to have limited success?

Certainly, the sense of urgency had much to do with dispensationalists' strong commitment to missions. With the possibility of so little time left, missionaries had to get busy. Robert Speer, secretary of the Presbyterian Board of Foreign Missions from 1891 to 1937, became a premillennialist during his college days at one of Moody's Northfield conferences and noted later how "life seemed altogether changed for me in that hour." Part of his personal transformation was an increased desire to reach the lost with the gospel before it was too late. According to Speer, dispensationalists' anticipation of the Lord's return motivated them to stay morally upright, made them more tolerant of others, and increased their zeal for sharing the gospel.[44]

Of course, Speer could get away with calling premillennialists "tolerant" in 1903, while no one would have thought of using the word twenty years later, when most dispensationalists had adopted fundamentalism's militant and separatistic style. But at the turn of the century, they showed a much softer side and could be downright cooperative. Like many other evangelicals, dispensationalists were often willing to cut denominational corners for the sake of missions. They knew that with little time remaining, they would have to combine forces with other evangelicals in the missions movement at the end of the nineteenth century.

But dispensationalists' understanding of the missionary mandate was different from that of other evangelicals. To put it simply, premillennialists believed that God never intended to save the world before the second coming of Christ, only a small part of it. In the present dispensation, God wanted to "visit the Gentiles, to take out of them a people for his name" (Acts 15:14). C. I. Scofield called this verse "the most important passage" in the New Testament because it showed clearly "the distinctive work of the present, or the church age. . . . The Gospel has never anywhere converted all, but everywhere has called out some."[45] The church's duty was evangelization, by which premillennialists meant the widespread and rapid spreading of the gospel to nonbelievers, not Christianization, which included the gradual transformation of social, political, and educational institutions along Christian lines. To be sure, dispensationalists wanted conversions. That is why they evangelized. But they did not envision a gradual transformation of the world through the spread of the gospel to individuals and institutions. Christianization would come, dispensationalists were convinced, but not until King Jesus defeated his enemies and sat on David's throne in Jerusalem.

Dispensationalists, then, were clearly working with a new theory of missions. Adoniram Judson Gordon understood the difference and felt no need to apologize for it. God's purpose for this dispensation was the gathering of the relatively few elect from the nations, not the Christianization of the entire world.[46] This meant that the church needed to put its energies into preaching the gospel, not "civilizing" the masses through various Christian educational, social, or economic projects. From Gordon's perspective, Christianizing did not work anyway. "We look in vain in the history of the ancient and the modern mission for examples of the heathen being slowly prepared, to and through culture, for the acceptance of Christianity; while conversely there is no lack of examples that the systematic way through civilization to evangelization has been not only a circuitous but a wrong way."[47]

Many found this emphasis rather curious and wrong. Most American evangelical missionaries at the end of the nineteenth century believed that Christianizing the "heathen" overseas included civilizing them in the ways of the West. After all, the Christian message had produced a superior Western culture, which was full of industry, learning, and economic prosperity. Even someone like Speer, whose premillennialism waned in his later years, believed that "there is a false imperialism which is abhorrent to Christianity, and there is a true imperialism which is inherent in it."[48] Premillennialists shared notions of America's cultural superiority and "the moral equivalent for imperialism,"[49] but they did not have enough time to do much about them. Evangelization, not civilization, was their calling. According to A. T. Pierson:

> Our Lord's coming furnishes a motive to world-wide evangelism in emphasizing duty rather than success, and our commission rather than apparent results. . . . Thus while premillennialism is charged with cutting the nerves and sinew of Foreign Missions, it in fact supplies their perpetual incentive and inspiration in teaching us that duty is ours, results God's.[50]

William J. Erdman said much the same thing: "It is not the purpose now between the first and second coming of His Son to convert all the nations. That conversion lies beyond the Second Coming. . . . Therefore, let us not be discouraged, but adapt ourselves to the purpose of God. Let us not in the least think Christianity or the Holy Spirit to be a failure."[51]

Contrary to the critics, then, dispensationalism did not lessen commitment to missions; if anything, the movement intensified missionary zeal, but with a difference. Dispensationalists used their considerable network of publications, educational institutions, and churches to create a vital missionary movement of their own, which in many ways rivaled the missionary program of the older evangelical denominations.

As already noted, premillennialists were masters of the media. Their magazines kept readers well supplied with missionary news and reminders that those who believed in the second coming had a large stake in the evangelization of the world: "And this gospel of the kingdom shall be preached in all the world for a witness unto all nations; and then shall the end come" (Matt. 24:14). The *Truth,* the *Watchword, Our Hope,* the *King's Business,* the *Institute Tie,* the *Christian Workers Magazine,* and *Moody Bible Institute Monthly* all carried regular features on missions. Even though the *Missionary Review of the World* served a much broader clientele, its editor, A. T. Pierson, was a leader in the new premillennial movement and constantly demonstrated how his eschatology informed his outlook.

The close connection between dispensationalism and missions was also carefully nurtured in the Bible institutes, many of which started out as missionary training schools. Considered by many to be the first of such schools was A. B. Simpson's Missionary Training School, which was founded in 1882 to train men and women for urban and foreign missions.[52] In 1888, Adoniram Judson Gordon became chairman of the executive committee of the American Baptist Missionary Union, which made him responsible for providing Northern Baptist missionaries for the newly acquired British Baptist mission in the Congo. Unable to find sufficient numbers of missionary recruits for the new work, Gordon took matters into his own hands. At the urging of H. Grattan Guinness, a popular British Bible teacher who had already founded a missionary training school in London in 1872, Gordon opened the Boston Missionary Training School in 1889.[53]

Even dispensationalist institutions not founded chiefly for missionary training purposes emphasized foreign service. At schools such as Moody Bible Institute (Chicago, 1886), Practical Bible Training School (New York, 1901), Northwestern Bible and Missionary Training School (Minneapolis, 1902), Bible Institute of Los Angeles (1908), Philadelphia School of the Bible (1914), Prairie Bible Institute (Alberta, 1922), and Columbia Bible Institute (South Carolina, 1923), missions education and awareness were important parts of the program.[54] The Bible institutes hired former missionaries as faculty, sponsored missions conferences for their students, booked visiting missionaries and missions executives to speak in chapel, and plastered the walls with maps of the world to show where missionary work was taking place—and where the need was greatest. According to one observer of campus life at Prairie Bible Institute, "They ate, drank, studied, slept, and sang missions morning, noon, and night."[55] It is not surprising, then, that these dispensationalist schools were both recruiting stations and boot camps for missionary service.

Dispensationalists also played an important role in the founding of the Student Volunteer Movement (SVM). In 1886, D. L. Moody sponsored a four-week summer Bible conference at his Mount Hermon School in Northfield, Massachusetts, for leaders of the intercollegiate YMCA. One of the conference's organizers, Luther Wishard, hoped to make missionary service a main theme of the gathering and recruited a number of students who were already interested in serving overseas. Shortly after the conference convened, these students asked A. T. Pierson, whom Moody had scheduled to lecture on "The Bible and Prophecy," to give a special talk on missions. As a leader in Presbyterian missions and the editor of the *Missionary Review of the World,* Pierson clearly knew his topic. During his lecture titled "God's Providence in Modern Missions," he traced on a map how God had opened doors around the world during the last quarter century and argued that with careful planning and spiritual resolve, a new wave of missionary volunteers could finish evangelizing the world by 1900.

Few lectures ever got such immediate and dramatic results. On the spot, over a hundred students committed themselves to missions after college graduation. Following the conference, many of the "Mount Hermon Hundred" organized groups on their own campuses to recruit additional volunteers. Traveling squads of college men and women went from campus to campus with the same message. By the next summer's conference in 1887, the Mount Hermon Hundred had grown to over one thousand. By the following year, the number had doubled again. Such a response required organization, so the Student Volunteer Movement for Foreign Missions was founded to manage the flood of enthusiastic recruits. The SVM adopted as its motto a phrase that Pierson had used in his 1886 lecture: "the evangelization of the world in this generation." Two young Ivy Leaguers were chosen to lead the new organization, John R. Mott as chairman and Robert Speer as traveling secretary. By 1910, roughly five thousand student volunteers were serving overseas.[56] Not all of them were dispensationalists, but many who fired up their initial enthusiasm and mobilized them for their unprecedented missionary push were convinced that their work was part of God's dispensational plan for the ages.

Dispensationalism's most important contribution to the missionary enterprise was the "faith missions" movement.[57] Unlike denominational mission boards, the faith missions were voluntaristic, independent of any formal ecclesiastical support or control, ecumenical, and nondenominational. Originally, the "faith" in faith missions referred to the financial policy they adopted. They refused to solicit directly for funds, trusting instead that God would provide, an approach that many of them have had to reconsider in more recent times. The faith missions focused on evangelization, not Christianization or civilization, and thus were in line with premillennialist concerns and strategy.

Most American faith missions followed the model established by J. Hudson Taylor, an entrepreneurial British evangelical who established a new way of doing mission work. Born in Yorkshire, England, of pious Methodist parents, Taylor left for China in 1853 with the China Evangelization Society. He served for seven years, but ill health forced his return to England in 1860. Through this missionary experience, Taylor found his calling: an abiding concern for the unreached people in the vast interior of China. In 1865, he started a new missionary agency, the China Inland Mission (CIM), without denominational support. He lectured throughout England, presenting the challenge of reaching inland China with the gospel. At first he called for 24 volunteers, two for each of China's unevangelized provinces. In 1875, Taylor called for 18 more, then 70 in 1881 and 100 in 1886. By 1895, the China Inland Mission numbered 641 missionaries and 462 Chinese helpers who served in 260 stations and outstations. Such numbers made the CIM the largest missionary agency of its time.

The CIM was built on Taylor's premillennialist principles, and it sought the evangelization of the largest number of people possible in the shortest period of time. Because of such urgency, the CIM ignored denominational differences, was open to people with little formal education, and opted for local control rather than establishing a missions bureaucracy in Great Britain. Its goal was to present the gospel in areas where it had not been preached before. Its priority was evangelization; for the most part, it left church building and education to others. Probably the most revolutionary thing about the CIM was its precarious financial base: Taylor sent out recruits in hopes that God would provide for them financially over the long haul.

It did not take long for American dispensationalists to adopt Taylor's method. In 1888, at D. L. Moody's invitation, Taylor came to America to speak at the Northfield and Niagara Bible conferences. Everywhere he went he described his "faith mission model," and audiences responded with enthusiasm and sizable donations. At Northfield, he was present at the founding of the Student Volunteer Movement. His North American tour was a roaring success: He returned to England with enough money to support eight new CIM missionaries for a year and a list of sixty applicants for missionary service. By the end of 1888, Taylor was back in China with fourteen new American and Canadian recruits.[58]

The key to the CIM's work in North America was Henry W. Frost, a devout Presbyterian who became a dispensationalist at one of the Niagara conferences. Frost had wanted to go to China, but Taylor recognized his entrepreneurial spirit and in 1889 appointed him secretary-treasurer for the CIM's work in the United States and Canada. Between 1888 and 1917, Frost sent out 239 North American missionaries (147 women and 92 men) and raised over $1.5 million. Most of these recruits were premillennial (but not necessarily dispensational), though the CIM was flexible enough to include a number of evangelical amillennialists as well.[59]

Next to the China Inland Mission, probably the most successful American premillennial faith mission was the Christian and Missionary

Alliance, which was founded in 1887 with the merger of the Christian Alliance and the Evangelical Missionary Alliance. The real force behind the CMA was A. B. Simpson, a Presbyterian premillennialist from Canada who left his affluent New York City church to work among the poor and unchurched.[60] The Christian and Missionary Alliance today has all the trappings of a denomination, but in the beginning it was a voluntary association for the advancement of home and foreign missions and drew support from throughout American evangelicalism. The CMA, to use more modern terminology, was an early example of a "parachurch" movement, a specialized organization that operated outside normal church structures to accomplish a well-defined task. Even before the merger, Simpson articulated the characteristics of the movement:

> There is no antagonism whatever in the Alliance to any of the evangelical churches, but a desire to help them in every proper way and to promote the interests of Christ's kingdom. . . . Let us never forget the special calling of our Alliance . . . to hold up Jesus in His fullness . . . to lead God's hungry children to know their full inheritance of privilege and blessing for spirit, soul, and body . . . to witness to the imminent coming of the Lord Jesus Christ as our millennial king.[61]

What held the Alliance together was a zeal for foreign missions, a concern for the needs of the poor and disinherited, and a commitment to what Simpson called the "four-fold gospel"—conversion, entire sanctification, divine healing, and the premillennial second coming. After 1892, the Alliance sent out between seventy and one hundred missionaries a year.[62]

The CIM and the CMA marked the beginning of an extensive premillennial missions network that more or less operated outside the normal denominational missions track.[63] In 1890, Fredrick Franson, one of the many admirers and imitators of Moody among Scandinavian immigrants in the late nineteenth century, founded the Scandinavian Alliance Mission (later the Evangelical Alliance Mission or TEAM). After hearing Taylor's call for one thousand volunteers for China, Franson mobilized a number of small Scandinavian immigrant denominations for his cooperative mission effort. In the same year, C. I. Scofield founded the Central American Mission, which was one of the first Protestant efforts in Latin America.[64] In 1893, Rowland V. Bingham, a Canadian premillennial evangelist, founded the Sudan Interior Mission (now SIM International), which eventually sponsored roughly one thousand missionaries, the largest Protestant contingent in Africa.[65] In 1895, Peter Cameron Scott, with help from A. T. Pierson, started the Africa Inland Mission (AIM) in Philadelphia.[66] Over the next two or three decades, many more organizations were founded.

As Joel Carpenter has pointed out, during the 1880s and 1890s, nearly all evangelicals still found the denominational missionary societies welcoming and compatible with their concerns. Thus, "the faith missions functioned like auxiliaries, taking up the surplus volunteers who couldn't fit into the denominational programs."[67] But by World War I, many evangelicals had grown uneasy with denominational or ecumenical missionary organizations that were too inclusive of what they considered bad doctrine or misguided missionary practices. For dispensationalists, such suspicions were tied to fears of the coming great apostasy, when "Christendom," which included even the evangelical denominations, would fall prey to the spirit of the Antichrist. Thus, it made sense for dispensationalist faith missions to go their own way. In 1917, seven faith missions founded the Interdenominational Foreign Missions Association of North America (IFMA) and elected as its first president CIM's Henry W. Frost, who had already started denouncing any association with "unbelief."[68] Such a move was obviously intended to distance the faith missions from the more inclusive (and therefore suspect) Foreign Missions Conference of North America, which had organized in 1911 with fifty-two members, most of which were denominational missionary societies. The IFMA can be seen as one of the first organizational expressions of the fundamentalist-modernist controversy. When conservative evangelicals felt alienated from their own denominational mission boards, many of them turned to faith missions as the only theologically safe alternative. In other words, what started as an auxiliary to denominational missions in the 1880s and 1890s became for fundamentalists the preferred way—for some, the only way—to do missions in the 1920s and 1930s.

Dispensationalism did not stifle foreign missions; it encouraged it, even when it denied that missions could succeed. As one premillennialist said at a 1918 prophetic conference, "[A]t such an hour it is not for us to fold our arms and look up, to sigh over conditions around us, to pray to be caught away out of the wreck of this sin-cursed world. . . . I would not cross the street to talk to a crowd of premillennialists about the coming of the Lord unless they were looking for and hastening His coming by sending forth the gospel."[69]

In some ways, then, dispensationalism was a massive motivator, not a spiritual sedative. People who embraced its doctrine said they were energized by it. They became more aggressive evangelists, missionaries, and in limited ways seekers after righteousness, at both personal and social levels. But what difference did accepting dispensationalism make in the way people both viewed and interacted with the larger world, with the momentous current events that were transforming the geopolitical scene? That is the topic of the next chapter.

3

Dispensationalists and the Flow of History

Dispensationalists said they knew where the world was going. To them the future was carefully spelled out in the pages of the Bible. From the beginning of their movement, they believed they had uncovered a divinely inspired scenario of end-times events. God was in control, and God's redemptive purposes were being carried out in the world. If people had the correct perspective, they could trace God's purposes in the morning newspaper. There were strong forces at work in the world beyond any person or group's control. Beneath the headlines, a cosmic battle was being fought, one that would soon be brought to an end by the return of Jesus, who would defeat all God's enemies and establish, finally, God's righteous reign on the earth. Dispensationalists knew there was nothing anybody could do to stop the prophecies from happening and there was nothing they had to do to ensure their fulfillment.

The critics were correct, then, about one thing: This view of the future meant that even those who believed they knew what would happen next could do nothing to change things one way or the other. The expressed will of God would be done no matter who liked it or did not like it. So what were dispensationalists supposed to do in light of this guaranteed future? They could do nothing, except interpret the signs of the times and warn others about the wrath to come. They were to sit in the bleachers of history and tell others how the future game on the field was going to turn out. They were not responsible for the game's outcome; only God was. Their job amounted to understanding the already-declared game plan and sharing it with others.

But even such a limited task could be difficult. While dispensationalists had their well-developed scenario, the players on the field did not always seem to cooperate. Sometimes dispensationalists had a hard time making the stated scenario and the morning newspaper align properly. Some days were better than others. Dispensationalists were exceptionally good at making the events leading to and resulting from World War I fit their expectations, but they had a more difficult time making sense of the complex events that led to World War II. What follows demonstrates that for the first half of the twentieth century, dispensationalists were passive observers of world events, not shapers of them.

The Place of World War I in Biblical Prophecy

To see how dispensationalists fit World War I into their prophetic expectations, one must enter the labyrinth of their interpretive system. As already stated, premillennialists viewed the Bible as an elaborate storehouse of prophetic material just waiting to be unpacked and sorted through or (to change the metaphor) a complicated prophetic jigsaw puzzle just waiting to be put together. Since they believed that all parts of the Bible were equally inspired, any text was fair game in building their interpretive argument.

THE FOUR GREAT EMPIRES AND THE TIMES OF THE GENTILES

Premillennialists believed they were living in the "times of the Gentiles," which C. I. Scofield defined as "that long period beginning with the Babylonian captivity of Judah, under Nebuchadnezzar, [which shall] be brought to an end by the destruction of Gentile world power . . . [at] the coming of the Lord of glory."[1] To understand this period, dispensationalists juxtaposed two texts from Daniel: Nebuchadnezzar's dream of a huge statue (2:24–45) and Daniel's dream of four beasts rising out of the sea (7:1–28). Both visions, they believed, had to do with the four great powers that would rule in succession during the times of the Gentiles.

Nebuchadnezzar's statue consisted of four parts: a gold head, silver chest and arms, bronze belly and thighs, and iron legs and feet, which also contained a mixture of baked clay. According to Daniel's interpretation of the dream, each section represented one of four empires, with Nebuchadnezzar's Babylon as the first. Each of the four would exert absolute sway during its time, but the last kingdom would be compromised by its internal divisions, as illustrated by the mixture of iron and baked clay in the statue's feet.

Daniel's dream about four beasts from the sea indicated much the same message. The first beast was like a lion with eagles' wings. The second was like a bear. The third looked like a leopard with bird wings growing out of its back. The fourth and last beast had ten horns and was a terror to behold:

> After this I saw in the night visions, and behold a fourth beast, dreadful and terrible, and strong exceedingly; and it had great iron teeth: it devoured and brake in pieces, and stamped the residue with the feet of it: and it was diverse from all the beasts that were before it; and it had ten horns. I considered the horns, and, behold, there came up among them another little horn, before whom there were three of the first horns plucked up by the roots: and, behold, in this horn were eyes like the eyes of man, and a mouth speaking great things. . . .
>
> The fourth beast shall be the fourth kingdom upon earth, which shall be diverse from all kingdoms, and shall devour the whole earth, and shall tread it down, and break it in pieces. And the ten horns out of this kingdom are ten kings that shall arise: and another shall rise after them; and he shall be diverse from the first, and he shall subdue three kings.
>
> Daniel 7:7–8, 23–24

Dispensationalists believed that both prophetic visions predicted the rise and fall of the same four great world empires: Babylonia, Medo-Persia, Greece, and Rome. Of the four, the last was obviously the most important, since it would be in existence when "one like the Son of Man" came to break once and for all the Gentile powers and establish the messianic kingdom.[2] According to their reckoning, the last Gentile power in Daniel's vision was not the old Roman Empire of caesars and legionnaires but a new one consisting of a ten-nation confederacy (the ten horns) ruled by a powerful king (the little horn) who had crushed three former confederates in his rise to power. Premillennialists were certain that this "little horn" of Daniel's prophecy was the "beast" in Revelation 13, the "abomination of desolation" in Matthew 24 (cf. Daniel 9), and the "man of sin" in 2 Thessalonians 2—the Antichrist.[3] As head of the revived Roman Empire, he would wield tremendous power and be the central figure in the events of the end times.

The Revived Roman Empire

The identification of the last kingdom with the Roman Empire posed a bit of a problem. As every student of ancient history knows, the Roman Empire fell a long time ago (actually, it fell more than once) and no longer exists. How, then, could this prophecy be true? This is precisely what World War I did for dispensationalists: It showed them how the defunct Roman Empire could be re-formed in anticipation of Christ's return.

In the middle of the nineteenth century, when dispensationalists first started to predict this end-times scenario, the revived Roman Empire existed only in their heads and on their prophetic charts. Exactly how the nations of Europe would come together to constitute the Antichrist's empire was not known. At the beginning of the twentieth century, Europe's national boundaries did not come close to what was envisioned for the end. But World War I suddenly provided a way by which the maps of Europe might be redrawn. Only one month after the war broke out in Europe, Arno C. Gaebelein excitedly told the readers of *Our Hope* that "it is possible that out of the ruins, if this universal war proceeds, there will arise the predicted revival of the great confederacy of Europe."[4]

How would the war affect the national boundaries of the warring nations? What would happen to existing alliances? Could this be the beginning of the end? Before one could answer any of those questions, one had to deal with one more basic issue: To what extent would the boundaries of the new Roman Empire coincide with those of the old? Some premillennialists argued that since its religious authority would extend far and wide, the new empire would be much larger than the original. Most premillennialists, however, held on to their biblical literalism and insisted that the new Rome would occupy the original territory.

Completing the Prophetic Picture

If the war provided a plausible means by which the Antichrist's ten-nation confederacy could take shape, then interpreters could turn their attention to other parts of the jigsaw puzzle.

From dispensationalists' perspective, the Antichrist would brutalize the "saints of God" who opposed his blasphemous demand to be worshiped. Because of their basic hermeneutical decision that all earthly prophecies belonged to Israel and not the church, dispensationalists believed that the "saints" referred to a newly restored nation of Israel that would be regathered in Palestine. As we will see in a later chapter, the reestablishment of the state of Israel became a central concern of dispensationalists throughout the century, an event that transformed them from passive observers to aggressive activists on the prophetic field of play.

According to the prophetic picture, the Antichrist and the new Israel will make a mutual defense pact, under which Jews will reconstruct their ancient temple and restore the old sacrificial system. Three years after signing the treaty, the Antichrist will break it, enter the temple, suspend all sacrifices, declare himself to be God, and demand to be worshiped (Dan. 9:27). To carry out his blasphemous plans, the Antichrist will have the assistance of a false prophet who will compel worship of the beast through force, clever utilization of miraculous powers, and economic coercion (Rev. 13:11–18). For three and a half years, these two evil geniuses will oversee a reign of terror—the great tribulation—against all those who refuse to give their allegiance to the Antichrist.[5]

Despite the enormous strength of the Antichrist over his reconstituted Roman Empire, premillennialists went on, there will be spheres of political power not directly under his control. In the course of the Antichrist's reign, Israel's security will be challenged by a northern confederacy of nations, which will include Gomer, interpreted by dispensationalists as Germany (Ezekiel 38–39).[6] Early in their history, the Bible teachers also concluded that the northern confederacy would be under Russian control. This conclusion was based on Ezekiel's reference to Gog (38:2), the prince of Magog, whose territory included Rosh, Meshech, and Tubal, which dispensationalists believed referred to Russia, Moscow, and Tobolsk.[7]

Once they adopted this interpretation of Gog and Magog, dispensationalist Bible teachers never wavered from it, but few other scholarly interpreters of the Bible understood Gog and Magog in the same way. In addition to the reference in Ezekiel, Gog and Magog appear in other parts of the Bible. In Genesis 10:2 (cf. 1 Chron. 1:5), Magog is a grandson of Noah (along with Gomer, Tubal, and Meshech), while in Revelation 20:8, Gog and Magog are allies of Satan in his final rebellion against God following Christ's one-thousand-year reign on earth. Before the rise of dispensationalism, biblical interpreters identified Gog and Magog with a variety of groups. As Paul Boyer has pointed out, in the beginning of the Christian era, the Jewish historian Flavius Josephus believed that Gog referred to the Scythians. Three centuries later Augustine thought Gog represented all unbelievers. The mystic Joachim of Fiore and other medieval interpreters pointed to tribes beyond the Caucasus, while others understood Gog in terms of aggressive Islam, especially the Ottoman Turks of the thirteenth century. Most British and European prophecy writers of the past few centuries followed this Gog-as-Turk interpretation, including the Puritans in colonial New England.[8]

It was not until the nineteenth century that students of Bible prophecy started interpreting Gog as Russia. Much of the credit for this change goes to Wilhelm Gesenius, a German Hebrew scholar whose Old Testament lexicon (1828) read "Rosh" as an early form of "Russia," "Meshech" as

Moscow, and "Tubal" as the Siberian city of Tobolsk.[9] By 1836, Gesenius's lexicon had been translated into English and was selling in Britain and America. John Nelson Darby was an early convert to Gesenius's interpretation of Gog, and a number of other prophecy writers followed his lead.[10]

Though other Bible scholars found such connections completely insupportable, turn-of-the-twentieth-century American premillennialists found them irresistible. C. I. Scofield clearly misrepresented the scholarly consensus in 1909 when he said of Ezekiel 38, "That the primary reference is to the northern (European) powers, headed up by Russia, all agree."[11] From that time on, dispensationalists saw Russia and its northern allies as crucial players in the end times. When they drew their maps of anticipated prophetic events, the arrows for the king of the north always originated in Russia.

With the Antichrist in charge of a revived Roman Empire and Russia anchoring a separate northern confederacy, two major sections of the prophetic jigsaw were already in place. The rest of the details were relatively easy to put together: Doubting the Antichrist's willingness or ability to hold Israel for himself, the northern confederacy will attack the Holy Land (Ezekiel 38). Their aggression will be coordinated with an attack from the kings of the south (Dan. 11:40; Ezekiel 30), which most dispensationalist Bible teachers identified as an Arab/African alliance, probably headed up by Egypt. This pincers attack will provoke the Antichrist to defend beleaguered Israel, but before he can even dispatch his forces from Western Europe, God will supernaturally intervene and destroy the invaders (Ezekiel 39).

Premillennialists had agreed on the essentials of that prophetic outline long before war broke out in 1914. Dispensationalists were not personally threatened by these predicted events, however, because they believed that Christ would rapture the church before the Antichrist was revealed and the tribulation began. But most dispensationalists also believed that the church would remain long enough to see events moving in that direction. Sitting high in the bleachers, dispensationalists had a safe perch from which they could watch the nations take their assigned places on the field below. As they were about to discover, however, sometimes historical events did not always follow dispensationalists' expectations.

PREDICTING THE WAR'S OUTCOMES

The war provided dispensationalists with a vast supply of historical data that needed to be analyzed for prophetic relevance. First, there was the matter of national boundaries. Even a casual glance at a prewar map of Europe revealed premillennialism's predicament: The national boundaries in 1914 showed little resemblance to what dispensationalists expected to be in place in the new Roman Empire. Ireland had never been under Roman control, but now it was under the control of England, which had. Contemporary Germany had been Roman only in its territory west of the Rhine and south of the Danube rivers. While parts of Austria-Hungary had been under Roman jurisdiction, nearly all of its territory north of the Danube, an area equal to roughly half its holdings in 1914, had not. Before any new Roman Empire could arise, some drastic changes would have to be made.

Consequently, with maps and prophetic Scriptures in hand, premillennialists formulated a number of predictions about the war's outcome. Since Germany had not been a member of the original empire and did not seem to figure prominently in the prophetic future, except as part of the northern confederacy that would oppose the new Rome, it would probably lose the war, suffer national humiliation, and give up some of its western territory that had originally belonged to the old Rome. The Austro-Hungarian Empire would have to be broken up so that some of its Slavic provinces north of the Danube would be free to fall under the influence of Russia and its northern confederation. Russia, though now closely allied with powers formerly within the Roman Empire, would end that association with the West and eventually develop as an independent power with influence over other nations in northern and eastern Europe. The Ottoman Empire, whether as a result of the war or a later series of events, would eventually relinquish control over Palestine or at least allow the regathering of the Jews there. Ireland would gain its independence from Great Britain.[12]

As one can easily see, premillennialists' predictions were amazingly accurate. Germany lost the war, was forced to accept full blame for the conflict, was loaded down with reparations, and turned over some of its western territory, Alsace-Lorraine, to France. Austria-Hungary was partitioned into Yugoslavia, Austria, Hungary, and Czechoslovakia, and gave up additional territory to Romania, Italy, and Poland. Russia suffered two revolutions in 1917, made a separate peace with Germany, and terminated its alliance with the Western powers. The Ottoman Empire simply dissolved after the war, with Palestine passing to British control, and Ireland won its independence from England three years after the war. By any standard of measurement, premillennialists' record was extraordinary. James M. Gray seemed completely justified in declaring in a 1918 prophecy textbook: "Prophecy Changing the Map of Europe."[13]

Clearly, as some of their detractors might have pointed out, one did not have to be a premillennialist to arrive at similar predictions about the war and its outcome. Anyone familiar with the recent past knew that France and Germany had quarreled for decades over Alsace-Lorraine. Likewise, long-standing ethnic divisions and antagonisms in the Austro-Hungarian Empire made some kind of partitioning inevitable. But premillennialists' claims had not been based on a careful study of political, social, or military history. Premillennialists had come to their conclusions through the use of the Bible alone. The unfolding events in Europe fit well into the scheme they had constructed from biblical prophecies long before the war began. The significance of their predictions was their source, not just their accuracy. Premillennialists knew both what was going to happen and why.

Of course, there were some surprises too. No premillennialist before the war had seen the demise of the Russian Empire under the czar. The prophetic scenario included an empire on the rise, not one in disastrous decline. In the early stages of the war, the Bible teachers hailed the Russian victories over the Turks as a sign of things to come, when the king of the north would lead his northern confederacy into the Middle East to do battle against the Antichrist's ten-nation empire. Thus, when in 1917 Russia suffered two revolutions and came close to complete collapse, the Bible teachers were at a loss: How could Russia fulfill its end-times role when anarchy reigned?

Gaebelein thought that the chaos was only temporary. He was running a series of articles on the prophet Ezekiel in *Our Hope* during the Bolshevik Revolution and concluded that "Russia will eventually return to the old regime and will once more become a monarchy to fulfill her final destiny as made known in this sublime prophecy."[14] He and other interpreters reasoned that the fall of the czar was God's just punishment for his ill-treatment of the Jews but that eventually the Russian Empire would re-form so that Magog, the prince of Rosh, could play his assigned role. In time, however, the Bible teachers realized that a communist Russia was just as serviceable as an imperial one. It did not take long for dispensationalists to forget about the czar and turn their attention to the threat of atheistic communism as the ultimate fulfillment of biblical prophecy. By 1920, Gaebelein wrote that the head of the northern confederacy would be Soviet Russia.[15]

THE TEMPTATION TO GO TOO FAR

In light of such overall success, some premillennialists could not resist the temptation to venture into even more speculative territory. As many dispensationalists discovered, sometimes the devil was in the details of their prophetic analysis. In trying to read the signs of the times, some premillennialists clearly went too far.

Some interpreters could not imagine the war ending in a "natural" way. In 1915, with no end of the war in sight, F. C. Jennings predicted that only God could stop the fighting—by rapturing the church. He envisioned a war-weary world shocked to discover millions of people suddenly gone from homes, factories, and the battlefield. Bewildered and demoralized by the rapture, the warring nations would no longer be able to carry on. Into the resulting confusion would step a great leader to restore order and establish a new political unity in war-torn Europe—the Antichrist. Even though Jennings hedged his bets a bit by saying that God might choose to end the war in some other way, such speculation inevitably worked against the movement's growing respectability.[16]

Though most dispensationalists did not go as far as Jennings, they believed that the war was too significant not to be somehow directly connected to the end of the age. The *Weekly Evangel,* the newspaper of the newly organized Pentecostal Assemblies of God, detected in Revelation 16:14–16 a clear-cut chronology for the end times—war, rapture, and Armageddon: "For they are the spirits of devils, working miracles, which go forth unto the kings of the earth and of the whole world, to gather to the battle of that great day of God Almighty. Behold, I come as a thief. Blessed is he that watcheth, and keepeth his garments, lest he walk naked, and they see his shame. And he gathered them together into a place called in the Hebrew tongue Armageddon." The analysis continued: "We are not yet in the Armageddon struggle proper, but at its commencement, and it may be, if students of prophecy read the signs aright, that Christ will come before the present war closes, and before Armageddon. . . . The war preliminary to Armageddon, it seems, has commenced."[17]

Other premillennialists reverted to the old besetting sin of date setting, which had been historicist premillennialism's undoing in the nineteenth century. Dispensationalism supposedly had eliminated that temptation by insisting that God's prophetic timetable had been discontinued at Israel's rejection of Jesus and would not be resumed until the rapture of the church. The suspension of prophetic time supposedly made all millennial arithmetic impossible during the great parenthesis. But some dispensationalists seemed to forget their basic principles. William E. Blackstone unexpectedly resorted to the useless year-day theory and predicted the end of the time of the Gentiles sometime between 1916 and 1934. He denied that he was date setting because his calculations applied to Israel and not the church and thus did not technically predict the return of Christ. But other premillennialists rightly saw that setting a date for the one was essentially setting a date for the other. Seven months after Blackstone's analysis appeared, William J. Erdman wrote a disclaimer and warned against adopting old methods that had proven so fruitless in the past.[18]

Still other dispensationalists promised that the end would "occur in our generation. That is to say, that the man of average age now living, and all younger, barring the usual accidents of sickness and death, [will] witness this tremendous climax and transition."[19] In light of all that had been happening, such a statement did not seem especially risky in 1919, but it still committed premillennialists to a vaguely defined time limit, which in the end worked against them.

Wisely, most premillennialists showed remarkable reserve and stuck to the main outlines of their program. In fact, all during the war years, some leaders in the movement warned against reading too much into the events of the day. Reuben A. Torrey complained that everybody wanted to get into the prophecy game and were coming to reckless conclusions: "Even writers and papers that have hitherto shown no great interest in prophecy are now giving voice to the wildest explanations of current events supposedly from the standpoint of Bible prophecy."[20] After the British captured Jerusalem in December 1917, James M. Gray, one of the more levelheaded premillennialist teachers, cautioned his readers not to assume that the capture of the city necessarily meant that the nation of Israel would be restored immediately. The founding of a permanent state could be years in the future. At any rate, premillennialists should "beware of fanaticism, beware of letting down the bars of restraint in any direction whatever. . . . The kind of watching the Lord desires is quite consistent with the care of our households, the proper conduct of our business and especially just now the support of the government."[21]

Most premillennialists knew that the closer they stayed to the basic outline of their prophetic script, the safer they were. Was the war the biblical Armageddon? Gray denied it, since the battle prophesied in the Bible would occur in Palestine, not in the trenches of the western front, and it would be between the Gentile powers and the returning Son of Man, not the Central Powers and the Western Allies. Naturally, things could change rapidly, but until the church had been raptured and the Antichrist had formed his empire, it would be foolish to identify the war with Armageddon.[22]

Was Kaiser Wilhelm II the Antichrist? At the beginning of the war, Arno C. Gaebelein, a German immigrant himself, rather liked the Kaiser. He especially appreciated his reported religious orthodoxy and piety: "The Emperor has the reputation of being a sincere Christian, who reads the Word and is a praying man."[23] But after war broke out, Kaiser Wilhelm's piety seemed beside the point. As much as American dispensationalists disliked the Kaiser, they had to admit that he did not fulfill prophetic qualifications. He was not from the old Roman territory; he did not rule over a ten-nation confederacy; and he had not declared himself to be God. Anti-German dispensationalists would have to wait for someone else. The Kaiser did not qualify.[24]

If the war was not Armageddon and the Kaiser was not the Antichrist, then what was the war's ultimate significance? In 1916, Gaebelein observed that "the only thing a Christian can safely say about these unprecedented conditions among the nations is that these events fully confirm the characteristics of the age and its predicted end as revealed in the Bible and that all that is happening in a way prepares for the very end of the times of the Gentiles and the coming of the King."[25] In so many ways, the war proved to be a large step toward the predicted end of the age, but in the last analysis, it was merely the first among many great wars that would characterize the last stage of the times of the Gentiles. As bad as things were, the World War was just the beginning. As Jesus had said, "And ye shall hear of wars and rumours of wars: see that ye be not troubled: for all these things must come to pass, but the end is not yet" (Matt. 24:6).

Despite the constant temptation to say more, most premillennialists did not predict more than Gaebelein did in 1916. The war confirmed their interpretation of the Bible, indicated a definite realignment of nations in anticipation of the rise of the beast, and marked a beginning of more wars in the future. Their war record earned dispensationalists the best reception ever. But not everyone was pleased with premillennialism's growing popularity. Some people believed that dispensationalism was dangerous and needed to be stopped before it could make a bad situation even worse.

The Counterattack against Dispensationalism

As hard as it was to deny or disparage dispensationalism's interpretive achievements, some people tried. But belittling premillennialism's record was not easy. As its credibility increased, that of its critics invariably declined, at least in many people's eyes. Those who had promised good times ahead suddenly had to account for the slaughter of millions of people, the blood lust of the nations, and what looked like the imminent collapse of European civilization.

Looking on the Bright Side

Despite bad news everywhere, a few never-say-die optimists refused to concede anything to the premillennialists. For some postmillennialists, for example, not even a world war weakened their confidence in the coming millennium. James H. Snowden compared the war to the Protestant Reformation. Just as the Reformers had shattered the power of ecclesiastical tyranny in the sixteenth century, so the Christian soldiers of the Allied Powers were wielding the sword of Christ in the twentieth, ridding the world of its last imperial tyrant, Kaiser Wilhelm II. In the long run, the war was not a serious setback to the coming of the millennium; it was an important, God-sent means to that very end. The war was God's way of bringing the millennium one step closer by exposing and eliminating humanity's darker side.[26]

Not everyone shared Snowden's approach, but still they wanted to look on the bright side, when they could find it. In the middle of 1915, the editors of the *Biblical World* asked its readers not to "paint the present situation . . . in too dark colors." While millions of people were fighting in the trenches, millions more were carrying on life as usual. Taking solace in the growing peace movement, the editors claimed that while "we have not made the world into the kingdom of God, we have made it much less the Kingdom of Satan." There may be tares in the field, but there is still more good seed than bad. "Let us count our liabilities if we must, but as sensible folk, let us count our assets as well."[27]

As the war came to an end, the days of such balanced optimism were long gone. Woodrow Wilson's Fourteen Points and his hopes for a transformed world and a lasting peace were shattered by the peace conference at Versailles. Many feared that the Great War had really not solved anything. Shailer Mathews of the University of Chicago reflected the widespread disillusionment after the war:

> The outbreak of war in 1914 shattered all optimism. Human nature was still untamed. A state could command the loyalty of its subjects in the face of interests that extended beyond the frontiers. It is easy now to be contemptuous of the optimism of pre-war liberalism, but when one recalls the elements of the world situation, it is not strange that we should have suffered illusion. Socialism, international labor movements, international commerce, international science, the Roman Catholic Church, Protestant Christianity, peace societies, the mixture of population, common culture, all seemed to insure the maintenance of peace. The outbreak of war did more than excite horror for itself. It argued a breakdown of forces which we believed were shaping up a new world order.[28]

Liberals may have been shattered by the war, but they were not about to accept premillennialism's rising popularity without a fight. Before the war, liberals did not see dispensationalism as a threat. But after the war broke out, they complained that premillennialists' "influence is permeating our churches"[29] and that dispensationalism's "injurious effect can already be seen in hundreds of churches throughout the United States."[30] Gaebelein quoted with a certain satisfaction the statement of the president of Auburn Theological Seminary: "The spirit of premillennialism is dividing the whole Protestant Church of America. . . . Here is a school of thought that is captivating the church of today."[31]

THE LIBERAL COUNTEROFFENSIVE

The liberals' counterattack began in 1917. In *When Christ Comes Again,* George P. Eckman portrayed premillennialists as eccentrics who were driven by a "strange perversity." He denounced their "proof texting," which amounted to gross mishandling of biblical prophecies in their original contexts. Even though dispensationalists claimed to be defending the Bible against liberal higher critics, Eckman warned that "the influence of the Bible can be injured by those of its alleged friends who either purposely or unwittingly pervert its teachings."[32]

In the same year, Shailer Mathews published *Will Christ Come Again?* certain that it would cause a storm of controversy. Distributed by the thousands by the American Institute of Sacred Literature, the booklet argued that

> historically minded students of the Bible distinguish between funda-
> mental Christian truths and the method and language used by the
> early Christians in expressing those truths. They believe that in order
> to realize these truths, the conceptions of those ancient men of God have
> to be translated into modern conceptions, exactly as the Hebrew and
> Greek language has to be translated into English.[33]

Thus, Mathews concluded that apocalyptic texts were "mistakes of early Christians" that were no longer binding on modern believers. When premillennialists argued that Christians in every age were bound to accept the inspired teachings of the Bible, "this logically ought to include belief in a flat earth, the perpetuation of slavery, the submission to rulers like Nero." Christians should move beyond such "Judaistic hopes."[34]

In 1918, the controversy heated up considerably. Shirley Jackson Case, Mathews's faculty colleague down the hall at the University of Chicago Divinity School, published *The Millennial Hope,* in which he traced the history of millennialism to show that apocalyptic movements emerge during times of crisis. Thus, to use the book's subtitle, the current wave of premillennialism in America was "a phase of war-time thinking." A year later Case took a more exegetical approach in *The Revelation of John* to demonstrate that the Apocalypse was an outgrowth of specific sociopolitical problems at the end of the first century, which meant that premillennialists were wrong to seek prophetic fulfillments in modern times.[35]

In 1919, James H. Snowden published two more important anti-dispensationalist polemics, *Is the World Growing Better?* and *The Coming of the Lord: Will It Be Premillennial?* He criticized dispensationalism from a number of angles. Christendom's historic creeds contained nothing approaching dispensationalism, and only a few contemporary scholars accepted its teachings. It used a superficial and misleading approach in regard to difficult biblical passages, selecting only those verses that supported its position or could be twisted to its advantage. Snowden characterized dispensationalism's view of the millennium, with its restored temple and blood sacrifices, as militaristic, Judaistic, pessimistic, and detrimental to the social dimensions of the Christian gospel.[36]

In 1920, George Preston Mains published *Premillennialism: Non-Scriptural, Non-Historic, Non-Scientific, Non-Philosophical.* He called premillennialists devout but misguided Christians whose teachings appealed to the unlettered and literalistic wing of the church. He called dispensationalism pessimistic, detrimental to missions, essentially Jewish in its view of the millennium, and mysteriously well-endowed for its massive propaganda campaign. Mains also condemned premillennialism's false "psychology of history," which saw only decay and decline ahead for the human race.[37]

In the same year, Harris Franklin Rall, professor of systematic theology at Garrett Biblical Institute in Evanston, Illinois, published a study entitled *Modern Premillennialism and the Christian Hope,* which was an expanded version of three articles he had published in *Biblical World.* Rall accused premillennialists of literalism, spiritualizing the text when it suited their purposes, unrestrained fancy in the use of typology and allegory, and a failure to understand texts in their original historical context. Premillennialists, he concluded, had a higher loyalty to their system than to the Word of God, which they twisted because of their mistaken views of biblical infallibility and verbal inspiration.[38]

Did the liberal counteroffensive do any good? Most likely, it made little difference. Despite their impassioned and well-argued critiques, the liberals failed to diminish dispensationalism's strong grassroots appeal. Dispensationalism provided worried and bewildered evangelicals with a clear, biblical explanation of what was happening and what would happen next. Case understood something about the appeal of millennial beliefs: They helped Christians to "maintain their faith in the triumph of righteousness at times when life's ills seemed overwhelming and no other way of escape seemed open."[39] In times of crisis, people wanted assurances and answers. Dispensationalists provided them, no matter what criticisms their opponents leveled against them.

Probably more significant in accounting for premillennialism's growing popularity during the war years was that its outline of the end times had an uncanny way of making sense. Liberals could protest all they wanted about the nature of Jewish apocalyptic literature in the intertestamental period or the necessity of reinterpreting ancient cosmological views of reality using modern terms. But they could not change the fact that to many people the new premillennialism had been able to explain the signs of the times.

For the most part, then, premillennialists could afford to ignore the liberal attacks against them. They, not the liberals, spoke the language of laypeople. They knew how to make complicated texts as plain as day. They were willing to let the facts speak for themselves.

The Attack on Premillennialists' Patriotism

The critics of premillennialism did manage to find dispensationalism's most vulnerable spot: If they were true to their principles, premillennialists could not be wholehearted supporters of the American war effort. During the super-patriotic and militaristic war years, some people accused premillennialists of being unpatriotic and even anti-American. As early as 1917, dispensational Bible teacher Harry A. Ironside claimed that "men of unflinching integrity and loyalty to the Word of God have been branded as secret political agents, and their books, so far as possible, proscribed by these audacious and unprincipled leaders in the apostasy."[40]

In the middle of 1918, Mathews edited a series of anti-premillennialist articles in the prestigious *Biblical World*. In his piece "The Premillennial Menace," Case accused premillennialists of not wanting America to win the war. Under normal circumstances, one could ignore premillennialism as a harmless fancy, he said, "but in the present time it would be traitorous negligence to ignore the detrimental character of the premillennial propaganda." According to Case, dispensationalism opposed the American war effort. "This type of teaching strikes at the very root of our present national endeavor . . . [and] is fundamentally antagonistic to our present national ideal. . . . At the present moment, premillenarianism is a serious menace to our democracy and is all the more dangerous because it masquerades under the cloak of piety." Case accused dispensationalists of secretly supporting Germany since "a Teutonic victory ought to bring us nearer to the end of the present world."

Sooner or later, Case went on, the enemy will recognize "that to aid and abet the premillennial movement is one of the safest and most subtle forms of activity in which he can engage." Premillennialism constitutes a threat to national security because "with a thoroughness suspiciously Teutonic," the movement is spreading rapidly in such a way as "to threaten our national enthusiasm at one of its most vulnerable points." He cited the widespread circulation of premillennialist books and pamphlets, its publicity campaign, and its aggressive evangelistic work among soldiers as proof of its seditious designs. In conclusion, Case declared that

> of course the premillennialist does not oppose the war; what he opposes— always in principle and sometimes by overt act—is any hopeful effort to win this war and thereby so reconstruct international relationships that warfare may henceforth be eliminated as a factor in human experience. When someone becomes a premillennialist, he becomes a pronounced enemy of democracy and a serious menace to the nation's morale in this hour of its need.[41]

The most preposterous part of Case's attack was his assertion that the premillennialist movement was possibly funded by German secret agents. Seven months before his article appeared, Case had suggested to the *Chicago Daily News* that premillennialists were getting two thousand dollars per week to spread their views around the country. "Where the money comes from is unknown, but there is strong suspicion that it emanates from German sources. In my belief, the fund would be a profitable field for governmental investigation . . . for if the belief spreads many would not be able to see the need of fighting for democracy."[42]

The charges were outrageous, and Case offered no evidence to substantiate them. Even some opponents of premillennialism thought that he had gone too far.[43] But the charges were serious and got premillennialists' attention. Suddenly, dispensationalists had some explaining to do.

DISPENSATIONALISTS FIGHT BACK

In normal times, such charges would have been too ridiculous even to acknowledge, but in the emotion-charged atmosphere of World War I, premillennialists had to answer them. Public sentiment was easily aroused against everything German. The nation's mood was well summarized in the words of Teddy Roosevelt: "He who is not with us, absolutely and without reserve of any kind, is against us, and should be treated as an enemy. Our bitter experience should teach us for a generation . . . to crush under our heel every movement that smacks of the smallest degree of playing the German game."[44]

Fellow Chicagoan James M. Gray responded to Case's accusations by citing the patriotic efforts of his Moody Bible Institute. On the day war was declared, he said, the American flag was run up the institute's flagpole, there to remain until final victory was won. The school gladly opened its doors for the sale of Liberty Bonds, and Moody students regularly canvassed to raise money for the Red Cross. Moody students had joined the army, and a few of them had died in the war. The institute stood firmly for dispensational truth, but it also felt its "duty to be the support of the government to the last dollar and the last man."[45]

Reuben A. Torrey compared Case to the prosecutors in the Salem Witch Trials in the 1690s. Thanks to such stupid scaremongering, one "faithful brother . . . [was] arrested and put in jail because of preaching the return of our Lord. The accusation brought against him was that of treason, or disloyalty to the President." Torrey provided no verifiable details of the incident but strenuously denied the charges that premillennialism was unpatriotic. If any disloyalty exists, he suggested, it can be found in Hyde Park at the University of Chicago, not on the north side at Moody Bible Institute: "While the charge that the money for premillennial propaganda 'emanates from German sources' is ridiculous, the charge that the destructive criticism that rules in Chicago University 'emanates from German sources' is undeniable."[46]

Evidently, some premillennialists were getting a bit edgy. They claimed that their literature had been confiscated and that their Bible teachers had been harassed. But such accounts were never substantiated and may never have happened. At times, the premillennialist press attempted to calm nerves and provide assurances that premillennialists and their doctrine were not in trouble with the government. In 1919, for example, the *Christian Workers Magazine* reported that official army sources denied that William E. Blackstone's popular *Jesus Is Coming* had been banned from army camps, as had been widely reported.[47]

DISPENSATIONALISM AND DEMOCRACY

The liberals were right about one thing: Many dispensationalists could not give unflinching support to America's war aims to make the world safe for democracy. According to dispensationalism, the spread of democratic governments was a sign of the end of the age. When viewed eschatologically, democracy possessed the seeds of its own destruction—the corrupting power of sinful human will. The rise of modern democracies was God's way of proving that humankind was incapable of governing itself. People who put faith in democratic institutions discover sooner or later that sinful humanity is incapable of governing itself. Changing the system, ensuring equal access to political power, and putting government in the hands of the people only compound the problems that all human governments face. According to biblical prophecy, too much democracy will lead to anarchy, which will cause people to turn to an authoritarian leader who can guarantee law and order—the Antichrist.[48]

If pressed, premillennialists had to admit that the very foundation of America's democratic government was corrupt. In 1915, in a question and answer section in the *Christian Workers Magazine,* James M. Gray declared that the idea that "governments receive their just powers from the consent of the governed" was false. "Democracy (self-government) is the antithesis of autocracy—God's ideal of government. . . . Self-government whether in an individual or in a nation is abhorrent to God's order for the creature." Gray asserted that when "scripturally viewed, the basis on which our government rests is false, that the ideal government is an absolute monarchy where Christ is the monarch," and that it was inconsistent for a Christian "to make himself part of a system whose principle is the apotheosis of man."[49] In light of the coming reign of King Jesus, C. I. Scofield even went so far as to declare himself a "monarchist."[50]

Taken by themselves and in isolation, such statements may lead one to the wrong conclusion. Dispensationalists were not counterrevolutionaries working for the overthrow of the government. They were speaking in eschatological terms, comparing the perfection of the coming age to the limitations of their own. Even though premillennialists longed for the ideal government under King Jesus, they realized that in the meantime they had to do the best they could. Therefore, in the same article in which he rejected the theoretical foundations of American democracy, Gray advised that "when a Christian finds himself one of a democracy, his duty to God . . . requires that he fulfill his obligations as a citizen whether it be in depositing a ballot or shouldering a gun. He may do both these things, and yet in spirit not be a part of that system to which they belong."[51]

Nevertheless, dispensationalist rhetoric could sound alarming and even subversive. In 1914, Reuben A. Torrey frequently urged his fellow premillennialists not to get caught up in the wave of uncritical patriotism that was sweeping the country:

> To love a country simply because it is one's own country and to stand by it no matter of what injustice it is guilty towards other and weaker nations is radically and thoroughly unchristian. The sentiment, "My country, may she always be right, but my country whether right or wrong," has been quoted and requoted until some almost seem to think it a portion of the Word of God. It is a thoroughly vicious statement. It justifies the most unjustifiable wars and the most devilish conduct in war. We should love our country . . . but we should not love our

country at the expense of other countries. We should not justify our country when she is in the wrong. We should not join hands with the multitude of our countrymen to do evil to other nations. We should seek the peace and prosperity and welfare of other lands as well as our own. We should not seek to always put the best construction on our own acts and the worst construction on the acts of other nations. The law of love should be the law of nations as well as the law of the individual. The fair-sounding word "Patriotism" is often used as a cloak for the basest and meanest conduct. In Christ Jesus there is neither Jew nor Greek, Barbarian, Scythian, German, Englishman, Russian, or American, we are all one in Him (Gal. 3:28; Col. 3:11).[52]

Torrey did not stop there. He argued against making military training mandatory in the public schools, criticized the "war madness" behind the massive military buildup, and, when war seemed inevitable in early 1917, sadly conceded that "no real Christian can relish the suffering that will come to real Christians on both sides."[53]

Even America's declaration of war did not put an end to Torrey's prophetic critiques. When Wilson announced that Americans were fighting to make the world safe for democracy, Torrey said that "this may sound well for a Fourth of July celebration and as an appeal to thoughtless people," but "there are many Americans who would refuse to fight for Wilson's ideals."[54] In an editorial in the July 1917 issue of the *Christian Workers Magazine,* Gray stated that "we are with [President Wilson] in considering this to be the present duty of the nation. But we are reminded by the inspired prophets that the ascendancy of democracy, though certain, is not lasting." Eventually, even the democracies will gladly turn themselves over to the Antichrist and make war on the returning Christ and his saints.[55]

Other premillennialists voiced similar concerns about entering the war and took a pacifist stance. In 1916, the *King's Business* of the Bible Institute of Los Angeles editorialized that a vote for Teddy Roosevelt in the upcoming election was a vote for war and advised against it. The next year the magazine used a long quote from Bertrand Russell and reprinted a sermon by Henry Sloane Coffin, the liberal Presbyterian leader, that opposed America's involvement in the European war.[56] In September 1917, *Our Hope* published an article that asked, "Should a Christian go to war?" and answered no. Christians have no business fighting to improve the world's corrupt system, the article reasoned, though during a national crisis believers may serve in noncombatant roles, as clerks, ambulance drivers, and hospital workers.[57]

These views show that when premillennialists were true to their eschatology, they could give only tentative allegiance to their government's war effort. In fact, had they been entirely honest, premillennialists would have admitted that, in the long run, America would be part of the Gentile powers destroyed at the second coming. Despite their personal love of country, consistent premillennialists acknowledged that, apart from Israel, God was committed to no nation. Like it or not, the United States was a part of the worldly system that was passing away. Since most dispensationalists could not find America explicitly mentioned in biblical prophecy, they did not have to publicize it, but every honest dispensationalist knew that it was true.[58]

Despite this initial reticence, most dispensationalists caught the war fever during 1918. For example, there was an abrupt change in the editorial policy of the *Christian Workers Magazine* after America entered the war. At one time the editors of the magazine were scrupulous about presenting both pro and con views of America's involvement. In 1916, the magazine published a respectable article against America's participation in the war.[59] In 1917, it printed an article by a Mennonite pacifist back to back with an article by Gray that used Augustine's just-war theory to support the idea of America's going to war against Germany.[60] But as the attacks on premillennialists' patriotism increased and Americans joined the fighting, the magazine's policy changed. By early 1918, an editorial urged Christians to support the government by not "giving any unlawful encouragement to pacifists and slackers who are operating in some cases as an enemy in the rear."[61] By June of that year, Gray wrote that Christians had a righteous duty to fight against the forces of evil and described it as "our responsibility to God as the executioners of His avenging justice."[62]

Arno C. Gaebelein at *Our Hope* also had a change of heart. He had opposed America's going to war earlier, but by April 1918, he concluded that America was justified in fighting a defensive war against Germany. By July, Gaebelein stated that it was "the solemn duty of everyone to do all and to give all in this cause and stand by the government, so the hosts of evil may be speedily defeated."[63]

No one attending the large prophetic conferences in the spring and fall of 1918 could have missed the fierce patriotism of the speakers. Organizers of the Philadelphia meeting in May referred to their "cheerfully submitting to the powers that be" and their "absolute patriotism, absolute loyalty" to the American government.[64] In the call to the November conference in New York, the conveners wanted it plainly understood that they would not allow "any sentiment not in fullest loyalty to our country and her allies." In addition to paying special attention to the prophecies concerning the war and the Jewish people, the conference sponsors said they would call "attention to the great doctrines of the Gospel as a bulwark and a protest against the subtle skepticism of the German-made theology."[65]

Therefore, by the time Case charged premillennialists with a lack of patriotism, they had already turned the corner. Though their eschatological views had made some of them reticent about entering the war, by the time America joined the conflict, they were eager supporters. Germany led the forces of apostasy and threatened to destroy what was left of Christian civilization. In May 1918, the *King's Business* quoted approvingly a Christmas editorial from the *Courier-Journal* of Louisville: "The Kaiser boldly threw down the gage of battle—infidel Germany against the believing world—Kultur against Christianity—the Gospel of Hate against the Gospel of Love. Thus is Satan personified—'Myself and God.'. . . Never did Crusader lift battle-ax in holier war against the Saracen than is waged by our soldiers of the cross against the Germans."[66] No one in America was more pro-war and anti-German than the premillennialist Billy Sunday: "If you turn hell upside down, you will find 'made in Germany' stamped on the bottom."[67]

PROPHECY AND THE AFTERMATH OF WORLD WAR I

After America won the war, premillennialists could once again afford to apply their doctrines consistently. As it turned out, the peace was filled with prophetic possibilities too. During the peace talks, dispensationalists chose sides in accordance with their eschatological views.

How should devout premillennialists respond to the proposal for a League of Nations? On the basis of their prophetic expectations, they had little hope for any scheme to guarantee long-term peace. The league was noble in its intent, but it would utterly fail to bring peace to the world. The course of the age had already been established by God. The World War was only the beginning of troubles. In the New York prophetic conference of 1918, Torrey stated that while many people were placing their hopes in the league, "such hopes are delusive, they will end in disappointment and dismay." The league could bring about a deceptive, temporary respite from war, but "then the most awful universal war that this old world has ever seen will follow."[68]

While all premillennialists agreed that the league would ultimately fail to create a lasting peace, they were divided about its prophetic significance. Might it become the Antichrist's ten-nation confederacy, the revived Roman Empire? Gaebelein did not think so. For one thing, it contained too many nations to be the Antichrist's empire. To meet prophetic specifications, Gaebelein argued, the league would have to scale down to ten nations and expel all those not originally part of the first Roman Empire. I. M. Haldeman, on the other hand, believed that the league was fulfilling prophecy by helping to restore the old Roman boundaries and by "preparing the way for the final and desperate revival of Rome under the form of ten confederate nations, with its last kaiser, that dark and woeful figure, the man of sin, the son of perdition, the Antichrist."[69]

Regardless of where they stood on the particulars of that issue, dispensationalists agreed that the league was one more step toward the realization of the new Rome and the rise of the Antichrist. Therefore, they sided with Senator Henry Cabot Lodge against Wilson's attempt to commit America to the league, hoping against hope that nonparticipation might make things easier on America when Christ returned to judge the Gentile powers. Furthermore, in light of the continuation of "wars and rumors of wars," the United States would be ill-advised to consider any form of disarmament.[70]

The future was not bright. World War I was only the beginning of grief. All attempts to make a lasting peace would fail. No matter what people of goodwill did, much of Europe would inevitably realign itself according to the old Roman borders, move into a ten-nation confederacy, and fall under the spell of the last dictator. All of those things would take place "not because we wish it to be so, nor because of any prophetic insight given to us, but because we believe the statements of a very old and very much neglected book called the Bible."[71]

As usual, despite the dismal outlook, premillennialists could sound hopeful. While they saw no hope within the historical process, they were still optimistic about ultimate outcomes. "Then is there not hope? Yes, there is hope, a hope both sure and steadfast, a hope that is absolutely certain, a hope that is built upon the inerrant and infallible Word of Him that cannot lie."[72] Jesus is coming, and when he arrives, he will "speedily produce the end of the last war."[73]

Prophecy and the Rise of Totalitarianism

Since European national boundaries were redrawn after World War I, the next major prophetic development dispensationalists expected was the emergence of a new Roman Empire under the Antichrist. What they got was the rise of Italian, German, and Russian totalitarian regimes. Fitting them into their expectations was not always easy. In fact, one could say that dispensationalists were at best only moderately successful at interpreting the signs of the times during the 1920s and 1930s.

MUSSOLINI AND THE REVIVED ROMAN EMPIRE

For over a decade, dispensationalists speculated about Benito Mussolini as the Antichrist and Fascist Italy as the center of a new Roman Empire. Postwar Italian politics verged on the chaotic. Many Italians were bitter about the results of the peace conference, convinced that Italy had not received its just deserts. Others noted the growing power of the political left and feared that Italy might experience its own communist revolution. Mussolini knew that the road to political power required the elimination of the Catholic Popular Party and the Socialists, so in 1919 he organized his first "combat groups" *(fasci di combattimento),* through which he launched a campaign of intimidation and violence. Even though the Fascists occupied only a few seats in the Chamber of Deputies, Mussolini was appointed premier in October 1922. With him, a little political power went a long way. From his position at the head of the government, he skillfully used his Fascist supporters to bully the opposition. After a hefty dose of terror tactics during elections in April 1924, the Fascists obtained a majority of seats in the Chamber of Deputies. Once in charge, they deprived their opponents of their rightful seats in the chamber, dissolved all political parties but their own, and disallowed all political dissent.

Obviously, here was a man worth watching. Could he be the prophesied Antichrist? He seemed to meet the biblical criteria: He was charismatic, power hungry, militaristic, and expansionistic. He was also based in Rome, the expected capital of the revived empire. He had even shown the ability to make peace with what dispensationalists believed was the largest segment of apostate Christianity, the Roman Catholic Church, through the Lateran Treaty and the Concordat of 1929.

On account of Mussolini's substantial pedigree, by the mid-1920s many dispensationalists were speculating that the Antichrist was already on the world scene, making plans for a new Rome.[74] A number of prophecy journals carried the story of Mr. and Mrs. Ralph Norton, dispensationalist missionaries in Belgium who somehow arranged a face-to-face meeting with Mussolini. They asked him if he intended to reestablish the Roman Empire. Such a thing was impossible, he said. "We can only revive its spirit, and be governed by the same discipline." That was not the answer the Nortons were hoping for, so they explained to him the biblical prophecy about such a restored empire in the last days. This got Mussolini's attention. He wanted to know more: "Is that really described in the Bible? Where is it found?"[75] With the right information, who knows what he could accomplish.

While some dispensationalists were warming to the idea of Mussolini as the Antichrist, others were a bit more skeptical. While early signs certainly pointed in that direction, more prudent Bible teachers were willing to wait on Mussolini to see how he conducted himself on the world stage. Even if in the final analysis Mussolini proved not to be the prophesied man of sin, he certainly gave the world a glimpse of what the real one might look like later on. In 1933, James M. Gray speculated about the results of the struggle between the Fascists and the communists in Italy: "If we understand prophecy, it is Fascism that will win in the end, though possibly under another name, for the reason that superman when he appears will be a Mussolini on an international scale."[76] Gray set the prophetic bar pretty high. Only a few months later, he was willing to venture a much more definitive conclusion about the Italian leader:

> Whatever else may be true of Mussolini, he is not the Antichrist as some thoughtlessly imagine. Fascism . . . may aid in preparing the way for that superhuman despot, preparing it, that is, from the national or political side. But Fascism as Mussolini represents it is the protection of Italy from Vaticanism on the one hand, and Communism on the other. Therefore, for the present at least, it may be well to wish it succeeds.[77]

Gray, as it turned out, was right about Mussolini, and in time, just about everybody came around to his conclusion. Mussolini self-destructed as a candidate for the Antichrist with his reckless behavior. For example, when Mussolini's army invaded Ethiopia in 1935, Leonard Sale-Harrison declared that Mussolini had disqualified himself. With the exception of Germany and Fascist Spain, all Europe was outraged by his attack on hapless Ethiopia, and Mussolini's popularity plummeted. Sale-Harrison observed that while the Antichrist of biblical prophecy was a subtle, diplomatic, charismatic, and beguiling deceiver, Mussolini was obviously anything but. As a result, most of the nations that dispensationalists expected to join forces with the Antichrist in a new empire condemned Mussolini as a bully and an aggressor. His adventurism took him off dispensationalists' prophetic radar screen. Nevertheless, Sale-Harrison thought that Mussolini played an important role in moving Europe toward the end. "Italy has been welded into an armed camp, which will be useful in the hands of a stronger and more cunning dictator. In other words, the resurrection of ancient Rome, even in the eyes of the most superficial observer, is certain of accomplishment, and is rapidly moving towards its goal, as prophesied in Holy Writ."[78]

Most other Bible teachers agreed. Mussolini was only a "type" or forerunner of the Antichrist, for whom he prepared the way.[79] Louis S. Bauman, however, a pastor and part-time faculty member at the Bible Institute of Los Angeles, was still convinced that Mussolini was the man of sin. "Notwithstanding a present common belief, the mastermind of Europe today is not in Berlin. Neither is he in Moscow, nor in London. In our opinion, the mastermind of Europe is in Rome." Bauman was convinced that Mussolini had maneuvered himself into a no-lose position:

> Europe had not space enough for two Caesars. So the Roman Caesar invited the German Caesar down into his domain, tickled his vanity

in a glorious parade of honor, formed an "axis" with him, and sent him back to Berlin with all the swell and swagger of a Napoleon ready to "lick the world!" He promptly began trampling beneath his spurred boots the helpless states to the east. None knew better than Mussolini that this would sooner or later involve him in endless difficulties with his powerful neighbors.[80]

When Hitler's aggression drew England and France into the war, Mussolini held back his troops, waiting for the right moment to advance. Bauman predicted that Mussolini would become the protector of the Balkans, then eventually strike an agreement with France and England. The Roman Empire was on the way.

HITLER, NAZI GERMANY, AND THE SOVIET UNION

Dispensationalists also found it difficult to fit Germany and the Soviet Union into their scenario, though for a while it looked as though both countries were following the prophetic script perfectly. For nearly a hundred years, dispensationalists had predicted that Germany and Russia would be partners in the northern confederacy that would attack Israel during the great tribulation. This expectation came from their interpretation of Ezekiel 38 and 39, which described a devastating future battle between Israel and her enemies designated as "Gog" and "Gomer." Premillennialists believed that Gog referred to Russia and that Gomer referred to Germany.[81] Throughout the 1930s, however, dispensationalist interpreters seemed to have an insurmountable problem. Hitler was communism's worst enemy. How could Nazi Germany and communist Russia ever get together to play out their assigned prophetic roles?

Dispensationalists had little choice but to wait for history to take a turn. In 1932, the *Moody Bible Institute Monthly* reported that the deposed Kaiser Wilhelm of Germany had said that "like the Russians, we cling with all our roots to the East. . . . Germany's next kin is Russia."[82] Certainly, that is what dispensationalists wanted to hear, but there seemed little chance that such an alliance would happen soon, at least as long as Hitler and Stalin were in power.[83] In 1935, Bauman wrote, "Many German editors insist that Germany can never march with the Bolsheviki. But stranger things than that have happened. Strange forces are at work these days in a world more afflicted with revolution and devolution than with evolution. When the hour strikes, Germany will tramp, Hitler and his Fascist brownshirts notwithstanding, with . . . *Gog!*"[84] In 1938, Bauman seemed even more certain: "Those who know the 'sure word of prophecy' expect nothing less than that some day in the not far distant future, the seeming enemy nations, Russia and Germany, will shake hands, whether Stalin and Hitler do or not."[85]

Sometimes unlikely things happen. On August 23, 1939, Germany and the Soviet Union signed a nonaggression pact. Though they had been predicting an alliance between Gomer and Gog for decades, many dispensationalists seemed surprised that the prophecy would be fulfilled by Hitler and Stalin. Certainly, Bauman could claim prescience, since he had been predicting a Nazi-Bolshevik alliance for a number of years. But other dispensationalists also claimed credit. Though he had not foreseen the rise of national socialism and communism per se, Arno C. Gaebelein in 1940 reminded the readers of *Our Hope* that he had predicted a German-Russian alliance in *Harmony of the Prophetic Word* in 1907.[86]

Whether most dispensationalists saw it coming or not, the Nazi-Soviet nonaggression pact elated Bible teachers. While they had been at a loss as to how such an alliance might happen, evidently God had not been deterred in the least. In fact, looking back, dispensationalists believed that God had providentially set them up to receive the news of the fulfillment. For example, five months before the pact was signed, dispensationalists had scheduled a prophetic conference for November 5–12, 1939, in New York City. Gaebelein believed that God had led the organizers to set up such a meeting so that they would be together to explore and exult in the Nazi-Soviet pact. He noted how in the past God had led him and others to schedule other conferences at the most opportune times. For instance, a few months before the outbreak of World War I in 1913, premillennialists had met in Chicago to discuss the signs of the times. In 1918, prophetic conferences in Philadelphia and New York had considered the consequences of the end of the war and other major events, such as the fall of the Ottoman Empire and the pledge to restore a Jewish home in Palestine. When conference planners scheduled their meeting for November 1939, they had no idea that they would be meeting at such an auspicious time. Gaebelein thought that the New York meeting might be their last: "For all we know, this may be the last prophetic conference which will be held, for 'our gathering together unto him' cannot be far away."[87]

Premillennialist euphoria was short-lived, however, because the nonaggression pact did not last long. In June 1941, Hitler launched a massive *blitzkrieg* against Russia. Those who had seen the nonaggression pact as the beginning of the northern confederacy were stunned. In response to this reversal of fortunes, there was "just one big awkward silence" from the prophetic experts.[88] One exception was the *Weekly Evangel*: "There are some prophets who are suffering no casualties. They are inspired writers of Bible prophecy. Their words shall be fulfilled. We may err when we forecast just how and when they will be fulfilled, but in God's own time the entire prophetic plan shall be complete."[89]

At no time during this long period did dispensationalists do anything to make their expected prophetic scenario come out right. There was no need to. God was in control of history, so sooner or later everything would work out as the prophecies indicated. That was good news, because sometimes dispensationalist Bible teachers misunderstood what was happening around them. Rank-and-file dispensationalists were forgiving and forgetful during the decades between the wars. They stuck by their leaders even when they misread the signs of the times. The Bible teachers did not seem especially bothered by their failures either. Events were changing so fast that there was little time for apologies. There were more books to write and more conferences to organize and attend. A few leaders realized that they were backtracking on prophetic interpretations and became rather sensitive about it. In 1942, after so many early speculations about the restored Roman Empire and the northern confederacy proved to be mistaken, William Culbertson, the new president of Moody Bible Institute, offered a curious defense. He pointed out that while students of prophecy had been mistaken in the past, they were not nearly so wrong as those who deny prophetic truth. "Suppose there are some eccentrics in the realm of prophecy. What does that prove? Suppose some sincere enthusiast expressed an opinion made ridiculous by current history. What of it? Scientists have not thrown science on the scrap heap because some theories of other days are now discarded."[90]

True enough, but such assurances hardly addressed the problem. Leading Bible teachers, not just a few eccentrics, had been "made ridiculous by current history." Furthermore, the Bible teachers were not scientists who tried out various theories about obscure natural phenomena. They were students of the "sure word of prophecy," which they believed was an infallible guide for unraveling present and future events. Smart dispensationalist preachers and teachers never claimed omniscience for themselves, but few showed much humility or tentativeness either. During times of crisis, people wanted guarantees, not speculations that might have to be revised from time to time. Still, the erring dispensationalist Bible teachers never suggested that they should climb down from the bleachers and move onto the field to make sure that the players fulfilled their assigned roles. They did not seek ways to guarantee expected outcomes. Instead, they tried new interpretations.

Besides, as important as the identification of a revived Roman Empire or a northern confederacy might be, neither constituted the linchpin of the prophetic scenario. That honor belonged exclusively to the Jews and the restored Jewish state. Everything depended on Jews carrying out their assigned prophetic role. In the long run, prophecies concerning the Jews and Israel were much more important. As would soon become apparent in the years following World War II, nothing tempted dispensationalists to leave the relative safety of the stands like the founding and survival of a restored Jewish state.

4

The Complicated Relationship between Dispensationalists and Jews

From its beginning in the brain of John Nelson Darby, dispensationalism put Jews on center stage. The Jews were God's chosen people, and God had important work for them to do right up to the end of the age and the return of Christ. Long before Zionism organized in the 1890s to promote the establishment of a Jewish homeland, dispensationalists envisioned a restored Israel as ground zero for end-times events. In the streets of Jerusalem and in the rocky hills and plains surrounding it, the drama of the Antichrist, the great tribulation, and the battle of Armageddon would unfold. The surviving Jewish remnant would welcome the returning Jesus as their true Messiah, then witness his victory over all his and their enemies. The ensuing millennial age would be Jewish through and through. King Jesus would rule the world from David's throne in Jerusalem, not far from the restored temple, where the bloody sacrifices of ancient Israel would be performed daily. In short, all of dispensationalism's hopes for the future were riding on the Jews.

All that was in the future. What about Jews in the present? Dispensationalists' relationship to real, live Jews was complicated and in some ways paradoxical. On the one hand, in the nineteenth and early twentieth centuries, no one was more supportive of Jewish nationalistic aspirations than American dispensationalists. In the late twentieth and early twenty-first centuries, dispensationalists consistently supported a restored Jewish state. They monitored the beginnings of Zionism and the first Jewish attempts to colonize the Holy Land. A few of them publicly promoted Jewish aspirations or tried their own hand at colonizing the Promised Land. During World War I, dispensationalists cheered the demise of the Ottoman Empire; the issuance of the Balfour Declaration, which committed the British government to the idea of a Jewish homeland; and the capture of Jerusalem by the British—all of which they thought had profound prophetic significance.

On the other hand, no other Christian group was more dedicated to targeting Jews for conversion than dispensationalists. Like other evangelicals, dispensationalists believed that everyone needed to put their faith in Jesus to be saved, but for dispensationalists, the evangelization of the Jews had important prophetic significance as well. They believed that at Christ's return "all Israel would be saved," but they also felt an obligation to launch an unprecedented evangelistic mission to save as many Jews as possible before the end arrived. Dispensationalists were certain that no mission to the Jews could succeed without their particular interpretation of Scripture and their understanding of the Jews' place in God's end-times program. As a result, dispensationalists founded dozens of Jewish missionary organizations, even though the going was usually tough and the results were almost always minimal.

Dispensationalism and the Restoration of the Jews

As already noted, dispensational premillennialists believed that God had two distinct peoples, Israel and the church. The original divine plan concerned only the Jews, with whom God made a series of covenants. Throughout Israel's long history, God kept these covenants, but the Jews occasionally broke them and suffered accordingly, most notably in the destruction of Jerusalem and the exile to Babylon. Nevertheless, God still had plans for Israel. Right on schedule, 483 years after the survivors' return from Babylonian exile, God sent the Messiah to save the people from their enemies and establish David's royal line forever. But most Jews rejected the Messiah, which caused an abrupt change in plans. God temporarily set Israel aside, suspended prophetic time, and formed a new people, the church.

Despite this new program, God still intended to fulfill all promises to Israel. In the nineteenth century, most dispensationalists believed that the final restoration of Israel and the conversion of the Jews would occur together, at the return of the Messiah. Nevertheless, most dispensationalists believed that the return of the Jews to the Holy Land could begin at any time. Consequently, dispensationalists were constantly on the lookout for signs that Jews were returning to the Holy Land to establish their own nation.[1]

THE ORIGINS OF ZIONISM

At about the same time that dispensationalists began predicting the restoration of Israel, there was a revival of nationalism among the dispersed Jews of Europe. The Zionist movement, which arose in the last decade of the nineteenth century, had many forerunners. By the 1850s, men such as Judah Alcalay, Avi Hirsch Kalisher, and Moses Hess had called for the colonization of Palestine, but with little success. Many Jews in Western Europe had already begun trying to assimilate into the dominant culture. Thanks to the Enlightenment's emphasis on reason and tolerance, thousands of Jews had left their ghettos and entered the European mainstream. Assimilationists believed that this emancipation required changes in their religious and communal practices. The result was Reform Judaism, which reinterpreted the Torah in terms of modern life, looked askance at or rejected outright parts of the rabbinic tradition, and even set aside belief in a personal Messiah who would lead Jews back to the Promised Land. By the middle of the nineteenth century, growing numbers of European Jews were satisfied to call Germany or France or Poland home and to leave it at that.

In the 1880s, however, a new wave of anti-Semitism swept over Europe, calling into question many of these assimilationist sentiments. Though anti-Jewish feeling arose nearly everywhere, Russia was the center of violent discrimination. Jews there and elsewhere were subjected to a series of repressive laws and widespread state-supported violence. These events shocked Jews who believed that European culture had moved beyond such Jew hatred, and responses to it varied. Some Jews became political radicals, intent to fight fire with fire. Others decided to work harder at assimilation, confident that they could avoid the fate of Russian Jews.

Another response was the revival of Jewish nationalism. In *Auto-Emancipation* (1882), Leo Pinsker argued that Jews needed their own homeland in order to guarantee their survival and called on Jews to abandon dreams of assimilation and to organize to secure a Jewish state. The response was not overwhelming, but a couple of years after the book's publication, supporters convened a Jewish congress in Kattowitz, Prussia, to consider the feasibility of founding a new state. Results were meager, but delegates did decide on a location (Palestine) and an approach (gradual colonization).

Over the next decade, the Love of Zion *(Hibbat Zion)* movement, as it came to be called, managed to settle twenty-five thousand Jews in the Holy Land, mainly in agricultural colonies, for which most of the immigrants were ill-suited. Much to the newcomers' surprise, the Jews who were already there did not welcome them with open arms. In their way of life and motivation for being there, the immigrants seemed unorthodox and too political. In the end, even supporters had to admit that the settlement strategy had not lived up to expectations, but it was a start.

Most European Jews were content to stay where they were, convinced that despite the occasional outbreak of persecution and discrimination, the future belonged to assimilation, not anti-Semitism. Many of those optimists were stunned in 1895 by the so-called Dreyfus Affair. Captain Alfred Dreyfus, a Jewish officer on the French General Staff, was accused and convicted of spying for Germany. Anti-Semitic riots broke out across France, and the army purged pro-Dreyfus sympathizers from the ranks. Because there was ample evidence that the charges against Dreyfus had been trumped up, the French president pardoned Dreyfus in 1899. By then, however, many Jews had given up on assimilation and were being carried along by a new wave of Jewish nationalism—Zionism—founded by the Hungarian-born journalist Theodore Herzl.

Following extensive research on the "Jewish Question," Herzl repudiated gradual colonization in favor of another approach. In *Der Judenstaat* (*The Jewish State,* 1896), he argued that European nations were eager to be rid of their Jews and would, with a little encouragement, take the initiative in founding a new Jewish state. In 1897, Herzl pulled together the first Zionist Congress in Basel, Switzerland, where unity evaporated in the inevitable debate over strategy for achieving statehood. Undaunted by such division, Herzl tirelessly traveled from capital to capital, seeking support in high places for Zionism. Palestine proved to be the big sticking point. The Ottoman Empire controlled the region and fiercely resisted the suggestion that it turn over part of its territory to anyone, especially to Jews. After Turkey shut the door on further negotiations over Palestine, Herzl sought an alternative. He proposed to the Zionist Congress of 1903 that it consider Uganda in British East Africa, which had been suggested by the British colonial secretary Joseph Chamberlain. The ensuing controversy almost tore the gathering apart. Herzl quickly backtracked and reaffirmed his commitment to Palestine, but the fallout lasted longer than he did. Herzl died in 1904, completely worn out at the age of forty-four.

After Herzl's death, the Zionist movement continued to be torn by internal dissension over strategy, but there were many outside pressures too. Socialists objected to the way Zionism drained off Jewish money and energy from their causes. Ultra-orthodox Jews preferred to wait for God to reestablish Israel through the coming of the Messiah rather than engage in human schemes for doing so. Assimilated Jews refused to forsake their hard-earned status in European society for what they considered a sentimental dream. On the eve of World War I, international Zionism had only 130,000 members, a small percentage of the world's Jews. Likewise, after decades of labor, the Love of Zion movement had established only fifty-nine small colonies in Palestine. Clearly, not all Jews welcomed or accepted Zionism's dream of a Jewish state.[2]

This was certainly true in America, where the Jewish community was deeply divided by different cultures, histories, and approaches to modernity. Jews were among the first Europeans to journey to the New World. Included in Columbus's 1492 crew were a number of Marranos, Spanish Jews who had converted to Christianity to escape the Inquisition but practiced their old faith in secret.

In 1654, a small Jewish community settled in Dutch New Amsterdam. How they got there is an intriguing and complicated story. When Spain and Portugal expelled the Jews in the 1490s, the exiles scattered far and wide. Many of them eventually ended up in Holland, which at the time was the most religiously tolerant nation in Europe. In 1630, the Dutch took Brazil away from the Portuguese, and a number of Dutch Jews moved to the New World. When the Portuguese recaptured Brazil in 1654, they expelled the Jews.

While some of the exiles returned to Holland, others chose to resettle on islands in the Caribbean or in Dutch New Amsterdam, which, after some reluctance, allowed them to stay. Ten years later, the Jews found themselves suddenly under English rule when the British took over the colony and renamed it New York. By the American Revolution, a number of Jewish communities had been established from Massachusetts to South Carolina. These communities were Sephardic, so-called because of their common roots in Spain and Portugal. By 1820, there were roughly five thousand Sephardic Jews in America, out of a total population of thirteen million.

A new wave of Jewish immigrants overwhelmed this small but stable Sephardic population. Between 1820 and 1880, as many as four hundred thousand German Jews, or Ashkenazim, came to America. Many of these immigrants had already embraced Reform Judaism and assimilationist goals. They eagerly tried to make their synagogues look more Protestant or even to pass as middle-class Gentiles. Not surprisingly, the more traditional Sephardim viewed the newcomers as a serious threat to religious orthodoxy and the integrity of their close-knit communities. Yet it did not take long for the Ashkenazi community to dominate American Jewish life.

A third wave of Jewish immigration overwhelmed the German Jewish establishment. Between 1880 and the outbreak of World War I, when immigration law changed to a quota system, 1.7 million Jews came to America. Unlike the earlier Sephardim and Ashkenazim, the third wave was from Eastern Europe, where brutal persecution and institutionalized anti-Semitism had created a completely different outlook. Unlike the earlier Jewish immigrants, Russian, Romanian, Polish, and Bulgarian Jews had no dreams of assimilation and little desire to be associated with American Protestants and their culture. The new immigrants preferred to stick together in big-city neighborhoods and reproduce, where possible, Old World ways of life. Now the American Reform Jews were on the defensive as Orthodox Judaism and Conservative Judaism, another variety of Jewish religious life, gathered new members from the Eastern European immigrants.

Zionism played out differently in these diverse communities. Many American Jews had little in common with the latest immigrants. European-style anti-Semitism was virtually unknown in the United States. Though American Jews did have to contend with occasional outbreaks of homegrown nativism, they had little fear of a knock on the door at midnight or officially sanctioned pogroms. Thus, any political movement based on the need for protection against the ravages of state-sponsored anti-Semitism seemed irrelevant in the American context.

Nevertheless, Jewish nationalism grew in America during the 1880s. A number of Love of Zion societies were established during the decade, but they were organized primarily as bulwarks against total assimilation, not as catalysts for Jewish immigration to Palestine. Most groups were content to study Hebrew and Jewish history and send money to aid the colonies in the Holy Land. In fact, if it had not been for the publication of Herzl's *Der Judenstaat,* the Love of Zion movement might have died out completely in the United States.

The Reform movement was especially resistant to any attempt at resettlement. Reform Jews separated being Jewish (i.e., belonging to a distinctive, self-conscious ethnic "nation") from practicing Judaism (i.e., following the Jewish religion as someone else might follow Presbyterianism). Judaism did not need a political state of its own to be a viable religion; one could practice the Jewish faith and still be a red-blooded American. They proclaimed the United States as their Zion and warned that support for a Jewish homeland in Palestine might be interpreted as disloyalty to America.

Consequently, most of the Reform rabbinate in the United States rejected the idea of a Jewish state, though some were open to the idea of Jewish colonization for those who needed to flee repressive conditions.

Orthodox Jews loved Zion too but insisted that if God wanted to restore the Jews, he could do it without the help of secular, nonobservant Zionists. Similarly, most Conservative Jews liked the idea of a restored Israel but were wary of the Zionists' political strategies. As a result of such divisions, by the start of World War I, only roughly twenty thousand of America's 1.5 million Jews belonged to Zionist societies.[3]

DISPENSATIONALISM AND ZIONISM

It is not surprising, then, that around the turn of the twentieth century, dispensationalists seemed more committed to a new Jewish state in Palestine than most American Jews. For decades they had been predicting the restoration of Israel, so when some Jews started taking steps in that direction, dispensationalists gave them their full attention and sometimes active support.

Premillennialist journals kept close watch on anti-Semitism in late-nineteenth-century Europe and commented on how such treatment fed the ancient Jewish longing for Jerusalem.[4] Premillennial reporters and conference speakers noted the founding of the Love of Zion movement and frequently filed stories on their newly established colonies in Palestine. They also kept statistics on the slow but steady growth of the Jewish population there and often speculated about when the Jewish immigrants would start constructing a new temple in Jerusalem.[5]

The premillennialist press praised the publication of Herzl's *Der Judenstaat* in 1896, and a few reporters even managed to attend the second Zionist Congress in Basel in 1898 to keep dispensationalists back home fully informed.[6] They also covered other Zionist congresses and judged them on the basis of how they measured up to dispensationalists' prophetic expectations.

Despite their intense support of Zionism, most dispensationalists did not believe it was the ultimate fulfillment of biblical prophecy concerning the restoration of Israel. The problem was that Zionism was a political and nationalistic movement, not a religious one. Zionism was a return to the Promised Land *in unbelief.* In 1905, Arno C. Gaebelein warned that

Zionism is not the divinely promised restoration of Israel. . . . Zionism is not the fulfillment of the large number of predictions found in the Old Testament Scriptures, which relate to Israel's return to the land. Indeed, Zionism has very little use for arguments from the Word of

God. It is rather a political and philanthropic undertaking. Instead of coming together before God, calling upon His name, trusting Him, that He is able to perform what He has so often promised, they speak about their riches, their influence, their Colonial Bank, and court the favor of the Sultan. The great movement is one of unbelief and confidence in themselves instead of God's eternal purposes.[7]

On that particular point, Gaebelein and other premillennialists sounded like Orthodox Jews, who also complained about the religious indifference of most Zionists. But if Zionism was not about the ultimate restoration of Jews to Palestine, it was, according to dispensationalists, the first link in a chain of events that would lead to the end of the "times of the Gentiles," the revelation of the Antichrist, and the glorious return of Jesus Christ. If Zionism was not the end, it was at least the beginning of the end.[8]

Most dispensationalists were satisfied to be mere observers of the Zionist movement. They watched and analyzed it. They spoke out in favor of it. But seldom did they become politically involved to promote its goals. There was one exception to the general pattern, however, in the person of William E. Blackstone, one of the most popular dispensational writers of his time.[9] Blackstone was born in Adams, New York, and grew up in a pious Methodist home, where he was converted at the age of eleven. He failed to qualify for combat duty in the Civil War, so he joined the United States Christian Commission, a religious social service organization, and ended up working at General U. S. Grant's headquarters. Immediately after the war, he married and moved to Oak Park, Illinois. There he became a great success in building and property management and an active layman in the Methodist Church.

Blackstone never went to college or seminary, but he was an avid student of the Bible and religious literature. Evidently, he learned his dispensationalism from friends in Chicago's extensive evangelical network. Blackstone became a close associate of premillennialist leaders such as D. L. Moody, James H. Brookes, and Horatio Spafford, who eventually founded the American colony in Jerusalem. By the late 1870s, Blackstone had become an enthusiastic promoter of dispensationalism and had written prophetic literature for distribution to "potential converts." In 1878, he published *Jesus Is Coming,* which outlined in rather simple terms what all dispensationalists expected to occur and showed how various current events qualified as signs of the times leading to the second coming.

Blackstone was a popularizer, not an original thinker. His understanding of Bible prophecy followed closely that of C. I. Scofield. The beauty of his book was its straightforward and clearly written style, which made it easy for laypeople to understand the complexities of the dispensational system. As a result, the book became one of dispensationalism's early best-sellers. *Jesus Is Coming* went through many printings and three editions during Blackstone's lifetime, and each version was longer than the one before. The first edition in 1878 contained 96 pages, the second in 1888 had 160, and the last in 1906 grew to 256. Eventually, the book was translated into 42 languages. Probably no dispensational Bible teacher of his time had a larger popular audience.[10]

Like all dispensationalists, Blackstone believed in the restoration of the Jews, but unlike most of them, he was not content to sit back and watch events unfold on their own. He wanted to make things happen. In 1888–89, Blackstone made an extensive tour of Palestine. He visited the colonies of Jewish pioneers and believed that they were portents of Christ's speedy return. After he returned home, Blackstone committed himself body and soul to the cause of a Jewish state.

Blackstone was a bridge builder. In 1890, he organized and chaired the first conference between Christians and Jews in Chicago. The meeting was held at the First Methodist Episcopal Church and drew an impressive cross section of Chicago's Christian and Jewish leadership. When Blackstone and a few other speakers began to promote the restoration of the Jews in Palestine, most people in the audience found the idea fanciful and unnecessary. One of its most adamant opponents was Reform Rabbi Emil G. Hirsch: "We modern Jews do not wish to be restored to Palestine. We have given up hope in the coming of a political personal Messiah. . . . We will not go back . . . to form again a nationality of our own."[11] While conferees were divided on the subject, they were united in their concern for persecuted Russian Jews. Blackstone saw to it that resolutions of sympathy were passed and copies forwarded to the czar.

During the following year (1891), Blackstone's compassion for oppressed Russian Jews led him to sponsor an amazing "memorial," which began with a simple question: "What shall be done for the Russian Jews?" After briefly discussing the situation in Europe, Blackstone offered his own answer:

> Why not give Palestine back to them again? According to God's distribution of nations, it is their home—an inalienable possession from which they were expelled by force. . . . Why shall not the powers which under the treaty of Berlin in 1878 gave Bulgaria to the Bulgarians and Servia to the Servians now give Palestine back to the Jews? . . . We believe this is an appropriate time for all nations, and especially the Christian nations of Europe, to show kindness to Israel. A million exiles, by their terrible sufferings, are piteously appealing to our sympathy, justice and humanity. Let us now restore to them the land of which they were so cruelly despoiled by our Roman ancestors.[12]

Blackstone combed Chicago, New York, Boston, Baltimore, Washington, and Philadelphia to collect signatures in support of his petition. Though he probably could have obtained more, he stopped at 413 names, including many prominent Americans. Among those who endorsed the memorial were Melville Fuller, chief justice of the United States Supreme Court; Chauncy Depew, United States senator from New York; Thomas Reed, Speaker of the House of Representatives; the mayors of Chicago, New York, and Boston; and a number of other elected officials and judges. Leading journalists from the *Chicago Daily News,* the *New York Times*, the *Washington Post,* the *Philadelphia Times,* and the *Chicago Tribune* also signed the document, as did a number of the nation's most recognizable business leaders, including Cyrus McCormick, John D. Rockefeller, and J. Pierpont Morgan. It made no difference to Blackstone that such people signed for humanitarian, not dispensational, reasons. They were doing God's work whether they realized it or not. On March 5, 1891, he forwarded the memorial and signatures to President Benjamin Harrison and Secretary of State James Blaine and urged them to take the lead in establishing a new Jewish state.

In October 1891, Blackstone wrote an article entitled "May the United States Intercede for the Jews?" which received wide circulation around the country. In it he wrote that

> there is one spot toward which the eye of the Jew has turned . . . his loved Palestine. There is room there for two or three millions more people, and the ancient scriptural limits of the country would largely increase its capacity. The rains are returning, agriculture is improving, its location promises great commercial possibilities, and only an independent, enlightened and progressive government is needed to afford a home for all of Israel who wish to return.[13]

Blackstone's memorial and article, it must be remembered, were written one year before the first Love of Zion societies were formed in the United States, five years before the publication of Herzl's *Der Judenstaat,* and six years before the first Zionist Congress was convened in Basel.

Blackstone's memorial set off a fierce debate within the American Jewish press. The editors of *Ha Pisga,* the *American Hebrew*, and *Menorah* were more or less favorable, while the editors of the *Jewish Messenger, American Israelite, Jewish Voice,* and the *Reform Advocate* opposed the memorial's program.[14] As already shown, most Reform Jews openly opposed efforts to create a new Jewish state, though there were a few exceptions. In fact, a small number of Reform rabbis signed Blackstone's resolution. Overall, the memorial received a favorable reception from Orthodox and Conservative Jews, who still anticipated the coming of the Messiah.

Political Zionists were predictably the most enthusiastic, though most did not understand the dispensationalism that underlay Blackstone's work. Those who were familiar with the details of Blackstone's prophetic views were not especially troubled by them. Zionists were willing to overlook dispensationalism's predictions about "the time of Jacob's trouble" and the Jews' future conversion to Christ because they needed all the help they could get in the present.

Though the memorial got plenty of press coverage, President Harrison and Secretary Blaine virtually ignored the document, and the little diplomatic notice it received faded quickly. A few American diplomats did comment on Blackstone's memorial, but none was enthusiastic or even positive. To seasoned diplomats, the proposal was naive and unworkable. Rather typical was the response of the American consul in Jerusalem, Selah Merrill, a devout Christian, whose laconic appraisal reflected political realities more than prophetic ones: "Turkey was not in the habit of giving away whole provinces for the asking."[15]

Such reticence did not deter Blackstone. In 1903, he induced the Chicago Methodist Preachers Meeting to pass a similar resolution, which he forwarded to President Teddy Roosevelt along with the original 1891 memorial. Again, there was no response. Then in 1916, a year before the Balfour Declaration, Blackstone sponsored another memorial, which was virtually the same as his previous ones. This one was intended for President Woodrow Wilson, the son of a Presbyterian minister, whom Blackstone hoped would be more inclined to help the Jews.

Blackstone did not go for the big numbers this time, and the signers of the 1916 memorial were not nearly as impressive as those who signed in 1891. Among the most prominent were Andrew White, president of Cornell University and former United States ambassador to Russia; businessman John Wanamaker; the General Assembly of the Presbyterian Church; the Presbyterian Ministerial Association; the Baptist Ministers' Conference of Chicago; and Shailer Mathews of the University of Chicago.[16] A distinguished delegation of church leaders presented the memorial to President Wilson, who received it gladly—and actually supported the Balfour Declaration when it was issued the following year.

Such advocacy opened many doors for Blackstone. He became friends with a number of leading Zionists, including Nathan Straus, Stephen Wise, Jacob De Hass, and Louis Brandeis. True to form, Blackstone kept his Jewish friends well supplied with dispensational literature, including some material that he suggested ought to be hidden away until *after* the rapture of the church so that those left behind could understand what had happened and turn to Jesus. Blackstone even felt free to insert himself into Zionist business, if he thought he could help.[17] For example, when Herzl's commitment to Palestine as the location of the coming Jewish state faltered, Blackstone sent him a marked copy of the Old Testament, showing in typical dispensationalist fashion all the passages that pointed to the Holy Land.[18]

Zionists liked and trusted Blackstone. Of all the dispensational Bible teachers who predicted the restoration of Israel, only he was ready to give active support to the cause. A 1918 Zionist Conference in Philadelphia acclaimed Blackstone a "Father of Zionism," and in 1956, on the seventy-fifth anniversary of Blackstone's memorial to President Harrison, the citizens of the state of Israel dedicated a forest in his honor.[19]

THE AMERICAN COLONY IN JERUSALEM

As adamant as Blackstone and other dispensationalists were about the restoration of the Jews to Palestine, they never suggested that fellow dispensationalists should settle there. But some of them did. In 1881, Horatio and Anna Spafford and a group of sixteen friends from Chicago immigrated to Jerusalem in order to watch the unfolding of end-times events at close range. The story of their American colony is an intriguing one that has not been given the attention it deserves.[20]

Born in North Troy, New York, in 1828, Horatio Spafford moved to Chicago in 1856 and quickly established himself as a successful lawyer and real estate investor. In 1861, he married a Norwegian immigrant named Anna Larssen. They settled on Chicago's North Side and became prominent members of the First Presbyterian Church. Not long after they married, they became dispensationalists and close friends of Moody and Blackstone. The energetic Spafford soon became a well-known lay evangelist to the business community.

The Chicago fire of 1871 nearly wiped out the Spaffords. Horatio and Anna spent the next two years in feverish activity, working hard to recover their losses and assist the recovery of others. In 1873, they were in desperate need of rest and decided to take an extended European vacation. In late November, Horatio sent Anna and their four daughters ahead on the steamer *Ville du Havre,* while he remained behind to conclude a business deal. Off the coast of Newfoundland, their ship collided with another vessel and went to the bottom with 230 passengers, including all four Spafford girls. Of Horatio's family, only Anna survived.[21]

Nothing was ever the same for the Spaffords after that. They had three more children, but one of them, their only son, died of scarlet fever in 1880. The death of five children created a theological crisis for the Spaffords, who began questioning parts of their church's Calvinism. Leaders of their congregation accused Horatio of denying the doctrines of predestination and eternal punishment. After a lengthy and public controversy, the Spaffords were forced out of the church. But they were not destitute of supporters. Most of their dispensationalist friends, including Blackstone and Moody, stood by them, as did a small group of intimates who had suffered similar tragedies. These "Overcomers," as they liked to call themselves, constituted most of those who moved to Jerusalem in 1881.

The pilgrims settled in the Muslim quarter of the Old City and organized themselves into a Christian commune. Following the disciples' example in Acts 2, they held all property in common, but unlike most early Christians, the "Spaffordites" (as they were sometimes called) made celibacy the house rule. The motivations of the settlers were complex, but dispensationalism was one of their main concerns. Their convictions about Bible prophecy shaped the way they lived and how they understood events around them. For example, for a while the group "went every day to the Mount of Olives with tea and cakes, hoping to be the first to offer the Messiah refreshment."[22] Likewise, when hundreds of penniless Jews from Yemen arrived in Jerusalem in 1882 and the Sephardic and Ashkenazi Jewish communities declined to help them, the Spaffordites concluded that they were members of the ten lost tribes of Israel who were supposed to return to the Holy Land just before the Messiah's second coming. Therefore, they assumed responsibility for them by providing tents, food, and other kinds of needed support. As a result, the Spaffordites became rather well known in Jerusalem and were generally accepted by their Jewish and Arab neighbors.

Horatio died in the late 1880s, and Anna became the undisputed leader of the community. She had a charismatic and domineering personality, claimed to receive visions from God, and liked to dress completely in white and be called "Mother." Under Anna, the colony flourished. For the next thirty-five years, nothing much happened at the colony without Anna's say-so.

The colony became a stopover for famous visitors to the Holy City. In 1883–84, the British general Charles "Chinese" Gordon spent almost a year in Jerusalem studying Bible history and archaeology (tourists still visit Gordon's Calvary and Garden Tomb) and frequented the colony often. Blackstone stopped in during his extended visit to Palestine in 1889 to see his old friends, and Moody did the same in 1892. In 1899, Selma Lagerlof, the celebrated Swedish writer and first female Nobel Prize winner for literature, spent some time at the colony, then wrote a highly favorable novel, *Jerusalem,* about what she saw there.[23] A. E. Thompson of the Christian and Missionary Alliance moved to Jerusalem in 1903 to become pastor of the American Free Church. He visited the colony often and became a friend and supporter. In 1904, fifteen hundred delegates came to Jerusalem for the Fourth Sunday School Convention.

The colony acted as unofficial host for the convention, thereby generating much goodwill and even some financial support from the visitors.

What enabled the colony to survive economically was the arrival in 1896 of seventy Swedish immigrants from Chicago and another thirty-seven from Dalarna, Sweden. Both groups had ties to the still powerful Swedish revival and were deeply interested in dispensationalism. One of the Swedes from Chicago explained their reason for coming: "We wished to go there when God brought the Jews back; we wanted to see the prophecies fulfilled."[24] The coming of the Swedes swelled the colony's size to roughly 150. Even more important than numbers were the skills the Swedes brought to the colony. In no time, they started a dairy farm, a bakery, a furniture store, a shop for tourists, a photography studio, and other ventures, including a children's hospital and a number of medical clinics. A guest house for visiting friends was eventually turned into a hotel that operates to this day.

There were other changes too. After twenty years of neglecting the education of their children because Anna believed the Lord's return was imminent, in 1903, the colonists started a school, which soon became the school of choice for the children of missionaries and foreign diplomats in Jerusalem. In 1904, the colony dropped its controversial celibacy rule. Mother Spafford claimed she had been instructed by divine revelation to do so, but there were other more mundane reasons. The Swedes never liked the rule and complained about it, and the colony's second generation—the children of the founders—had reached marriageable age and were pressuring for change. Probably the most significant factor in Anna's decision to drop the rule was her daughter Bertha, who passionately desired to marry Frederick Vester, whose father was a German Lutheran missionary and wealthy merchant.

Though the colony survived as a religious community for over fifty years, it lived with almost constant controversy. Its practice of celibacy generated questions and endless rumors. The American consul in Jerusalem, Selah Merrill, disliked the colony's sexual and prophetic views and did everything he could for over twenty years to discredit it. Not long after their arrival, the Swedes criticized Mother Spafford's leadership, which could be tyrannical and harsh, and unsuccessfully challenged the unwritten rule that Americans made all the decisions and Swedes did all the work. In 1895, a contentious child custody dispute landed members of the colony in a Chicago courtroom and on the front pages of Chicago newspapers.

Eventually, the passage of time and the decline of premillennialist convictions did the colony in. Anna died in 1923, and the colony's ethos and viability declined. Disputes over finances and leadership split the ranks. Some people left the colony but stayed in Jerusalem, while others went home to America or Sweden. As is common in such communal experiments, the religious convictions of the second generation were different from those of the first. Bertha Spafford Vester and other children of the founders no longer watched the skies for the coming of Christ or viewed the return of Jews to Palestine as the fulfillment of Bible prophecy. In fact, by the 1930s, the colony ceased being primarily a religious community and started operating more like a family business. Without its original prophetic outlook, the colony's perspective on life in Palestine dramatically changed. After Anna's passing, the community identified more with the needs of the indigenous Arab population and considered Zionism a threat to Arabs' legitimate rights.[25]

Certainly, the story of the American colony in Jerusalem was unusual. American dispensationalists expected the Jews, not Protestant evangelicals like themselves, to return to Palestine. But the Spaffordites did demonstrate how powerful premillennial ideas could be. Some dispensationalists were willing to relocate in order to be present when God's promises to Israel were fulfilled.

THE BALFOUR DECLARATION AND THE CAPTURE OF JERUSALEM

As already shown, premillennialists believed that World War I played a major role in realigning European nations for the eventual fulfillment of biblical prophecy. But nothing during the war had greater prophetic significance for dispensationalists than the events occurring in the Middle East.[26] Changes in Palestine pointed to the restoration of a Jewish state.

As the Great War entered its final year, the attention of all premillennialists focused on the Holy Land. When the British changed the thrust of their eastern operations from Mesopotamia to Palestine, dispensationalists were confident that the fall of the Ottoman Empire was imminent and that prophecy was about to be fulfilled. By 1916, there was already widespread speculation in the secular press about the restoration of a Jewish homeland after the war, a fact not missed by dispensationalist observers. Premillennialist publications such as the *Weekly Evangel, Our Hope,* and the *Christian Workers Magazine* all noted these persistent rumors.[27] Even though British military prospects in the Middle East seemed rather dismal in early 1916, the editors of the Assemblies of God's *Weekly Evangel* were full of confidence: "As God is working with the nations, He will drive the Turk out of Palestine and cause his ancient people to take possession of it."[28]

Toward the end of 1917, fast-moving events heightened expectations. On November 2, as British forces fought their way into Palestine from the south, Lord Arthur Balfour, the British foreign secretary, wrote to Lord James Rothschild, a leader in the international Zionist movement:

> His Majesty's Government view with favour the establishment in Palestine of a national home for the Jewish people, and will use their best efforts to facilitate the achievement of this object, it being clearly understood that nothing shall be done which may prejudice the civil and religious rights of existing non-Jewish communities in Palestine or the rights and political status enjoyed by Jews in any other country.[29]

Barely five weeks after the Balfour Declaration was written, the Turks surrendered Jerusalem to British forces under General Edmund Allenby. The door seemed wide open for prophetic fulfillments. Here was the most substantial proof yet that the "times of the Gentiles" were drawing to an end: "Jerusalem shall be trodden down of the Gentiles, until the times of the Gentiles be fulfilled" (Luke 21:24). Dispensationalists did not seem to mind that control of the city had passed from one Gentile power (Turkey) to another (Britain). The important thing was that the new occupiers had already promised to undertake the establishment of a new Jewish state. For the first time in over two millennia, the Gentile grasp on Jerusalem was starting to loosen.[30]

The dispensationalist response to the declaration and the capture of Jerusalem was a combination of religious enthusiasm and smug "we told you so." Though he had been predicting the restoration of the Jews for years, A. B. Simpson seemed surprised and shaken by the Balfour Declaration. He wept openly when he read the declaration to his congregation and reflected on its prophetic significance.[31] Later, he was in Chicago to speak at a prophecy conference when he learned that Jerusalem had fallen to the British. He was overwhelmed by the news and had to retreat to his hotel room, where he wept for joy and prayed fervently for the redemption and restoration of Israel. After regaining his composure, he made his way to the Moody Tabernacle, where he delivered a stirring address on the fulfillment of prophecy in Palestine.[32] In *Our Hope,* Arno C. Gaebelein called the coming restoration of the Jews "the sign of all signs" and noted that the establishment of a new Jewish state had to come "some time" and that it was "impossible that this should not come to pass."[33]

Dispensationalists everywhere were energized by the news. Leaders quickly organized prophetic conferences to underscore the significance of the times in which they were living. In May 1918, a group of Philadelphia businessmen, largely motivated by the events in the Middle East, convened a prophetic conference that lasted three days and drew three thousand people. One of the high points of the conference was the address by A. E.

Thompson, who had been, until his expulsion by the Turks, the pastor of the American Free Church in Jerusalem. In part, he said that

> the capture of Jerusalem is one of those events to which the students of prophecy have been looking forward for many years. Even before Great Britain took possession of Egypt, there were keen sighted seers who foresaw the day when God would use the Anglo-Saxon peoples to restore Jerusalem. When the war broke out, there were some of us who were convinced that it would never end until Turkish tyranny was forever a thing of the past in the Holy City. When the city was captured, we felt very confident we could put one hand upon this great event which had stirred the heart of the whole Christian world, and laying open our Bible at many places in the Prophets say as confidently as Peter on the day of Pentecost, "This is that which was spoken by the prophets."[34]

Later that fall Gaebelein organized another well-attended prophetic conference at Carnegie Hall in New York, where speakers discussed recent events in the Middle East.

As the participants in the 1918 prophetic conferences indicated, the capture of Jerusalem and the issuance of the Balfour Declaration were in full accord with long-standing dispensational expectations.[35] At the New York conference, Gaebelein articulated the standard interpretation of those events: "To us true believers it is the sign that the times of the Gentiles are rapidly nearing their close."[36] If the times of the Gentiles were almost over, could the restoration of the Jews be far behind? Like many other dispensationalists in 1918, W. Fuller Gooch thought that the founding of the new Jewish state was just around the corner: "We are, therefore, likely to see in the near future a Jewish State in Palestine. It may be in a month or two, it may be in a year or two; but the intention is to restore the land to the people and the people to the land."[37]

Of course, as Gooch and others eventually discovered, establishing the state of Israel would take thirty years more and another World War to accomplish. Nevertheless, events in 1917–18 made dispensationalists confident that everything was moving ahead according to the Bible's clear predictions. Shortly after the end of World War I, W. W. Fereday spelled out what virtually all dispensationalists thought about the Balfour Declaration and the fall of Jerusalem to the British:

> Palestine is for the Jews. The most striking sign of the times is the proposal to give Palestine to the Jews once more. They have long desired the land, though as yet unrepentant of the terrible crime which led to their expulsion therefrom. November 2, 1917, was a red-letter day in the world's history when the British Foreign Secretary addressed his now

famous letter to Lord Rothschild on this subject. Prophetic Scripture supposes the Jewish people back in the land during the next crises. Thus in Rev. xi. a temple is divinely acknowledged in Jerusalem, and Daniel ix. 27 speaks of a treaty to be made by the head of the Western Empire with the people. Isaiah xviii. 1–6 distinctly speaks of an effort to be made by a maritime Power to restore the Jews to Palestine apart from God. . . . There is a mass of Prophetic Scripture yet to be accomplished, but no prophecy can be accomplished until Palestine is again in Jewish hands. Prophecy revolves around the despised Jew: and if Jewish restoration is imminent (as it appears to be), how near we must be to the fulfillment of every vision![38]

Dispensationalism and the Mission to the Jews

Dispensationalists saw a close connection between the restoration of the Jews to Palestine and their coming to Christ. At the 1878 prophetic conference in New York, Bishop William R. Nicholson of the Reformed Episcopal Church made the connection: "Previous to the coming of the Lord . . . it will be still as rejecters of Christ and rebellious to God, that they will occupy their land." Once there, Jews will rebuild the temple and observe its ancient rites, but they will still be under God's curse. "The object of their gathering is ultimately their conversion, but primarily, their chastisement and suffering." After being reduced to a remnant during the great tribulation, the Jews "will look on Him whom they have pierced. . . . They shall mourn for their sins. . . . They will believe in the Lord Jesus Christ, and they shall be forgiven; not forgiven only, but accepted in the preciousness of that Name which they and their nation had rejected and abhorred." In the end, after the eschatological dust settles, all Israel (the tiny remnant that remains) will be saved. In the meantime, Jews are spiritually lost unless they accept Jesus as Lord and Savior.[39] Though dispensationalists did not expect the wholesale conversion of Jews until the return of Christ, they believed that converting a few Jews now was an important sign of things to come.

This perspective explains why dispensationalists welcomed nationalistic aspirations of Jews while at the same time targeting their community for aggressive evangelization. No one better illustrates how premillennialists held the two together than William E. Blackstone. At a 1918 Zionist mass meeting in Los Angeles, Blackstone had the chutzpah to give an altar call:

I am and for over thirty years have been an ardent advocate of Zionism. This is because I believe that true Zionism is founded on the plan, purpose, and fiat of the everlasting and omnipotent God, as prophetically recorded in His Holy Word, the Bible. . . . There are only three courses open to every Jew. . . . The first is to become a true Christian, accepting Jesus as Lord and Saviour, which brings not only forgiveness and regeneration, but insures escape from the unequaled time of tribulation which is coming upon all the earth. . . . Second—become a true Zionist and thus hold fast to the ancient hopes of the fathers, and the assured deliverance of Israel, through the coming of their Messiah, and complete national restoration and permanent settlement in the land which God has given them. It is true that this leads through unequaled sorrows, as prophesied notably by Jeremiah. . . . [Third—] these are the *assimilants*. They are the Jews who will not be either Christians or Zionists. They wish to remain in the various nations enjoying their social, political, and commercial advantages. . . . Oh, my Jewish friends, which of these paths shall be yours? . . . God says that you are dear unto Him. . . . He has put an overwhelming love in my heart for you all, and therefore I have spoken thus plainly. Study this wonderful Word of God . . . and see how plainly God Himself has revealed Israel's pathway unto the perfect day.[40]

BEGINNINGS OF THE DISPENSATIONAL MISSION TO THE JEWS

American Protestants began evangelizing Jews early in the nineteenth century and for the most part targeted Jews the same way they targeted other immigrant groups.[41] But once dispensationalists set up their own networks, they began to focus much of their energy on the establishment of new missions to the Jews that were rooted in their prophetic views of them as the chosen people who would play a crucial role in the events of the last days. In fact, from the 1880s to the 1910s, dispensationalists founded dozens of such Jewish missionary organizations.[42]

What made these missions different from those founded by mainline Protestants was the underlying conviction that God was not finished with the Jews as a national entity. Dispensationalists' missionary message was always tied to their prophetic teachings about a restored Israel and the Jews' central role in the end-times events. In fact, premillennialists claimed that their prophetic emphasis was the key to successful Jewish evangelism. Unlike most other evangelicals who believed that the church was the New Israel and that Jews had already had their day, dispensationalists were able to assure Jews, especially Orthodox Jews, that their greatest days were still ahead and that all of God's prophetic promises to them would be kept.

Dispensationalists believed that missionaries who could not make such assertions were evangelizing with one hand tied behind their backs. James H. Brookes once observed that "no man is fit to preach to the Jews unless he believes in the personal [second] coming of the Messiah." Since "most Jews, except those who have been utter infidels, confidently expect to be restored to the land of their fathers, it is most important to show them that their hope is founded upon the coming of Messiah."[43] Arno C. Gaebelein shared these sentiments. In 1914, he stated that

> a Christian who does not believe in the second coming of Christ is therefore wholly unfit to deal with the Jews. More than that, the church-missions among the Jews which are run with the un-scriptural post-millennial argument are a dead failure. The true way to present the Gospel to the Jews is to show them the truth of the two advents in the Old Testament, and also how the New Testament looks forward to the second coming of Christ and the establishment of the Kingdom.[44]

One of the first dispensationalist missions to the Jews was founded by William E. Blackstone and some of his friends in Chicago in 1887. First called the Chicago Committee for Hebrew Christian Work, the mission changed its name to the Chicago Hebrew Mission in 1889. Two years later it was incorporated as the first Jewish mission in the state of Illinois. The mission moved frequently during its first few years, for a time occupying space in Jane Addams's Hull House on Halsted Street. Because most of its intended audience were recent immigrants, the mission offered programs geared to their needs. Eventually, the mission had its own reading room, industrial school, temporary home for new Jewish converts, and day nurseries for the children of working mothers that were located in different places around the Jewish section of Chicago. In 1906, the mission had a staff of twenty-three who conducted preaching services, mothers' meetings, a kindergarten, house-to-house visitation, and literature distribution.[45] The mission eventually had its own publication, the *Jewish Era,* and sponsored regular Conferences on Behalf of Israel, in which noted dispensationalists analyzed Jewish aspects of biblical prophecy. One of these conferences was held at Moody Church in November 1915 and drew seventeen thousand spectators over four days. Leading dispensationalists such as James M. Gray, Robert McWatty Russell, A. E. Thompson, A. B. Simpson, John Timothy Stone, B. B. Sutcliffe, and William E. Blackstone participated.[46]

Another successful premillennialist mission to the Jews was New York City's Hope of Israel Mission, which, after 1892, was under the leadership of Gaebelein. Although the mission was originally affiliated with the Methodist Church Extension Society, Gaebelein eventually severed all relationships with the Methodists.[47] The mission conducted preaching services on Saturday afternoons on the Lower East Side; published three monthly papers in Yiddish *(Tiqweth Israel),* German *(Unsere Hoffnung),* and English *(Our Hope);* and tried to provide free medical services for the poor whenever possible. The real strength behind the mission, however, was Gaebelein, who personified the passion and technique of dispensationalist missionaries in search of Jewish conversions.

Gaebelein immigrated from Thuringia, Germany, in 1879, in part to escape compulsory military service. Though raised a Lutheran, once in America he joined the Methodists and became a minister in their German Conference, serving churches in New York, New Jersey, and Maryland.[48] He first encountered dispensationalism in the early 1880s when he read some prophetic literature and attended the first Niagara Bible Conference. In 1887, he left parish work to do Jewish evangelism full-time. His work among the Jews of New York seems to have played a role in his acceptance of dispensationalism, for he found that it gave him an edge in doing evangelism: Dispensationalism's belief in the regathering of Jews to Palestine and the restoration of David's throne appealed to Orthodox Jews especially.

Gaebelein was essentially self-taught, though he did do a year's study at Johns Hopkins University during a pastorate in Baltimore. He learned Hebrew and Yiddish in order to debate with the rabbis on the Lower East Side. After joining the Hope of Israel Mission in the early 1890s, he conducted spirited lectures on Saturday afternoons, in which he agreed to answer all questions on the messiahship of Jesus or the future of Israel according to Bible prophecy. In fact, he acquired such an expertise in the Talmud and other rabbinic literature and spoke such flawless Yiddish that he often had difficulty convincing his audiences that he was not a Jew trying to pass as a Gentile. Under Gaebelein's leadership, the mission expanded to Baltimore, Philadelphia, Pittsburgh, St. Louis, and, for a while, Jerusalem. Despite such success, in 1904, Gaebelein left the mission to devote all his time to editing, writing, and speaking.[49]

Eventually, nearly every major American city with a substantial Jewish population had some kind of evangelistic witness to the Jews, most of which were either founded or heavily supported by premillennialists: Hebrew Messianic Council, Boston, 1888; Brooklyn Christian Mission to the Jews, 1892; San Francisco Hebrew Mission, 1896; St. Louis Jewish Christian Mission, 1898; New Covenant Mission to the Jews and Gentiles, Pittsburgh, 1898; New York Hebrew Christian Association, 1903; and Hebrew Christian Mission to the Jews, Newark, 1904, to name only a few.[50] By the turn of the century, there were dozens of dispensational missions to the Jews in operation.

MISSIONARY METHODS

In general, the methods used in these missions organizations were the same ones employed to reach other immigrant groups. In the more successful operations, the emphasis was on programming: They had reading rooms, social centers, kindergartens, day care centers, sewing and home economics classes, English tutorials in which the New Testament was the only textbook, public lectures on a variety of religious topics, door-to-door visitation, literature distribution by hand and through the mail, and open-air meetings. But missions to the Jews were more difficult and required more sensitivity than did evangelistic efforts among other newcomers. As one might expect, Jewish immigrants who had just come from pogroms and anti-Semitism in Europe were not eager to encounter Christian missionaries in the United States. Memories of forced baptisms and religious persecution were too fresh in their minds for them to welcome the work of Christian evangelists. Some Jews considered any kind of evangelism anti-Semitic and intent on destroying the Jewish community. Consequently, Christian missionaries to the Jews faced an extremely difficult task.

Missionaries who conducted open-air meetings in urban neighborhoods had especially hazardous duty, as can be seen in the account of one street meeting in Chicago conducted by students from Moody Bible Institute. Using a standard evangelical approach, the students tried to conduct their service from the back of a "gospel wagon," which was a modified flatbed truck used as a platform. Soon over a thousand irritated Jews gathered, shouting "disconcerting questions" and insulting the students. Charles Meeker, the director of practical work, or field education, at Moody Bible Institute, had "told the speakers not to get into any wrangles over these questions, but to adhere closely to their testimony and lay the claims of Christ upon the audience with all the power at their command; and no matter how much they disliked or resented it, they should not hesitate to use the name of Jesus freely." But the more the missionaries stuck to their program, the angrier the crowd became. At one point, Meeker sent two of his students to look for a policeman to provide some protection.

Finally, Meeker and the students started their strategic withdrawal under "an avalanche of watermelon rind, banana peelings, overripe tomatoes, and other edible fruit." Such treatment might have scared off some evangelists, but according to Meeker, the encounter "in no way dampened our ardor or quenched our desire to give the gospel to the Jew." Despite everything, Meeker claimed, some Jews were converted to Christ that day. In no time, Meeker's students were on the streets again.[51]

As the Moody students' experiences made clear, missionaries to the Jews had a number of practical issues to consider: Who, for example, had the best chance of reaching Jews with the gospel—sympathetic Gentile missionaries or converted Jews? Both had strengths and weaknesses.[52] Sometimes Jews gave Gentile missionaries a better hearing than Jewish converts, who were reviled as traitors. But the most sensitive issue in the dispensationalist mission to the Jews was the best way to evangelize Jewish children. As evangelicals had learned from decades of revivalism, the young are easier to reach with the gospel than the old. The same was true for Jewish children, who were often embarrassed by the Old World ways of their parents and eager for something new.

At times Christian missionaries camouflaged their evangelistic intentions behind sewing, cooking, or singing classes. Unsuspecting Jewish parents let their children attend without knowing what the teachers were really up to. On one such occasion, at least, that strategy backfired. The missionaries in charge unwisely opened the program with a hymn whose words took the children completely by surprise:

> As soon as we expressed in the hymn the word Jesus, the children simultaneously, as though done by magic placed their fingers in their ears and refused to sing or to listen. Some of them began to hiss, and some of them decided not to stay. They were shocked, they were horrified, and some were ready even to weep and to run home. Their teachers were puzzled and perplexed. But we kept on singing; and after a little, the children would gradually withdraw their fingers from their ears and listen. When they recognized that the word Jesus was not being expressed, they would keep their fingers out till we came to that word, and again that performance was gone through with.[53]

Such a rocky start did not mean permanent failure. A few months later, those same children sang "What a Friend We Have in Jesus" as they rode in open trolleys through Jewish neighborhoods on their way to a mission-sponsored outing in the country.

Some of the opponents of evangelizing Jewish children accused Christian missionaries of openly encouraging the children to deceive their parents or of purchasing parental cooperation through some kind of financial assistance. More scrupulous missionaries made sure they had parental permission before taking their children to evangelistic meetings. If everything was above board, missionaries discovered, some parents were willing to let their children attend.[54]

SCANDALS

As though those built-in problems were not enough, dispensational missions to the Jews occasionally suffered the embarrassment of public scandal. A case in point is the controversy surrounding Leopold Cohn, founder of the Williamsburg Mission to the Jews in Brooklyn, New York. According to his autobiography,[55] he was born in Hungary in 1862 of Orthodox parents. After becoming a rabbi at the age of eighteen, Cohn began to study prophecy in the Hebrew Scriptures without any knowledge of Jesus of Nazareth or the New Testament. The more he studied the Talmud, however, the more confused he became. In 1892, he arrived in New York to work among Jewish immigrants, hoping to continue his own studies of messianic prophecy. Shortly after his arrival, he attended a meeting in which a Christian missionary spoke about the coming of the Messiah. Cohn obtained a New Testament in Hebrew but did not make the connection between the Yeshua (Jesus) of the Gospels and the Christ of Christianity. When a fellow rabbi pointed it out, it was already too late. Cohn converted and was baptized in June 1892. He studied Christian theology in Scotland, had a painful reconciliation with his family, then returned to New York in 1893 to share the gospel with fellow Jews.

He opened a storefront mission, but the going was tough. After three years of struggle, Cohn secured the financial backing of the Baptist Home Missions Society (BHMS) and the Church Extension Society, and the mission prospered. Cohn conducted Bible studies, evangelistic lectures, child evangelism, and a free medical dispensary. In time, his work spread beyond Brooklyn to Coney Island, Philadelphia, Pittsburgh, Los Angeles, and Buffalo.[56]

Cohn's troubles began in 1907, when he began feuding with the Baptist Home Missions Society over issues of money and control. The dispute finally broke into the open when Cohn, acting independently of the BHMS, secured a ten-thousand-dollar donation from Frances J. Huntley. BHMS board members claimed that Cohn had acted improperly and that the donation rightly belonged to the society. Cohn agreed to turn the donation over to the BHMS if Miss Huntley so directed, but she deferred. The BHMS severed all ties with Cohn and warned its constituents that Cohn "has alienated some of his best supporters by his refusal to have any supervision of his work in any way whatever. . . . His insulting language and his bad temper and general management of the work have alienated many of his best friends." They advised potential supporters not to donate any more money.[57] Cohn changed the mission's name to the American Board of Missions to the Jews and quickly turned the mission into the biggest and most influential Jewish mission of its day. The more successful Cohn became, however, the more opposition he faced.[58]

In 1913, Cohn found himself embroiled in an even larger controversy. Yiddish newspapers in New York reported that Cohn had lied about being a rabbi in Hungary and that Cohn was not even his real name.

According to the newspapers' sources, he had been an innkeeper in his native land and had been forced to flee when he was accused of murder. Cohn's supporters claimed that Jews in New York had raised ten thousand dollars to discredit Cohn because of his missionary successes and had hired a young man to go to Hungary to bribe Cohn's hometown sheriff into making the false accusations.[59]

On top of these charges, during an appearance in the Brooklyn Municipal Court in December of the same year, Cohn admitted that he owned a country estate in Connecticut, another home in New York City, and other real estate holdings. Because Cohn, when making financial appeals, had often claimed that he was nearly destitute, many were disturbed by the news and began to question Cohn's ethics and the legitimacy of his mission work.

By 1916, James M. Gray was under pressure to stop advertising the mission in Moody Bible Institute's *Christian Workers Magazine.* Realizing that Cohn's future ministry was at stake, Gray put together a special investigatory committee to look into allegations that Cohn had mishandled funds. The committee included respected evangelical members of the business and religious communities.

The committee rented rooms in the Williamsburg YMCA and invited everyone with pertinent information to come forward. Cohn's lawyers were allowed to cross-examine witnesses. After seven weeks, the committee issued its findings: "As a result of these weeks of painstaking inquiry, the committee has found no evidence which could be substantiated which affords a reasonable basis for any of the charges made by his accusers."[60] Shortly thereafter, Gray reported to his own readers that Cohn was innocent of all charges and had always acted legally. Cohn had been wrongly accused by his enemies, and his mission deserved generous support.[61] The mission survived and prospered, especially after Cohn turned control of the mission over to his son Joseph.

Despite Cohn's vindication by the committee, the outcome did not reduce the widespread belief among Jews that those who tried to proselytize them were really con men and charlatans. Sometimes converts themselves provided sensational exposés about the missionaries. One such person was Samuel Freuder, who had come to the United States from Hungary in 1883. He graduated from Hebrew Union College in 1886 and served as a Reform rabbi in Georgia. After a crisis of faith, Freuder moved to Chicago in 1891. There, under the influence of Blackstone's Chicago Hebrew Mission, he converted to Christianity and was baptized. He then took up ministry studies at Chicago Theological Seminary. Following ordination as a Congregationalist minister, he became a missionary to Jews in Boston in 1894.

Freuder was a troubled man. After only five months at the Boston mission, he quit to go into secular business. After a series of jobs, Freuder decided to lecture on prophetic and evangelistic themes. Eventually, he transferred to the Protestant Episcopal Church and joined the staff of Grace Episcopal Church in New York City. By 1908, however, Freuder was extremely unhappy and disillusioned with Christianity, so he resolved to break from it by publicly repudiating his conversion.[62]

He waited until June 1908, when he was scheduled to speak on "Christ and the Talmud" at a Hebrew Messianic Conference at Boston's Park Street Church. Instead of speaking on the assigned topic, Freuder declared to a stunned audience that he was leaving the Christian faith and ministry. He told the gathering, "You don't know what it means and costs for a Jew to be baptized—the rended soul, the disrupted family, the desertion of friends, the loss of respect." In conclusion, he pronounced a curse on himself if he ever preached in a Christian pulpit again. In his letter of resignation to his bishop, Freuder stated that missionaries to Jews would lose their jobs if their manipulative techniques were widely known, which would force them to "turn their faking abilities into some business channels less destructive of true manhood and morality."[63]

In the published version of his story, Freuder wrote that to retain the support of their contributors, missionaries falsified the results of their work. They also frequently took advantage of their new converts by thrusting them into the public eye as spiritual trophies. Most of the missionaries in Freuder's portrayal appeared to be thoughtless and exploitative manipulators who did not understand anything about the price Jews paid to convert. Freuder's analysis was obviously overdone, but it did reflect the prevailing Jewish view of Christian evangelism.[64]

Most Christian missionaries to the Jews were much better than Freuder claimed. They were sensitive to criticism, especially the kind that questioned their integrity. In fact, some of them openly criticized the manipulative methods of fellow missionaries who "bought converts" by misleading them into believing that there were financial benefits to accepting Christ. One case in point was Herman Warszawiak, a Polish-born Jewish missionary in New York City in the 1890s. Warszawiak converted to Christ in Germany, on his way to America from Warsaw, then diverted to Scotland for theological training. He came to New York in 1890 and went to work for the New York Mission and Tract Society. He was young, handsome, and a charismatic speaker who regularly drew hundreds of hearers on the Lower East Side during his Saturday afternoon sermons. While other missionaries to the Jews plodded along, Warszawiak qualified as a celebrity whose star was rising fast.

In 1895, he struck out on his own, founding the American Mission to the Jews. Every Saturday he preached in the auditorium of the Presbyterian Church at Henry and Market streets. To advertise his meetings, he distributed handbills in Yiddish: "Whoever comes this Sabbath afternoon to our meeting at 19 Market Street will receive a free ticket to a wonderful electric picture exhibition. Come and secure free tickets. The collection of pictures is highly interesting. The tickets to be purchased will cost 50 cents."

Warszawiak's marketing strategy was way ahead of its time. What people today might consider a rather run-of-the-mill come-on scandalized people at the end of the nineteenth century. Gaebelein, whose mission competed with Warszawiak's, accused him of trying to buy converts for 50 cents each.[65] To make matters worse, when Warszawiak sought ordination through the New York Presbytery in 1896, he was turned down, largely on the testimony of a well-known "anti-vice crusader" who said he had seen Warszawiak frequenting a "house of vice" in Weehawken, New Jersey. Even his own Fifth Presbyterian Church removed him from membership over these and other charges. Though the church later reversed its decision, the damage was done. His mission and his reputation were ruined. What is significant about the Warszawiak case is that he was not done in by Jewish critics[66] but by fellow missionaries and church members who disapproved of his methods—or maybe his success.[67]

While some missionaries were less than honest or overly aggressive, the majority seemed sincerely concerned about the spiritual condition of Jews. Some missionaries claimed that *they* were the real victims, not the Jewish converts. All missionaries were occasionally victimized by Jewish "seekers" who took advantage of them. Even Freuder admitted that some Jews came to the missionaries for financial assistance. A feigned interest in the gospel message and a hard-luck story sometimes moved missionaries to help financially. In some cases, dishonest Jews passed the word on to their friends, who used the same scheme.[68] Even Gaebelein confessed to being fooled by so-called converts who refused baptism at the last minute when they realized there was no cash payoff.[69] In the early days, the life of a missionary to the Jews was not easy.

THE MATURING OF JEWISH MISSIONS

Over the years, Jewish missions became much more sophisticated. From their founding in the 1880s through World War I, the missions focused on the needs of newly arrived Jewish immigrants. But by the 1920s, the Jewish community in America had changed dramatically, requiring missionaries to adjust to the different needs of the second generation. American-born children of Jewish immigrants did not look at things the way their parents did and were becoming Americanized. The missions needed to understand the complexity and diversity of the Jewish community and to raise the quality of their evangelistic endeavors. The real initiative for the improvement of the missions came from the missions themselves. The Hebrew Christian

Alliance of America, to which dozens of Jewish missions belonged, lobbied the conservative evangelical community for the establishment of a special educational program for the training of missionaries to the Jews. In 1923, such a program opened at Moody Bible Institute in Chicago. The alliance collaborated with the institute in hiring the first professor of Jewish studies, Joel Levy, then his replacement, Solomon Birnbaum, after Levy's untimely death. The curriculum consisted of studies in Jewish history, religion, and culture; Hebrew; Yiddish; and the best practices in Jewish evangelism. In addition to these specialized courses, students were required to take classes in preaching, religious education, Bible, theology, and messianic prophecy—all from a dispensational perspective. This program of study lasted two years, with fifteen weeks of fieldwork in one of Chicago's Jewish neighborhoods. Under successive leaders such as Max Reich, Nathan Stone, and Louis Goldberg, the Jewish studies program at Moody Bible Institute produced hundreds of well-trained leaders in the Jewish missions network.[70]

Even Jewish critics noticed the increasing quality in the work of the mostly Gentile missionaries. In the early days of Jewish missions, opponents criticized missionaries' poor understanding of Jewish ways of life, religious practices, and rich literary and oral heritage. Even Jews who may have been drawn to the Christian message were put off by the "missionary Yiddish" used in sermons and tracts, which was inferior and sometimes laughable. Clearly, Gaebelein's Yiddish ability was the exception, not the rule. But when missionaries undertook the systematic study of Hebrew and Yiddish, such criticisms were more difficult to make, especially after the publication of two excellent Yiddish translations of the New Testament in 1941 and 1949.[71]

With such an emphasis on training, it did not take long for missionaries to acquire expertise and sensitivity about Jewish life and religion. Eventually, seasoned missionaries produced manuals and practical guides on a variety of topics, demonstrating their growing understanding of the people they were trying to evangelize. These books contained accurate portrayals of Jewish history, culture, and religious life, including well-nuanced discussions about variations of belief and practice within the American Jewish community. Such knowledge was required, according to these manuals, to reach Jews with the gospel. Some evangelistic techniques were more effective than others, and authors passed along tried-and-true methods and those biblical passages that were most persuasive.[72] Typical of such manuals were Albert Huisjen's *Home Front of Jewish Missions* and *Talking about Jesus to a Jewish Neighbor;* Henry J. Heydt's *Studies in Jewish Evangelism* and *The Chosen People Question Box II;* Daniel Fuchs's *How to Reach the Jew for Christ;* and Jacob Gartenhaus's *How to Win the Jews* and *Winning Jews to Christ.*[73]

FINDING A HOME FOR JEWISH CONVERTS

No matter how hard they tried, Christian missionaries could do little to ease the culture shock of their converts. As Freuder's story illustrates, to most Jews, conversion to Christ meant a total repudiation of ethnic, religious, and even family identities. Certainly, that is how most Jews looked at conversion: Accepting Jesus meant rejecting Judaism; becoming a believer in Christ meant an end to any claim to being a Jew. Jewish converts often reported being expelled from their homes and considered dead by their families and friends.[74] Under such conditions, missionaries frequently had to find them new homes, jobs, and social contacts. Essentially, then, converts felt they had no alternative but to lay aside their Jewishness and enter the Gentile world.

But was such a drastic break from Jewish identity absolutely necessary? Could converts come to Christ and retain certain Jewish practices? Was there a way to be both Jewish and Christian at the same time? Did Jewish converts always have to join a Gentile evangelical church, or could they develop their own Jewish-Christian congregations? Leaders of Jewish missions struggled with such questions from the 1880s on.

In the early days of dispensationalist missions to the Jews, a few missionaries believed that converts should retain their Jewishness by joining newly established "messianic" (i.e., Jewish-Christian) congregations. Gaebelein believed that the New Testament itself authorized such an approach. Appealing to Acts 15, he observed that

> when the Christian church was founded at Jerusalem, these first Jewish Christians were nationally so narrow-minded that they believed that the Gentiles must first become Jews and be circumcised before they could gain admission to the church of Christ. It would be the same narrowness of opinion now, at the end of the church age, if Christians were to demand that the Jewish people must first enter one of the [Gentile] churches before they could have a part in the Kingdom of God.[75]

Such a position had far-reaching consequences. Gaebelein believed that Jewish converts could retain some of their traditional religious practices. When outlining the principles of his Hope of Israel Mission in 1898, he insisted that

> the Jew has no need whatever of the organization or institutions of historical [i.e., Gentile and denominational] Christianity. All he needs is personal, saving faith in his own Jewish Messiah, the Christ of God, nothing more. And all that was divinely given him through Moses he has full liberty to retain and uphold as far as possible when he becomes a believer in Jesus Christ.[76]

Gaebelein clearly believed that one of the goals of Jewish missions should be the formation of new congregations that were Christian in belief but Jewish in style and expression. Here was an appeal for a fully contextualized Jewish Christianity.

Gaebelein shared the views of Ernest F. Stroeter, a former professor at the University of Denver who joined the Hope of Israel Mission in the 1890s. Like Gaebelein, Stroeter was a German immigrant and a Methodist. He also believed that Jewish converts did not have to join evangelical congregations and lay aside their Jewish customs and observances. They were free to maintain their Jewish way of life, including keeping the law of Moses and observing the traditional Jewish holy days. As long as they believed in Jesus Christ, they could live out their new faith in appropriate ethnic ways. Stroeter was direct: Christian missionaries who herded their converts into Gentile churches were treating them worse than heathens, who were never required to give up their ethnic or cultural identity in order to become Christians.[77] Greeks did not stop being Greeks when they accepted Christ as Savior; Swedes remained Swedes; and Germans in the New World were free to establish German congregations. So why were Jews stripped of their culture when they became believers in Jesus? To correct this abuse, Gaebelein and Stroeter started a new congregation where Jewish converts could feel at home.

Most other missionaries to the Jews considered the founding of separate Jewish-Christian congregations highly controversial. In fact, the movement to establish Hebrew-Christian congregations was quashed almost as soon as it began. For example, though they believed Jews were God's chosen people and would play a central role in the end times, missionary pioneers such as Blackstone and Cohn strongly urged their converts to attend evangelical churches, fully aware that the experience could be shattering to them. New converts returned from their initial forays into the Gentile evangelical world in culture shock. They told tales of being served ham at church suppers, having to sing "Onward Christian soldiers, marching as to war, with the cross of Jesus going on before," or hearing offhanded anti-Semitic remarks. Recent immigrants from Eastern Europe often found such things too much to bear.[78] Already cut off from their Jewish culture, they also felt out of place in their new Christian culture.[79] In a word, they were marginalized: To Jews they were Christians, and to Christians they were Jews. They were stuck between two religious traditions.[80]

The missionaries were sympathetic with the converts' plight, but most of them felt bound by their theology to prohibit the continuation of Jewish practices. The missionaries granted the existence of ethnic churches among other immigrant groups, but they thought Jews were in a special category. Being German or Swedish or Greek did not specify another religion as being Jewish did. Jewish ethnicity and Jewish religion seemed intricately bound together. The missionaries were caught in the same argument that raged in the Jewish community: What does it mean to be Jewish? Is Jewishness rooted in ethnicity or in religious practice? If Jews themselves had different answers to those questions, then it is not surprising that missionaries were confused. Most missionaries played it safe: They decided not to allow anything that might compromise the gospel of grace. If people are saved by grace through faith and not by works, then keeping the law of Moses is both unnecessary and dangerous. That was precisely what Paul warned against in his letter to the Galatians, converts who turned their backs on grace to live once again under the law. Such notions were nothing more than "Judaizing," something the New Testament condemned. Stroeter complained that his ideas were misunderstood and insisted that Jewish converts who kept kosher were still under grace, not law. Jewish holy days pointed to God's faithfulness to Israel and were appropriate for believing (i.e., Christian) Jews to remember and observe.[81] But most dispensationalists feared that unless converts completely gave up their old way of life, they might be tempted to return to it. Keeping the law and living under grace were incompatible.

Even Gaebelein could not swim against that swelling tide for long. Shortly after he and Stroeter went public in favor of developing a distinctly Jewish form of Christianity, he repudiated the idea.[82] He was in good company. During the Hebrew Christian Alliance of America's third annual conference in 1914, delegates discussed the issue of the cultural identity and religious practices of converted Jews. By an overwhelming majority, the conferees rejected a resolution that approved of Jewish Christians observing the feast days of Judaism. The delegates voted to close "the doors once for all to all Judaizing propaganda" and recommended that only the pure gospel of grace be preached.[83] None of this changed Stroeter's mind. He parted company with Gaebelein and the Hope of Israel Mission and moved to Dusseldorf, Germany, where he continued to evangelize Jews his own way.

While most missions to the Jews decided against founding distinctive Jewish-Christian churches, there was a significant exception, the Presbyterian Church in the U.S.A.[84] Starting in 1845, the General Assembly authorized the Board of Foreign Missions to evangelize the Jews, but its efforts were rather halfhearted and inconsequential. Thanks especially to the acceptance of dispensationalism by a small but significant segment of the denomination, the desire for Jewish missions grew. By 1920, dispensational Presbyterians lobbied for the creation of a Department of Jewish Evangelization under the Board of Home Missions. The department's first director was an avowed dispensationalist named John S. Conning, who clearly stated his premillennialism in a book and periodical of the same title, *Our Jewish Neighbors.*[85] The department established mission centers in New York (Brooklyn and the Lower East Side), Newark, Philadelphia, Chicago, Omaha, Los Angeles, and San Francisco that functioned more like community centers than storefront missions. They offered varied programs geared to reach the increasingly Americanized second generation of Jewish immigrants. In many respects, these centers resembled the YMCA or the newly established Young Men's Hebrew Association (YMHA). The department also set up three summer camps for Jewish young people in New Jersey, Illinois, and California. Though Conning and his successor, Conrad Hoffman, were Gentiles, they made sure that the field missionaries were Jewish and knew how to create viable support communities for the new converts.

The Presbyterian work was well funded and was remarkably successful. By the early 1930s, the Department of Jewish Evangelization could count roughly two thousand Jewish converts, most of whom joined already existing Presbyterian churches. But some of the converts, with the department's encouragement and support, founded their own Jewish-Christian Presbyterian congregations. These were mild to moderate attempts at contextualization. On the walls was the star of David, not the cross, and on the church calendar were Hanukkah and Passover, which were observed with a decidedly Christian theological spin. In most other respects, however, the congregations functioned as rather typical conservative evangelical Presbyterian churches in which preaching often centered on the place of the Jews in Bible prophecy and the nearness of the second coming.

These Jewish-Christian Presbyterian congregations were strongest and most numerous in the 1930s and 1940s, then began to decline in the 1950s. A few of the congregations in Los Angeles, Chicago, and Philadelphia are still in existence. What caused the others to decline? By the 1950s, theological changes within the Presbyterian Church in the U.S.A. seriously called into question the targeting of Jews for evangelization. According to Yaakov Ariel:

> The rise and fall of the Presbyterian missionary work among the Jews is, in many ways, an amazing development. Within a generation, the denominational policy reversed, and the task of propagating the Christian gospel among the Jews was completely abandoned. This turn of events reflected the larger developments in the mainline churches, which defined themselves more and more in liberal terms. The initial American Protestant impetus for missionizing the Jews came from a prophetic reading of the Bible and an understanding of the Jews as historical Israel, God's first nation. Such voices, which were strong in the early decades of the century among Presbyterians, had died out

almost completely by 1960. Other views advocating recognition and dialogue gained the upper hand. Ironically, it was in an interim period in the history of the church, when the liberal agenda was gaining ground but not completely dominant, that the missionary work among the Jews flourished. The premillennialist views were on the decline yet still alive and very influential in shaping the Presbyterian agenda. The eventual decline of the missionary agenda was inevitable considering the prevailing trends in the denomination.[86]

The Presbyterians were not the only ones to prefer interfaith dialogue to evangelization. The winds of liberal theology blew strongly in other mainline churches and brought the same result. As a result, by the middle of the twentieth century, the evangelization of the Jews belonged almost exclusively to the dispensational missions. These enterprises had successfully transitioned from their early storefront strategies, which were ideal for immigrant Jews, to the more serviceable community centers that reached the increasingly Americanized second or even third generation. By the 1930s, most urban Jews were used to seeing the missionaries in their neighborhoods and even receiving their services. Most Jews had learned to pay them little attention. They wrote off the few converts the missionaries were able to attract as troubled and insignificant in the total scheme of things. According to Ariel's analysis of this between-the-wars period, there was even a grudging respect and tolerance within the Jewish community for the missionaries, who had worked hard to build cordial relationships with Jewish leaders. As a result, the Jewish missions were no longer seen as a threat to the community. Besides, the meager success of the missionaries was a minor irritant in comparison to the rise of organized anti-Semitism at home and abroad.[87]

For their part, dispensationalists saw no contradiction in supporting the drive for a new Jewish state and evangelizing Jews at the same time. Their understanding of Bible prophecy made both an imperative. They saw themselves as uncompromising friends of the Jewish people: Only they fully understood that Jews were still God's chosen ones and that they would play a crucial role at the end of history and the second coming of Christ. Dispensationalists showed their support for Jews by affirming Zionist aspirations and telling them about Jesus, their true Messiah. Fellow Christians who did not anticipate a restored Jewish state or undertake the evangelization of the Jews were at odds with God's prophetic purposes.

What good did all this missionary activity do? Did dispensationalists actually convert many Jews? Accurate figures are hard to come by because both the missionaries and the Jews who opposed them had a stake in inflating statistics. The missionaries needed big numbers to satisfy their supporters, and Jewish leaders needed a serious threat to rally their defenses. Ariel estimates that most missionaries had only a few dozen Jewish converts after decades of hard labor, which in the eyes of many looked like "a failure in comparison to the amount of work and hope that the missionaries had invested" in the missionary enterprise.[88]

Despite the meager results, dispensationalists cared deeply about their mission to the Jews. Dispensational laypeople financially supported the missions, most of which were independent of direct denominational support. In the long run, it seems, results were not always the primary concern. The dispensational mission to the Jews had symbolic value too. According to Ariel, "One can find in the accounts of dispensationalist missionaries to the Jews satisfaction and rejoicing over the mere existence and functioning of a missionary enterprise. For the dispensationalists, spreading the Gospel among the Jews was thus an aim in itself, regardless of how many people were converted."[89] The fact that there was such a mission had eschatological significance for dispensationalists. According to one Jewish convert who became a missionary to his own people, converted Jews were a "pledge of the final salvation of all Israel."[90] The numbers of converts did not matter.

5

Dispensationalism's Dark Side

Though Jews played a central role in dispensationalism's expectations for the future, dispensationalists still had mixed feelings about them. Jews were God's chosen people and heirs to all the prophetic promises, but for good reasons, most of their history had been marked by suffering and persecution. The glory of Israel was past and future. Present Jews were living under the power of Satan and were contributing to the decline of the present age. Historian Yaakov Ariel noted this ambivalence: "On the one hand they are God's chosen nation to whom the biblical prophecies refer. They will be restored to their ancient land and serve as the central nation in the millennial kingdom. On the other hand, as they have refused to recognize Jesus as their Messiah, their character reflects obnoxiousness and rebellion. Their road to glory is paved with suffering and destruction."[1] In short, before the end came, Jews would experience their worst persecution ever.

Of course, individual Jews could escape the "time of Jacob's trouble" by accepting Jesus Christ as Lord and Savior, thereby being raptured with the church before the tribulation began. That is what dispensationalist-run Jewish missions were all about: to save as many Jews as possible before the end. But even then, dispensationalists knew that the vast majority of Jews would not convert. Most Jews would remain in "unbelief" and keep their rendezvous with the Antichrist, experience unprecedented persecution, and die in huge numbers. Those lucky enough to survive the horror would repent at Christ's coming and finally accept him as their Messiah.

This was dispensationalism's "dark side." Premillennialism's view of the future had negative as well as positive elements and was both bad and good news for Jews. Of course, dispensationalists did not feel responsible for the content of their message—it came directly from the Bible—only for its delivery to those who needed to hear it. But no group of people could feel responsibility for disseminating such a message without being shaped by it themselves. Accordingly, dispensationalists on occasion expressed both hostility toward Jews and indifference to their suffering. For example, while dispensationalists condemned anti-Semitism as a grievous sin against God, they believed it was a necessary part of God's plan. Thus, while they denounced it, they did not think they could do anything to stop it. Such a stance often came across as apathy. As a theological or social construct, dispensationalism was not inherently anti-Semitic. Dispensationalists were sincere when they condemned Jew-baiting and warned that God had a special place in hell reserved for those who mistreated the chosen people. Premillennialists honestly believed that they were the Jews' best friends. In fact, some historians have argued that dispensationalists' prophetic views made them inherently philo-Semitic.[2] Nevertheless, at times dispensationalists, like the anti-Semites they condemned, blamed Jews for the mess the world was in.

In 1910, I. M. Haldeman, a prominent Baptist pastor in New York City, wrote in his *Signs of the Times* that "as a nation, [the Jews] crucified their king, and the nations have crucified them." Jews faced universal contempt for the way they "took advantage of their foes, cheated when they could, and lied themselves out of threatened danger." No matter where they called home, Jews "bear upon them the mark and stamp of the alien."[3] That was a typical way for dispensationalists to think about Jews: While they condemned anti-Semites in forceful terms, they often accepted anti-Semites' analysis of why Jews were despised in the world. This perspective made dispensationalists remarkably susceptible to anti-Semitic conspiracy theories and Nazi propaganda during the 1930s. Even when they successfully placed Adolf Hitler and the Holocaust within their prophetic framework, the dark side remained: What lay ahead for Jews was far worse than anything they had experienced in the past. Before all Israel was saved, most Jews would have to be destroyed.

Dispensationalists and Jewish Conspiracy Theories

Nowhere is dispensationalists' dark side more clearly seen than in their use of *The Protocols of the Elders of Zion* during the 1920s, 1930s, and 1940s. The *Protocols* contained an alleged series of secret proceedings in which

Jews plotted to take over the world. The manuscript outlined an elaborate conspiracy to undermine civil government, disrupt international economy, and destroy Christianity.[4] Throughout the *Protocols* were statements such as the following:

> By the severity of our doctrines, we shall triumph and shall enslave all governments under our super-government. . . . Do not think that our assertions are without foundation: note the successes of Darwinism, Marxism and Nietzscheism *engineered by us.* The demoralizing effects of these doctrines upon the minds of the Gentiles should already be obvious to us. . . . We will present ourselves in the guise of saviours of the workers from oppression when we suggest that they enter our army of Socialists, Anarchists, Communists, to whom we always extend our hand under the guise of the rule of the brotherhood demanded by the human solidarity of our social masonry.[5]

The *Protocols* caused a sensation when it first appeared in Europe and America after World War I. A number of American newspapers printed selections, but Henry Ford made the *Protocols* his special project. He serialized it in his *Dearborn Independent,* then published the entire document as *The International Jew.*[6] Because it provided such clear evidence that sinister Jews were masterminding a global conspiracy to destroy Christian civilization, the *Protocols* quickly became an important weapon in anti-Semitism's growing arsenal. Given their view of the future, dispensationalists were interested in what the *Protocols* had to say, but they differed in their response to it.

DISPENSATIONALISTS' FIRST REACTION TO THE *PROTOCOLS*

A few dispensationalists believed that the *Protocols* was a crude, anti-Semitic forgery. Joseph Hoffman Cohn, who succeeded his father, Leopold, as the head of the American Board of Missions to the Jews, called the document an obvious fraud and condemned Ford for disseminating such anti-Semitic propaganda. Cohn published his own point-by-point refutation of the *Protocols* conspiracy theory[7] and warned of the dire consequences in store for anyone who stirred up trouble against God's chosen ones. "It is our business to show to the Jews only love, and the best way that we can show that love is to give them in abundant measure the message of the Gospel of the Lord Jesus Christ; we ought also to protest on every occasion possible against any outbreak of hatred against the Jews."[8]

But other dispensationalists thought there might be something to the *Protocols.* Charles C. Cook of the Bible Institute of Los Angeles wrote an article entitled "The International Jew" for the institute's *King's Business*. He announced the authenticity of the *Protocols*, then added some anti-Semitic observations of his own:

> The Jewish race is morally fully capable of doing all that is charged against it. It is at present rejected of God, and in a state of disobedience and rebellion. . . . As a race Jews are gifted far beyond all other peoples, and even in their ruin, with the curse of God on them, are in the front rank of achievement; but accompanying traits are pride, overbearing arrogance, inordinate love for material things, trickery, rudeness and an egotism that taxes the superlatives of any language. Oppressed are they? Indeed, and subject to injustice more than any other race, and yet never learning the lesson of true humility . . . for the unregenerated Jew usually has a very unattractive personality. There is a reason for his being *persona non grata* at resorts and in the best society; who can deny it?[9]

Moody Bible Institute's James M. Gray believed that the *Protocols* was "a clinching argument for premillennialism and another sign of the possible nearness of the end of the age." But he was concerned about the way the document was being used by anti-Semites. He declared in no uncertain terms that "anti-Semitism is evil and has no place in our Christian civilization" and issued dire warnings of hellfire to anyone persecuting the Jews. Nevertheless, he also felt constrained to add that the prophets of the Old Testament said worse things about Israel than any modern anti-Semite did. Despite the persecutions that could arise based on the *Protocols*, Gray had to admit that the *Protocols* sounded authentic. The conspiracy was "Satan's counterfeit of God's purposes" for the end of the age.[10]

Arno C. Gaebelein referred to the *Protocols* four times in *Our Hope* in the early 1920s and was certain that the conspiracy it described had been predicted by the Bible centuries before. He said that he could not be absolutely sure about its authorship, but he felt strongly that it had come "from the pen of apostate Jews" whose influence he could also detect in Russian Bolshevism and other revolutionary movements around the world. He was especially struck by how many Jews were involved in the illegal liquor business and how many criminals had Jewish last names, facts that fit well with the conspiracy's plan to undercut society's morals and stability. Gaebelein believed there was something especially loathsome about the chosen people doing such things. Since God expected more from them, their sins were worse than other people's. "There is nothing so vile on earth as an apostate Jew who denies God and His Word."[11]

This initial fascination with the *Protocols* was short-lived. After a flurry of interest and speculation in the early 1920s, it quickly dropped out of the dispensationalists' repertoire for a decade. Why were some of the leading Bible teachers so interested in the document? The answer is rather simple. As Gray made clear, the *Protocols* seemed to support what dispensationalists had been saying all along—that toward the end of the present age, civilization itself would hang in the balance and Jews would increasingly find themselves on center stage in the cosmic drama. Dispensationalists knew that the world was going to get worse and worse before Jesus returned and that the Jewish people would experience their worst persecutions ever. Therefore, when the *Protocols* was published and opposition to the Jews increased, dispensationalists thought they saw the fulfillment of Bible prophecy.

Dispensationalists were also attracted to the *Protocols* because it was useful in making distinctions between good and bad Jews. This perspective can be seen in Gaebelein's statement that "there is nothing so vile on earth as an apostate Jew who denies God and His Word." Gaebelein and other dispensationalists claimed that they loved Jews, and there is plenty of evidence to show that they did. But they clearly loved some Jews more than others. Dispensationalists found it was easy to love Orthodox Jews because they still believed in the coming Messiah, read the Bible prophecies with expectancy, and honored the Hebrew Scriptures. But they had little use for Reform Jews, whom they equated with "unbelieving" liberal Protestants, and the rising number of secular Jews. These were the vile apostate Jews to whom Gaebelein referred, the ones who stirred up trouble and provoked anti-Semitism. In this way, dispensationalists could use the same arguments as anti-Semites but claim that they were not being anti-Semitic: They were referring only to apostate Jews, not the Jewish people as a whole.

THE REVIVAL OF THE *PROTOCOLS*

In 1933, the *Protocols* experienced a revival in dispensationalist circles. A number of leading Bible teachers published sensational exposés on the Jewish-led conspiracy to destroy Western civilization.[12] Gerald B. Winrod was the dispensationalist most responsible for this renewed interest in the *Protocols*. Born in Wichita, Kansas, in 1898, Winrod had little on his résumé to suggest that he would become a significant fundamentalist leader in the 1930s. He had no formal theological training, never led a local congregation, and had no denominational affiliation or base of operations. But these were not major deficiencies in the rock-'em, sock-'em days of early fundamentalism. What he lacked in formal credentials he made up for in his aggressive and entrepreneurial style and his ability to make friends of influential people.

In 1925, Winrod founded the Defenders of the Christian Faith in Wichita to do battle against evolution and theological liberalism, then promoted the organization through its magazine, the *Defender,* which he edited. That venture soon opened other doors. Winrod began getting invitations to speak in fundamentalist churches and ended up on the program of the World's Christian Fundamentals Association. He made such a favorable impression there that in 1926 he became the extension secretary of WCFA, which meant that he became a close associate of the leaders in the interdenominational fundamentalist network. In fact, Winrod talked a number of fundamentalist movers and shakers into becoming "associate editors" of the *Defender* and listed their names on the magazine's masthead: William Bell Riley, pastor of the First Baptist Church of Minneapolis and head of a fundamentalist empire in the upper Midwest; Paul Rood, popular California evangelist; Paul Rader, former pastor of Moody Church in Chicago and sought-after evangelist; Charles E. Fuller, pioneer in radio evangelism and the future cofounder of Fuller Theological Seminary in the late 1940s; Mark Matthews, pastor of the First Presbyterian Church in Seattle; A. Z. Conrad, pastor of historic Park Street Church in Boston; and Oswald J. Smith, prominent fundamentalist pastor of the People's Church in Toronto. Such contacts made Winrod "a significant second-level figure" in fundamentalist circles and gave him an important platform for broadcasting his views.[13]

In 1933, the *Defender* published Winrod's evidence for the conspiracy outlined in the *Protocols.*[14] The Jews controlled the world's banking system, were responsible for bringing on both World War I and the depression, dominated FDR and dictated the terms of the New Deal, were in charge of the movie industry and thus responsible for the nation's decline in morals, and led the international communist movement. The "hidden hand" was everywhere. According to Winrod, a dispensational understanding of Bible prophecy and an awareness of the conspiracy revealed in the *Protocols* provided a clear picture of present world conditions.[15]

Shortly after Winrod's exposé, Gaebelein published *The Conflict of the Ages,* in which he carefully traced the "mystery of lawlessness" from the fall in the Garden of Eden to modern times.[16] For Gaebelein, history was a complex web of conspiracies. The *Protocols* was the last in a long line of sinister plots to pull down Christian civilization. Gaebelein praised Serge Nilus, the Russian who first published the *Protocols* in 1901, as "a believer in the Word of God, in prophecy, and . . . a true Christian." Gaebelein was certain that the document was no "*crude forgery.* Behind it are hidden, unseen actors, powerful and cunning, who follow the plan still, bent on the overthrow of our civilization."[17] The plot was now being carried out by Russian communists and their apostate Jewish allies.

Gaebelein believed he had evidence from a variety of sources to show that communism had Jewish roots and that the Bolshevik Revolution of 1917 had been masterminded by a well-trained, fanatical cadre of Jewish agitators. Karl Marx was a Jew; Vladimir Lenin had a Jewish mother; and Leon Trotsky, whose real name was Bronstein, had lived for a while on the predominately Jewish Lower East Side of New York before returning to Russia to become the "main instigator of this program from hell." Gaebelein also cited sworn testimony before a United States Senate subcommittee by George A. Simons, a former director of Methodist missions in Russia, and numerous news reports from the London *Times* and the French journal *L'Illumination*. All these proved the Jewish-communist connection. Even Jews themselves, Gaebelein observed, admitted to the ties between the two. According to the *Jewish Chronicles,* "The ideals of Bolshevism at many points are consonant with the *finest ideals of Judaism.*"[18]

For Gaebelein, the *Protocols* provided the undeniable link between Jews and the international communist conspiracy. "The most important fact is that throughout the twenty-four *Protocols* we have a *very pronounced re-statement of the principal theories of Illuminism and Marxism.*"[19] Furthermore, he thought that the current Jewish-communist conspiracy would eventually lead to the final confrontation between the forces of good and evil, Christ and the Antichrist, at Armageddon. Gaebelein made it clear that he did not believe that *all* Jews were involved in the conspiracy, but he was convinced that "bad" Jews now outnumbered "good" Jews.

Here we must draw attention to the fact that while there is an onsweeping apostasy in Christendom, there is also a corresponding Jewish apostasy, or rather infidelity. Any Christian will honor the orthodox Old Testament believing Jews, who still cling to the hope of a coming Messiah, and who pray for His coming and expect him. . . . But they are becoming less. The greater part of Jewry has become reformed, or as we call it, "deformed." They no longer believe in the law and in the prophets. The Messiah and the glorious future is looked upon as a delusion. . . . Turning away from the hope of their fathers and their own Scriptures, they become infidels and finally through their reaching out after material things and power they become a menace. The lower elements become lawless. As we have shown, these infidel Jews were prominent in the revolutionary propaganda during the nineteenth century. Karl Marx, the author of "The Communist Bible," was an infidel Jew, so was Lasalle and hundreds of others active in the socialistic-anarchistic and communistic activities. Trotsky and at least two score other leaders of the Russian revolution were apostate Jews. They make themselves felt in our country and in other civilized countries. Watching the names of those who were arrested in anti-government demonstrations, we find that a large percentage are Jews.[20]

Gaebelein believed that Jews were still under a "national blood-guiltiness" for killing Christ, a stigma that could not be wiped away until the second coming and the Jews' repentance for it.[21] Even then, more Jews would be lost than saved. He held out the most hope for the Orthodox. During the great tribulation, after the church has been raptured, "the orthodox Jews who have held on to the faith of their fathers, who pray for the coming of the Messiah King, whose eyes are [now] blinded that they cannot see, from them the veil will be removed." They are the prophesied remnant that will be saved at Christ's return, but most Jews will not be included. "The international Jews, the political-financial schemers, the lawless elements, who ridicule and hate religion of any kind and are atheists . . . these Jews will worship the beast. They reject the true Christ and accept the false Messiah."[22] They are doomed, and rightly so.[23]

Another major dispensational figure who promoted the *Protocols* in the 1930s was William Bell Riley, the Baptist leader from Minnesota. He first came across the *Protocols* in the 1920s and rejected it as fanciful and far-fetched. But a few years later he read it again and was struck by how accurately it explained what was happening all over the world.[24] In 1934, Riley published *The Protocols and Communism,* in which he argued that the same plot that had turned Russia communist was now at work in FDR's New Deal. "Today in our land many of the biggest trusts, banks, and manufacturing interests are controlled by Jews. . . . Most of our department stores they own. . . . The motion pictures, the most vicious of all immoral, educational and communistic influences, is their creation."[25] Visitors to Riley's First Baptist Church in Minneapolis got a steady dose of similar sentiments from the pulpit, so much so that Jewish leaders identified the church as one of the most important sources of anti-Semitism in the Twin Cities.[26]

Most dispensationalists at the time did not consider such views extreme.[27] Gaebelein's *Conflict of the Ages* got rave reviews in such leading fundamentalist journals as the *Moody Bible Institute Monthly,* Dallas Seminary's *Bibliotheca Sacra,* Donald G. Barnhouse's *Revelation,* and Charles G. Trumbull's *Sunday School Times.*[28] Winrod could point to a number of dispensational friends who believed more or less the same thing he did: James M. Gray of Moody Bible Institute; A. Z. Conrad of Park Street Church; and Keith Brooks of the Bible Institute of Los Angeles.[29] But promoting the *Protocols* in 1933–34 was not the same as speculating about it in the early 1920s. By the thirties, the *Protocols* was clearly identified with well-organized anti-Semitic groups at home and abroad. Why would dispensationalists, who so adamantly condemned anti-Semitism, embrace some of its most vicious arguments?

As we saw earlier, it was easy to make the Jewish conspiracy fit into the dispensationalist prophetic scenario. Already committed to a conspiracy theory of cosmic proportions, believers in Bible prophecy found the sinister plot in the *Protocols* well within the realm of possibility. Dispensationalists were willing to use whatever seemed to support their prophetic system.

There were other reasons for the *Protocols'* renewed popularity. The 1920s had been hard on people like the dispensationalists, and the 1930s looked as though they were going to be even worse. The modernists were in firm control of the old evangelical denominations, evolution was taught in the public schools, and morals were slipping rapidly. The economy was in a tailspin, and President Roosevelt was willing to take what many considered extreme measures to stop the depression. He had also promised to repeal Prohibition and extend diplomatic relations to the Soviet Union, which, of course, meant that America would be aligning itself with one of the evil empires of Armageddon. Dispensationalists watched the rise of dictatorships in Europe and the spread of communism at home.[30] Prophecy hounds who followed such developments with one eye on their prophetic charts found it hard to believe that "a situation like this just happened."[31] The Bible had predicted such a crisis immediately before Christ's return, and many devoted readers of Bible prophecy believed they understood the conspiracy that was behind it.

Because of their fears and resentments, it is easy to identify dispensationalists in the 1930s with other political extremists on the far right. Because dispensationalists were fierce anticommunists, they often endorsed and promoted right-wing sentiments and causes. Winrod, for example, used his organization to disseminate well-known right-wing and anti-Semitic materials, and other dispensationalists often quoted such materials in their writings. Riley published in the *Pilot* articles by Elizabeth Dilling, the author of *The Red Network* and *The Octopus,* which Ralph Lord Roy called "the most virulent anti-Semitic tract ever published in the United States,"[32] and a number of articles by Elizabeth Knauss, the author of *Red Propaganda in the Churches.*[33] In fact, in 1932, Knauss published an article in the *Pilot* in which she equated the international communist conspiracy with the plot outlined in the *Protocols,* scooping Winrod by two months. Gaebelein often quoted from the *National Republic,* a leading right-wing magazine, and allowed his name to be joined to E. M. Hadley's extremist Paul Revere Society, though by the late 1930s he denied that he had ever had any significant involvement with the group.[34]

THE BACKLASH AGAINST USING THE *PROTOCOLS*

Naturally, dispensationalists who exposed the international Jewish conspiracy expected an angry response from modernists, communists, and apostate Jews, but they were surprised by the strong rebuke from fellow fundamentalists. Not surprisingly, the biggest criticism came from Jewish-Christian colleagues, especially those engaged in missions to the Jews. In late 1933, the *Hebrew Christian Alliance Quarterly,* which represented many dispensational Jewish mission agencies, castigated the *Moody Bible Institute Monthly,* the *Sunday School Times,* and *Revelation* for promoting the *Protocols* and other anti-Semitic materials. Jewish Christians complained that people who believed in international Jewish conspiracies rarely made distinctions between good and bad Jews. All Jews, even Christian ones, suffered when people bought into conspiracy theories.[35]

Especially agitated by the renewed use of the *Protocols* was Joseph Hoffman Cohn of the American Board of Missions to the Jews. In 1933 and 1934, he alerted readers of his magazine, the *Chosen People,* that "there has arisen in recent months Christians and Christian Bible teachers who have been adding fuel to the fire of Jewish hate, and even fanning the flames!" He cited "another brother" who had "scavenged from the rubbish heap the old Henry Ford accusations against the Jews."[36] Cohn was a dispensationalist himself, but he blasted Bible teachers who claimed to be friends of the Jews then circulated unprovable and patently false charges against them.

Cohn saved some of his harshest criticism for Gaebelein's *Conflict of the Ages.* He published Elias Newman's scathing review and point-by-point rebuttal of Gaebelein's book,[37] as well as other critical comments from leading dispensationalists. For example, Harry A. Ironside, the pastor of Moody Church in Chicago, said he was grieved "to find that the *Protocols* are being used not only by godless Gentiles, but even by some fundamentalist Christians to stir up suspicion and hatred against the Jewish people as a whole."[38]

Cohn's criticisms were hard to ignore. Dispensationalists who had used the *Protocols* now had to defend themselves on their own turf. James M. Gray of Moody Bible Institute quickly got caught in the cross fire. In 1921, he had called the *Protocols* "a clinching argument for premillennialism,"[39] and in 1927, he had defended Henry Ford's decision to publish them in his *Dearborn Independent.* Ford "had good grounds for publishing some of the things about the Jews. . . . Mr. Ford might have found corroborative evidence [for the Jewish conspiracy] had he looked for it."[40]

By the end of 1933, Gray was under pressure to repudiate the *Protocols* and his use of it. At first he held his ground. Despite criticism from the *Hebrew Christian Alliance Quarterly,* he continued to affirm the document's validity and pointed out that Moody Bible Institute had always shown friendship to Jews by training missionaries to evangelize them. He agreed that anti-Semitism was a horrible sin but added that

Jews would suffer even worse things if they did not accept Jesus as their Messiah. Furthermore, he hinted that Jews were at least partly to blame for their ill-treatment. In support of his views, he cited an article in the *Hebrew Christian Alliance Quarterly* by Max Reich, the director of Moody's Jewish Missions program, which pointed out how many American Jews were becoming "de-Judaized without becoming Christian." As a result, they posed a major problem: "Without religion, the Jew goes down and becomes worse than others, as a corruption of the best is always the worst corruption." Gray also quoted Rabbi Elias Margolis, president of the Rabbinical Assembly of New York, who had recently observed that if Jews wanted justice and fair treatment from others, they had to be willing to give them in return.[41]

Such a defense did not put an end to the controversy. By the beginning of 1935, Gray and the institute were under attack from the *American Hebrew and Jewish Tribune,* the *Bulletin of the Baltimore Branch of the American Jewish Congress,* and even *Time* magazine.[42] Gray defended the institute in an address over MBI's radio station and eventually published his remarks in the institute's magazine. Gray did not deny that he had believed and used the *Protocols* himself, but he insisted that Moody had never officially promoted it. He said that he deplored its dissemination from any Christian source and called anti-Semitism "one of the most despicable, brutal and dangerous forms of racial hatred and antagonism known to mankind. . . . It is true that Jehovah has awfully cursed Israel for her sins, and His curse rests upon her today. But it is one thing for God to curse her and another thing for us to do so." Gray realized that using the *Protocols* had become more of a liability than an asset. While he never took back his claim that the *Protocols* was "a clinching argument for premillennialism," he suggested that the Bible alone contained everything that Christians needed to know about Jews and their end-times activities. "Therefore, in the present state of the public mind on this question, my advice to Christians would be this: Let us confine ourselves to the Bible and leave the *Protocols* alone."[43]

Other dispensationalists came to the same conclusion. *In Shirts and Sheets: Or Anti-Semitism, a Present-Day Sign of the First Magnitude* (1934), Louis S. Bauman admitted that the *Protocols* had become a divisive issue among dispensationalists, and so he decided to avoid using it. Even if it were true, he said, it reflected the views of only a few fanatical Jews and did not represent the whole race.[44] Four years later he published a more extensive country-by-country examination of anti-Semitism entitled *The Time of Jacob's Trouble* and did not even mention the *Protocols*.[45] By the late 1930s, other dispensationalists were ready to condemn the *Protocols* as an outright forgery that never should have been taken seriously, no matter how much it seemed to confirm prophetic expectations.[46]

A few dispensationalist Bible teachers steadfastly stuck with the *Protocols*. Winrod dismissed Cohn's criticisms, accused him of being overly sensitive, and denied that his own views could in any way be judged as anti-Semitic.[47] But many other dispensationalists thought that Winrod had gone too far. Within months of his article on "The Hidden Hand," the names of his prominent associate editors began disappearing from the *Defender*'s masthead. As Winrod devoted more time and energy to the Jewish conspiracy, many of his old friends began keeping their distance. Despite this loss of support, Winrod never wavered. Throughout the 1930s, he continued to attack FDR's New Deal and to blame every problem on Jews and communists. He became a candidate for the U.S. Senate in 1938 but lost badly in the primary. His dogged defense of Hitler and extreme right-wing movements eventually got him into trouble with the federal government. In 1942, he was one of thirty people indicted for sedition by a federal grand jury. When the judge died while proceedings were just getting underway, a mistrial was declared and Winrod went free.

Riley did not take criticism well either. He had been a boxer in college, so when Cohn attacked Riley's *Protocols and Communism* in 1934, the minister from Minnesota came out swinging. He denied that there was any anti-Semitic intent in his sensational revelations. He was simply telling the truth and following the Bible. Then he tried to turn the tables on Cohn by suggesting that Christian Jews like him should welcome such disclosures and not be swayed by their racial pride. Once someone made Riley's list, it was hard to get off. For the rest of his life, Riley tried to prove that Cohn was a religious con man who bilked his supporters of their money.[48]

Riley realized that many of his own constituencies did not understand or appreciate his views and that some of his own enterprises might suffer because of the controversy. In what was a rare experience for Riley, in 1936, he backed down. He suspended sales of *The Protocols and Communism*, but not because he no longer believed there was a Jewish conspiracy. According to his explanation in the *Pilot*, "He [this is Riley referring to himself in the third person] has not at all changed his opinion that the atheistic and international Jew is a world-menace, but he is entirely unwilling as the Executive-Secretary of the World's Christian Fundamentals Association to press a point on which the Fundamentalists were not agreed."[49]

Needless to say, such a halfhearted retraction did not satisfy his critics. In 1937, J. Frank Norris, Riley's old friend and copresident of the Baptist Bible Union, attacked him for promoting the *Protocols*. "I confess my amazement that certain intelligent outstanding Fundamentalist pastors have joined in this age-long and divinely-cursed persecution. One of the outstanding Fundamentalists of this hour has published many things that are nothing short of amazing."[50] Norris ran a fundamentalist Baptist empire of his own in Texas, was a consummate controversialist, and never imagined a conspiracy he did not like. But even he drew the line at anti-Semitism. Jew-baiting was both wrong and counterproductive. Using dispensational logic, he argued that God needed a large number of Jews to become evangelists after the church was raptured:

> Of all the peoples on earth that ought not to persecute Jews or any other race, it is that people called Fundamentalist Baptists. Those who believe in the Premillennial coming of Jesus Christ should certainly do everything in their power to help the Jew because we believe when Christ comes the Jews will be converted, and become the world's greatest evangelists—then why kill them off if they are to be the world's greatest evangelists?[51]

Norris, called by friends and foes alike the Texas Tornado, accused Riley of aligning himself with the Jew-hating enemies of God. In 1938, Norris published his own pamphlet repudiating the *Protocols* and covering his debate with Riley over the issue.[52] Not even being attacked by Norris kept Riley from pressing his anti-Semitic conspiracy theory. In 1939, three years after withdrawing *The Protocols and Communism,* Riley published *Wanted—A World Leader!* in which he presented an updated and even more vitriolic report on the international Jewish conspiracy.[53]

Gaebelein, the former missionary to the Jews, handled criticism differently: He did his best to ignore it. After getting blasted by Cohn in the *Chosen People,* Gaebelein called the attack "unfair and unjust" and warned that "nothing is gained by an attempt to whitewash the atheistic-revolutionary Jewish elements which are so strong everywhere today." Cohn had misunderstood him: He never intended to condemn the entire Jewish race, only the "international" or "lawless" or "apostate" Jews who served the interests of Satan. He was the Jews' best friend, not their enemy. Then he promised not to respond to such criticism again. "'The Conflict of the Ages' has the Lord's most gracious approval, and is wonderfully used in helping and blessing God's people everywhere. We are sorry that we had to mention this matter again."[54]

Gaebelein refused to apologize, but he had no desire to keep the controversy going. In 1934, he declined an invitation by Harold Morgan to debate the *Protocols* in public. Gaebelein continued to write and worry about the threat of communism and its connection to apostate Judaism, but he never mentioned the *Protocols* in print again.[55]

By the late 1930s, then, most dispensationalists wanted nothing whatsoever to do with the *Protocols.* Promoting the idea of an international Jewish conspiracy made them sound too much like anti-Semitic Nazis.

In fact, some dispensationalists repented for ever having used it at all. In 1938, Keith Brooks, a former associate of Winrod, organized the American Prophetic League in California to put as much distance as possible between dispensationalism and Nazi anti-Semitism. In 1939, Brooks published a "Manifesto to the Jews," which condemned the spread of pro-Nazi propaganda in the guise of biblical prophecy and asked fundamentalist leaders to go on record against the *Protocols* and its use. Over sixty well-known Bible teachers signed the manifesto.[56] But that did not solve the problem. Three years later Brooks again urged his fellow dispensationalists to "come clean" in order to "clear the church at large from the charge laid against it by unbelievers, that it had been a tool of Hitler and the Jew-baiters."[57]

Winrod and Riley never signed the manifesto. Gray died in 1935, four years before the manifesto was published. Gaebelein squeezed himself onto the list later, without ever letting the people who mattered most to him know about it.[58] Though Gaebelein had taken a public stand with sixty of dispensationalism's best-known leaders, he never informed his *Our Hope* constituency that he had done so or even acknowledged Brooks's crusade against those who had been taken in by Nazi propaganda. He continued to advertise and sell *The Conflict of the Ages* until his death in 1945, which made adding his name to the manifesto completely disingenuous.

Even Gaebelein's death did not put an end to his controversial book. His son Frank, who became a distinguished leader in the evangelical renaissance after World War II, advertised it in the pages of *Our Hope* and continued to sell it until 1953, when apparently supplies finally ran out. In 1982, David Rausch, Gaebelein's biographer, came out with a new edition of *The Conflict of the Ages* but edited out all the original references to the *Protocols*. That was necessary, Rausch explained in the introduction, because people today could too easily misunderstand what Gaebelein was driving at and erroneously conclude that he was anti-Semitic.[59]

Clearly, then, premillennialists did not need the *Protocols* to substantiate their understanding of the flow of history. The document was serviceable as long as it was not closely tied to organized anti-Semitism. But when using it made dispensationalists look bad, most students of prophecy quickly found it expendable. The last thing dispensationalists wanted was to be labeled anti-Semitic.

Dispensationalism's Interpretation of Hitler and the Holocaust

Dispensationalism's credibility depended on its ability to make sense of the flow of history. Dispensationalists' interest in the *Protocols* demonstrated that they could be taken in by a conspiracy theory that supported their prophetic view of things. In the end, most believers in Bible prophecy did not like the company that using the *Protocols* put them in. But dispensationalists did not really need the *Protocols*. Long before the document was published, dispensationalists were teaching that Jews would play an important role in the world's demise. As James M. Gray pointed out, the Bible taught everything believers needed to know about the Jews.

MAKING SENSE OF HITLER

Dispensationalists were vulnerable to Nazi propaganda in the years before war broke out. For a while, at least, they had a hard time figuring out what Hitler was up to, but once they placed Hitler and the Holocaust within their prophetic system, they were able to move ahead, as confident as ever that God's plans were coming to pass.

When Adolf Hitler became German chancellor in 1933, many dispensationalists struggled to understand him and what was really happening in Germany. They sifted through radically different evaluations of the situation, all purportedly from Christian sources. A few dispensationalist leaders actually visited Germany to check out conditions for themselves and left with different impressions. In the summer of 1934, Will H. Houghton, who would succeed Gray as president of Moody Bible Institute the following year, visited Germany and came home deeply concerned about the growing Nazi pressures on the churches and the worsening plight of the Jews.[60] Oswald J. Smith, the founder of the People's Church in Toronto, published the account of his 1936 tour of Germany in Winrod's *Defender.* He marveled at the wonderful spirit of the German people and their growing openness to evangelical Christianity. Smith did voice concern, however, that some innocent Jews might be suffering in Hitler's campaign against Jewish Bolshevism.[61] Arno C. Gaebelein took a trip to his native Germany in 1937. He described his impressions in a letter to William Bell Riley, who published it in the *Pilot*. Gaebelein condemned most American press reports about the "new Germany" as slanderous and erroneous. It was obvious to him that Hitler had been taking necessary steps to stop the spread of Jewish-inspired Bolshevism. "There is no question in my mind that Hitler was an instrument of God to save Germany and Europe from the Red Beast."[62]

One can also see the confusion in the pages of the *Moody Bible Institute Monthly* in 1934–35. Editor James M. Gray, caught in the middle of his own controversy over the *Protocols,* tried to keep abreast of the news coming out of Germany but found it contradictory. Gray did not like Nazis but decided to present as balanced a view of Hitler as he could.

In the July 1934 issue of the magazine, he printed a pro-Hitler letter to the editor from a German pastor who denied reports that Christian Jews had been excluded from German congregations, that Christians were supporting the boycott against Jewish businesses, and that there was no more reading from the Old Testament in church services. "This statement is one of the many lies which are being circulated among the different nations in order to find fault with the new republic in which we live and to arouse suspicions against its aims. . . . We are very thankful that we now have among our nation peace and harmony and this in a way as we never had it in the history of Germany."[63]

In the next issue, Gray published both pro- and anti-Hitler pieces in "The New Germany and the Evangelical Church." On one side, Paul Umlauf of Berlin denied that the new Nazi regime was hostile to religion. "Chancellor Hitler, in his national socialist program, has made it clear that he looks upon Christianity as the cultural foundation on which the new state must be built." Hitler had wanted the churches to run their own internal affairs, but they had failed to do so. Social Democrats and Marxists had infiltrated the churches to carry out their own anti-Nazi political agenda. "Thus the government was compelled to take a stand and to undertake the work which was the duty of the churches to attend to. . . . The ways of Providence are too difficult to understand; and if God thinks fit to do so, He will call upon the temporary powers to adjust any errors that may have crept into the government of the church." Umlauf believed that the crisis in the churches required the election of the reichsbishop and the appointment of Nazi commissars to monitor church life.[64] Martin Luther had argued much the same thing in the sixteenth century when he had called on German princes to take up the cause of church reform when the Roman hierarchy refused to get with the program.

On the other side was a reprinted editorial from the April 1934 issue of the *Bulletin of the Federal Council of Churches*. It described and condemned Nazi propaganda, threats, ruthless force, and deception in church affairs. It repudiated the forced election of the reichsbishop and the process of selecting new ministry candidates only from the ranks of the Hitler Youth. "The leaders of this frankly nationalistic and increasingly pagan organization made no secret of their desire to make God salute Hitler if He wishes to have an official place in German life."[65] Gray knew that his balanced editorial policy could be misinterpreted. In December 1934, he wrote, "We would not be interpreted as holding a brief for Herr Hitler and Nazism, but we always wish to be fair."[66]

Gray was more than fair. In fact, at times it was difficult to understand exactly what he was up to. In the fall of 1935, he published a letter to the editor from a German national living in Maryland. The writer identified herself as an old woman and a devout Christian who prayed for Christ's return. She praised the *Moody Bible Institute Monthly* for not misjudging Hitler, who, she had on good authority, was an avid Bible reader. She said that all her German relatives were also evangelical Christians who loved the führer, prayed for him, and refused to believe anything that his enemies published about him. Despite widespread newspaper reports to the contrary, the churches in Germany had complete freedom to preach Christ. "We believe that Christ will come soon and that He will be merciful to Hitler too. Hitler's father was a drinker, but Adolf lives with his mother and is a very good son."[67] Was Gray naively taken in, or was he merely sharing a laugh with his readers over a letter too ridiculous to be believed?

Gray also had problems sifting through reports of Hitler's campaign against the Jews. Soon after Hitler's rise to power in 1933, Gray advised readers of the *Moody Bible Institute Monthly* "to suspend their judgment about Germany's present dealings with the Jews until both sides have an opportunity to be heard." After affirming that he was against anti-Semitism in any form, Gray suggested that it was possible that Hitler was not guilty of everything of which he had been accused: "We learn from private sources, more than one, and worthy of respect at least, that the Jews in Germany are not being persecuted as a race, but that Communism organized by Russian Jews is being punished by Hitler. Former government positions, it is said, were held by Jews, and in every form of business they were given preference over Germans. Jewish artists, for example, always received the prizes in the art exhibits." Gray also had it on good authority that newspaper reports about bloody attacks against Jews were planted by Social Democrats or communists who wanted to defame the fuhrer. According to Gray's German source, over 90 percent of the alleged attacks on Jews were actually communist attacks against the Nazis. Gray believed it: "There are Jews and Jews just as there are Gentiles and Gentiles," and communists are adept at using "satanic propagandism" to achieve their goals.[68]

In the fall of 1935, the Nazis instituted the Nurnberg Laws, which forbade anyone with at least one Jewish grandparent from marrying or having sexual relations with Aryans. That started the systematic marginalization of Jewish citizens. By the end of 1938, Jews had been virtually excluded from government positions, the professions, and cultural life. By then it was clear to most dispensationalists what Hitler was up to, and equivocation stopped. Actually, some dispensationalists seemed to grasp the genocidal aims of the Nazis long before the liberal Protestant press did. By 1938, readers of dispensationalist magazines already knew what was going on in places such as Buchenwald.[69] Even Gaebelein, who had praised Hitler's handling of the communists, understood what evil he was capable of. He had been following the career of the Nazi leader since 1930, three years before he had become German chancellor, and had predicted dire consequences for German Jews if Hitler ever gained political power.[70] From 1937 through the end of the war, Gaebelein kept readers of *Our Hope* well informed of the Nazi program to eliminate Jews from Germany and the rest of Europe.[71]

Only a few dispensationalists were willing to believe the best about Hitler after 1935. Like Gray, William Bell Riley had waited before passing judgment on the new Germany. Though he had been strongly anti-German during World War I, Riley decided this time to "be fair toward a once-hated enemy."[72] Riley applauded Hitler's early efforts to keep the Jewish conspiracy from turning Germany communist. He quoted with approval Hitler's belief that "the Jew is the cause and beneficiary of our slavery. . . . He has ruined our race, rotted our morals, corrupted our traditions, and broken our power."[73] Given such sentiments, Riley refused to criticize Hitler openly and defended American pro-Nazi groups such as William Dudley Pelley's Silver Shirts.[74] In 1939, Riley published *Wanted—A World Leader!* which was his most virulent anti-Jewish book.[75] Only when war with Germany seemed inevitable did Riley stop making pro-Hitler and anti-Semitic statements. In 1941, he published *Hitlerism: Or the Philosophy of Evolution in Action,* in which he called Hitler the "beast man." But nowhere in the book did he ever criticize Hitler's brutal treatment of the Jews.[76] Gerald B. Winrod's dogged defense of Hitler and extreme right-wing advocacy never stopped. Even his indictment in 1942 for sedition by a federal grand jury did not end his anti-Semitism. Only his death in 1957 stopped his warnings of the worldwide Jewish conspiracy.[77]

MAKING SENSE OF THE HOLOCAUST

How did dispensationalists react when they realized Hitler's genocidal plan for the Jews? Instinctively, they sought to fit it into their already-accepted prophetic scenario. Long before the Nazi persecutions began, dispensationalists had warned that there was terrible suffering ahead for the Jews. In 1923, Arthur W. Pink predicted that before they could experience the glories of fulfilled prophecy, Jews would have to atone for "the murder of Christ." Just as the Old Testament had demonstrated over and over, Israel's God would not destroy the people for their sins but would "chasten them as a father would a wayward child." Thus, when the scope of the Nazis' persecution became known in the late 1930s, dispensationalists interpreted it as part of this long-prophesied pattern. In 1937, Charles G. Trumbull, the editor of the widely popular *Sunday School Times,* wrote that the Jews were being punished in Germany for their "deliberate, persistent, and continued apostasy," just as they had been judged by God at other times in their history.[78]

Louis S. Bauman, a careful recorder and fierce opponent of anti-Semitism in the late 1930s, tried to understand the Nazi assault on Jews in terms of such biblical precedent. Just as God had used Nebuchadnezzar's evil and ruthless Babylonians to punish the chosen people in the Old Testament, God was using Hitler's Nazis to carry out later dimensions of the divine plan. But God would judge the persecutors too, when their awful work was done. God intended the Jews to suffer, but God would also deal with those through whom the suffering came.[79] In this way, dispensationalists could see the Nazis playing a role in the prophetic plan at the same time they viewed Hitler and his men as monsters who deserved to be damned by God. Keith Brooks followed such reasoning: "While God has permitted anti-Semitism to be the rod of correction upon His ancient people, the fact remains that for those who participate in this persecution, there are no more burning warnings in the Word of God."[80] Shortly after the war, Lewis Sperry Chafer, dispensationalism's greatest theologian in the 1940s, wrote about this paradox: "Jehovah may chasten His people and even use the nations to that end, but invariably judgment falls on those who afflict Israel." God had promised Abraham that those who blessed Israel would be blessed, and those who cursed it would be cursed (Gen. 12:3). That promise "has never failed in its fulfillment, nor will it fail to the end of human history on the earth."[81] According to this logic, one could say that in the complex divine drama, God could both use the evil that men did to carry out divine purposes and punish them for doing it.

Dispensationalists took some solace in the fact that no one, not even Hitler's henchmen, could actually succeed in eliminating the Jewish people. In 1934, at the beginning of the Jews' real troubles in Germany, one dispensationalist was rather sanguine about the situation: "Jew haters never learn anything from history. . . . Anti-Semitism is futile because it is fighting against God. . . . The Jewish people are indestructible."[82] In 1940, after the Nazi program had turned murderous, Henry Anderson felt confident that God had too much riding on the Jews to let them all be annihilated. The God of Abraham might permit the Jews to suffer severely, but God would prevent their extinction. God's entire prophetic program hinged on getting them back to Palestine to reestablish a Jewish state, where, ironically enough, they would experience even worse persecution in anticipation of Armageddon and the second coming of Christ.[83]

Since dispensationalists saw the Holocaust as part of God's prophetic plan, they believed there was nothing anyone could do to stop it. But that did not mean that dispensationalists were to sit idly by and do nothing. Their response was complicated but consistent: They both grieved for the Jews in their suffering and rushed to take spiritual advantage of their plight. In 1939, a who's who of dispensationalist leaders scheduled for December 1 an international day of prayer for the suffering Jews. For what were the participants supposed to pray? Oddly, the organizers did not suggest praying for the persecutions to stop. Instead, they urged people to pray for Jewish conversions: "Workers among the Jews in America, Europe, Palestine, and other lands agree that the hearts of the chosen people are more open and receptive to the Word of God and the gospel message today than ever before. The terrific persecutions in Europe, the troubles in Palestine, and the ever-increasing anti-Semitism throughout the world have softened their hearts and made them long for security and rest of soul." Under such dire conditions, the best thing Christians could do for the Jews was to send them more New Testaments and missionaries.[84] That was also the basic response of the many missions to the Jews: In the midst of the Jews' horrible persecution, God had given the church an unprecedented opportunity to reach them for Christ. As one of the missions advertised in 1943, "These Jewish persecutions may be in God's providence our opportunity to win them to Christ and show that we really care."[85]

Dispensationalists widely believed that the spreading crisis had two unintended consequences: It had made Jews more open than ever to the claims of Christ, and it had increased their longing for a Jewish homeland in Palestine. Harry Rimmer believed that Nazi persecutors were accomplishing more than they realized. "By driving the preserved people back into the preserved land, Hitler, who does not believe the Bible and who sneers at the Word of God, is helping to fulfill its most outstanding prophecy."[86] Will H. Houghton of Moody Bible Institute reported that fear of an impending German invasion in the summer of 1939 had prompted a mass turning to Christ among Warsaw's Jewish youth. "Perhaps that is the reason the Devil saw to it that Warsaw was wrecked and the Jews scattered."[87] Dispensationalists never produced any statistics to back up these claims or any arguments to explain how being persecuted by Gentiles made Jews more accessible and amenable to Christian evangelists, but in such claims dispensationalists utilized all their interpretive powers. Hitler's actions fulfilled both God's punitive and merciful purposes.

There was a humanitarian side to dispensationalists' response as well. In early 1939, the *Moody Monthly* carried an article entitled "An Appeal for Persecuted Israel," which presented an accurate and horrifying picture of Jewish life under the Nazis. It declared that the lives of well over six million European Jews, including over one million Jewish Christians, were in peril. The appeal called Christians to action: "God is calling his people to show forth mercy, sympathy, love, and substantial help to the Jews and to the Jewish Christians of Central Europe. Under no circumstances would we differentiate between races or religions in an appeal for help. All belong to the great suffering human family."[88] To meet such crying needs, a number of prominent evangelicals organized the Friends of Israel Refugee Committee. Based in Philadelphia and administered by a number of Christian business and church leaders, the committee solicited funds to alleviate the suffering of Jews, regardless of their religious convictions. The committee ran a number of additional ads, soliciting funds to provide emergency food and housing for displaced Jews.[89] Of course, by then there were not many Jewish refugees to help. In 1940, most European Jews were beyond the reach of both Christian missionaries and humanitarians.

The Last Great Holocaust

As bad as things were for the Jews, the Holocaust in Central and Eastern Europe was only a foreshadowing of the great tribulation of the end times. Gaebelein warned that the suffering of the Jews in the Holocaust would pale in comparison to their future suffering under the Antichrist.[90] He was reflecting bedrock dispensationalist teaching. The Jews' worst times were coming.

Starting with John Nelson Darby, dispensationalists viewed the coming great tribulation as the "time of Jacob's trouble" (Jer. 30:7). Their predictions of this period were gleaned from numerous Old and New Testament passages (Deuteronomy, Jeremiah, Ezekiel, Daniel, Zechariah, Matthew, 2 Thessalonians, and Revelation) that were stitched together like a huge prophetic quilt. There was no uniformity in the way dispensationalist experts described this time. As anyone who delves into the labyrinth of dispensationalist interpretation quickly discovers, readers of the sure word of prophecy did not always agree on how the pieces fit together.[91] But one can make some generalizations about how dispensationalists viewed the coming tribulation and the Jews' role in it.

John Walvoord, a leading dispensationalist teacher of the late twentieth century, summarized what lay ahead for those Jews who returned to Israel in search of safety in their own homeland:

> Israel is destined to have a particular time of suffering which will eclipse any thing that it has known in the past. . . . Heartrending as it may be to contemplate, the people of Israel who are returning to their ancient land are placing themselves within the vortex of this future whirlwind which will destroy the majority of those living in the land of Palestine. The searching and refining fire of divine judgment

will produce in Israel that which is not there now, an attitude of true repentance and eager anticipation of the coming of their Messiah.[92]

The tribulation would be a period of judgment through which the Jewish people would have to pass to make them ready to repent of their unbelief and receive their Messiah. None of this could take place without the removal of the church in the rapture. Once that was accomplished, Daniel's seventieth week could begin and prophesied events could be fulfilled. Following is a summary of what dispensationalists believed would happen next.

The "time of Jacob's trouble" will begin with the emergence of the Antichrist as the savior of Israel and the protector of the peace. Tensions in the Middle East will make Israel desperate for peace, and the charismatic new leader of the revived Roman Empire will deliver. Writing in 1974, Walvoord's description sounds especially relevant in light of events in the early twenty-first century.

> A peace settlement in the Middle East is one of the most important events predicted for the end time. The signing of this peace treaty will start the final countdown leading to Armageddon and then introduce the new world leader who will be destined to become the world dictator—the infamous Antichrist. According to Daniel 9:27, the last seven years leading up to the second coming of Christ will begin with just such a peace settlement. The same passage describes a covenant to be made between the nation of Israel and the prince who will rise to power (Daniel 9:26). While the details of the covenant are not given, it will be an attempt to settle the Arab-Israeli controversy which has focused world attention on the Middle East. It may well take the form of a forced peace settlement in which Israel returns much of the land conquered through war in exchange for strong international guarantees for Israel's safety and prosperity.[93]

Once the peace is made, Jews will experience a revival of peace and prosperity. They will resume their ancient sacrificial system in a restored temple, feel secure behind their borders, and relish their new place in the world order. But all that will abruptly change. Though the new leader of the West is powerful, not all nations are under his dominion. Three and a half years after the peace treaty is signed, a new crisis will arise: Russia and its northern alliance will combine with certain "kings of the south," which dispensationalists have historically understood as an Arab/African alliance, to launch an attack on Israel (Daniel 11). Before the Antichrist can marshal his forces to protect Israel, however, God will intervene and supernaturally destroy five-sixths of the invaders in the field (Ezekiel 38–39). With Russia and its northern and southern allies miraculously destroyed, the Antichrist's forces will contend with an invasion of a huge army (two hundred million strong) from the "kings of the east" (some dispensationalists put this invasion at the end of the tribulation). The ensuing war will be terrible, with one-third of the human race being destroyed (Revelation 9).

With hostile nations thus eliminated, the Antichrist will achieve world domination. Once he controls the world, his behavior toward Israel will change. He will enter the temple in Jerusalem, set up his own image there ("the abomination that causes desolation" [Dan. 12:11]), and demand that all the world worship him. The Antichrist will also require as an act of loyalty that people receive the "mark of the beast" on their hands or foreheads. Without it, people will not be able to buy or sell (Revelation 13).

At that point, many Jews will decide that their only hope for the future lies in God and the coming Messiah. In fact, 144,000 of them, 12,000 from each of Israel's twelve tribes, will become missionaries to the world, preaching the gospel of Jesus and warning of the wrath to come (Revelation 7). These Jewish evangelists will have enormous success. According to Milton Lindberg:

> Not only will these transformed Jews have a hearing, but as Revelation 7 indicates, their preaching will result in "a great multitude, which no man could number, of all nations, and kindreds, and people, and tongue" coming out of the Great Tribulation, having "washed their robes, and made them white in the blood of the Lamb." What a mighty revival will result when these enemies of Jesus Christ become His devoted servants![94]

The Antichrist will respond to such defiance by ordering a bloodbath. He will target not only Jewish evangelists and their converts but also Jews in general. Thus, the second half of the tribulation will be horrific, the worst time the Jews have ever experienced. According to Hal Lindsey, "a numberless multitude" of Jews will die, including the 144,000 evangelists. This persecution will be much worse than the one under Hitler. The Antichrist's brutality will make the Nazis "look like Girl Scouts weaving a daisy chain."[95] Another interpreter made a similar comparison between the Holocaust of Hitler and that of the Antichrist:

> It took Hitler to turn the Jews toward Palestine. It will take a greater Hitler to turn them to God. . . . Antichrist's persecution will be much more terrible than Hitler's. Hitler used gas chambers; he got rid of six million Jews; but Antichrist's purpose will be to do away with all Jews of all nations. That many Jews cannot be driven into gas chambers, but they could be driven into Egypt. Egypt has great deserts where

Jews could be sent to die and their bones would not clutter up good ground.[96]

Historian Paul Boyer notes that dispensational teachers expressed a "telling ambiguity" about the ultimate source of this horrible judgment against the Jews. "Taken as a whole, the genre sees Jews as victims of both God's loving judgment and Satan's hatred. While some writers say God will unleash the invasion foretold in Ezekiel 38 to punish the Jews for worshiping Antichrist, others view it as Satan's revenge for their refusal to bow down to the Beast!"[97] Whether God or the devil is behind the persecution, the results will be the same. Most Jews (the favorite estimate is two-thirds, after Zech. 13:8) will perish. The remnant that remains will witness the world's worst battle at Armageddon, where the Antichrist will summon the nations to destroy Israel once and for all. Before the Jewish remnant can be destroyed, however, the Messiah will return with his raptured church to defeat the Antichrist and his legions. The Jewish remnant will hail him as their rightful Savior and king, then join with Jesus to reestablish David's throne and purify the temple for the inauguration of the millennial kingdom.[98]

Evaluating Dispensationalism's Dark Side

What should we make of all this? Dispensationalism was not inherently anti-Semitic any more than it was pro-Hitler, though it could appear to be both thanks to the extremism of certain Bible teachers. As the above evidence shows, there were major disagreements among dispensationalists concerning the existence of an international Jewish conspiracy. Some interpreters were drawn to the notion, while others vehemently opposed the idea. There were personal and political differences among them that make generalizations dangerous. While all dispensationalists believed in the unraveling of Christian civilization, not all of them were willing to blame the Jews for it. Historians who have studied anti-Semitic fundamentalists frequently trace their nasty attitudes to bitterness brought on by personal misfortune and failure.[99] Yet despite their individual and psychological issues, dispensationalists who used the *Protocols* believed that the document matched their understanding of Bible prophecy.

Dispensationalism was sufficiently ambivalent toward Jews and their place in God's prophetic plan that adherents could go in a number of directions. As George Marsden has observed, between the two world wars, fundamentalists "could be both pro-Zionist and somewhat anti-Semitic, favoring the return of the Jews to Israel, which would lead eventually to their conversion; yet in the meantime especially distrusting apostate Jews."[100] Dispensationalists could evangelize Jews, support their nationalistic aspirations, condemn anti-Semitic attacks on them, and blame at least some of them for the world's ills—all at the same time. In retrospect, one wonders why such conspiracy-minded dispensationalists did not have a severe case of cognitive dissonance.

Dispensationalists faced an enormously difficult task. Since they believed that the Bible presented a precise scenario of where history was going, they felt obligated to explain what was happening and what it all meant. The times were obviously apocalyptic, which meant that the Bible teachers were under pressure to give a comprehensive account of the signs of the times. They knew the world would fall prey to a sinister and Satanic deception, and their own experience proved that the righteous could be temporarily outmaneuvered by God's enemies. Dispensationalists, therefore, tried to make sense of the world with their Bibles in one hand and their newspapers in the other.

Sometimes their efforts backfired. So intent were they to prove that their reading of the Bible was correct that they too quickly accepted what appeared to be corroborating evidence. They grabbed the idea of an international Jewish conspiracy because it seemed to fit well with what they already believed. It did not work. As many of their fellow dispensationalists eventually recognized, one could not legitimately condemn anti-Semitism and promote the arguments of anti-Semites simultaneously. The likes of Winrod, Gaebelein, and Riley wanted to have it both ways, but other dispensationalists would not let them do it. Wrapping themselves in the prophetic pages of the Bible did not absolve them of taking responsibility for what they taught. Using dispensationalism to support conspiracy theories did not make these arguments any less reprehensible. During the 1930s and 1940s, one had to be terribly naive to think that one could sound like a Nazi and not be criticized for it.

Despite these negative elements, the record shows that dispensationalists had gained credibility with large numbers of conservative Protestants by their apparent ability to fit together biblical prophecy and current events. Shortly after World War II, the most important prophetic expectation was fulfilled. The state of Israel was founded in Palestine. Here was verification that they had interpreted the Bible correctly and that the return of Jesus was imminent.

6

The Founding and Expansion of Israel

D ispensationalists could get away with being confused about events between and during the world wars, but they could not afford to be wrong about the regathering of the Jews in Palestine. As already shown, the return of God's chosen people to the Holy Land was key to their understanding of Bible prophecy. Without a restored Israel, there could be no Antichrist, no great tribulation, no Armageddon, and no triumphant second coming of Jesus. With a restored Israel, all of those things were not only possible but guaranteed.

As things turned out, dispensationalists were not wrong about the founding of a new Jewish state, though the path to its establishment did not exactly conform to their expectations. At almost every turn the difference between their well-publicized prophetic scenario and the historical realities in the Middle East were noticeable. Thanks to the unrelenting opposition of the Arab majority, the British began reneging on the Balfour Declaration almost as soon as they issued it. In the 1930s, Great Britain proposed the partitioning of Palestine into Jewish and Arab states, then suggested a single state under a coalition government. Neither proposal, however, proved to be practically workable or remotely close to dispensationalists' predictions. Even when Israel won its independence in 1948, its territorial holdings were far less than Bible teachers expected.

Despite these disappointments along the way, dispensationalists remained confident that sooner or later, one way or another, all the promises to Israel would be fulfilled and the events of the end times would come to pass. Thus, Bible teachers were strong supporters of the expansion of Israel and especially the taking of the Old City of Jerusalem in the Six-Day War of 1967. Because the acquisition of more territory was part of the divine plan, most dispensationalists saw no reason to dwell on the ethical implications of Israeli actions in the Middle East, though some Bible teachers warned against adopting an "ends justifies the means" attitude concerning everything that happened in the Holy Land. Despite the often messy complications of the founding and expansion of Israel, dispensationalists were sure that everything was finally in place for the playing out of history's last phase.

On the Road to Statehood

Dispensationalists viewed the founding of the state of Israel in 1948 as the mother lode of prophetic fulfillment, but getting there was not easy. As their experience in the 1920s, 1930s, and 1940s made clear, detecting the signs of the times could be difficult. Even the exhilaration brought on by the Balfour Declaration in 1917 was tempered in the decades that followed by events in the Middle East. While most dispensationalists believed that the new state of Israel would be restored shortly after World War I, the realities of Arab and Jewish conflict and the inability of the British to do anything about them put such hopes on hold. Yet through it all, dispensationalists continued to believe that a Jewish state was part of the prophecy leading to the return of Christ and the end of the age.

THE BALFOUR DECLARATION AND THE BRITISH MANDATE

The prophetic hopes of dispensationalists soared in the last year of World War I. On November 2, 1917, the British issued the Balfour Declaration, which promised their help in the "establishment in Palestine of a national home for the Jewish people." Five weeks later, Jerusalem fell to the British army under General Edmund Allenby. Suddenly, all things seemed possible, including the rapid restoration of a Jewish state and the second coming of Jesus. Almost as suddenly, however, these prophetic hopes were dashed by a series of unexpected historical developments.

Dispensationalists tended to have a rather truncated view of the events they judged to be prophetic fulfillments and viewed history in instrumental terms. They studied past and current events to find those that fit their expected prophetic scenario. Because they believed they understood where history was going and the unseen forces that were moving it along, history contained few real surprises. Dispensationalists rarely showed any interest in mining the complexities of historical cause and effect or the often unexpected consequences of human behavior. In other words, they had a decidedly ahistorical view of history and liked to "proof text" it in order to match it to their anticipated plan. Once dispensationalists placed an event into their prophetic jigsaw puzzle, it was difficult for them to take it out.

But things are never quite that simple, and the Balfour Declaration was a perfect case in point. That important piece of the puzzle did not suddenly materialize out of thin air. It was the result of a long history of British involvement in the Middle East, and what proved exasperating to some dispensationalists were the many complications that followed its issuance.

For decades before World War I, the European powers maneuvered to take advantage of the distressed and declining Ottoman Empire, which the Russian czar had called the "Sick Man of Europe." Britain, France, and Russia had numerous clashes, both diplomatic and military, over one another's aspirations for Ottoman territory. As the British Empire expanded, so did its interests in the Middle East. To secure access through the Red Sea to its empire in East Africa, India, and the Far East, the British purchased the Suez Canal in 1876. Two years later, under the terms of the Cyprus Convention, Great Britain promised to protect Turkish territories in Asia, which was simply another way of protecting its own growing interests there. By the turn of the century, then, it was clear that the English had a substantial stake in the territory from the Nile to the Euphrates River. British designs on Ottoman territory were obvious to the Turks too, who eventually turned to Germany for protection when the new kaiser, Wilhelm II, seemed more supportive and less threatening. As it turned out, by aligning with the Central Powers at the beginning of World War I, the Ottoman Empire sealed its own fate, which opened the door to even greater British expansion.[1]

In other words, the British had aspirations in Palestine long before and after the issuance of the Balfour Declaration. In her study of England's centuries-long fascination with the Holy Land, historian Barbara W. Tuchman argued that the British interest in Palestine was rooted in both political and religious ideas.[2] Many British statesmen in the nineteenth century thought of the Holy Land primarily in biblical terms. The prime example of such thinking was Anthony Ashley Cooper, Earl of

Shaftesbury, who spent his long career in government service weaving together his dispensational prophetic views and the needs of the British Empire.[3] Lord Shaftesbury advocated the restoration of the Jews to the Holy Land as early as 1839. Also influential was F. Laurence Oliphant, a member of Parliament whose book *The Land of Gilead* (1880) called on Britain to help resettle persecuted Jews from Russia and Eastern Europe in Palestine. Most British politicians were not as well-grounded in Bible prophecy as Shaftesbury and Oliphant, but widespread biblical literacy in nineteenth-century England ensured that Zionist leaders received a polite and even positive hearing from the beginning of their movement. Chaim Weitzmann, Theodore Herzl's successor as the leader of international Zionism (and the future first president of Israel), taught chemistry at Manchester University and became fast friends with a number of leading British politicians, including Arthur James Balfour, who served in various government posts before becoming foreign secretary during World War I. Balfour had been raised on heavy doses of what Tuchman called "the Hebraism of the Bible." According to Balfour's niece and biographer, Balfour's lifelong interest in the Jews "originated in the Old Testament training of his mother and in his Scottish upbringing. . . . He always talked eagerly on this and I remember in childhood imbibing from him the idea that Christian religion and civilization owe to Judaism an immeasurable debt, shamefully ill repaid."[4]

Balfour's declaration was not an impulsive undertaking. For a year before issuing it, Balfour consulted endlessly with British politicians and Zionist leaders and wrote numerous drafts until the British government finally reached a consensus regarding its terms. According to Tuchman's careful analysis, underlying the declaration was a complicated set of motives.

> They [the British] did it because they meant to take Palestine anyway for its strategic value; but they had to have a good moral case. The timing is important. . . . Allenby's army had already begun its advance into Palestine in October, had taken Beersheba on the 31st, and was at the gates of Jaffa. Jerusalem would be next and was in fact taken five weeks later, on December 8. The awful moment when a British army would enter the Holy City had suddenly become a reality. The Balfour Declaration was issued to dignify that approaching moment, not only in the eyes of the world, but especially in the eyes of the British themselves. And not only the moment, but also the future. For the British meant not only to take Palestine, but likewise, by one expedient or another, to hold it. . . . This was the purpose that the Balfour Declaration served: it provided the effective moral attitude, the good case. It appealed to the imaginative side of the national

character. In short, it allowed Britain to acquire the Holy Land with a good conscience.[5]

The British promised to lend their considerable support to the creation of a "national home for the Jewish people." The precise wording of the statement is important. It did not say a "national *state* for the Jewish people." The framers of the declaration consciously avoided using the language of statehood, and even the Zionists avoided insisting on it. "National home" seemed less provocative. After all, at the same time the British were negotiating with Zionists, they were also talking to various Arab factions and the French about their future roles in the post-Ottoman world.[6] During the war, different British diplomats, including T. E. Lawrence ("Lawrence of Arabia"), Sir Mark Sykes, and Sir Henry McMahon, negotiated with Arab leaders such as the old but influential Sherif Hussein of Mecca and his two sons, Faisal and Abdullah, about founding an Arab nation. The British promised the Arabs independence if they supported them in the war against Turkey and the Central Powers. The hopeful Arabs were unaware that in 1916 Britain and France had secretly signed the Sykes-Pinot Agreement, in which they promised to divide the Ottoman Empire between them after the war.

It seems that conflicting promises were made on all sides and that the various factions were purposely vague to preserve future maneuverability. The inevitable result was widespread misunderstanding and double-dealing. In a nutshell, the British believed they had been clear that Arab "independence" would be under a British protectorate and would not include Palestine, while the Arabs believed they had been equally clear that any consideration of relinquishing Palestine was contingent on Britain granting them true independence elsewhere after the war. Each side had ample reason to feel betrayed and misled. It was only a matter of time before the terms of the Balfour Declaration became the great sticking point in the region.[7]

The Paris Peace Conference, which ended World War I, decided things in favor of the colonial powers by essentially turning the sentiments of the Balfour Declaration into international law. In 1920, the victorious Allies met at San Remo to determine the final disposition of the Ottoman territories. In 1922, their decisions were confirmed by the League of Nations in the establishment of British mandates for Palestine, Transjordan, and Iraq and French mandates for Syria and Lebanon. Under the mandate system, France and Britain were supposed to take steps to lead the people in their territories toward full independence. The league's mandate for Palestine, however, authorized the British to "secure the establishment of the Jewish National Home" and to facilitate Jewish immigration to the land.[8] Again, the word *state* was not used in the mandate, though leaders in the British government later said that they understood that statehood would be "a matter of gradual development in accordance with the ordinary laws of political evolution." British prime minister David Lloyd George, another politician raised on Bible prophecy,[9] remembered that while no one expected a Jewish state to be set up immediately, they did expect Palestine to become a Jewish commonwealth within the British Empire if the Jews "responded to the opportunity afforded to them and . . . [became] a definite majority of the inhabitants." Winston Churchill, a member of the war cabinet that originally approved the Balfour Declaration, wrote in 1920 that he anticipated "the creation in our lifetime by the banks of the Jordan of a Jewish State under the protection of the British Crown."[10]

Key to these expectations was a massive influx of Jewish immigrants to create a Jewish majority in Palestine. What about the Arab population that at the time of the Balfour Declaration made up 93 percent of the total? The formulators of the declaration tipped their hats to this unnamed majority: "it being clearly understood that nothing shall be done which may prejudice the civil and religious rights of existing non-Jewish communities in Palestine." The league's mandate went into great detail concerning the Jews but failed to mention the Palestinian Arabs by name, referring to them obliquely as "other sections of the population" or "various peoples and communities" whose rights and status needed to be protected.[11]

Looking back, one can only marvel at such an omission, especially when Wilson's Fourteen Points and the Paris Peace Treaty emphasized the importance of self-determination. The British had not thought through the effects of Jewish immigration on the resident population of Palestine. As time went on, it became obvious that making a home for the Jews without stepping on the rights of the Palestinians would be extremely difficult, if not impossible.

Such practical matters made little difference to dispensationalists. Whatever the motives of the British or the reaction of the Palestinian Arabs, premillennialists never doubted that the Balfour Declaration and the League of Nation's mandate would result in a Jewish state, which, of course, was all they really cared about.

Conflicts over Holy Ground

The problems in Palestine were rooted in religion as well as in politics and real estate. The three Abrahamic religions called Palestine home, and their pilgrim roads crisscrossed the Holy Land and converged in Jerusalem.[12] For Jews and Muslims, no site in Palestine was more sacred than the thirty-five-acre Temple Mount or Al-Haram al-Sharif (the Noble Sanctuary), where Israel's first two temples once stood and Islam's Dome of the Rock and Al-Aqsa Mosque now stand.[13]

The first temple was built by King Solomon in the mid-tenth century B.C., probably over a huge outcropping of rock believed to be Mount Moriah, where Abraham came close to sacrificing his son Isaac (Genesis 22). This structure was destroyed in 587 B.C. by the army of King Nebuchadnezzar, which carried off its sacred utensils and a large number of surviving Jews to Babylon. Seventy years later, King Cyrus allowed many of the exiles' descendants to return to Jerusalem to rebuild the temple. This second temple stood for almost five hundred years, though it occasionally fell into disrepair and was desecrated by the Seleucid king Antiochus Epiphanes in 167 B.C.

The Maccabees defeated Antiochus's forces and cleansed the temple a few years later, but in 63 B.C., the Roman general Pompei conquered Jerusalem. In 37 B.C., the Romans set up an Idumean, Herod, as their vassal "King of the Jews." To curry favor with his less-than-loyal Jewish subjects, Herod undertook a vast refurbishing of the second temple. Workers leveled the hilly terrain of the Temple Mount in order to double the size of the esplanade and outer courtyards of the temple. Such an undertaking required extensive excavation of the site and the construction of massive retaining walls. Herod died in 4 B.C., but the work on the temple continued until A.D. 64. Herod's temple was the one Jesus knew, worshiped in, and angrily cleansed. Its glory, however, was short-lived. Within two years of the temple's completion, the Jews revolted against their Roman occupiers. General Titus besieged then destroyed Jerusalem in A.D. 70. The Romans razed the temple and carried off its treasures to Rome as spoils of war, a depiction of which can still be seen on the triumphal Arch of Titus in the Roman Forum. The only things that remained of Herod's temple complex were the retaining walls. For Jews, the Western Wall remained sacred.

Roughly sixty years later, Emperor Hadrian decided to rebuild Jerusalem as a Roman city, complete with pagan temples and shrines. News of Hadrian's intentions led to another Jewish uprising, the Bar Kokhbar Revolt of A.D. 131. When it ended four years later, Hadrian constructed his temples and expelled all Jews from Aelia Capitolina, his name for the new Jerusalem.[14] By then Jews had already figured out how to practice their religion without a temple and its blood sacrifices, but Jews did not put the memory of their temple completely behind them. Many of them still believed that when the Messiah came, he would build a glorious third temple on the very spot of the previous two.

After the fourth-century rise of Constantine, the Roman Empire's first Christian emperor, Jerusalem became a destination for Christian pilgrims. The emperor's mother, Helena, explored Palestine in 326 to find the holy places of Christianity. Her entourage found what it was looking for: Without much effort, it identified the place of Jesus' birth, his place of execution, his tomb, and even the true cross. Constantine made sure that appropriate churches and basilicas were built at or over these sacred sites, but he and subsequent Christian emperors left the Temple Mount alone. After all, Jesus had predicted the temple's destruction: "There shall not be left here one stone upon another, that shall not be thrown down" (Matt. 24:2). For obvious reasons, Christians had no interest in rebuilding the temple, which the death and resurrection of Jesus had superseded in importance. Under Christian auspices, then, the Temple Mount became the garbage dump for the Holy City.

All that changed with the coming of Islam in the seventh century. A Muslim army conquered Jerusalem in 638, and Omar, the second caliph after Mohammed, asked the Christian patriarch where the temple had stood. When he arrived at the Temple Mount, he was shocked to find that it was a rubbish heap. He ordered it cleared and built a mosque at its southern end, where today's Al-Aqsa Mosque now stands. In 691, Caliph Abd al-Malik ibn Marwan constructed the Dome of the Rock over the rocky outcropping believed to be the site of the two Jewish temples. The rock had a different significance for Muslims: They believed it was the site where Abraham had almost sacrificed *Ishmael* (not Isaac) and the spot from which Mohammed had ascended to heaven, as can be seen by his footprint left in the rock.[15] Inside the dome were mosaic inscriptions from the Koran obviously meant for Christians: "Do not say things about God but the truth! The messiah Jesus, son of Mary, is indeed a messenger of God. . . . So believe in God and all the messengers, and stop talking about a trinity. . . . Verily God is the God of unity. Lord Almighty! That God would beget a child?" According to Gershom Gorenberg, the construction of the Dome of the Rock also carried an unmistakable message for Jews: "The Dome stands where everyone knew the Temple did. Islam, the building says, is the culmination of Judaism and Christianity."[16] The Dome of the Rock is now considered the third holiest shrine in Islam, the Western Wall is the holiest site in Judaism, and in that part of Christianity that understands the Bible and the future in dispensationalist terms, the Temple Mount is an essential piece of real estate for second-coming events.

TROUBLE LEADING TO STATEHOOD

As soon as the British mandate was established, Palestinians began resisting it. By then it was obvious that the British were serious about establishing a Jewish homeland in Palestine and would not keep their promise regarding Arab independence. In 1920, Palestinian Arabs rioted over the British government's liberal Jewish immigration policy, which they rightly believed was intended to create a Jewish majority as a necessary step toward a Jewish state.

When the British appointed Sir Herbert Samuel as high commissioner for Palestine under the mandate, he inherited from the Turks elaborate rules for regulating Jewish access to the Western Wall. Not wanting to rock the boat, Samuel retained them: While Jews could pray at the wall, they were not allowed to do anything to alter the site, such as set up benches, erect religious symbols, or even blow the shofar, the sacred ram's horn. Jews could worship there only if they did not offend their Muslim hosts. Maintaining the status quo was especially important to Hajj Amin Al-Husseini, the mufti of Jerusalem, the chief authority on Muslim law in Palestine. Al-Husseini believed that the Jews intended to expand their privileges at the Western Wall as part of a grand scheme to set up a synagogue there or even to take over the Al-Aqsa Mosque. He and his fellow Muslims had been watching the Zionists form an organizational framework on which they could build their own state. The Jews had set up their own militia (the *Haganah*) and a proto-parliamentary body consisting of representatives from their trade unions and the *kibbutzim,* agricultural communities set up to make the land productive. The Jewish Agency, which sought to oversee all Jewish enterprises in Palestine, represented the entire Jewish community, or *Yishuv,* to the British high commissioner. It was only a matter of time before something triggered a violent confrontation.

On Yom Kippur in 1928, Jews at the Western Wall erected a divider to separate men and women at prayer, which, technically speaking, was not allowed by the old rules. The Jewish worshipers insisted that the divider was required to preserve proper decorum during worship. The Arabs saw it as a desecration of the sacred precincts of the Al-Aqsa Mosque and a sign of Jewish subterfuge. When the Arabs appealed to the high commissioner, the British took down the divider and scuffled with Jewish worshipers. Following this incident, Al-Husseini began an emotional public campaign to alert the Arab population of the ongoing Jewish threat and issued a call to be ready to protect the Western Wall and the mosque it supported from Jewish abuses. Under the mufti's auspices, Muslims occasionally drove their livestock through the narrow opening in front of the wall to disrupt Jewish worshipers. Jews countered by flying the Zionist flag, the star of David, in defiance. Here was a disaster waiting to happen.

It finally did on August 16, 1929, when a Jewish boy kicked a soccer ball into an Arab garden. A fight broke out, and the boy was stabbed to death. The Jewish population in Jerusalem was outraged. Following the boy's funeral, angry Zionists marched to the Western Wall to protest the murder. The mufti countered with a fiery sermon about Jewish threats to Arab rights. During the next week, armed Arab peasants from the hinterlands began arriving in Jerusalem, and on August 22, they started attacking Jews throughout the Old City. The violence spread to the suburbs and into the countryside. In Hebron, sixty-seven Jews were killed, including a number of women and children. The Jews fought back as they were able, and the British had to call in reinforcements from Egypt to restore order. By the end of the rioting, Jews had suffered 133 dead and 339 wounded; the Arabs, 110 dead and 232 wounded.[17] According to Gorenberg, "For the British, Friday, August 16, 1929, was the day that the Palestine Mandate began to come undone."[18] For the Jews and Arabs of Palestine, the day marked the end of any hope for a peaceful coexistence.

Throughout the 1930s, the Arab and Jewish communities in Palestine pulled farther apart. Arabs continually worried about the growth of the Jewish population. At the time of the Balfour Declaration, Jews numbered roughly 83,000, or about 7 percent of the total population. By 1922, the Jewish population had grown to 14 percent, and by 1933, it was up to 19 percent. Between 1933 and 1938, over 217,000 Jews immigrated to Palestine, most of them fleeing from Nazi Germany. By 1939, Jews numbered over 400,000 or approximately 28 percent of the population.[19] Arabs also complained bitterly about the steady loss of their land. Starting in 1901, the Jewish National Fund (JNF) began purchasing land for Jewish settlement and agricultural purposes. In many cases, the sellers were absentee Arab landlords who had been renting their land to local Arabs. The JNF always retained title to the land it purchased and made sure that only Jews lived or worked on it, thereby eliminating Arab jobs and displacing Arabs whose families had been on the land for generations. As Jewish immigration and funding for such land purchases increased during the 1930s, Arabs felt the squeeze.

Serious anti-Zionist riots broke out in 1931, then again in 1933–34. In 1936, Arabs called a general strike, which turned into widespread civil disobedience, then violent civil unrest. What began as an anti-Zionist demonstration quickly became a full-blown anti-British rebellion. When attacked, most Jews responded with measured restraint, but some chose brutal retaliation and even terror tactics to counter the violence against them. The instigators were from the *Irgun Zvai Leumi,* a violent resistance group that had been formed out of the more radical elements of the *Haganah* (the Jewish militia) in 1931.

The British quickly put together a royal commission under Lord William Peel to evaluate the causes of Palestine's unrest and to suggest a solution. The commission held sixty-six meetings. The Arabs boycotted the proceedings until the fifty-sixth meeting. When Al-Husseini finally had his say, he argued that the root cause of the conflict was religious: "The Jews' ultimate aim is the reconstruction of the temple of King Solomon on the ruins of the *Haram al-Sharif*, the *Al-Aqsa* Mosque and the Holy Dome of the Rock."[20] The Peel Commission issued its final report in 1937. It found little hope for resolving the deep divisions between Jews and Arabs apart from partitioning Palestine into separate Jewish and Arab states: "But while neither race can justly rule all Palestine, we see no reason why, if it were practicable, each race should not rule part of it. . . . Partition seems to offer at least a chance of ultimate peace. We can see none in any other plan."[21] The commission also suggested that Jerusalem remain under a British mandate to ensure that all parties could have access to the holy places.

The Zionists wanted more land than the Peel Commission offered but finally and reluctantly declared their willingness to accept the plan. The Arabs rejected the notion outright. The Arab rebellion, which had been suspended during the commission's deliberations, resumed in October 1937 and lasted until the end of 1938. In the last phase of the revolt, the British partnered with the *Haganah* to put down the rebellion and exiled a number of Palestinian leaders, including Al-Husseini. He ended up spending part of World War II in Nazi Germany, where he met with Hitler and "repeatedly exerted himself to prevent Jewish emigration from the territories of Germany's allies."[22]

Despite their practical alliance with the Jews, in the waning days of the Arab revolt, the British reversed their position again. In May 1939, they issued a White Paper that proposed phasing out Jewish immigration over five years (unless Arabs agreed to welcome more Jews, which seemed unlikely), stopping Jewish land purchases, repudiating the plan for partition, and advocating the creation of an independent state ruled jointly by Arabs and Jews. For all practical purposes, Balfour was dead.

The British had a way of devising plans that few liked but themselves. The Arabs favored the idea of cutting off Jewish immigration and land purchases but were not about to accept joint rule. The Jews, with some justification, felt betrayed by the British. The policies of the White Paper were still in effect when World War II started. Given the alternative, most Jews supported Great Britain in the fight against Nazi Germany, but some Jews decided that the British were their biggest enemy and launched a terrorist campaign against them. In 1940, Abraham Stern founded *Lehi,* a terrorist organization with extreme elements from the *Irgun.* The Jewish terrorists shot British policemen, set bombs in public buildings, hanged British soldiers in retaliation for executing *Lehi* operatives, and tried unsuccessfully to assassinate the British high commissioner, Sir Harold MacMichael. When Stern was killed in 1942, Yitzhak Shamir took over. More moderate Zionist leaders condemned such tactics, but they could not deny that they were bearing fruit. Under such blistering pressure, the British were getting close to repudiating their own White Paper. In fact, Chaim Weitzmann was negotiating with Prime Minister Winston Churchill about a new partition plan when Jewish terrorists assassinated Lord Moyne (Walter Edward Guiness), the British minister for Middle East affairs, in Cairo. That act ended any further negotiations. Zionist leaders were so enraged at the Stern Gang (as the British called *Lehi*) that they began cooperating with the British to eradicate the organization.

When the war ended, things got even worse. According to the provisions of the White Paper, the British allowed only a trickle of Jewish immigrants from war-ravaged Europe. The British navy actually intercepted and deported shiploads of Jewish survivors of the death camps, even sending some of them back to Germany. Such a policy was bound to backfire. In America, both the government and the general public condemned the British position. Now even moderate Zionist leaders were in favor of an armed uprising against British rule. In early 1946, the British tried to end resistance through mass arrests of members of the Jewish Agency and the *Haganah,* but resistance increased, especially from the more radical *Irgun* and *Lehi.*

The year 1947 was a crucial turning point for the British. In February, they finally gave up on finding a resolution to the Palestine problem and referred the situation to the newly established United Nations. In July, the *Irgun,* under its new leader, Menachem Begin, blew up a wing of the King David Hotel in Jerusalem, where the British army was headquartered, killing ninety people and wounding forty-five. In October, President Harry Truman demanded that the British lift their restriction on Jewish immigrants and endorsed for the first time the concept of a "viable Jewish state" in Palestine.[23] In November, the General Assembly of the United Nations approved a resolution to partition Palestine into Arab and Jewish states, with Jerusalem under international control. The Jews accepted the plan, but the Arabs rejected it. Britain announced that it would not be responsible for enforcing the U.N.'s partition plan and that it intended to depart Palestine on May 15, 1948. Without Arab agreement and British assistance, the United Nations' partition plan could not possibly work.

Making Sense of Palestine with Bible Prophecy

Did the tumultuous events in Palestine lead dispensationalists to question their analysis of the signs of the times? Historian Dwight Wilson has shown that Bible teachers were often confused by changing Jewish fortunes under the British and therefore came to contradictory conclusions about their prophetic significance. Nevertheless, although history seemed to be going in the wrong direction, dispensationalists doggedly stuck to their belief in the coming Jewish restoration in the Holy Land.[24]

The riots in 1929 over the Western Wall were a serious wake-up call for dispensationalists, an unexpected challenge to their assumption that everything was moving toward the restoration of the Jews. Keith Brooks of *Prophecy* magazine tried to look on the bright side: Even though the British stupidly sided with the Arabs in the crisis, their action did not amount to a repudiation of the Balfour Declaration.[25] Other Bible teachers were equally disappointed in the British but stood firm in their confidence that nothing could stop the coming of the Jewish state. According to Agnes Scott Kent, "The end is determined. Palestine is for the Jew. . . . The Abrahamic Covenant, not the Balfour Declaration, is the Jewish Magna Charta to the land of Palestine."[26] In the *Moody Bible Institute Monthly,* Aaron Judah Kligerman argued that the restoration of Israel had already begun with the Balfour Declaration and would continue until a new nation was formed, despite occasional political disputes and even bloodshed. "Be as these may, I believe that 'he that scattered Israel will gather him, and keep him, as a shepherd doth his flock.'"[27]

Only occasionally was a premillennialist writer willing to hold Jews at least partly responsible for the trouble they were having in Palestine. J. A. Huffman believed that "there has been fault on both sides. . . . It is well known that the Jews themselves were partly to blame for the riots of 1929. But this does not justify the Arab for his falsehoods which helped to incite the trouble, nor for the murder of men, and even women and children, of which he is guilty." Nevertheless, "the Jewish nation is to have a future in Palestine."[28]

As dispensationalists soon discovered, the 1929 riots were not an aberration or an isolated incident; they marked the beginning of an escalating and deepening conflict between the Jewish and Arab communities. The road to restoration was not going to be easy. As the British, Zionists, and Arabs careened from one failed solution to another, dispensationalists struggled to make sense of it all. Especially confusing to them was the British insistence after 1937 that partition was the only way to resolve the conflict. The partitioning of Palestine into Jewish and non-Jewish sections had never been part of the dispensationalist prophetic scenario. The Promised Land had been promised to Jews, not Arabs.[29] Here was one of those unexpected historical developments that did not fit the biblical plan. Not surprisingly, Bible teachers were divided over how to interpret such an unanticipated problem. They universally opposed the idea of partition, though a few speculated that as an intermediate step it could be part of God's plan. The depth of dispensationalists' ambivalence can be seen in the pages of the *Weekly Evangel,* which during the early 1940s contained articles that took different interpretive positions on the question of partition: Either it was a reasonable step toward the Jewish occupation of all of Palestine, or it was a serious blunder by nations that God would judge at Armageddon.[30]

When the British White Paper of 1939 proposed a single state in Palestine ruled by a coalition government, Bible teachers again tried to fit the proposal into their scenario. The *Weekly Evangel,* which had already taken pro- and anti-partition positions, put in a good word for a coalition government: "No hope for a peaceful solution is seen apart from a co-operative program in which Jews and Arabs work together and rule the country in a coalition government."[31] For a while, Arno C. Gaebelein argued that under present circumstances the best the Jews could hope for was assured political representation in the emerging United Arab Republic.[32]

In the end, however, most dispensationalists recognized that a partitioned state was better than no state at all. While they had not seen it coming on their prophetic charts, partitioning could be God's way of doing things. T. DeCourcy Rayner articulated what became the standard view in a 1947 *Moody Bible Institute Monthly* article: "The Jews will eventually be given not a partitioned Palestine, but the whole of the land, and ultimately the whole of Trans-Jordan as well."[33] Partition was possibly the first word, but it would not be the last word in Palestine.

Of course, there was a way out of the interpretive quagmire if dispensationalists wanted to take it. Bible teachers could reopen the old debate over whether the Jews' return would be in "belief" or in "unbelief." In the nineteenth century, dispensationalists overwhelmingly believed that the final restoration would not occur until *after* the second coming, when Jews who survived the great tribulation would accept Jesus Christ as their true Messiah and would return to the Promised Land to reign with him for a thousand years. After the founding of Zionism, however, dispensationalists were faced with the possibility that significant numbers of Jews might return to Palestine prior to Christ's return and without faith in Jesus. Some interpreters had even decided that the push to establish a Zionist state was not part of the prophetic scenario; the real Jewish restoration would come later, after Jesus returned. If premillennialists argued this way, the failure of the British and the Zionists to set up a Jewish state was not a prophetic disconfirmation, since God had never promised to set up a secular Jewish nation before Christ came back.

On the other hand, dispensationalists could suggest that while Zionism was not the complete fulfillment of Bible prophecy, it was a partial fulfillment, a harbinger of things to come, a first step in a much longer process that would culminate in the conversion of the Jews and their flocking to King Jesus. Eventually, most dispensationalists chose this alternative, but the choice was not an easy one. The difficulty can be seen in the pages of the *Weekly Evangel*. In 1940, one writer was certain that "God swore that Israel should be re-gathered in her own land, unconverted, in the latter days. Ezekiel 36:24–38."[34] But the following year the editors argued the opposite:

> We all have been thrilled to watch the rebuilding of Palestine and the return of many Jews to that land through the efforts of Zionism. But let us remember that Zionism alone is doomed to ultimate failure. God's Word teaches that 'Jerusalem shall be trodden down of the Gentiles, until the times of the Gentiles be fulfilled.' Luke 21:24. Not until Christ returns will the Jewish nation go to Palestine as a whole, nor will the Jews get full sovereignty over the land. Jewry needs to know this.[35]

In 1948, on the eve of Jewish statehood, the *Weekly Evangel* was once again adamant but would soon be proved wrong again: "The Zionists will never get the Promised Land by their own political schemings and their own armed might. They will get it when they welcome Jesus of Nazareth back to earth as their Messiah."[36]

As the coming of a Jewish state looked inevitable, most dispensationalists were willing to make the needed adjustment in their interpretation. The *Sunday School Times* early on concluded that the Jewish restoration included an initial return in unbelief.[37] Even Arno C. Gaebelein, who for years had insisted that Zionism was not the fulfillment of biblical prophecy, was willing to endorse a Zionist state as a first step toward the authentic fulfillment: "That the Jewish people will be restored to their land in the end is inevitable, since God has so decreed in His Word (Jer. 23:7, 8). That restoration will be a restoration in faith. Now the Jews are seeking to go to Palestine in unbelief. Is there Scripture that leads us to suppose that their efforts will succeed? Yes, although we do not know when it will be."[38]

Another important question for dispensationalists in the years before Israel's statehood was whether the fulfillment of Bible prophecy always trumped questions of justice and international law. Even during the 1930s, much of the debate over Palestine had to do with who had legitimate claims to the land, Jews or Arabs? Did the end (restoring a Jewish state in Palestine) justify the means (displacing Arabs from their homes)? James M. Gray of Moody Bible Institute thought so. He admitted that when it came to securing a Jewish homeland, "the ordinary rules of statesmanship do not work." The Jews do not have to "be governed by the principles that maintain in a democracy like the United States. . . . The Jews were, are, and always shall remain a peculiar people, and the reason why a 'reversion' should be 'sanctioned' in their case, and why it certainly will come to pass, is because Jehovah has so ordained it."[39]

Rarely in their interpretations did Bible teachers grapple with the practical or legal issues involved in acquiring such large swaths of Arab territory. Overwhelmingly, premillennialists rejected all Arab claims to Palestine. God owned the Promised Land and had deeded it to the children of Abraham through Isaac, not Ishmael. The current conflict between Arabs and Jews was nothing more than the continuation of the biblical feud between Isaac and Ishmael, the half-brother sons of Abraham. According to the Bible, then, God chose the Jews but rejected the Arabs.[40] The descendants of Ishmael were usurpers who were being controlled by communist, Nazi, or even satanic influences.[41] Arab antipathy against the gospel was even more serious. According to Keith Brooks, "The Arab and Moslem world is not only anti-Semitic, but is out and out anti-Christ."[42]

In light of such pervasive anti-Arab thinking, it is surprising that any dispensationalists were willing to take Arab claims seriously. One exception was W. F. Smalley. Not long after the riots of 1929, he published "Another View of the Palestine Situation" in the *King's Business* and argued that the predicament in Palestine was much more complicated than most dispensationalists recognized. Since both Jews and Arabs had obtained Palestine through conquest, neither could claim rights to it on that basis alone. Furthermore, just as the British had made promises to the Jews about a national homeland, they had promised Palestine to the Arabs before issuing the Balfour Declaration. The heart of Smalley's argument had to do with commonsense fairness and the principle of self-determination: "It is easy to forget that Palestine has, after these years of freedom for Jewish immigration, some 163,000 Jews as over against about 635,000 so-called Arabs. Shall the minority rule?" What would the residents of present-day California do if a foreign power decided they should relinquish their land to descendants of the Indians who had lived there before white settlers came? "It is altogether likely that the inhabitants of California would do as much as the Arabs do today." Smalley was a dispensationalist who believed in the eventual restoration of the Jews, but he had a hard time believing that God would approve of such an unjust approach as the Balfour Declaration. "I want to see the Jew given every right that the Arab has, but I do not like to see three-quarters of the population threatened with being ruled by the other one-fourth."[43]

The challenge for dispensationalists was staying true to their reading of the Bible while at the same time facing the ethical issues involved in the Arab-Zionist dispute. In an article in the *Sunday School Times,* T. A. Lambie struggled over two contradictory truths: God had given the land to the Jews, but the Arabs had legitimate legal rights to the same territory.

> Of course the [Arab] inhabitants of the land do not want them [the Jewish immigrants]. Neither did the Canaanites of old want them, nor the Jebusites, nor any of the inhabitants of the ancient land, and yet they came and they are coming again. God has decreed it. It must be so.
>
> Of course their right to the land cannot be maintained apart from God. . . . The Arab people in the land do have rights from almost every human viewpoint. These rights can never be ruthlessly trampled under foot, and it is difficult to imagine their having a change of heart and becoming willing to admit the Jews.
>
> An irresistible force seems to be meeting an immovable body and how God's purpose for Israel will work out in its inflexible course we can only wonder. It will be worked out, and all that most of us can do about it is to watch, to pray, and to believe.[44]

One can detect a cognitive dissonance here: If one spent too much time thinking about it, one could honestly see the Arab side of the argument. For the sake of staying true to the divine plan, however, one simply had to lay aside such concerns. In the final analysis, dispensationalists believed that Bible prophecy settled the issue. The Arabs had to adjust to God's plan for them, which did not include possessing Palestine in the end times. Of course, no one really expected the Arabs or their supporters to accept this view of things. Dispensationalists were being quite consistent: They believed that *all* nations except Israel would suffer the consequences of being at cross-purposes with the divine plan. Of course, not everyone viewed the complex issues of the Middle East in this way, and issues of fairness and rightful claim to the land would continue to challenge premillennialists for decades to come.

Independence and Expansion

Despite efforts by Great Britain and the United Nations, no partition plan was acceptable to the Arab majority, which was unwilling to give up any of its land for a Jewish state. Britain declared its intention of defending its interests until its departure date in May 1948 but would not enforce any resolution of the conflict, including the U.N.'s. While they prepared to leave Palestine, the British did nothing to stop the increasing level of violence between Arabs and Jews. Everyone knew that diplomacy would not decide the outcome of this dispute. Both sides prepared for the war that now appeared to be inevitable.

The Birth of the State of Israel

In November 1947, after the U.N. approved the resolution for partition and the Arab side rejected it, the war for Israeli independence began, with each side attempting to secure territory before the British pullout. A turning point in this struggle occurred in April 1948, when *Irgun* forces under Menachem Begin attacked the Arab village of Deir Yassin near Jerusalem and killed 250 civilians. The Arabs retaliated by attacking a Jewish medical convoy on the way to the Hadassah Hospital and Hebrew University on Mount Scopus, killing 77 doctors, nurses, students, and patients. Terror spread on both sides. As a result, Arabs began to leave areas with a sizable Jewish population, especially around Jaffa and Tel Aviv, fearing that they too would be massacred. By the middle of May, over 300,000 Arabs had either fled or been driven from their homes, depending on who is doing the telling, most seeking protection in neighboring Arab countries.[45] By the end of the war, the number of Arab refugees had increased to over 700,000, which was roughly the size of the entire Jewish population.

On May 14 in Tel Aviv, David Ben-Gurion declared the birth of the state of Israel. The next day the British lowered the Union Jack and left Palestine. Armies from Syria, Lebanon, Iraq, Transjordan, and Egypt invaded and began attacking Jewish strongholds, hoping to destroy the state of Israel before it could take root. The Arab forces had the advantage in numbers of troops, better artillery, and more aircraft, but their efforts were not coordinated and faltered quickly. Though Israel's survival seemed likely after only a few days, thanks especially to the United States' rapid recognition of Israeli statehood, a fierce battle raged over Jerusalem. The Jews tried to occupy the city immediately after the British withdrawal but were prevented by the quick arrival of the Transjordanian Arab Legion, commanded by British general John Glubb. A U.N.-brokered cease-fire went into effect on June 11 but lasted less than a month. Two more cease-fires followed, but they did not hold either. With each renewal of the conflict, the Israelis expanded the territory under their control. Finally, in the winter and spring of 1949, separate armistices were signed between Israel and the Arab states that had attacked it, with the exception of Iraq. Shortly thereafter, Israel became a member of the United Nations, with questions about the status and return of the Arab refugees left unresolved.

The new Israel contained upper Galilee in the north, the coast line from Lebanon to the Gaza Strip on the west, and the Negev in the south, which was much more territory than had been included in the original U.N. partition proposal. All of the West Bank of the Jordan River, the biblical Judea and Samaria, remained in Arab hands. In 1950, the West Bank was annexed by the Hashemite kingdom of Jordan (with the addition of the West Bank, the "trans" was no longer needed). A year later, agents of Al-Husseini assassinated Jordan's King Abdullah while he visited the Al-Aqsa Mosque in Jerusalem. Standing next to King Abdullah when he was killed was his young grandson Hussein, who later became king of Jordan himself.

Jerusalem was never internationalized, as proposed in the original U.N. resolution. Ironically, while Palestine was not partitioned, Jerusalem was. It remained a divided city, half Israeli and half Jordanian, with a no-man's-land and a "green line" separating the two parts. The Jordanians maintained control over East Jerusalem, including the Old City, the Temple Mount, and the Western Wall, to which Jews were denied access. The Israelis controlled the newer suburbs of West Jerusalem and began moving their government offices there. Israel, it seemed, was there to stay.

THE BIGGEST FULFILLMENT, ALMOST

It was not as much as dispensationalists had predicted during the previous century, but Jews finally had their own state in Palestine, including part of Jerusalem. Premillennialists were utterly amazed. Louis T. Talbot of the Bible Institute of Los Angeles summed up the prevailing premillennialist view: "I consider it the greatest event, from a prophetic standpoint, that has taken place within the last one hundred years, perhaps even since 70 A.D., when Jerusalem was destroyed."[46] The *Weekly Evangel*'s editor was likewise overwhelmed by the emergence of a new Jewish state: "We well may wonder whether we are awake or lost in sleep merely having a very exciting dream. . . . Beloved, it can't be long until our blessed Lord takes us home to be forever with Him. . . . Oh, joy unspeakable!"[47]

Once Jews had their own state in Palestine, dispensationalists understandably stopped speculating about whether God intended a partial return of the Jews in unbelief. Now even Arno C. Gaebelein was sure that the new state was the beginning of the Jews' final restoration. The *Weekly Evangel,* so ambivalent before about the Zionist state, was also quite certain: "God is permitting them to return to the land He promised them, there to plead with them, to deal with them firmly, and eventually to turn them to Himself." According to the *King's Business,* "The nation is to be born, the people are to return to their land in unbelief, great prosperity will come and, climaxing these conditions, will be the personal appearance of the greatest Jew of all time, the Lord Jesus Christ."[48]

While dispensationalists were thrilled that Jews had their own state, they were still perplexed about its boundaries: The new nation that had been declared in May 1948 looked nothing like the maps of ancient Israel found in the back of their Bibles or hanging on the walls of their Sunday school rooms. Even before independence had been declared, dispensationalists had speculated about the geographical extent of a new Israel. In his 1935 publication, *Rebuilding Palestine according to Prophecy,* George T. B. Davis suggested that eventually the restored Jewish state would have to expand beyond its historic, biblical borders to accommodate the large number of Jews who would want to live there. God promised Abraham the territory "from the river of Egypt unto the great river, the river Euphrates" (Gen. 15:18), which would be sufficient space for all the world's fifteen million Jews.[49] The *Weekly Evangel* was even more generous in its calculations. By expanding the Promised Land to two hundred thousand square miles, there would be room for over two hundred million Jews, though the editors never explained where so many Jews would come from.[50] Twelve years later, the *Weekly Evangel* referred to a story in *Time* magazine in which the new Israeli prime minister Ben-Gurion said that he believed that one day Israel's population would approach ten million. When asked if the current size of Israel was large enough for such a population, the prime minister answered, "I doubt it." The author concluded that the Jews would not be satisfied until they possessed all of Palestine and probably Transjordan too. "That young nation has already fought for and won desired lands and will continually wage successful gains until God's original promise is fulfilled completely."[51]

Even more disconcerting to premillennialists was the fact that the new Israel did not control all of Jerusalem. For over a hundred years, dispensationalist Bible teachers had been instructing the faithful that at the second coming Jesus would set his foot down on the Mount of Olives and enter Jerusalem through the Eastern (or Golden) Gate on the Temple Mount, all of which remained under Muslim control in 1949. Before, during, and after World War II, dispensationalist writers speculated about the building of the third temple: They believed that plans already existed for its construction, Jews were seriously raising money for the project, clandestine Jewish seminaries were training priests in how to conduct the blood sacrifices, and some "irresponsible Jews" were plotting to destroy the Dome of the Rock to make way for the reconstruction.[52] In 1952, an editorial in the *King's Business* spelled out dispensationalists' concern about unfinished prophetic business: "Next in order for Israel will be the complete jurisdiction over Jerusalem, the destruction of the Mosque of Omar [i.e., the Dome of the Rock], the building of a great temple and the re-establishment of their ancient worship."[53] Clearly, then, for Jesus to return, all of Jerusalem needed to be in Jewish hands. According to the *Weekly Evangel,* "When the Jews gain control of Jerusalem, the times of the Gentiles will be ended."[54]

As impressive as the restoration of Israel was from a prophetic perspective, dispensationalists were not yet satisfied. Israel needed to expand its borders, take control of the entire city of Jerusalem, and maintain its sovereignty against all efforts of the United Nations and its Arab enemies to restrict, control, or even eliminate it. In the 1950s and 1960s, dispensationalists had ample opportunity to see their predictions come to pass.

THE SUEZ CRISIS OF 1956

The first opportunity Israel had to increase its territory was during the 1956 Suez Crisis, which Israelis referred to as the Sinai Campaign. Following its war for independence in 1948–49, Israel had been unable to secure permanent peace treaties with any of its Arab neighbors. While the Israelis had hoped that the armistice with Egypt, Lebanon, Syria, and Jordan would be the first step toward permanent peace, the Arabs viewed it as nothing more than a temporary truce and continued to threaten the existence of the Jewish state, boycott its goods, and close the Strait of Tiran and the Suez Canal to its shipping. Such saber rattling played well on the Arab "street" (i.e., public opinion), but the Arab masses did not know that their leaders were secretly negotiating with Israel. The demands of the Arab leaders varied: Husni Za'im of Syria offered to take three hundred thousand Palestinian refugees in return for half of the Sea of Galilee. King Abdullah of Jordan wanted Israel to provide a corridor between his new West Bank territory and the Mediterranean Sea. King Farouq of Egypt offered Israel peace in exchange for the Negev, which constituted nearly two-thirds of Israel's territory. But all that behind-the-scenes conversation achieved nothing: Israel was unwilling to give up land (or sea) for peace, and the Arab leaders never risked going public with their peace efforts for fear of reprisals from their people. In fact, their fears were well-founded. Within a few years of Israeli independence, Husni Za'im was overthrown and put to death in Syria, King Abdullah of Jordan was assassinated in Jerusalem, King Faisal of Iraq was dismembered by an enraged mob in Baghdad, and King Farouq of Egypt was deposed by a military coup.[55]

Out of the political chaos of the Arab world emerged Gamal Abdel Nasser, Egypt's new leader. He quickly became a serious problem for all the major parties in the Middle East. The conservative Arab dynasties condemned his espousal of socialism as heresy and worried about his ability to rouse the Arab masses with his fiery nationalistic and anti-Zionist rhetoric. The British resented their loss of presence and control over the Suez Canal. Nasser had maneuvered them into evacuating the canal zone and then had unilaterally nationalized the waterway. The British also resented the way Nasser bullied their most significant allies in the Arab world, Iraq and Jordan. The French blamed Nasser for fomenting the revolt against their rule in Algeria. Israel was deeply concerned about Nasser's support of guerilla raids into its territory by the *fedayeen* ("self-sacrificers" in Arabic) and his continuing refusal to allow Israeli ships to pass through the Suez Canal and the Strait of Tiran. Such concerns dramatically increased in September 1955 when Nasser announced an enormous arms deal with the Czechs that included "more tanks, guns and jets than those amassed by all the Middle East's armies combined."[56]

In their mounting desperation, Britain, France, and Israel decided to attack and depose Nasser before he had a chance to realize the full benefits of his new military superiority. They concocted a plan that in retrospect looks both fanciful and foolhardy. At the end of September 1956, the three countries agreed on a scheme that included the following: "Israeli forces would feign an assault on Suez, thus providing the Europeans with an excuse to occupy the Canal, ostensibly to protect it. In return, the Israelis would receive air and naval support as its forces destroyed Egypt's army in Sinai and opened the Straits of Tiran."[57] The three countries believed that Nasser could not survive such a loss of face and territory. Supplied with new arms from the French, on October 29, 1956, Israeli paratroopers under Moshe Dayan dropped into the Sinai Desert, only thirty miles from the Suez Canal. In eight days, the Israeli Defense Force (IDF) drove the Egyptian army from the Gaza Strip and the Sinai, thereby opening up the Gulf of 'Aqaba to Israeli ships. As planned, the British and the French seized the Suez Canal, then, on cue, threatened both Egypt and Israel with retaliation if they did not stop fighting. It did not take long for the international community to figure out what was really going on.

Militarily, the plan worked brilliantly, but politically, it was a complete disaster. The world condemned the Israeli attack and the European intervention. The day after the war started, the United States went to the United Nations Security Council with a proposal for an immediate cease-fire and a withdrawal to the old armistice lines. When France and Great Britain vetoed the resolution, the United States got it passed by an emergency session of the General Assembly. Then the Soviet Union threatened to launch an attack against the three invaders if they did not comply. Thanks to the work of Canadian foreign minister Lester Pearson, the United Nations Emergency Force (UNEF) was sent as peacekeepers to the region to provide a buffer between Egyptian and Israeli armies. As a result, France and Britain quickly evacuated the canal zone, but Israel was reluctant to give up territory it considered so vital to its national security. The two superpowers strongly condemned Israel's resistance. The United States threatened to suspend all aid—financial and otherwise—to Israel, and the Soviets renewed their threat to use military force. Israel had no choice but to withdraw from occupied Sinai and Gaza in March 1957, once it received assurances that its ships would not be impeded in the Gulf of 'Aqaba and that the *fedayeen* raids would stop.[58]

Most dispensationalists fully supported the Israeli attack on Egypt and severely criticized the stance taken by the U.S. government. George T. B. Davis thought that America's anti-Israel policy put the United States in great danger:

> Is the United States to be the next nation to fall from her present exalted position through her failure to help Israel in this crucial hour when she is surrounded by foes bent on her destruction? We are standing at the crossroads at this very moment! Will our leaders believe God's Word and take the road of blessing that will lead our nation to still greater glory and victory; or will we forsake God's Word and take a stand against the Jews and so bring upon us terrible judgments of God as in the case of Egypt, Spain, Germany and Great Britain?

Davis and his fellow premillennialists knew that God blessed those who blessed Israel and cursed those who cursed Israel. In his view, American policy in the recent crisis amounted to a curse. The United States had put its need for Arab oil before its obligation to support Israel in the outworking of the divine plan. "Is the oil of the Middle East more important than the blessing of God? As a nation let us take a firm stand to help and strengthen the Jews in the State of Israel."[59] Such sentiment was common among dispensationalists: America's own security and well-being were at stake in such matters. Since they believed that Bible prophecy made Israeli expansion inevitable, dispensationalists expected wars to continue as Israel extended its borders at Arab expense.[60]

Some dispensationalists were beginning to catch on to the complexities of the Middle East situation. Possibly the isolation and widespread condemnation that Israel experienced after its invasion of Sinai was part of the divine plan too. After all, the prophets had predicted that in the last days Israel would find itself surrounded on every side by hostile powers and that the decisive battle of Armageddon would include nations intent on destroying Israel once and for all. Thus, Israel's miscalculation was actually an important step in setting up the end-times antipathy of the nations. William L. Hull took this line in his 1964 book, *Israel—Key to Prophecy*. He argued that Israel's action in the Suez Crisis and America's strong condemnation had actually set up Russia's future invasion of Palestine, which would be another step toward Armageddon and the return of Christ. Thus, even though America should have supported Israel, its failure to do so had served God's plan extremely well.[61]

The Suez Crisis prompted another lively discussion among evangelicals about the issue of prophetic fulfillment and ethics. While the Suez Crisis was still smoldering, *Christianity Today,* the new flagship magazine of the post–World War II evangelical renaissance, published a revealing debate between Oswald T. Allis and Wilbur M. Smith over recent events in the Holy Land. Allis was a highly regarded Old Testament professor from Princeton Theological Seminary who approached his topic without dispensationalist understandings of the present or the future. In his article "Israel's Transgression in Palestine," he expressed deep sympathy for what Jews suffered in the Holocaust but condemned Jewish actions in the Holy Land. He stated that Jews had no right "to take possession of a large part of Palestine and to force hundreds of thousands of Arabs out of it. . . . Two wrongs do not make a right." He fully understood why the Arabs were incensed by the Jewish occupation of their land and their intention to settle more and more Jewish immigrants in it. Allis believed that Christians should resist lending their support to such an unethical undertaking: "Should Christians be willing to plunge the nations into a third world conflict just to restore unbelieving Jews to, and maintain them in, a land from which they were driven nearly two thousand years ago? We believe the verdict of history will be, No! May God grant that this verdict not be written in rivers of blood." For Allis, Israel was "an unjust restoration."[62]

Wilbur M. Smith was considered a dispensationalist intellectual, one of the founding professors of Fuller Theological Seminary. His article "Israel in Her Promised Land" presented a standard premillennialist defense of Israel. He argued that the Bible authorized the restoration of the Jews, whose presence had made a once barren land burst with productivity. In contrast, the Arabs had been "a curse to the land," as centuries of their occupation made clear. For Smith and his fellow dispensationalists, Israel's presence and expansion were simply part of God's plan of the ages. God promised the land to the Jewish people, and God never reneges on a promise. Bible believers needed to support God's plan no matter what, since not even the Antichrist would be able to stop what God had started in the Holy Land.[63]

Dispensationalists could always dismiss someone such as Allis because he had never learned to "rightly divide the word of truth" along dispensational lines. But dealing with someone like Paul S. Allen was more difficult. Allen was the president of Simpson Bible College, which was affiliated with the dispensational Christian and Missionary Alliance. Allen believed in Bible prophecy and the fulfillment of all God's promises to Israel, but like the non-dispensationalist Allis, he was deeply bothered by what was happening in Palestine. "God does not need to use questionable methods in bringing about the fulfillment of prophecy." While Allen believed that the Jewish restoration had been prophesied, he pointed out that Israel had been founded "in unbelief." "Possibly that unbelief will encourage methods incompatible with the Christian sense of justice." In other words, Christians were not obligated to approve of whatever Israel did, even though their actions could contribute to the fulfillment of prophecy. "The Israel of today must justify its acts, not in terms of its ultimate destiny (which is not universally recognized or accepted) but in terms of the moral conscience of the nations of today." Christians were not to lose sight of the fact that the ends did not justify the means. "If Israel's reactions to probing along its borders seem out of proportion to the provocations suffered—admittedly a two-eyes-for-an-eye policy of retaliation—the Christian is duty-bound to apply the measuring stick of moral values as he knows them."[64]

Here was an attempt to grapple with the ambiguities and even the contradictions within God's prophetic plan. While the future was determined and history would reach its prophesied end, Christians were not obligated to support and approve of everything that happened along the way. While Allen stated that "God does not need to use questionable methods in bringing about the fulfillment of prophecy," the fact was that sometimes in the past God had apparently done exactly that. As the Old Testament made clear, God used the evil that people did to further the divine plan (one remembers the Babylonians as instruments of God's judgment against Israel), but, according to Allen, believers were not to be a party to such evil when it occurred. Allen seemed to be saying that it was possible to see the founding and the expansion of Israel as parts of God's plan without approving of the methods used by the Israelis to achieve them. This amounted to condemning the methods but cheering the results. For most dispensationalists, such a way of looking at things was too tortured and raised too many questions about God's ways in the world. In practical terms, what was one to do with such a perspective: speak out against Israel's unethical behavior and thereby give comfort and support to its enemies, then affirm that the results of such unethical behavior were part of God's promises? It was much easier to give blanket support to Israel, then let God worry about the means by which the divine plan unfolded. For most dispensationalists, then, it was enough to know that God was in control of events and had much more work to do in the Middle East.

THE SIX-DAY WAR OF JUNE 1967

To Jews and dispensationalists alike, the year 1967 turned out to be as miraculous as 1948. In the decade after the Suez Crisis, Israel experienced significant growth and what passed for relative peace. Its population grew to roughly three million, and its relationship with the United States under presidents Kennedy and Johnson deepened. The Israeli economy was robust, and the IDF grew in size, armaments, and élan to the point where most Israelis believed they could handle whatever the Arabs threw at them. Yet the pressure against them also increased during this period.

In 1958, there was a violent revolution in Iraq and attempted coups in Lebanon and Jordan. Nasser sought closer relations with the Soviet Union, then stunned the world by uniting with Syria to form the United Arab Republic, a pro-Soviet socialist state. This union lasted until only 1961, when a military takeover in Syria broke it apart. Two years later, after another coup, Syria became the most aggressive Soviet surrogate in the region. In the meantime, Egypt became bogged down in a civil war in Yemen. Though the anti-Israel/pro-war rhetoric emanating from Arab capitals remained constant and fierce, in the early 1960s, there was little chance of Arabs mounting a coordinated attack against the Jewish state.

In 1964, Nasser brought together leaders from Arab states in the region to form the United Arab Command in an attempt to standardize Arab military hardware and prepare for a final war of liberation in Palestine. Planners estimated that the UAC would not be ready to attack until 1967. Again, this attempt to unify Arabs against Israel did not get off the ground because Western-supplied Arab states did not want to standardize weapons with those supplied by the Soviets, and none of the armies wanted to put themselves under Egyptian command.

Arab unity withered under the heat of old and new rivalries. Syria took the initiative in provoking Israel long before the Arab states were ready to go to war. In 1964, Syria attempted to dam up the headwaters of the Jordan River to thwart Israel's plans to divert its water to irrigate the Negev. As expected, the Israelis bombed the Syrian earthworks, which provoked a Syrian response, then an Israeli response, then responses ad infinitum. Syria also became the primary source of guerilla strikes against Israel, which escalated dramatically in late 1964. Syria then attempted to destabilize Jordan by launching *al-Fatah* (a violent anti-Israeli guerrilla band founded by Yasser Arafat in 1965) terrorist attacks against Israel from Jordanian soil, which brought on stiff retaliation by the IDF in Jordan's West Bank territory—and a crackdown by King Hussein against the more radical Palestinian activities in Jordan.

By mid-1966, the region was even more destabilized due to increasing Soviet arms sales to Syria and its encouragement to step up Syria's anti-Israel propaganda. In October, Egypt and Syria signed a new defense treaty that essentially put Israel in a vice. Following additional guerrilla strikes against Israeli settlements, the IDF attacked the most vulnerable target, Jordanian forces on the West Bank, provoking an angry response from the United States, which saw King Hussein as the best hope among Arab leaders for peace in the region. Other Arab states vilified Jordan for refusing to allow Iraqi and Saudi troops to be stationed on the West Bank, thereby not protecting Palestinians adequately.

Arab rhetoric for war was clearly pushing Arab regimes toward a conflict they were not ready to fight. When a border skirmish in the Golan Heights turned into a mini air war between Israeli and Syrian fighter jets in April 1967, the Syrians were easily bested—over the skies of Damascus for all to see—but the Egyptians did not rally to Syria's defense, demonstrating how feeble their defense pact really was. Nevertheless, Nasser believed that he had to make a stand in the Sinai to prevent what the Arab world believed was an imminent Israeli attack on Syria. In the middle of May, Egypt moved a substantial military force into the Sinai and closed down the Strait of Tiran to Israeli ships, which Israel considered an act of war. Nasser also secured the departure of the United Nations Emergency Force, the peacekeepers who had stood between Egyptian and Israeli forces in the Sinai and Gaza. The stage was set for full-scale war.

The mood in Israel turned to despair as Israelis awaited what many feared would be another Holocaust and the destruction of the nation. Israel used the next three weeks to call up reserves and get ready for a multi-front war. Then on June 5, the Israelis made a preemptive strike against the Egyptian air force and essentially destroyed it on the ground in a matter of hours. Egyptian government-controlled radio falsely broadcast that the attacking Israeli air force had been annihilated and claimed an Egyptian victory, which made Jordan and Syria eager to enter the fray. In the meantime, the Israelis, under General Ariel Sharon and others, broke through Egyptian defenses in the Gaza Strip and the Sinai and drove quickly to the Suez Canal, which prompted most of the Egyptian army to retreat to Cairo. Though pockets of strong Egyptian resistance remained, Israel had essentially neutralized its most formidable enemy in two days. The IDF next engaged Jordanian forces on the West Bank and Syrian forces in the Golan Heights, effectively driving them from those territories as well.[65]

The capture of Jerusalem was the single biggest story of that incredible week. On Wednesday morning, June 7, the third day of the war, the IDF surrounded the Old City of Jerusalem, then entered it from the northeast through St. Stephen's (or Lion's) Gate. It was a short distance from there to the Temple Mount. Jordanian troops put up a fight, but the IDF overwhelmed them quickly. Soon hundreds of Israeli soldiers were swarming over the sacred site. A few of them raised an Israeli flag on the Dome of the Rock, but their real objective was the Western Wall.

The Israeli troops, however, did not know how to get there. Jews had not been to the wall for nineteen years and had never been able to access it from the Temple Mount. An old Arab man gave them directions through the Mughrabi Gate. As the soldiers moved down the stairs to the base of the wall, they met up with other Israeli soldiers who had fought their way into the Holy City through the Zion Gate to the west. Hundreds of hardened Israeli soldiers then converged on the wall, weeping, singing, and dancing. The IDF's chief rabbi, Brigadier Shlomo Goren, arrived with a Torah scroll in one hand and a shofar in the other. It was the first time anyone had blown the shofar at the wall since 1929.[66]

Now that the Israelis controlled the Temple Mount and the wall, they had to decide what to do with them. According to Major General Uzi Narkiss, who had led the Israeli attack on the Old City, the initial reaction of Rabbi Goren was less than charitable. After stepping off what he believed were the outlines of the second temple, the rabbi urged General Narkiss to blow up the Dome of the Rock and clear the site once and for all, but the general refused. In fact, the Israelis moved quickly to assure Muslims that their holy places would be safe in an Israeli-controlled Jerusalem. Moshe Dayan, the Israeli defense minister, went to the Temple Mount the afternoon of its capture and ordered the lowering of the Israeli flag from the dome. He then conferred with Muslim leaders. Dayan promised that while officially the Temple Mount would remain in Israeli hands, Muslims would retain full control of their holy places there. Dayan insisted that the ban against Jews visiting the mount must be lifted, though he agreed that Jews would not be allowed to set up a place of worship there. Their holy site would be the Western Wall, over which Muslims would no longer have any control. Later on a rabbinic ruling forbade Jews from even visiting the Temple Mount for reasons of ceremonial purification (more on that later). In practical terms, that was the only way to prevent a holy war pitting Israel against the entire Islamic world.

While Muslims were relieved to retain control over the Dome of the Rock and the Al-Aqsa Mosque, they were outraged by what Israelis did to the area in front of the Western Wall. The war ended on Saturday, June 10. At midnight, dozens of bulldozers entered the Old City and went to work on the Arab Mughrabi neighborhood, which fronted the wall. By morning all the homes were gone, and hundreds of Arab people were homeless. The destruction was necessary, according to Israeli officials, to accommodate all the Israelis who wanted access to their most sacred space. Three days later, two hundred thousand Jews filled the newly created plaza to celebrate the holiday of Shavuot.

For even secular Jews, the recapture of Jerusalem was a religious experience. For centuries, Jews had been praying at their annual Passover

Seder that it would be celebrated "next year in Jerusalem." The desire to occupy Jerusalem's Old City was seared into Jewish consciousness, for many the most powerful symbol of Jewish identity and peoplehood. Now the Old City was theirs. For religious Zionists such as Rabbi Tzvi Yehudah Kook, however, the capture of the Temple Mount and the Western Wall was a prophetic sign of the nation's imminent redemption, which included the arrival of the Messiah.[67] By the end of June, the Israeli parliament (Knesset) announced the "reunification" of Jerusalem, which amounted to the formal annexation of Arab East Jerusalem, including the Old City and the Temple Mount.[68] The Israelis swore that whatever happened in the other occupied territories, they would never relinquish Jerusalem again.

By any measurement, the Israeli victory was overwhelming. The Egyptians had lost up to 15,000 soldiers, and another 5,000 had been wounded. Jordan's figures were 700 killed and 6,000 wounded or missing. Syria's dead numbered 450, with about 1,800 wounded. Israel counted 800 dead and about three times as many wounded. While Arabs held 15 Israeli POWs, Israel held 5,000 Egyptians, 550 Jordanians, and 365 Syrians. The Arab states also lost significant amounts of their military hardware, especially their combat aircraft. Egypt, for example, lost 85 percent of its war planes on the first day, including all of its bombers. As many as 250,000 Palestinians on the West Bank fled their homes for Jordan when the fighting started, many of them becoming refugees for the second time. The Syrian civilian population also evacuated the Golan Heights. As a result of the war, Israel now occupied the Sinai, the Gaza Strip, the West Bank, and the Golan Heights, which made the country three and a half times its original size.[69]

Egypt, Jordan, Syria, and the rest of the Arab world were humiliated and enraged by the war's outcome. If anything, their animosity against Israel increased. Arab leaders, led by Nasser, immediately began calling for rearmament so that they could finish the war that Israel had begun. For a while, Israel hoped to use the occupation of Arab territory as leverage to jump-start serious peace talks. On June 19, the Israeli cabinet voted to explore the possibility of trading occupied land for bona fide peace with its Arab neighbors, but the Arabs quickly shut that door of opportunity. At a September summit in Khartoum, Nasser led other Arab leaders in stating their three no's: no recognition, no peace, and no negotiations with Israel.[70] Despite such intransigence, other nations began working behind the scenes to find a final solution to the Middle East crisis. Eventually, negotiations led to the passing of U.N. Security Council Resolution 242 in November 1967. The resolution affirmed two basic principles: "Withdrawal of Israeli armed forces from territories occupied in the recent conflict, and Termination of all claims or states of belligerency and respect for and acknowledgment of the sovereignty, territorial integrity and political independence of every State in the area and their right to live in peace within secure and recognized boundaries free from threats or acts of force." The resolution also affirmed the necessity of guaranteeing freedom of navigation in international waters, the just settlement of the refugee problem, and the setting up of demilitarized zones to guarantee territorial integrity.[71]

Israel accepted the resolution but insisted that its leaving of the occupied territories depended on the achievement of lasting peace with its neighbors. Jordan affirmed the resolution. Nasser equivocated. While publically approving it, he privately told his generals that he did not mean it and that they needed to prepare to take back lost territory by force. Iraq and Syria rejected Resolution 242 outright, since it required recognizing Israel's right to exist. It was obvious that there would be no lasting peace in the Middle East any time soon and that Israel had every intention of holding on to the territory it had gained during those incredible six days.[72]

DISPENSATIONALIST SUPPORT FOR AN EXPANDING ISRAEL

For dispensationalists, the Six-Day War was a miracle of God. According to L. Nelson Bell in *Christianity Today,* "That for the first time in more than 2,000 years Jerusalem is now completely in the hands of the Jews gives a student of the Bible a thrill and a renewed faith in the accuracy and validity of the Bible."[73] John F. Walvoord, president of Dallas Seminary and one of the most important dispensational Bible teachers of the 1960s and 1970s, considered the conquest of Jerusalem "one of the most remarkable fulfillments of biblical prophecy since the destruction of Jerusalem in A.D. 70."[74] A variety of authors in an issue of *Moody Monthly* devoted to the war were convinced that God had fought on the Israeli side and that with the taking of Jerusalem, Israel had moved one giant step closer to its rendezvous with the Antichrist, the return of Jesus, and its ultimate redemption.[75]

Dispensationalists' responses to the Six-Day War revealed old themes. Bible prophecy predicted a process leading toward the end of the age, and events in Israel proved that the process was underway and unstoppable. The most significant prophetic outcome of the war was the end of the "times of the Gentiles." For well over a century, premillennialists had been anticipating the time when Jerusalem would return to Jewish control after centuries of Gentile dominance. The capture of the Old City pointed to the prophecy of Luke 21:24: "Jerusalem shall be trodden down of the Gentiles, until the times of the Gentiles be fulfilled." Following the times of the Gentiles, events leading up to the "coming of the Son of Man" would quickly take place.[76] On day four of the Six-Day War, Moody Bible Institute's radio station, WMBI, broadcast a two-hour program on the war and its prophetic significance. The day before the broadcast, the IDF had occupied the Old City, which led a somewhat reticent faculty member, Alan Johnson, to conclude that if the Israelis could hold the Holy City, there was a good possibility that Christ's return could be just around the corner.[77]

Dispensational interpreters overwhelmingly justified Israel's expansion into Arab territory on biblical grounds. An author in *Christian Life* claimed that occupation of the West Bank, Gaza, and Jerusalem was justified on the basis of Psalm 83:1–8, in which Israel's enemies plot to destroy the nation ("Come, and let us cut them off from being a nation; that the name of Israel may be no more in remembrance" [v. 4]), and Obadiah 17–20, in which Israel triumphs over its enemies and takes their land ("But upon mount Zion shall be deliverance, and there shall be holiness; and the house of Jacob shall possess their possessions" [v. 17]).[78]

Bible teachers also warned that God would judge those nations that opposed Israel's right to the land. Biola College (the new name for the Bible Institute of Los Angeles) issued "A Proclamation Concerning Israel and the Nations" shortly after the end of the Six-Day War. After stating that "it appears that recent developments in the Middle East may be preparing the way" for the coming of the Messiah, the proclamation pronounced the familiar warning: "Throughout its history the nation Israel has been the object of opposition and attack by Satan the archenemy of God's purpose and program. Untaught and unholy men have unwittingly cooperated with the devil in this. It is our conviction that the true people of God should not be found in league with those who oppose the will and work of God for Israel."[79]

Biola's proclamation did not directly address the ethical issues involved in Israel's occupation of Arab territory, but other dispensationalists tried to do so. Charles C. Ryrie, prominent theology professor at Dallas Seminary, believed that eventually Israel would occupy all the land from the Nile to the Euphrates and saw the territorial gains in the June 1967 war as part of that process. At the same time, however, he realized that neither side was totally blameless: "And while the efforts of a political state may ultimately be used by God in the mysterious accomplishing of his purpose, his use of the wrath of men does not excuse that wrath or make right the wrongs that the state may commit. In other words, we must not assume that the end justifies the means." Like other Bible teachers before him who pondered God's ways in the world, he sought a biblical analogy to make his point. He found one in the crucifixion of

Jesus. God still held responsible those who conspired to send Jesus to the cross, even though his death was part of God's redemptive plan. "Likewise, the state of Israel is not relieved of its obligation to act responsibly in the community of nations even though the secret purpose of God may be brought to fruition through its actions. Any premillennialist's rejoicing over the apparent nearness of the Lord's return will have to be coupled with sadness over current issues."[80] What Ryrie did not discuss, however, was what Christians were to do when they saw Israel acting unjustly. His silence implied that there was nothing they could do, since the outcome was already determined by God. Certainly, one should not actively oppose Israeli injustice because that would be opposing God's plan. Again, a dispensationalist who was sensitive to ethical issues struggled to make sense of how prophecy was being fulfilled.

Despite Ryrie's caveat, sadness was not the most obvious emotion when premillennialists contemplated Arabs and their cause. In his book *Israeli/Arab Conflict and the Bible,* Wilbur M. Smith wrote of the "perpetual hatred" of the Arabs. "He [the Arab] cannot be said to be distinguished for amiability and love of peace. He personally shall be the aggressor against all others."[81] Charles L. Feinberg, the dean of Talbot Theological Seminary, portrayed Arabs as habitually belligerent. As a result, "God will in His own good time cast out the sons of Ishmael, despite all their devisings and intrigues, and will settle the sons of Isaac."[82] According to William Ward Ayer, "Arabs had lived in continual warfare with the rest of the world."[83] It was difficult to show sympathy for such people. More than ever, then, after the Six-Day War, dispensationalists saw Arabs as foils to God's plans in the Middle East and on the side of Satan and the Antichrist.

By 1970, therefore, dispensationalists were full of confidence. Despite great difficulties, the nation of Israel had been established and had expanded its borders in the Middle East. Antipathy and hatred for Israel was unquenchable among Muslim nations and the Communist Bloc. The threat of nuclear war was increasing. On the home front, American dispensationalists noted the unraveling of the American social order in what sociologist Francis Fukuyama called "the great disruption."[84] As bad as things looked elsewhere, inside the dispensationalist community, things had never looked better. In fact, Bible teachers were about to enter the glory days of their movement, in which they reached more people and developed more markets than ever before.

7

Dispensationalists Engage a Changing World

The founding and expansion of Israel propelled dispensationalists into a new period of visibility and success. Sure that prophetic confirmations were there for everyone to see, Bible teachers took their message into markets never penetrated before. As a result, Bible prophecy became a growth industry in the last three decades of the twentieth century. With confidence, premillennialists made their move into the popular culture by mastering mass media. Dispensationalists also entered the world of politics, which surprised outsiders and even themselves. After decades of viewing world events as spectators in the stands, premillennialists became not only more visible but also more involved. No longer content to be observers only, they descended to the playing field and became important participants in the world they were sure was rapidly passing away.

Entering the Mainstream: Dispensationalism and Popular Culture

After the Six-Day War, dispensationalists were sure that more than ever the world was ready for their message, and they pushed hard to bring it to as many people as possible. Their breakthrough occurred in the print media with the publication of Hal Lindsey's *Late Great Planet Earth* in 1970.[1] A flood of prophetic books followed Lindsey's, as did other kinds of media. By the early 1980s, Hilton Sutton's appraisal was beyond question: "Bible prophecy has come into its own."[2] In the decades that followed, it would have an impact far beyond its traditional clientele.

THE BREAKTHROUGH BOOK: *THE LATE GREAT PLANET EARTH*

The author of dispensationalism's breakthrough book was Hal Lindsey. Born in Houston in 1929 and raised in a nominally Christian family, he joined the Coast Guard during the Korean War after studying business for two years at the University of Houston. By his mid-twenties, Lindsey was a tugboat captain in New Orleans. Converted at twenty-six after a personal crisis, he then moved back to Houston, where he attended "Colonel" Bob Thieme's dispensationalist church. A few years later he sensed a call to the ministry and enrolled at Dallas Theological Seminary, even though he did not have a college degree. At Dallas, Lindsey honed his premillennialism under dispensational giants such as John F. Walvoord, Charles C. Ryrie, and Dwight Pentecost.

Lindsey graduated from seminary in 1962, then became director of the Campus Crusade for Christ chapter at U.C.L.A. Lindsey quickly emerged as an impressive figure on campus. He was young, built like a football player, and, thanks partly to his soothing Southern drawl, an engaging speaker. Students who got close to him were amazed by his knowledge of current events and the Bible, which he could read in Hebrew and Greek. He was also well-versed in the revolutionary youth culture that was sweeping college campuses in the 1960s. Despite his rigorous theological training at Dallas Seminary, Lindsey had a knack for translating his message into vivid, everyday language that communicated clearly to the "now generation."

In the late 1960s, Lindsey turned his attention to Bible prophecy. In the spring of 1968, a number of area Campus Crusade chapters sponsored a lecture series on the end times. Five evenings in a row, Lindsey spoke in the grand ballroom of the student union at U.C.L.A., drawing larger crowds each night. From the same stage on which Timothy Leary had promoted the use of LSD and Angela Davis had preached Marxist revolution, Lindsey carefully explained God's plan for the ages, the restoration of Israel, the rapture of the church, the rise of the Antichrist, the great tribulation, and the battle of Armageddon. He showed how key prophetic passages predicted current events, traced on huge maps future battle plans, and made his case that the end was near. His motives were blatantly evangelistic. He pressed home the same question that dispensationalist preachers had always asked: Do you want to be left behind when Jesus comes? Scores of college students made commitments to Christ, which was the point of the lecture series. Lindsey clearly was on to something: Bible prophecy resonated with young people faced with the hard realities of Vietnam, the threat of nuclear war, and the breakdown of American institutions. As he would soon discover, Bible prophecy also resonated with parents who were deeply disturbed by the social revolution picking up speed all around them. Lindsey reworked his lectures, then published them as *The Late Great Planet Earth.*[3]

Lindsey followed the same prophetic plotlines that dispensationalist Bible teachers had been using for over a century. What made Lindsey's book different were the times in which it was published. Earlier authors could only point to future fulfillments, but Lindsey claimed that the puzzle pieces of prophecy were already falling into place for all to see. Such arguments were not possible before 1948 and 1967. Lindsey's ability to make connections between the Bible's prophecies and current events gave his book power to attract an audience. For many people, reading *The Late Great Planet Earth* was like getting an advance copy of tomorrow's newspaper.

Lindsey believed that the nations were lining up according to biblical predictions. Israel was back in Palestine and in control of Jerusalem. European nations were forming a common market, which would soon morph into a revived Roman Empire. The Soviet Union, Iran, and the Arab world were the sworn enemies of Israel and could easily combine forces to attack. The Chinese were ready to flex their growing military might and move into the Middle East. There was widespread talk in Israel about rebuilding the temple. The existence and proliferation of nuclear weapons made the kind of rapid and widespread slaughter the Bible predicted possible if not probable. There were other signs of the times as well: a decline of morality; a proliferation of drug use; a rejection of authority and the scourge of lawlessness; the spread of religious apostasy, the occult, and Eastern religions; an increase in the number of earthquakes, famines, epidemics, and the like. In other words, all the elements needed to flesh out dispensationalists' expectations were present, and Lindsey fit them together in a sensational there's-no-doubt-about-it style.

The founding of the state of Israel in 1948 was the key to understanding everything else. Lindsey's crucial text was the Olivet Discourse (Matthew 24), in which Jesus revealed the signs leading up to his coming at the end of the age: "Now learn a parable of the fig tree; When his branch is yet tender, and putteth forth leaves, ye know that summer is nigh. So likewise ye, when ye shall see all these things, know that it is near, even at the doors. Verily I say unto you, this generation shall not pass, till all these things be fulfilled. Heaven and earth shall pass away, but my words shall not pass away" (vv. 32–35).

Like other dispensationalists before him, Lindsey believed that the fig tree was the symbol for Israel. Thus, Lindsey concluded, "When the Jewish people, after nearly 2,000 years of exile, under relentless persecution, became a nation again on May 14, 1948, the 'fig tree' put forth its first leaves." Now the implications of Jesus' other words were obvious: "This generation shall not pass, till all these things be fulfilled." Lindsey asked then answered the crucial question: "What generation? Obviously in context, the generation that would see the signs—chief among them the rebirth of Israel. A generation in the Bible is something like forty years. If this is a correct deduction, then within forty years or so of 1948, all these things could take place. Many scholars who have studied Bible prophecy all their lives believe that this is so." Israel's founding "has now set the stage for the other predicted signs to develop in history. It is like the key piece of a jigsaw puzzle being found and then having the many adjacent pieces rapidly fall into place."[4]

For all its apocalyptic flash and fury, *The Late Great Planet Earth* was primarily an evangelistic exercise. Lindsey wrote the book to lead people to Christ and encourage believers in holy living. "As history races toward this moment, are you afraid or looking with hope for deliverance [in the rapture]? The answer should reveal to you your spiritual condition. One way or another history continues in a certain acceleration toward the return of Christ. Are you ready?"[5] He concluded the book with another evangelistic appeal: "If you are not sure that you have personally accepted the gift of God's forgiveness which Jesus Christ purchased by bearing the judgment of a holy God that was due your sins, then you should do it right now wherever you are. . . . Right at this moment, in your own way, thank Jesus for dying for your sins and invite Him to come into your heart."[6] His word to believers was also tried-and-true dispensationalist advice. They should submit to the Holy Spirit's guidance, read the Bible daily, share the gospel with others, and be ready for the rapture, whether it occurred now or later. "We should plan our lives as though we will be here our full life expectancy, but live as though Christ may come today."[7]

Unlike other dispensational books from the past, Lindsey's book found its way into "secular" bookstores, drugstores, airport newsstands, and supermarkets. The times were right for such a book because American popular culture was suddenly awash with interest in the supernatural and the paranormal. Shelf stockers sometimes had a hard time deciding where to put the book. Did it belong in the religion section, next to the Bibles and devotional materials? Or, given its sensational subject matter and style, should it be displayed with books about pop-culture fads such as ESP,

UFOs, pyramid power, astrology, parapsychology, out-of-body experiences, and the occult? Maybe it belonged in the section on science fiction or pseudo-science or among the other books warning of some impending economic or ecological catastrophe? Even some non-dispensationalist Christians had difficulty telling the difference between Lindsey's book and Erik Von Daniken's *Chariots of the Gods* or Immanuel Velikovsky's *Worlds in Conflict.*[8] National bookstore chains such as B. Dalton and Waldenbooks created a new section to accommodate titles they judged to be more or less in the same genre: "Prophecy, New Age, and Occult."[9] Yet no matter where Lindsey's book was displayed, it sold. According to the *New York Times*, *The Late Great Planet Earth* was the best-selling nonfiction book of the 1970s. Eventually, it was translated into over fifty languages and sold more than thirty-five million copies.[10] No other dispensationalist in history had ever generated such an audience.

Lindsey became a one-man prophecy conglomerate. A film version of *The Late Great Planet Earth* appeared in commercial theaters in 1978. Narrated by Orson Welles, the movie was done in documentary style, with various religious, military, diplomatic, and scientific experts painting more or less the same picture of a world careening out of control on its way to certain doom. As usual, Lindsey concluded the film with an evangelistic appeal to accept Christ before it was too late. He also produced a steady stream of audio- and videotapes, appeared on countless Christian radio and cable TV programs, led tours to the Holy Land, published prophecy newsletters, and for a while was the pastor of a local church not far from the U.C.L.A. campus.

Despite his diversification into all aspects of the prophecy business, Lindsey never strayed far from the printed page. He continued to write books, twenty-eight at last count, which were mainly updates or variations of *The Late Great Planet Earth.*[11] Though none came close to the success of his first book, they certainly kept his name and particular view of the future before the public. Lindsey claims that he has sold over forty million books. In the mid-1990s, Lindsey founded his own company, Western Front, Ltd., to publish his writings.[12] He also has his own website, which features "News You Can Use to Wake the 'Dead'" (www.hallindseyoracle.com).

Lindsey's success opened the door for other dispensationalist teachers and writers. After the Six-Day War but especially after *The Late Great Planet Earth*, the Bible prophecy field exploded. Virtually all the celebrity clerics of the so-called electronic church taught the gospel of premillennialism, including Oral Roberts, Rex Humbard, Kenneth Copeland, Jimmy Swaggart, Jerry Falwell, and Jim Bakker. Various "prophecy in the news" programs aired on commercial and cable TV: Charles Taylor's *Today in Bible Prophecy,* Stuart McBirnie's *News Commentary,* and *Jack Van Impe Presents.* New media enterprises such as Paul Crouch's Trinity Broadcasting

Network (TBN) and Pat Robertson's Christian Broadcasting Network (CBN) featured premillennialist teaching morning, noon, and night. In addition to the new exposure on cable television, dispensationalism continued to expand its reach into the culture through a flood of new publications and other products. By the 1990s, premillennialists had their own version of the Amazon.com online bookstore, armageddonbooks.com, where one could find a huge selection of dispensationalist books, DVDs and VHS videos, prophecy charts, and other materials, plus links to 280 prophecy websites. One no longer had to go to Sunday school to learn about the Antichrist, Armageddon, and the last days. Bible prophecy was now one more rest stop on the information superhighway.[13]

THE NEW RECORD SETTER: LEFT BEHIND

None of the new wave of prophecy writers ever came close to Lindsey's sales numbers until Tim LaHaye's Left Behind fiction series hit stores in the mid-1990s. Lindsey tried his hand at writing a novel about the end of the world (*Blood Moon,* 1996), but LaHaye quickly dominated the field of prophecy fiction. Born in 1926 in Detroit, LaHaye graduated from Bob Jones University and became a Baptist minister, first in Minneapolis, then in El Cajon, California. LaHaye was a Christian entrepreneur who left his mark on the San Diego area. Not only did his church grow rapidly, but he also founded a number of Christian schools, including Christian Heritage College.

LaHaye was a busy man, but not too busy to write books. Like Lindsey, LaHaye knew how to analyze the culture and speak to it. His first success in publishing came in the area of self-help and psychology. He wrote books about overcoming depression, managing anger, understanding the male temperament, learning self-control, and living the Christian life. He and his wife, Beverly, wrote a rather graphic sex manual for Christians, *The Act of Marriage: The Beauty of Sexual Love,* which sold over 2.5 million copies.[14] His *Battle for the Mind,* which warned of the pervasive threat of secular humanism, was one of the New Christian Right's opening salvos.[15] In fact, LaHaye was a founding board member of the Moral Majority, and he and Beverly started conservative Christian organizations of their own: the American Coalition for Traditional Values (1984) and Concerned Women for America (1979).[16]

LaHaye also wrote a number of books about Bible prophecy starting in the early 1970s.[17] Afraid that belief in the pretribulation rapture was slipping in evangelical circles, in the early 1990s, LaHaye cofounded the Pre-Trib Research Center, which sponsored academic conferences on dispensationalism and published a *Pre-Trib Newsletter.*[18] In the mid-1980s, he attempted a novel about the second coming but was unhappy with the results. If LaHaye was ever going to write such a novel, he would need help. By the mid-1990s, he had found the perfect partner in Jerry Jenkins, who had already authored 140 Christian books. LaHaye provided elaborate notes on prophetic passages and chronology, which Jenkins then turned into exciting plotlines involving a winsome cast of characters. The result was a projected twelve-volume adventure series that followed a group of people through the horrific seven years of the great tribulation.

The plot centers on Rayford Steele, a commercial airline pilot with a roving eye whose recently converted wife is a student of end-times prophecies. Rayford is clearly not interested, at least until the unthinkable happens. While he is piloting a jumbo jet from Chicago O'Hare to London, the flight attendants make a chilling discovery: Dozens of passengers (including everyone under age twelve) are missing. Spread over their now-empty seats are their clothing, jewelry, and even dental fillings and surgical pins. It is as though their bodies simply vaporized and went elsewhere. Soon Steele's 747 is ordered back to O'Hare, where Rayford finds a world in chaos. Thanks to missing pilots and air-traffic controllers, planes are going down all over the globe, and freeways are clogged by accidents due to driverless cars. CNN reports that it is the same everywhere: People in large numbers have gone missing, and the resulting panic is spreading. Rayford manages to get home only to find empty beds where his wife and son had spent their last night on earth. Grief stricken, Rayford finally puts two and two together: The rapture has occurred. All true Christians, including his loved ones, had been caught up in the air, just as the Bible said they would be. He and everyone else have been left behind.

Rayford soon teams up with Buck Williams, a senior writer for a major news weekly, plus Rayford's former chief flight attendant and an unconverted minister who had, to his enormous embarrassment, been left behind too. As the truth of their situation sinks in, they make commitments to Christ, then decide what to do next. Rayford and Buck recruit a small band of recent converts, including Rayford's college-age daughter, to resist the evil forces that are gathering all around them. Soon this "tribulation force" finds itself in the thick of things. Because of his recently acquired spiritual insight, Buck is not duped by the charismatic new leader of the U.N., Nicolae Carpathia, who is really the Antichrist. Like apocalyptic Forrest Gumps, Rayford, Buck, and the tribulation force seem to be everywhere and witnesses to everything of prophetic importance, thanks in large part to Rayford's appointment as the Antichrist's personal pilot. While other new Christian converts are tortured and killed, the tribulation force battles behind the scenes and somehow survives. In volume after volume, the dispensationalist scenario unfolds. There is no shortage of explosions, plagues, and mass martyrdoms. Wars break out, natural disasters occur with increasing regularity, and the landscape is littered with millions of dead. Getting left behind is clearly not for the faint of heart.

Published by Tyndale House of Wheaton, Illinois, installments in the Left Behind series have sold in the multi-millions. The first volume, aptly titled *Left Behind,* sold 7 million copies. The second *(Tribulation Force)* sold 4.1 million. Volumes 3 through 9 *(Nicolae, Soul Harvest, Apollyon, Assassins, The Indwelling, The Mark,* and *Desecration)* each sold in the 3 to 3.5 million range. Volume 9, *Desecration,* was the best-selling novel in 2001, and volume 10, *The Remnant,* had a first print run of 2.75 million. So far, then, LaHaye and Jenkins have sold close to 50 million copies. Volume 11, *Armageddon,* hit bookstores in April 2003, and volume 12, *Glorious Appearing,* appeared in March 2004. The authors have also promised a prequel and a sequel to the series. With such sales numbers, LaHaye and Jenkins have replaced Lindsey as the best-selling dispensationalist authors of all time. *Time* magazine estimates that each author has earned over $50 million in royalties, and the end has not yet arrived.[19]

The popularity of the book series generated an extensive Left Behind product line that is available through its own Tyndale House–sponsored website.[20] There is a comic book version called Graphic Novels, audio books, a dramatic audio series, a video series, a Left Behind calendar, and the promise of Left Behind apparel and collectibles. There is also a twenty-six-book Left Behind series for kids about four teenagers who become believers, then band together to evade the Antichrist for the seven-year tribulation. According to Jenkins, the kids' books combine accurate teachings about the end times with a "coming of age" twist since the teens grow into adulthood during those perilous times. These books are popular too, with over ten million copies sold.

Such an unprecedented success story for Christian fiction is largely due to the relatively new marketing strategies adopted by Christian publishers, including Tyndale House. Until recently, Christian books were pretty much confined to "religious" bookstores, but thanks to marketing-savvy book agents who now regularly represent successful evangelical authors, things have changed considerably. Leading the pack of Christian marketers is Alive Communications, Inc., whose agents know how to get the best deals for authors like LaHaye and Jenkins, thereby prodding their publishers to behave more like the bottom-line driven companies who never put ministry over money. Christian publishing houses, many of which have been taken over by secular publishing or communications companies, have begun using tried-and-true sales and marketing techniques to get their products into mainstream outlets such as Dalton Books, Barnes and Noble, Borders, Wal-Mart, Target, and Sam's Club. Thanks to such strategies, even dispensationalist books are now available everywhere.[21]

About the only part of the LaHaye-Jenkins juggernaut that was not a runaway success was *Left Behind: The Movie*. Not long after their first book was published, LaHaye and Jenkins optioned film rights to Namesake Entertainment, an independent Christian film company in Louisville. Namesake unsuccessfully shopped the idea for a *Left Behind* film to major studios in Hollywood, then with time running out on its option contracted with Cloud Ten, a Canadian Christian film company, to produce the movie. Cloud Ten had experience making other prophecy films, most notably the trilogy *Apocalypse* (1998), *Revelation* (1999), and *Tribulation* (2000). Later on LaHaye claimed that Namesake and Cloud Ten promised him a big-budget (forty-million-dollar) Hollywood blockbuster with big-name actors and Spielberg-quality special effects by January 1, 2000.

The result was something considerably less than that. Cloud Ten's budget for the film was only $17.4 million, far more than any other Christian movie ever made but considerably less than needed to produce the kind of film LaHaye wanted. That price tag got barely recognized actors (the exception was Kirk Cameron, who had starred in the 1980s TV sitcom *Growing Pains*) and less than convincing special effects. By typical Hollywood standards, *Left Behind* looked like a B movie. To make matters worse, the film's producer, Paul Lalonde, decided to put the movie out first in video in October 2000, hoping that word of mouth publicity would generate a huge response when the film was released in theaters later on. The videos sold well ($3 million worth by the end of 2000), but they did not produce the kind of interest that Lalonde had expected. On its opening weekend in February 2001, the movie earned only $2.5 million. Sixteen other movies did better at the box office on the same weekend. Good reviews were rare, and some were quite devastating.

Evidently, LaHaye saw it coming. Long before *Left Behind: The Movie* was finished, LaHaye fumed about the quality of the film, its late release date after Y2K fever had dissipated, and its controversial and widely ridiculed "video-first" marketing strategy. In fact, four months before the video version of the movie even came out, LaHaye sued Namesake Entertainment and Cloud Ten for breach of contract.[22] A federal judge dismissed the case,[23] but clearly it was easier to write a series of best-sellers than to make a quality Hollywood film about the tribulation.

As with other pop-culture phenomena, the Left Behind series generated spin-offs. Tyndale House made a deal with Teckno Books, worldwide publishers of Tom Clancy, Robert Ludlum, Dean Koontz, Isaac Asimov, and others, to distribute a new series of trade paperbacks starting in late 2003. *Apocalypse Dawn* was the first in a series of military thrillers by Mel Odom, the author of a series of novels about Buffy the Vampire Slayer. *End of State* by Nessa Hart launched a new line of political thrillers.[24] While the spin-offs will include cameo appearances by the main characters of Left Behind, they will feature new casts of beleaguered Christians trying to survive the great tribulation.[25]

Tim LaHaye likewise has made post–Left Behind plans. In early 2002, he dropped Rick Christian of Alive Communications, who had worked out his deal with Tyndale House, and hired Michael Ovitz of Artists Management, one of Hollywood's leading literary agents. Ovitz got LaHaye a forty-five-million-dollar, four-novel deal with Bantam Dell. Jerry Jenkins, who had actually written the Left Behind novels, was not part of the contract.[26]

The Left Behind books obviously hit a nerve in American culture. The terrorist attacks of September 11, 2001, pushed many people toward an apocalyptic view of their own times. "A *Time*/CNN poll finds that more than one-third of Americans say they are paying more attention now to how the news might relate to the end of the world, and have talked about what the Bible has to say on the subject. Fully 59 percent say they believe the events in *Revelation* are going to come true, and nearly one-quarter think the Bible predicted the Sept. 11 attack." *Time* reporter Nancy Gibbs thinks the impact of the books has been as much political as spiritual.

> To some evangelical readers, the *Left Behind* books provide more than a spiritual guide: they are a political agenda. When they read in the papers about the growing threats to Israel, they are not only concerned for a fellow democratic ally in the war against terror; they are also worried about God's chosen people and the fate of the land where events must unfold in a specific way for Jesus to return. That combination helps explain why some Christian leaders have not only bonded with Jews this winter as rarely before but have also pressed their case in the Bush White House as if their salvation depended on it.[27]

The 1980s: The Dispensationalists Go Political

Actually, dispensationalists combined prophecy and politics long before Left Behind came along. Between *The Late Great Planet Earth* and Left Behind, large numbers of dispensationalists changed their minds about political involvement, deciding it was time to stop being spectators in the stands and to get down on the field to participate in the divine drama that was being played out there.

FINDING POLITICAL IMPLICATIONS

As soon as Bible teachers embraced the results of the Six-Day War as fulfillment of Bible prophecy, the political implications of dispensationalism became apparent. Lindsey wasted no time in taking the insights of his *Late Great Planet Earth* to those who might profit most from such information. He consulted with groups of military planners at the American Air War College and the Pentagon who were interested in his analysis of the Middle East and the coming of World War III. Did such people adjust their military plans to bring them in line with dispensationalism? There is no evidence that they did so, but one cannot help but marvel at the fact that Lindsey got access to them. *The Late Great Planet Earth* was also translated into Hebrew and made widely available in Israel, which was highly unusual for a Christian book. According to Lindsey, it "caught on like wildfire. A great many copies circulated among military men and government officials as well."[28] Such exposure showed that Lindsey and other dispensationalists were ready to think through the practical political implications of their views.

Lindsey's *1980s: Countdown to Armageddon* was one of the first examples of how dispensationalists could blend prophecy and politics if they put their minds to it. Much of the book was a retrospective analysis of *The Late Great Planet Earth*'s predictions. Lindsey was more than satisfied with the accuracy of his earlier study. The Soviet Union had continued to expand its power and influence in the 1970s, as its invasion of Afghanistan in 1973 showed. The Middle East was still a powder keg: In 1973, Israel barely survived the Yom Kippur War, and OPEC challenged the West by temporarily reducing its oil output, thus creating long gas lines and fears for the future in the United States. The Iranian Revolution under Ayatollah Khomeini in 1979 was a new destabilizing force in the Middle East, and in the same year, the common market added its tenth member nation, which made it ready for a takeover by the Antichrist, who was alive and probably holding down a seat in the common market's parliament.[29]

There were surprises in the 1970s too. Lindsey never anticipated the strong peace initiatives of Anwar Sadat in 1971 or his unprecedented trip to Israel in 1977. The Camp David Accords, brokered by President Jimmy Carter in 1978, resulted in an Egyptian-Israeli peace treaty, which included the return of the Sinai to Egypt after the removal of all Israeli settlements there. The accords even laid a framework for a more comprehensive peace in the region later on, hinting that Israel would have to give up additional land for peace.[30] The accords certainly looked like a reversal of the trends established in 1967. With the return of the Sinai and the lessening of tensions in the region, there was a growing possibility of prophetic disconfirmation. Yet Lindsey was not deterred.

He predicted that the Camp David Accords would not last long and that architects for Middle East peace such as Begin and Sadat were doomed to failure or possibly even worse. The Arab world would never accept a real peace with Israel, Lindsey assured his readers in 1980, and he pointed out that Sadat was "in constant danger of being assassinated by militant Arabs," which is exactly what happened the year after Lindsey's book was published.[31]

Following his predictions in *The Late Great Planet Earth,* Lindsey confirmed America's decline during the 1970s.[32] He pointed to its loss of military and diplomatic dominance in the world and regretted that the United States had not used its nuclear power in the late 1940s and 1950s when it had overwhelming strategic superiority.[33] Lindsey knew who was responsible for America's precipitous decline: the Council on Foreign Relations and the Trilateral Commission. The Council on Foreign Relations had controlled the U.S. State Department for almost four decades. The Trilateral Commission, "an international group of the western world's most powerful bankers, media leaders, scholars and government officials bent on radically changing the world in which we live," was responsible for the 1976 election of Jimmy Carter, who in turn loaded his administration with Trilateralists. The result was ominous: "The Trilateral movement is unwittingly setting the stage for the political-economic one-world system the Bible predicts for the last days."[34]

Likewise, political liberalism all but destroyed America's traditional moral and political values. Since FDR's New Deal, the democratic, capitalistic, free-enterprise system had been under attack. A "free lunch mentality" had given rise to an out-of-control welfare system and the spread of socialistic ideas.[35] Such things were prophesied and therefore inevitable. Lindsey affirmed his earlier prediction that by the time the Antichrist emerged on the world scene, America would be a second-rate power thanks to a communist takeover, a surprise nuclear attack, the economic dominance of the European Common Market, or its spreading moral and spiritual corruption. "So from the standpoint of Biblical prophecy, the U.S. must fade from its place of leadership for the west and its former supreme superpower status."[36]

So why not leave it at that, as he had in *The Late Great Planet Earth?* Why not find some consolation in knowing that America was following the prophetic script? Or better yet, why not rejoice that the Bible had once again been proven true by its prophecies? In a clear departure from his earlier work, Lindsey wanted it both ways: He knew that America's decline was certain, but he wanted Christians to do what they could to delay the inevitable. "If some critical and difficult choices are made by the American people right now, it is possible to see the U.S. remain a world power. We could become an equal ally of the European confederation, with each dependent on the other. In that way, America could keep much of its sovereignty and freedom."[37] Specifically, Lindsey advised his readers to demand a rebuilding of the American military: "I believe that the Bible supports building a powerful military force. And the Bible is telling the U.S. to become strong again. A weak military will encourage the Soviet Union to start an all-out war."[38] He urged his fellow citizens to eliminate the influence of the Council on Foreign Relations and the Trilateral Commission: "I believe it is high time for the citizens of this country to clean this 'elite' group out of the Department of State and replace it with some people with common sense and courage." He also challenged Christians to use their power at the ballot box to elect the right kind of leaders who could delay America's rendezvous with disaster: "We need to clean house in Washington and elect a Congress and a President who believe in the capitalist system." If American Christians act now, "America will survive this perilous situation and endure until the Lord comes to evacuate His people."[39]

THE NEW CHRISTIAN RIGHT AND THE DEMISE OF THE SOVIET EMPIRE

Lindsey was not the only premillennialist to issue a call to political action in the late 1970s and early 1980s. Many dispensationalist pastors, Bible teachers, and laypeople mobilized to form the New Christian Right to wage culture war on liberals, feminists, gays, pornographers, Hollywood, and all other perceived destroyers of traditional values. Premillennialists Jerry Falwell, Ed McAteer, and Pat Robertson used their growing media-based networks to recruit large numbers of believers for organizations such as the Moral Majority, the Religious Roundtable, and, later on, the Christian Coalition.[40] Of course, such sudden political involvement raised a number of questions: Why would dispensationalists feel compelled to make things better when they knew they had to get worse before Jesus returned? Why declare culture war if signs of cultural decay were expected in the end times? Why organize politically when they knew from Bible prophecy that such efforts were doomed to failure?

Probably the most obvious answer is that dispensationalists were made up of more than their prophetic convictions. They were citizens, considered themselves patriots, and had social and political views that were or were not logically connected to their prophetic beliefs. On one level, then, politically engaged premillennialists were simply responding to what they believed were serious challenges to their traditional way of life. As already shown, earlier dispensationalists occasionally entered the political fray if they believed the cause was achievable in the short-term and did not interfere with their primary calling to save souls. Believing in Bible prophecy did not keep them from standing up for what they thought was right. They knew the world was going downhill, but they still felt free to speak out or even organize against evil. The president of Moody Bible Institute called such political work "giving the Devil all the trouble we can till Jesus comes."[41] Nobody expected to solve social problems permanently, only to hold corruption in check temporarily.

Can the unprecedented levels of political activism in the 1980s be explained in the same way? By the late 1970s, many conservative American Christians were deeply disturbed by what they considered the moral decline of their society. They pointed to the sexual revolution, the growing acceptance of homosexuality, the breakdown of the traditional family, increasing crime and drug use, the spread of abortion on demand, the outlawing of prayer in school, and the exclusion of religious faith from the public square.[42] A sociological study of the Moral Majority in Arkansas and Indiana showed how dispensationalists justified political action under such conditions. Most of the members surveyed were dispensationalists from the Bible Baptist Fellowship (Falwell's denomination) who had deep misgivings about the efficacy of politics and made evangelism the church's first priority. Nevertheless, when they concluded that the chaos in American life was inspired by Satan, they felt they had a moral obligation to speak up, to "fight the good fight," even if the conflict could not be finally won until Jesus returned. "By participating in the battle, they side with the forces of God."[43]

Based on the echoes of Lindsey's arguments, one could suspect another reason for their willingness to get involved politically: In the 1970s and 1980s, American dispensationalists suddenly realized that the world they were living in was falling apart much sooner than they had expected. They knew that America was going to decline, but they did not want it to happen while they were still present to suffer the consequences. If they could postpone the suffering and misery until after Jesus came, then the world and its troubles would belong to somebody else—those left behind.

As the New Christian Right got organized, most observers identified its rank and file as fundamentalists or conservative evangelicals without picking up on their beliefs about Bible prophecy. With the election of Ronald Reagan in 1980, however, premillennialists found themselves with unprecedented access to power, and it did not take long for the news media to detect premillennialists in the new administration. In early 1981, during an appearance before the House Interior Committee, secretary of the interior James Watt was asked if people should be taking steps now to guarantee that natural resources would be available for their children. Many people found his answer curious and even shocking:

"Absolutely. That is the delicate balance the Secretary of the Interior must have, to be a steward for the natural resources for this generation as well as future generations. I do not know how many future generations we can count on before the Lord returns; whatever it is we have to manage with a skill to have the resources needed for future generations." The press jumped all over Watt, who was a devout Pentecostal, inferring that his view of the second coming precluded any interest in planning for the future.[44] Sometime later, Caspar Weinberger, Reagan's secretary of defense, admitted, "I have read the Book of Revelation, and, yes, I believe the world is going to end—by an act of God, I hope—but every day I think time is running out."[45]

As the 1984 presidential election approached, political reporters hotly pursued the connection between premillennialism and right-wing politics, especially after Reagan's own dispensationalist beliefs began to surface.[46] In April, a widely circulated article in the *Washington Post* concluded that, thanks largely to his prophetic views, the president believed that a "Nuclear Armageddon" was inevitable.[47] Then 175 public radio stations carried a documentary titled "Ronald Reagan and the Politics of Armageddon," which explored similar themes.[48] In October, the Christic Institute of Washington, D.C., presented evidence in a news conference that American foreign policy was being unduly influenced by dispensationalists.[49] During the second presidential debate, Marvin Kalb of NBC News put the question to Reagan: "Do you feel that we are now heading perhaps for some kind of nuclear Armageddon, and do you feel that this country and the world could survive that kind of calamity?" People close by heard First Lady Nancy Reagan gasp at the question, but the president shot back his answer: "No one knows whether Armageddon is 1,000 years away or the day after tomorrow." He added that he had "never seriously warned and said we must plan according to Armageddon," though he admitted that he had discussed the matter with various theologians who believed that "the prophecies are coming together that portend that."[50]

That exchange put Bible prophecy on the media's radar screen. *Time, Newsweek,* the *New York Times,* and other newspapers ran stories on the popularity of Bible prophecy and again asked if people with such views were influencing American foreign policy.[51] Reporters noted that Reagan first called the U.S.S.R. the "evil empire" at a meeting of the National Association of Evangelicals, where many if not most people in the audience would have understood such a reference in prophetic terms.[52] In short, the media reflected the growing concern that holding such views undercut any effort to bring about lasting peace or even arms reduction and that such beliefs could even turn Armageddon into a self-fulfilling prophecy.[53]

Once the media knew where to look, they found plenty of evidence that Bible teachers believed nuclear war was part of God's plan. As historian Paul Boyer has pointed out, premillennialists in the 1970s and 1980s were consumed with the cold war and the threat of nuclear weapons.[54] After World War II, Bible teachers started working atomic bombs into their prophetic scenarios, and Lindsey updated and expanded their predictions in *The Late Great Planet Earth* and its sequel, *There's a New World Coming.*[55] According to Boyer, Lindsey

> relentlessly turned the Bible into a manual of atomic-age combat: Zechariah's image of human flesh consuming away portrays "exactly what happens to those who are in a thermonuclear blast"; "fire and brimstone" means tactical nuclear weapons; the falling stars and stinging locusts of Revelation are warheads fired from space platforms and Cobra helicopters spraying nerve gas; the scorching heat and awful sores mentioned in Revelation describe the effects of radiation as observed at Hiroshima and Nagasaki.[56]

Lindsey turned such biblical language into thermonuclear weaponry, believing that the ancient prophets were incapable of understanding the horrific visions of twentieth-century mass destruction that they had received. It was thus up to modern interpreters of the Bible to translate what Daniel, Ezekiel, and John the Revelator witnessed in their prophetic visions of the future.

Not all Bible teachers agreed on when or how nuclear war would come, but they all agreed that the divine plan included widespread nuclear annihilation. Following Revelation's prediction that one-third of the world would be consumed by fire in one of God's coming judgments, one dispensationalist specified which nations would suffer nuclear attack: Israel; the old Persian Empire of Iraq, Iran, and West Pakistan; Ethiopia; Libya; the U.S.S.R. and the rest of the nations in the Warsaw Pact; the ten European nations controlled by the Antichrist; and the United States. He even did the math to show that their combined area amounted to exactly one-third of the earth's land surface. Most Bible teachers held out little if any hope for America in the end times. As one dispensationalist predicted in 1985, the United States "is going to be destroyed by fire! Sudden destruction is coming and few will escape. . . . A hydrogen holocaust will engulf America—and this nation will be no more."[57]

Did dispensationalism's beliefs about the inevitability of nuclear war directly impact American foreign policy, as many people feared? In his careful analysis of this question, Boyer argued that decades of Bible teachings about the end of the world conditioned millions of people to believe that future horrors were unavoidable, part of some divine plan. But he did not believe that dispensationalists had as much direct influence on policy making as their critics often charged. Premillennialism's political influence was more indirect and subterranean: It created a certain passivity about the inevitability of military buildups, failed peace talks, deepening crises, and nuclear war. If such things were going to happen no matter what, then there was no use trying to do anything about them. One could add that when things were moving in the right direction, dispensationalists were usually content to sit back and let them happen. Boyer believed, however, that dispensationalists did have a direct political impact in other areas. When they decided to "fight the good fight" against the gathering end-times evil in American culture, their political muscle was formidable: "In these years [the 1980s] the premillennial eschatology that had saturated grassroots religious culture for decades converged with a larger rightward thrust in American life in a synergistic process that . . . transformed the political landscape."[58]

Despite Boyer's assertions about premillennialist passivity, during the 1980s, dispensationalists strongly supported American rearmament in the face of the Soviet threat. While they believed that nuclear war was inevitable, they preferred not to have the bombs fall while they were still around. As Lindsey had proposed in 1980, if America took aggressive military steps, it could possibly hold the dogs of atomic war at bay until Jesus returned to evacuate his followers. No one knew whether Reagan consciously followed this game plan, but his policies certainly were in line with such hopes. Leaving the earlier strategy of detente behind, Reagan denounced the Soviet Union as a dangerous totalitarian state that needed to be resisted at all costs. He then undertook the largest military buildup in U.S. history and proposed the development of "Star Wars," the Strategic Defense Initiative, a high-tech missile defense system that threatened to eradicate the older doctrine of mutual deterrence. The ensuing arms race produced unprecedented budget deficits at home but probably also contributed to the Soviet system's collapse and its rapid movement toward democratic reforms.[59]

Changing the Subject

Many times in its history dispensationalism had to contend with the unexpected. At times history took a surprising turn, but Bible teachers showed an amazing resilience. They were flexible, able to adjust when necessary, regroup, and move ahead. Since so much seemed to be riding on the role of Russia in the end times, the collapse of the Soviet Empire in the late 1980s was obviously a problem for prophecy pundits, but as usual, Bible teachers were more than up to the challenge.

THE NEW WORLD ORDER

As a result of the policies of the Reagan years, dispensationalists felt much better about the kind of America in which they had to live until the rapture, but the collapse of the Soviet empire in the summer of 1989 was much more than dispensationalists expected or even wanted. While some dispensationalist teachers believed the Soviets could be restrained until the rapture, none believed that the entire evil empire would come crashing down. For many decades, Bible teachers had identified the Soviet Union with Gog and Magog of Ezekiel 38–39 and after World War II had seen the Soviet Bloc in Eastern Europe as the coming northern confederacy. The Soviets' huge stockpile of nuclear weapons had also been a crucial part of Bible teachers' message. What did the demise of the evil empire and the decline of the nuclear threat do to dispensationalist credibility? To outsiders, at least, they meant prophetic disconfirmation on a huge scale. The mainstays of post–World War II prophecy teaching were suddenly gone.[60] It was as though someone had removed key pieces of the prophetic jigsaw puzzle. What were Bible teachers to do now?

Some dispensationalists held their ground and insisted that the changes on the world scene were only temporary. Once adamant that their interpretations were verified by the morning newspapers, the never-say-die Bible teachers now insisted that people should not believe everything they read there. Despite all appearances to the contrary, the Soviet Empire was not finished, only biding its time. The changes were an illusion.[61] Jack Van Impe, Hal Lindsey, Stuart McBirnie, and others staked out their state of denial early: They scoffed at Mikhail Gorbachev's efforts at *glasnost* and *perestroika* as clever ploys to get the Western powers to drop their guard and provide financial aid. After the Soviets rebuilt their economic and political systems, they would reactivate their empire and once again assume their assigned role in Bible prophecy. Without exactly explaining why, Van Impe claimed that "Russia's new role is the predicted final plan developing before our very eyes at breakneck speed. These shocking events are giant steps toward . . . WORLD WAR III and then, ARMAGEDDON." In 1990, Salem Kirban wrote about a Russian "Trojan horse" meant to deceive the world into believing that it was no longer a threat to world peace. Yet it was difficult to maintain this hopeful emphasis on the former Soviet Union while its economic and military might continued to deteriorate for all to see. With irony and sarcasm, Paul Boyer observed that Bible prophecy's "popularizers have little difficulty absorbing minor blips on the radar screen of history such as the collapse of the Soviet menace, the demise of the Cold War, and the waning of the nuclear threat."[62] In the long run, claiming that the huge geopolitical changes taking place did not really matter or were not what they seemed was a losing proposition.

If denial did not work, dispensationalists could always change the subject, which is what most of them did. Suddenly, their attention shifted to the coming New World Order. The notion of a one-world government was common in dispensational prophetic circles. With the status of the Soviets and their allies now in question, the New World Order loomed as the next big thing to watch for. David Hunt, for example, argued in *Global Peace and the Rise of Antichrist* that the demise of communism actually facilitated the emergence of a one-world government because people felt they now had the opportunity to create global peace. Into such a situation the Antichrist would emerge as the ultimate peacemaker.[63]

No prophecy teacher changed the subject any better than Pat Robertson. Born in Virginia in 1930, Robertson was the son of a U.S. senator and a graduate of Washington and Lee universities, Yale Law School, and New York Theological Seminary. Ordained a Southern Baptist minister, Robertson eventually became a Pentecostal and a pioneer in Christian broadcasting. In the early 1960s, he founded the Christian Broadcasting Network (CBN). Then in 1975, he established what is now called Regent University in Virginia Beach. Given his enormous media base, he emerged as one of the early leaders of the New Christian Right. In 1980, he sponsored the Washington for Jesus Rally, which attracted over two hundred thousand people. He worked hard to mobilize conservative evangelicals through voter registration drives and the founding of a number of organizations, the Christian Coalition being the most significant. He was even a short-lived candidate for the Republican presidential nomination in 1988 and remained a significant force in Republican politics through the 1990s and into the new century.[64]

For most of the 1980s, Robertson sounded a lot like Hal Lindsey. He made prophetic teaching a regular feature on his *700 Club*. He more or less followed the dispensationalist scenario, seeing the Soviet Union and the new European Union as major players in end-times events. Like Lindsey, he fiercely opposed Soviet expansionism, urged the U.S. government not to negotiate disarmament treaties with the Soviets, and gave unqualified support to Israel. He even indulged in date setting when he announced on the *700 Club* that Jesus would return by the end of 1982.[65]

After the collapse of the Soviet Empire, he changed gears and began focusing on the New World Order. Sounding a bit like old-guard conspiracy theorists Arno C. Gaebelein and Gerald B. Winrod in the 1930s (though without their anti-Semitism or use of *The Protocols of the Elders of Zion*), Robertson unraveled a worldwide conspiracy of bankers and internationalists whose sinister plan for world domination had been passed down through the Freemasons and the Illuminati. America was currently in the grip of such conspirators through the Council on Foreign Relations, the Trilateral Commission, and the Federal Reserve Board, which together controlled "the establishment" in the United States. This cabal intended to undercut American sovereignty by promoting a one-world government through the United Nations and controlling the world's economy. According to Robertson, the antidote to this scheme consisted of safeguarding America's independence from foreign control, returning to American traditional values, as exemplified in the Ten Commandments and the Golden Rule, and eliminating the Federal Reserve System's control over the nation's money supply.[66]

Instead of fitting the coming New World Order into the standard dispensational scenario, Robertson utilized a different biblical motif, the age-old conflict between two different streams of humanity. On one side were the true descendants of Abraham, the people of faith whose lives were rooted in love and obedience to God; on the other side were those who "based their lives on human potential, human ability, and human rebellion against God and His order." Such people ended up worshiping animals, the stars, demons, and even one another. At one point, they tried banding together into a one-world government against God. The result was the building of the ancient tower of Babel (Gen. 11:1–9). Such unity among those opposed to God and the people of faith was so dangerous that God confused their speech and scattered them far and wide.[67]

This first failed attempt to unify humanity against God took place in Babylon, along the Tigris and Euphrates rivers. In the early 1990s, Robertson detected another attempt to create a New World Order in the same location. The Gulf War's prophetic significance was that the United Nations authorized military action against Iraq, which Robertson claimed was the "first time since Babel that all of the nations of the earth acted in concert with one another."[68] Such a united effort was an ominous sign for God's faithful people because the one-world system "will set spiritual forces into motion which no human being will be strong enough to contain."[69]

In his description of this coming New World Order, Robertson referred only passingly to the premillennial view of prophecy. Behind the New World Order was the dragon of the Book of Revelation, who would work through the leader of the one-world government to persecute Israel, then begin persecuting the world's Christians. (Robertson believed that the rapture would occur *after* the great tribulation, which meant that all Christians would suffer under the Antichrist.) Though Robertson referred to this evil leader as the Antichrist, he avoided using other typical dispensationalist prophetic terminology. There was no mention, for example, of the rapture, the great tribulation, the revived Roman Empire, the northern confederacy, or the battle of Armageddon. Robertson did predict, however, that Israel would be the focus of the wrath of the nations and would be pressured to give up land for peace.[70]

What would happen next? According to Robertson, once the Christian United States was safely out of the way, Satan would empower the leader of the New World Order.[71] That was why American Christians needed to become active now: to prevent the "humanistic-occultic branch of humanity" from achieving their New World Order anytime soon. Robertson's Christian Coalition had a strategy to "sweep the one-worlders out of contention in the public policy arena in a short time." Robertson believed that the 1990s would be the crucial decade to turn back the tide of the one-world conspiracy in the United States. While he believed in "the miraculous power of concerted, believing prayer to alter world events" and the ultimate victory of God's world order at Christ's return, he also believed that the struggle between the two parts of humanity was inevitable.[72] As Robertson's book *The New World Order* made clear, Robertson was much more interested in stopping the forces of one-worldism than in explaining or proving the elaborate dispensationalist system.

MILITANT ISLAM AND THE GULF WARS

Like Robertson, other Bible teachers started turning their attention away from the Soviet Empire and toward other things, specifically the Middle East and Islam. While "the Turk" (during the existence of the Ottoman Empire, almost everybody's shorthand for Islam) had played a major role in the prophetic scenarios of other millennial movements,[73] dispensationalists had always believed that Russia and its northern confederacy would be Israel's worst enemies in the end times. To be sure, Muslims figured into the final assault on Israel as Russian allies, the "kings of the south" in Daniel 11:4–45, but Russia was clearly the main story. Starting in the mid-1970s, however, Bible teachers began watching Islam's growing role in world affairs. In response to the OPEC-inspired oil crisis of 1973, Dallas Seminary's John F. Walvoord reflected this new emphasis in *Armageddon, Oil, and the Middle East*, which sold 750,000 copies.[74] Other dispensationalist teachers soon "rediscovered" Islam in Bible prophecy too, especially after the 1979 revolution in Iran under Ayatollah Khomeini. In 1980, Lester Sumrall published *The Holy War Jihad: The Destiny of Iran and the Moslem World* to show how fundamentalist Iran would eventually align itself with Russia in the final assault on Israel, even though at the time it was obvious that Shiite Muslims were fierce opponents of the Soviets because of the Soviet invasion of Afghanistan.[75] The Ayatollah was not the Antichrist, but his fanatical ruthlessness was a foretaste of things to come. In 1989, one prophecy pundit predicted that militant Islam could turn out to be more important than most students of prophecy had believed: "The Muslims have declared war on the West, the United States, and especially the Christians. . . . The Muslim faith . . . could turn out to be the 'beast system.' . . . We will keep you posted."[76]

The Iraqi invasion of Kuwait in August 1990 came at just the right time. In one sense, the Persian Gulf War put dispensationalists back in business. Zondervan Publishing Company reported an 83 percent increase in the sales of the venerable *Late Great Planet Earth,* even though the 1970 book reflected a world much different from the one in 1990. According to Bantam Books, its mass-market edition of Grant Jeffrey's *Armageddon—Appointment with Destiny* was its "hottest single religious title" in the fall of 1990. John F. Walvoord's rather stodgy *Prophecy Knowledge Handbook* had a surge in sales, as did his updated and reissued *Armageddon, Oil, and the Middle East Crisis.*[77] In fact, after decades of popularity in dispensationalist circles, Walvoord suddenly found himself the center of attention in the secular media. He appeared on CNN, CBN, and CBS and gave interviews on sixty-five radio stations on the prophetic significance of the Gulf War. Prophecy teachers preached to full auditoriums about the prophetic significance of the war. Newspapers across the country reported on the growing interest in Bible prophecy, with the *New York Times* concluding in 1991 that it was at "fever pitch."[78]

Now was the time for dispensationalists to connect the dots between Iraq and Bible prophecy. Before Iraq's invasion of Kuwait, few Bible teachers had paid Iraq much mind. Lindsey's *Late Great Planet Earth* was silent on Iraq, and his *1980s: Countdown to Armageddon* predicted that Iraq would become part of Syria and would restore its broken relationship with the Soviet Union.[79] With the Gulf War, however, Bible teachers found another interpretation: Iraq was really the Book of Revelation's Babylon. In chapters 17–18, John the Revelator recounted his visionary encounter with a woman sitting "upon a scarlet colored beast, full of names and blasphemy, having seven heads and ten horns" (17:3). The woman herself was dressed in purple and scarlet and covered with jewels. She held a golden cup brimming with "abominations and filthiness of her fornication" (17:4). On her forehead was written, "MYSTERY, BABYLON THE GREAT, THE MOTHER OF HARLOTS AND ABOMINATIONS OF THE EARTH" (17:5). To make matters even worse, she was drunk "with the blood of the saints, and with the blood of the martyrs of Jesus" (17:6).

The standard dispensationalist approach had been to understand the "great whore of Babylon" in symbolic terms. According to *The New Scofield Reference Bible:*

> There are two forms which Babylon is to have in the end-time: political Babylon (Rev. 17:8–17) and ecclesiastical Babylon (Rev. 17:1–7, 18; 18:1–24). Political Babylon is the beast's confederated empire, the last form of Gentile world dominion. Ecclesiastical Babylon is all apostate Christendom, in which the Papacy will undoubtedly be prominent; it may very well be that this union will embrace all the religions of the world. Although some hold to a literal rebuilding of the city of Babylon . . . the evidence seems to point to the symbolic use of the name here. . . . Ecclesiastical Babylon is the "great harlot" (Rev. 17:1) and is to be destroyed by political Babylon.[80]

In short, political Babylon was the Antichrist's revived Roman Empire, and ecclesiastical Babylon was the apostate religion of the last days.[81] Most dispensationalist Bible teachers had taken this approach. In *The Late Great Planet Earth,* Lindsey described this apostate religion as a mixture of astrology, mind expansion, witchcraft, ecumenism, and drug-induced hallucinations.[82] But Lindsey and other dispensationalists were also intrigued by the reports that Saddam Hussein had plans to rebuild the ancient city of Babylon only sixty miles from Baghdad. Such information led some Bible teachers to believe that they should interpret Revelation's references to Babylon in more literal terms.[83]

When Iraq invaded Kuwait, the pendulum of interpretation started swinging toward the literal-Babylon approach. Charles Taylor quickly issued a book and cassette titled *Saddam's Babylon the Great* and declared, "That city in Iraq has to be rebuilt because the BIBLE DECLARES IT."[84] Charles Dyer of Dallas Seminary was probably the leading proponent of the belief that Babylon would be rebuilt by Saddam so that it could be destroyed by the returning Christ. His 1991 book, *The Rise of Babylon,* featured Saddam Hussein on the cover and promptly sold three hundred thousand copies.[85] Jack Van Impe liked the idea of a reconstructed Babylon too and reasoned that since ancient Babylon had been conquered by the Medo-Persian Empire in the sixth century B.C., modern-day Iraq should be seen as part of Iran (the new name for Persia, as mentioned in Ezek. 38:5), which would join the soon-to-be reconstituted northern confederacy.[86] Probably the most telling piece of evidence that dispensationalists were taking Babylon more literally was found in the plotline of the Left Behind series. When the Antichrist, Nicolae Carpathia, assumed control of the United Nations, he renamed it the Global Community and moved its headquarters to the New Babylon, which had been constructed on the site of its ancient predecessor in the Iraqi desert.[87] Such flexibility of interpretation allowed Bible teachers to maintain their audience when other parts of their prophetic system did not seem to be doing nearly as well.

Though breathless with enthusiasm, in the end, most of the noted Bible teachers showed some restraint. For example, in the early 1990s, nobody identified Saddam Hussein as the Antichrist or the Gulf War as Armageddon. But Bible teachers were convinced that the war was an important step toward the end, especially in the way it concentrated the world's attention on the Middle East in general and Israel in particular. Lindsey was not definite, but he believed that the second coming was only a few years away. Van Impe predicted the end of the world in 1996, based on a long-repudiated method of prophetic calculation from the second century. He argued that world history would last six thousand years because God created the world in six days and "one day is with the Lord as a thousand years" (2 Peter 3:8). Van Impe accepted Bishop Ussher's date for the creation of the world in 4004 B.C., then added six thousand years, which gave him A.D. 1996. With the date so close, no one was going to quibble about what happened to Gog and Magog and the northern confederacy.[88] Charles Taylor came to the conclusion that most of his colleagues had reached: "That which is transpiring is a shuffling of the nations to get them in proper position" for the events leading up to Christ's return.[89]

In comparison to the flurry of prophetic speculation at the beginning of the Gulf War of 1991, Bible teachers were quite restrained when Gulf War II began in March 2003. A number of newspaper reporters went looking for prophecy pundits to make connections between the second Gulf War and the end times. For the most part, they came up empty-handed. Bible teachers were much more reluctant in finding fulfillments.[90] One of the exceptions was Irvin Baxter, founder of *Endtime* magazine. He stated that the second war with Iraq would result in the deaths of millions as a result of Iraq launching missiles of mass destruction in retaliation against its neighbors and terrorists killing millions of Americans with portable nuclear weapons. Furthermore, according to Baxter, other nations would try to take advantage of the diversion of Iraq to settle old scores: China would possibly attempt to regain control of Taiwan, or India would try one more time to take control of Kashmir. Baxter expected the resulting nuclear exchange to bring on World War III and the death of one-third of the world's population.[91]

But for many dispensationalists, the second war with Saddam was a bit too much like "been there, done that." Whatever things may have looked like in 1992, most interpreters did not see anything new looming eleven years later. A pastor in Arizona who was teaching a class on the Book of Revelation when the war broke out was especially struck by the prominence of the River Euphrates in Bible prophecy and its significance in war strategy. "I don't think anyone can deny God is putting his hand on history," he said. Another pastor believed that we were getting close "to the time when the Lord will say enough is enough." Even so, he was cautious: "Things are coming together according to the Bible, but we should not be looking for signs. Instead, we should be getting ready."[92] A Baptist pastor from Maine expressed a common notion about the war's significance without getting too specific: "It is my opinion that the invasion is biblically significant as it relates to the last times. It could be a trigger to the rise of the Antichrist and the battle of Armageddon."[93]

The more academic shapers of dispensational thought were equally slow to stick their necks out concerning Gulf War II. Mark Bailey, the president of Dallas Theological Seminary, reported that while his faculty had been in high demand for major media interviews after the war broke out, he sensed that there was less excitement in 2003 than in 1991. "With this new conflict and the absence of Israeli events, the discussions seem less speculative." Furthermore, Bailey did not see anything specific in Bible prophecy about the United States or Iraq, so it was useless to speculate about the prophetic meaning of this particular conflict. He also rejected all talk about Saddam being the Antichrist or setting a date for the second coming. "Don't assume. The end is not yet. Jesus says that even with war and the rumors of war and famine, that is not the end. Even if you think you're in the middle of that seven-year build up of tribulation, you can't presume to know when it will happen. We heed the warnings of Christ not to speculate as to time and not to speculate about identities."[94]

As things turned out in Gulf War II, keeping the lid on prophetic speculation was a wise choice. With the regime change in Iraq, the chances of rebuilding Babylon became slim. At best, Saddam Hussein was only a minor blip on the radar screen of biblical prophecy. The easy defeat of Iraq and the long-term unknowns about the American presence in the Gulf region, however, will keep all eyes focused on the Middle East. It is too early to determine the long-term implications of the second Gulf War, which should provide prophecy pundits with plenty to think about in the years ahead.

One of the most interesting ways of gauging how dispensationalists were reading the signs of the times during Gulf War II, or any other time for that matter, was the Rapture Index, an online analysis of biblical prophecy that bears a striking resemblance to the Dow Jones Industrial Average. Founded in 1995 by Todd Strandberg, the Rapture Index evaluates forty-five prophetic categories such as earthquakes, mark of the beast technology, wars and rumors of war, famines and pestilence, ecumenism and religious apostasy, and date setting. Each category is ranked from one to five, depending on whether it is increasing or decreasing. Thus, the higher the score, the faster the world is approaching the end. According to Strandberg, anything higher than a score of 145 means "Fasten your seat belts." At the beginning of Gulf War II, the index was 174, which was lower than the all-time high mark of 182, which was recorded following September 11, 2001.[95] At the beginning of Gulf War II, Strandberg stated, "People are anticipating a rerun of 1991. When we went in that time, we were anticipating a major loss of life and we lost very few. Some envisioned it as a major event in prophecy. So now, most of us think that this won't be a major event either. The Bible predicts that things get so bad in the end times that if Christ doesn't come back, there will be no flesh saved. It will obviously get much worse than this before the end." Still, Strandberg has watched the number of hits to the site increase to roughly 250,000 per month, which is nothing compared to what he expects later on: "I believe that when the Rapture takes place, there is going to be a horrendous surge of people looking for what happened. The hits are going to be in the millions."[96] Thanks to Strandberg, those who are left behind will have somewhere to go to find out not only what happened but also what will happen next.

If Strandberg is correct, he will never know how many people access his RaptureReady.com website. He and the millions of other dispensationalists will not be here after Jesus raptures the church. But most dispensationalists are not content to sit back and wait for the rapture. Israel, the crown jewel of prophetic speculation, the key piece in the apocalyptic puzzle, always seems to be in danger. Increasingly, dispensationalists want to do what they can to protect Israel, to make sure that it will be where it is supposed to be to carry out its unique role in the end times. Since 1967, but especially since the late 1970s and early 1980s, dispensationalists have left the stands and have entered the field of play to make sure that everything follows the divine script until Jesus comes.

8

Dispensationalists Organize to Support Israel

The biggest story in the years following the Six-Day War was not that Bible teachers could adjust their interpretations when necessary. They had been doing that for decades. The most significant development among dispensationalists was the way they organized to support Israel in the face of the forces arrayed against it. Now that Jews were "home" in the land of Israel and had expanded beyond its 1948 borders, dispensationalists became actively committed to keeping them there. No longer content to study their Bibles and predict the future, many premillennialists were ready to take steps to make prophecy happen.

Early Stages in a New Alliance

Israelis and dispensationalists started building their special relationship shortly after the Six-Day War. An important sign that something new was underway was the Jerusalem Conference on Biblical Prophecy, which was held June 15–18, 1971. The organizer for the event was a minister from Pennsylvania named Gaylord Briley, who promoted the gathering as a "ringside seat at the second coming." Gaylord convinced a number of evangelical media personalities and pastors of large churches

213

to support the enterprise by scheduling Holy Land tours before and after the proceedings. As a result, roughly fourteen hundred people attended the conference, which Carl F. H. Henry, the editor of *Christianity Today,* called the largest Christian gathering in Israel since its independence in 1948. Sessions were held in Jerusalem's convention center, which the Israeli government made available free of charge. The highlight of the conference came on its first day, when the venerable David Ben-Gurion, Israel's first prime minister, welcomed the participants to Jerusalem and spoke about Israel as the land of the Bible, a message obviously intended to connect with the audience. The conference program contained a few non-dispensationalist speakers, to be sure, but most of the presenters used the Bible to show that Israel's existence and expansion were part of God's plan for history and that God's people needed to lend their support to the new state.[1]

TOUR BUS DIPLOMACY

The Jerusalem Conference on Biblical Prophecy marked the beginning of a great harvest of evangelical tourism to Israel, which over time became the foundation on which the strong relationship between dispensationalists and Israel was built. After he became prime minister in 1977, Menachem Begin began urging American evangelicals to come to Israel and often showed a personal interest in helping leaders put together their own package tours. In 1981, Begin convinced Assemblies of God evangelist David Lewis of Springfield, Missouri, to establish his own travel agency (Lewis Tours) to promote such tours, and soon other evangelical leaders were making plans to bring their constituents to Israel too.

The pattern for such religious/political pilgrimages was established early. During the early 1980s, the Israeli Ministry of Tourism actively recruited evangelical religious leaders for "familiarization" tours at no cost to them. In time, hundreds of evangelical pastors received free trips to the Holy Land. The purpose of such promotional tours was to enable people of even limited influence to experience Israel for themselves and be shown how they might bring their own tour group to Israel. Needless to say, the Israeli Ministry of Tourism was interested in more than tourist dollars. Here was a way of building a solid corps of non-Jewish supporters for Israel in the United States by bringing large numbers of evangelicals to hear and see Israel's story for themselves. The strategy caught on, and hundreds of tours were arranged according to the agreed-upon modus operandi: Tourists were to fly only on the Israeli airline El Al, employ only tour guides licensed by the Israeli Ministry of Tourism (required by government regulation after 1981), and use only Israeli ground transportation companies.[2] These tours were not the traditional religious pilgrimages that allowed people to "walk where Jesus walked" in the land of the Bible. They were a calculated attempt to win Christian friends for Israel through a strong evangelical-Israeli network.

Soon the airport at Tel Aviv was flooded with evangelical tour groups from America. Dozens of travel agencies helped evangelicals arrange tours to Israel, and many of them used Bible prophecy in their marketing. For example, Joshua Travel sponsored "Bible Prophecy Tours" led by Jimmy and Judy DeYoung, residents of Jerusalem who conducted tours geared to demonstrate the place of Israel in God's plan of the ages.[3] Another such group was SOR International/Ruth Sims Tours, which advertised itself as a "nonprofit organization dedicated to the education of the believers in the Biblical significance of God's Covenant with the Jewish people and the Nation of Israel." According to one satisfied customer, SOR tours focused on "the fulfilment of God's prophetic word today."[4] Some dispensationalist missions to the Jews made getting people to Israel an important part of their ministries. Chosen People Ministries (the new name of the American Board of Missions to the Jews), Ariel Ministries, and the American Messianic Fellowship regularly conducted tours to Israel. Zola Levitt, a Messianic Jew whose successful television ministry is headquartered in Dallas, set up his own travel agency, Travel Experience International, to handle the various kinds of tours to Israel that he sponsored.[5]

Other dispensationalist leaders also became regular tour leaders to Israel. Chuck Smith, the founder of the Calvary Chapel movement, was a frequent visitor whose tours featured mass baptisms of believers in the Jordan River. The Israelis granted him permission to set up chains along the banks of the river, like those used to guide crowds through lines at Disneyland, so that large numbers of the faithful could be accommodated while waiting to be immersed at the very spot where, according to tradition at least, John the Baptist baptized Jesus at the beginning of his ministry. But baptisms were only part of the story of these tours: Chuck Smith was a firm believer in Bible prophecy and Israel's place in it, and he conducted his tours accordingly.[6]

Probably no premillennialist group was able to link tourism and political support for Israel more successfully than the International Christian Embassy of Jerusalem. In 1980, when Israel essentially annexed all of East Jerusalem into the state of Israel, thirteen nations moved their embassies from Jerusalem to Tel Aviv, in protest of what they considered Israel's violation of international law. Into the former Chilean embassy moved the International Christian Embassy of Jerusalem, which, despite its name, had no real diplomatic standing. The ICEJ was the creation of an international group of self-identified Christian Zionists who believed that God wanted them to offer visible and effective support to the Israeli government in its time of need. According to the embassy's staff, the ICEJ was "founded in 1980 as an evangelical Christian response to the need to comfort Zion according to the Scriptural mandate: 'Comfort, comfort my people, says your God. Speak tenderly to Jerusalem, and proclaim to her that her hard service has been completed, that her sin has been paid for, that she has received from the Lord's hand double for all her sins' (Isa. 40:1–2)." The ICEJ claimed that it supported Israel

> because we love her, are indebted to her and seek to obey God's word. We are not trying to fulfill an end time agenda, but are standing on biblical principles. We proclaim a message to Zion that her modern day restoration is not a historical accident, but the fulfillment of God's word (Ezekiel 36:24–26; Luke 21:24). A time of great glory awaits Israel even though dark times may precede the break of day. Vision will not fail and from a Jewish Jerusalem, the Lord's law will go out and the "nations shall not learn war anymore" (Isaiah 2:1–4).[7]

The embassy was established and maintained by dispensational and charismatic sources from all over the world. Currently, the ICEJ has forty branch offices in North and South America, Europe, Africa, Australia, and the Far East and has a staff of sixty-five in Jerusalem.

What does the embassy actually do? Over the years, the embassy has developed a number of social service programs in Jerusalem, including a nursing program for Israelis in need of home care and the Jerusalem Ministry Center, which specializes in helping new immigrants to Israel, especially those from the former Soviet Union, get established. But the ICEJ is by far best known for its annual Feast of Tabernacles conference and celebration, which consistently attract five thousand Christians from around the world to celebrate the Jewish festival of Succoth. For seven days, Christian "pilgrims" gather in the International Convention Center in Jerusalem and other venues around the city for a variety of events. Included are elaborate worship and praise sessions in the evenings, which are led by international choirs, orchestras, and dancers; seminars during the day that have a "special focus on the prophetic perspective of Israel, the Church, and eschatology"; and a special desert celebration in the Ein Gedi wilderness that features a "Middle Eastern-style barbeque meal."

For many participants, the highlight of the week is the Jerusalem March, when conferees parade through the streets of the Holy City, waving their national and Israeli flags to "comfort Israel." The *New York Times* covered the 1999 march and reported that according to Israeli authorities, the ICEJ's Feast of Tabernacles is consistently the largest foreign religious gathering in Israel year after year. The pilgrims are hard to miss. On the day of the 1999 march, they assembled with their signs written in Hebrew and dressed in their native costumes. Alongside Dutch Christians walking in wooden shoes and gypsies wearing their colorful dress were American Christians in "Oklahoma for Israel" T-shirts and a contingent of Native Americans who had painted the star of David on their leather shields. The marchers sang Christian and Israeli songs, waved pro-Israel placards, and did their best to show the Israelis who lined the streets that Christians from around the world pray for and support them against their many enemies. According to Ehud Olmert, the mayor of Jerusalem, the ICEJ marchers are "the most wonderful guests that this city has."[8]

The embassy has always claimed that its work is religious, not political, but among Christian Zionists, the line between the two is often hard to distinguish. For example, embassy leaders always refer to occupied territories by their biblical names of Judea and Samaria to make the point that they belong to the Jewish people by divine decree. The ICEJ's office in Washington, D.C., has lobbied the U.S. government for years to get the American embassy moved from Tel Aviv to Jerusalem as a statement that the Holy City should remain united under Israeli control forever. The embassy and its branches also work hard to squelch diplomatic efforts to trade land for peace by supporting the right of Israelis to establish settlements anywhere they choose in the West Bank and Gaza. Israeli politicians understand the power of the ICEJ to influence Christians and their governments. Israeli prime ministers (Barak was the one exception in 1999) never fail to show up at the Feast of Tabernacles celebration to thank the pilgrims for their support and to spur them on to greater efforts on behalf of Israel.[9] Rather typical of prime ministerial comments were those of Benjamin Netanyahu in 1998:

> I came here to thank you for your support in our great endeavor. It has been consistent. It has been unreserved. And I have to tell you, from my point of view, as Prime Minister of Israel, it has been very, very effective. Thank you. The state of Israel is stronger because of your support and it needs this strength to resist undue pressure and threats. You know, and we know, that this is support for a just and good cause. I said we have come back to our ancient homeland. Our claim to this land is based on the greatest and most incontrovertible document in creation—the Holy Bible. It's the Bible that has given us the deed to this land. It is on the basis of the Bible that the Christian world and so much of the international community have recognized our right to it.[10]

At the 2002 Feast of Tabernacles, Prime Minister Ariel Sharon struck a similar chord: "I said we are ready to do many things, to take many steps, to make many compromises . . . in areas which are a part of the cradle of the Jewish people. There is one thing we will never do: we will never make any compromise when it comes to our security and the very existence of the State of Israel, and for that we need you and we need your support." He went on to conclude: "I would like to thank you again for everything—for your friendship and for your solidarity, which are so important to us. I also have a message that I would like you to take home: send more people like you to visit Israel."[11]

In a nutshell, Sharon summarized the goals of the ICEJ: to provide strong and unbending support to Israel against all pressures to compromise its national security and to bring more evangelical tourists to the Holy Land to hear and accept the Israeli cause. Of course, most evangelical tourists to Israel come because they *already* believe these things, but getting them to the land of the Bible solidifies and emboldens them to stand up for Israel like never before. Bible prophecy points them to these conclusions, and visiting the state of Israel for themselves affirms them.[12]

The ICEJ has also sponsored four International Christian Zionist Congresses, where like-minded people from all over the world come together to seek ways of shoring up and extending Israel's hold on all of the Holy Land. The congresses were held in 1985, 1988, 1996, and 2001.

JERRY FALWELL'S ISRAELI CONNECTIONS

Probably no one better illustrates the way the relationship between American dispensationalists and the state of Israel developed than Jerry Falwell. After the Likud Party's rise to power in the late 1970s, Falwell became good friends with its leaders, including Prime Minister Begin, and quickly became one of Israel's most loyal supporters in the United States. The courting of Falwell followed a familiar pattern. In 1978, Falwell was invited to the Holy Land at the Israeli government's expense. During his visit, he demonstrated his solidarity with Israel by planting some trees, which became known as the Jerry Falwell forest. A year later, Falwell returned to Israel, again at the government's expense, and in a public photo op endorsed the Likud Party's strategy of building Israeli settlements throughout the West Bank. The Israelis valued Falwell's friendship: In 1980, Prime Minister Begin awarded him the Vladimir Jabotinsky Medal, named after the right-wing Zionist leader of the early twentieth century. Shortly thereafter, the Israeli government gave him a Windstream jet to make his comings and goings easier. One should remember that the Falwell-Likud relationship developed at the same time that Falwell was pulling together his own Moral Majority in the United States. In other words, Israel found Falwell just as his star was rising within the fundamentalist-evangelical political resurgence. The

Israelis knew they could count on Falwell. In 1981, after the Israelis launched a preemptive strike against the Iraqi nuclear reactor, Begin called Falwell first for support, and he gave it. He contacted his large network of supporters and made the case for Israel. Likewise, Falwell was a vocal defender of the Israeli invasion of Lebanon in 1982.[13]

Along with speaking out for Israeli causes, Falwell continued to promote tours to Israel to build a popular base of support for the Jewish state. In 1982, Falwell brought roughly forty evangelical leaders from his Moral Majority to Israel for a familiarization tour in hopes that they would later bring their own sizable constituencies to Israel. Throughout the 1980s and 1990s, he used his extensive church and political ties to sponsor many other tours of his own. Falwell even made building strong ties with Israel an important part of the educational mission of his Liberty University in Lynchburg, Virginia. In 1998, thanks to a four-million-dollar donation to cover all expenses, he brought three thousand freshmen from the university to Israel for a study tour. According to the Religious News Service, the tour "was an outgrowth of Falwell's close relationship with Israeli Prime Minister Benjamin Netanyahu."[14]

What happened on these Falwell-sponsored tours? One investigative reporter, Grace Halsell, wrote a book about her experiences on two of Falwell's tours to Israel in the 1980s.[15] The first tour in 1983 had 630 participants; the second in 1985 had 850. Such numbers constituted something like a "prophetic expeditionary force" as the tourists moved from one site to the next. All along the way, Halsell detected an overt and consistent theological and political point of view among most of her fellow tour members and all of the guides and special lecturers. She was struck by the fact that the tour contained relatively little about the life and teachings of Jesus but much about the rights of Israel in its struggle with the Palestinians. Though the tour went into Palestinian Christian areas such as Nazareth and Bethlehem, guides avoided any real discussion of the standing of the Palestinians or the perspectives of Arab Christians. Over and over, guides and special lecturers instructed tour members that God had given Israel to the Jews and that the Palestinians were obstacles to God's purposes. Though some people on the tours requested opportunities to meet and even worship with fellow Christians in Israel, most of whom would have been Palestinians, tour leaders made sure such contacts never took place.[16] As a result, Halsell concluded that the tour was not about "real times in a real place where real people" lived. Rather it was about "the Holy Land as an Edenic fulfillment of God's promises to only one group of people." The others simply did not matter or even exist.[17]

The tours had no trouble finding time to meet with Israeli government officials, however, including generals, cabinet officers, and political leaders such as Begin and Shimon Peres. On both tours, Halsell reported, Falwell hosted banquets to honor Israeli leaders. At the 1983 banquet, Falwell honored Defense Minister Moshe Arens, and in 1985, he recognized Ariel Sharon, who had recently overseen the highly controversial invasion of Lebanon and would later become Israel's prime minister.[18] It was obvious that Falwell and Israeli leaders, especially those from the Likud Party, liked and supported one another.

Falwell has continued his unwavering pro-Israel commitments. Recently, Falwell said, "We are very pro-Jewish, pro-Israel. I would say evangelicals are the very best friends Israelis have in the whole world outside their own family. Evangelicals are more committed to Israel than some of the American Jewish community." Like other dispensationalists before him, Falwell believes that such commitments are rooted in the Bible. "Basically God promised to bless those who blessed the children of Abraham and curse those who cursed Israel. I think history supports the fact that he has been true to his word. When you go back to the pharaohs, the Caesars, Adolf Hitler and the Soviet Union, all those who dared to touch the apple of God's eye—Israel—have been punished by God. America has been blessed because she has blessed Israel."[19]

Of course, terrorism and the continuing Palestinian *intifada* (the widely used Arabic word for "uprising") have played havoc with tourism in Israel. The high water mark for tourism was 2000, when 2.7 million people went to the Holy Land. The numbers would have been even higher, but after the terrorist attack on the *USS Cole* in October of that year, tourist numbers took a dramatic dip. In 2001, the figures were even worse, thanks to the 9/11 attacks in the United States and the increase in the number of suicide bombings in Israel. In the summer of 2002, the U.S. State Department warned Americans that the continued violence in Israel made travel there dangerous. As a result, many tour companies simply stopped scheduling trips to the Holy Land.[20] Still, some dispensationalists continued to go, as the International Christian Embassy of Jerusalem's Feast of Tabernacles attests.

The Pro-Israel Dispensational Network

Getting American evangelicals to travel to Israel was only half of the Israeli strategy. The other half was to create a politically engaged, pro-Israel force among conservative American Christians in the United States. Shortly after the Six-Day War, elements within the Israeli government saw the potential power of the evangelical subculture and began to mobilize it as a base of support that could influence American foreign policy. Targeting Christian conservatives was a departure for Israelis. From Israel's founding in 1948, liberal Protestants had seemed like more natural allies of the Jewish state, given their more-or-less progressive political views, which corresponded to those of most American Jews. The National Council of Churches and other liberal Protestant groups generally had been supportive of the new state, but over time, they had become more critical of Israel, especially after Israelis occupied Palestinian land after the 1967 war.[21] At the same time, Israelis noticed that American fundamentalists seemed to present a solid front of support for everything the Jewish state did.

Shortly after the Six-Day War, the Israeli government sent Yona Malachy of its Department of Religious Affairs to the United States to study American fundamentalism and its potential as an ally of Israel. Malachy was warmly received by fundamentalists and was able to influence some of them to issue strong pro-Israeli manifestos. He reported in an influential book that conservative American Christians were fiercely friendly to Israel and were not afraid to say so.[22] In the mid-1980s, there was a discernible shift in Israeli political strategy. The American Israel Public Affairs Committee (AIPAC), the Jewish state's major lobbying group in Washington, D.C., started realigning itself with the American political right wing, including Christian conservatives. According to one AIPAC insider, "We are becoming more 'neo-conservative.' We want to broaden Israel's support to the right—with the people who do not care about what is happening on the West Bank but care a lot about the Soviet Union."[23] Historian Paul Boyer noted the same trend: "As liberal Protestant support eroded, Israel played its fundamentalist card. Privately ridiculing premillennialist readings of prophecy as those of a six-year-old child, they recognized an important political block and dealt with it accordingly."[24] Israel's timing was perfect. It began working seriously with American dispensationalists at the precise moment that American fundamentalists and evangelicals were discovering their political voice in the rise of the New Christian Right.

PRO-ISRAEL ORGANIZATIONS, POLITICAL AND OTHERWISE

American dispensationalists liked the attention and were willing to be wooed by the Israelis. Bible teachers were quick to discover that their new standing on the world political stage was largely defined by their access to prominent leaders. As already shown, tour groups led by the likes of Hal Lindsey, Jerry Falwell, Pat Robertson, Oral Roberts, and others got VIP treatment in Israel by Israeli government officials. This was especially true after the rise of the Likud Party. Prime Minister

Menachem Begin seemed especially available to American evangelicals, hosting them individually or in groups. On one occasion he met with sixty evangelicals at once, and at other times he was willing to let prominent Bible teachers share their interpretations of Bible prophecy with him. It is not difficult to imagine the thrill that dispensationalist leaders felt at having such access to the leaders of Israel. Suddenly, they were not just observers of prophetic fulfillment; they were a part of it. One dispensationalist recounted eleven meetings with Begin, his "old friend," including one in 1984 at the Waldorf-Astoria in New York City, where the prime minister welcomed leaders of the National Association of Religious Broadcasters and the National Association of Evangelicals.[25]

In return, dispensationalists did their part by organizing their constituents to support Israel in a variety of ways. One of the earliest organizations of this type was Christians Concerned for Israel, which eventually changed its name to the National Christian Leadership Conference for Israel. Founded by David Lewis and other dispensationalists, the NCLCI eventually became more ecumenical, including both Catholics and mainline Protestants. The organization claims not to involve itself in Israel's internal politics. Instead "it tries to influence public opinion in America by encouraging Christians generally and people of influence particularly to learn about Israel and respect the right of Israelis to live as they choose in the peace and security of their homeland."[26]

How does the NCLCI exert influence? It schedules conferences, organizes letter-writing campaigns, places advertisements in newspapers, and puts on large public rallies. In April 2002, for example, the organization held a pro-Israeli rally on the Mall in Washington, D.C. Its list of speakers was impressive: Governor George Pataki of New York; Bill Bennett; Elie Wiesel; former prime minister Benjamin Netanyahu; radio talk-show host Janet Parshall; Deputy Secretary of Defense Paul Wolfowitz; representatives Dick Armey and Dick Gephardt; senators Harry Reid, Arlen Specter, and Barbara McKulski; and former New York City mayor Rudolf Giuliani.[27] David Lewis still serves as the chairman of the organization's board of directors, and its message remains compatible with dispensationalist sentiments: Israel has a right to all of its land, including the West Bank, Gaza, the Golan Heights, and Jerusalem; the Palestinians are not really interested in peace; and the United Nations and the United States must stop pressuring Israel to give up land for peace.

Another organization of this type is Christians for Israel. It called the founding of Israel in 1948 a "major landmark in the history of the world." Israel is the fulfillment of biblical prophecies, "which in turn brings the return of our Lord Jesus Christ that much closer!" The goal of the organization is "to alert everyone to these magnificent facts, while at the same time offer practical help to the Jewish people."[28] Like most of the prophecy-oriented organizations of this kind, Christians for Israel packages its politics in educational and humanitarian activities. It promoted familiarization tours to Israel for pastors and other spiritual leaders and conducted its own group tours to the Holy Land. It made available on its website pro-Israeli and anti-Palestinian articles and news stories and issued a monthly newsletter on issues pertaining to the Middle East. It also urged its supporters to buy Israeli products, which it made available through Internet links.

But its main thrust has been to assist Jews from the former Soviet Union in immigrating to Israel, thus fulfilling the biblical prophecy about the restoration of the Jews to the Holy Land prior to the last days. In partnership with the Jewish Agency of Israel and a British bus company (Good News Travels), the Exobus program recruits Jews in Ukraine, then transports them safely to the nearest airport for a flight to Israel. The Jewish Agency provides the plane tickets, and Christians for Israel provides the buses and other logistical support. The organization solicits donations to cover expenses, $135 for an individual and $660 for a family. The Exobus program claims that it assists 1,200 Jews per month to immigrate to Israel (65,000 since the program began). The organization's concern does not stop there, however. When the immigrants arrive in Israel, Christians for Israel refers them to Joseph Storehouse, a Christian humanitarian aid center that provides supplies for getting settled in Israel.

Underlying the work of Christians for Israel is a firm commitment to a dispensational understanding of the restoration of Israel and its role in events leading to the return of Christ. It aligns itself with other Christian organizations that believe likewise. For example, it helped to promote the Interfaith Zionist Leadership Summit, which was held at the Omni Shoreham Hotel in Washington, D.C., in May 2003. The announced purpose of the gathering was to ensure Israel's survival in the face of the Palestinian jihad and terror campaign and to reject the "road map" being proposed by the United States, the European Union, Russia, and the United Nations for the establishment of a Palestinian state.

Claiming to be the largest organization of its kind is the National Unity Coalition for Israel, which was founded in 1990 as Voices United for Israel. In that year, a Jewish woman named Esther Levens from Kansas City and her Christian friend Allen Mothersill decided to establish a pro-Israel, interfaith study group. Their action was prompted by the Bush administration's decision to make loans to Israel contingent on the Israelis not permitting any new settlements on the West Bank. Levens was surprised by the level of support for Israel she found among evangelicals, so she set out to network as many evangelical and Jewish organizations as she could locate. In the end, she claimed to have assembled a coalition of two hundred such organizations (two-thirds of which were evangelical), representing forty million people.

In 1998, Levens's organization sponsored two large conferences in Washington, D.C., at which then prime minister Netanyahu spoke. In the April gathering, over three thousand people assembled, including Ralph Reed of the Christian Coalition, Kay Arthur of Precept Ministries, Jane Hanson of Women's Aglow, and Brandt Gustavson of the National Religious Broadcasters. Jerry Falwell and Pat Robertson endorsed the meeting but could not attend. The meeting was held the day before Netanyahu was scheduled to meet with President Clinton, who was pressuring the prime minister to trade land for peace. Making it obvious that he preferred pro-Israel evangelicals to the president, Netanyahu declared that "we have no greater friends and allies than the people sitting in this room."[29]

The position of the National Unity Coalition for Israel is clear: It calls on the United States to stop funding and negotiating with Yasser Arafat and his Palestinian Authority and opposes "the establishment of a Palestinian state within the borders of Israel." It "pledges our support by sending our prayers, by communicating our support to Prime Minister Ariel Sharon and his cabinet, by visiting the Land whenever and as often as possible, and by continuing to tell Israel's remarkable story to our friends, our communities, our elected officials, and our media."[30]

The organization's media committee has consulted with Israeli government officials in developing promotional and educational materials for use in American media markets. In addition, the coalition has assembled a vast communications network to get its message across. For example, it publishes a monthly "Eye on Israel Newsletter" and sends as-needed emails, "Chutzpah Action Alerts," to its constituents to encourage them to email, fax, and phone President Bush, Prime Minister Sharon, members of Congress, media outlets, and others. As a result, the organization claims to be able to mount a "Virtual March on the White House" at almost a moment's notice. The coalition also maintains a bureau of experts on Middle Eastern affairs and sponsors a clergy network through which it distributes a clergy manual containing information about Israel, current events, and suggestions for influencing others on behalf of Israel. It also creates a steady stream of press releases and calls for press conferences. In short, the National Unity Coalition for Israel is a well-organized and well-funded advocacy group for Israel.

Politically speaking, the coalition is rather homogeneous, but religiously, it is amazingly diverse. While the majority of coalition members are evangelical Christians, the remaining Jewish element ranges from Orthodox to Reform. According to Levens, what holds the coalition together is a shared commitment to Israel and its current government and a tacit agreement not to press religious differences.

The Jerusalem-based Bridges for Peace is another educational/charitable organization that is guided by its view of Israel's place in Bible prophecy. Founded in 1976 by G. Douglas Young, Bridges for Peace has developed into a ministry with a worldwide reach, maintaining offices on six continents. It publishes a bimonthly magazine, *Dispatch from Jerusalem,* a monthly *Israel Teaching Letter* on Christianity's Hebraic roots, and a weekly "Update from Jerusalem," which it distributes via email. In addition, it sponsors conferences, workshops, seminars, prayer groups, and makes available an endless supply of news and information on its website. It also operates a Galilee Study Center near the Sea of Galilee. Through these and other activities, it tries to build bridges of understanding and support for Israel within the evangelical Christian community.

Bridges for Peace is also committed to practical ministry within Israel itself. It founded the first and largest food bank in Israel, Operation Ezra, which distributes up to fifty-five tons of food a month to Israel's needy, whose numbers are evidently increasing. For twenty dollars per month, donors can supply the nutritional requirements for an individual, for eighty dollars, the needs of a family of four. The organization's Adoption Program supplies school books to poor children, and its Operation Rescue helps Jews in the former Soviet Union obtain passports, visas, transportation, and temporary lodging so they can immigrate to Israel. The organization sees such activities as part of its end-times obligation to Israel. Clarence Wagner, Bridges for Peace's current CEO, puts it this way: "We are seeing Bible prophecy being fulfilled before our eyes. Would you agree with me that God has not brought His people home for them to starve and lack their basic needs?" One of the organization's promotional pieces is aimed at prophecy believers: "Don't just read about prophecy when you can be part of it."[31]

Another hands-on approach is illustrated by the Christian Friends of Israeli Communities, founded in 1995 by Colorado Springs businessman Ted Beckett. He founded CFIC to provide "solidarity, comfort, and aid" to the 220,000 Jewish settlers who have set up communities in the occupied territory, or, as Beckett prefers to call it, Judea, Samaria, and Gaza, by linking them with evangelical congregations in the United States. He started his ministry after Israel's Labor Party government stopped funding the settlements in 1993 to spur on the peace process. Beckett believed this action ran counter to the clear teachings of the Bible. "Our movement is designed to give encouragement to these settlers and to say that these lands were promised to them."[32]

As of the late 1990s, Beckett had successfully paired roughly 40 churches and settlements. His goal is to find an evangelical church partner for every Jewish settlement that wants one, which he estimates to be about 110 out of the current 150 settlements. CFIC trains each congregation to set up a links team, which not only establishes contact with its assigned settlement but is also responsible for fund-raising, lobbying, and letter writing on behalf of Israel. It does not take long for the congregations and settlements to establish pen pals, email exchanges, and other practical projects through which American Christians can show their emotional and financial support. Beckett is adamant that the Israeli settlements are part of God's prophetic plan and thus deserve support and protection from Christians: "Judea and Samaria is the Biblical name for the center of the Holy Land also called the Mountains of Israel, even though the media calls this area the 'West Bank.' Those settlers who choose to live there are fulfilling prophecy and are pointing the way for the rest of the Jewish people back to their roots." The CFIC's position is reminiscent of the other pro-Israeli, prophecy-driven organizations:

> This Biblical region was given to Abraham, Isaac, Jacob, and their descendants forever, 4,000 years ago. Because of sin, disobedience and unbelief, most Jews were driven from the land around 70 A.D. However, in 1948 Israel was reborn as a sovereign nation and in 1967, the 'West Bank' was reunited with the rest of the nation in the prophetic, miraculous Six Day War. There was never any attempt to form a Palestinian State while the land was under Arabic control.[33]

Probably the most publicized and successful partnering relationship has been between Faith Bible Chapel of Arvada, Colorado, and Ariel, an Israeli settlement on the West Bank. The church has had a long commitment to Israel. In fact, in May 2003, it held its twenty-fifth annual Israel Awareness Day, with former Republican presidential candidate Gary Bauer as the featured speaker. It has sponsored numerous tours to Israel and has a person on its pastoral staff whose responsibility includes nurturing the church's Israeli connections.

Ariel has a population of fifteen thousand, but it was languishing after Itzak Rabin's Labor government cut off support for settlements in the early 1990s. Faith Bible Chapel stepped into the gap and adopted Ariel as its own special project. The church provided money for a new library, equipment for a health clinic, and additional material and financial support. Ariel's major, Ron Nachman, has become a minor celebrity in dispensationalism's pro-Israel network. Through his connections with Faith Bible Chapel and Beckett's Christian Friends of Israeli Communities (he serves as a member of Beckett's Israeli Advisory Board), he has been able to raise "a few million" dollars (he will not say exactly how much) through speaking tours to the United States. Nachman is a secular Jew and a member of the Likud Party. He is unconcerned about the motivations of American dispensationalists who contribute to his town's welfare. Places such as Ariel need all the help they can get. But the help cuts both ways. Ariel has become a base of operations for prophecy-driven Christian Zionists: In the late 1990s, Pat Robertson's CBN opened an office there.[34]

Faith Bible Chapel illustrates what a single congregation can accomplish when it makes supporting Israel a priority. Another example is Cornerstone Church, an independent congregation in San Antonio, Texas. The church's pastor is John Hagee, who has created an ecclesiastical empire in south Texas. Hagee is not only the founder and senior pastor of the 17,000-member Cornerstone Church but also the president and CEO of Global Evangelism Television, which broadcasts his church services over 120 television and 110 radio stations nationwide. He also conducts evangelistic crusades around the United States and the world through his John Hagee Ministries, which operates apart from the church.

Hagee is a dispensationalist who is committed to supporting Israel, as his many prophecy publications attest.[35] He has traveled to Israel twenty times and met personally with Prime Minister Begin. Hagee has made sure that both his church and his broader ministries connect with Israel. According to the church's statement of faith, "We believe in the promise of Genesis 12:3 regarding the Jewish people and the nation of Israel. We believe that this is an eternal covenant between God and the seed of Abraham to which God is faithful. Our church sponsors a Night to Honor Israel to express our love and support for the State of Israel and the Jewish people." John Hagee Ministries sponsors Exodus II, which seeks to help Jews in the former Soviet Union immigrate to the Holy Land. According to Exodus II's promotional material, a $300 donation will cover the expenses for one émigré. Hagee claims to have spent $3.7 million to relocate over six thousand Jews. This ministry is obviously an outgrowth of Hagee's prophetic beliefs. By contributing to the restoration of dispersed Jews, donors "become a part of Biblical prophecy." The pledge card on which donors indicate their level of financial support contains the following statement: "I want to be a part of the fulfillment of prophecy and the courageous effort to return Jewish families to their homeland."[36]

Another organization that functions as a part of the pro-Israel dispensationalist network is the International Fellowship of Christians and Jews, even though it was founded (1983) and is still run by an Orthodox Jewish rabbi named Yechiel Eckstein, the former codirector of Inter-religious Affairs of the Anti-Defamation League of B'nai B'rith.[37] Originally called the Holy Land Fellowship of Christians and Jews, the IFCJ specializes in fostering better understanding between Christians and Jews and mobilizing them for various humanitarian projects. Rabbi Eckstein is especially adept at making friends with evangelical Christians. According to Robert Dugan of the National Association of Evangelicals, "Probably no one in the Jewish community understands Evangelical Christianity better than Rabbi Eckstein."[38] In fact, one gets the distinct impression that most of the fellowship's supporters are evangelical Christians, not Jews. The overwhelming majority of the organization's endorsers are prominent evangelical leaders such as Jack Hayford, Lloyd Ogilvie, Charles Colson, Gary Bauer, Jerry Falwell, Pat Boone, Pat Robertson, W. A. Criswell, the late Bill Bright, and Bailey Smith, the former president of the Southern Baptist Convention who created controversy in the early 1980s when he declared that God did not hear the prayers of Jews.

Rabbi Eckstein has developed projects that evangelicals can support with enthusiasm. In 1992, the IFCJ started its On Wings of Eagles program, which has provided transportation costs for tens of thousands of Jews from the former Soviet Union and Ethiopia to go to Israel. Its Guardians of Israel project provides material assistance for the growing number of homeless and impoverished Jews in Jerusalem, many of whom are recent immigrants to Israel. Elderly, impoverished Jews who remain in the former Soviet Union receive food, in-home care, medical assistance, and heating fuel through the Isaiah 58 project. In early 2003, the IFCJ reported that it had raised forty-five million dollars over the previous three years in support of these humanitarian programs.

Rabbi Eckstein knows evangelicals and how to appeal to their prophetic sensibilities. As already shown, many dispensationalists have mobilized to help Jews return to Israel out of their conviction that the restoration of the Jews is part of God's prophetic plan for the end times. Thus, the following statement unquestionably resonates with the dispensationalist community:

> One of the *International Fellowship of Christians and Jews'* most rewarding achievements is providing caring Christians with significant opportunities to express their love for Israel and the Jewish people in fulfillment of the biblical promise to Abraham, "I will bless those who bless you" (Genesis 12:3). No matter what your particular interest as a new friend of the *Fellowship*, you will have the chance to participate in programs bringing blessing and help to thousands of people in need.
>
> For instance, your prayers and financial support will help us continue rescuing persecuted Jewish *émigrés* in the former Soviet Union, Ethiopia, and other countries, and bringing them to freedom and safety in Israel *in fulfillment of biblical prophecy* [emphasis added]. We also provide life-sustaining aid to two special groups of people: elderly Soviet Jews suffering dire need in the midst of a crumbling Russian economy and poverty-stricken residents of the holy city of Jerusalem.[39]

Where does the money come from for such projects? Rabbi Eckstein has produced fund-raising documentaries/infomercials about his fellowship's mission, which he shows on Christian cable television stations. The programs are extremely well done and are obviously made to appeal to prophecy believers. Without embracing the details of dispensational belief, Rabbi Eckstein's programs include code language that dispensationalists understand and accept. Included in each video are testimonials by leading evangelicals and famous Bible teachers, as well as grassroots supporters who share why they have contributed to On Wings of Eagles, Guardians of Israel, or Isaiah 58. Many of them speak about their love for the Jewish people and the importance of Israel in God's prophetic plans for the future. Though Rabbi Eckstein never directly affirms his supporters' prophetic understandings, he seems willing to allow others to appeal to them to fund his projects.

In 2003, IFCJ launched a Stand for Israel initiative, which was cochaired by Rabbi Eckstein and Ralph Reed, former head of the Christian Coalition. This project was clearly political. At IFCJ's first Washington briefing in April 2003, Christian leaders gathered to hear Israeli representatives talk about the current situation in the Middle East, the prospects for peace, and the serious dangers to Israel's safety and security. Attenders also heard from Attorney General John Ashcroft, radio talk-show host Janet Parshall, Richard Land of the Southern Baptist Convention, and representatives Tom DeLay and Tom Lantos, both of whom received the first Friend of Israel awards for their political support of Israel in Congress. The goals of the Stand for Israel campaign include mobilizing one hundred thousand churches and one million Christians to stand in solidarity and prayer for Israel. Those who join the campaign have been promised fax alerts on pressing issues and a well-funded media campaign.[40]

Over and over, the pro-Israel dispensationalist/fundamentalist network demonstrates the close connection between belief in Bible prophecy and certain political commitments concerning Israel. In October 2002, during its annual convention in Washington, D.C., the Christian Coalition sponsored a Solidarity with Israel Rally. At the gathering, which some observers said numbered ten thousand, Pat Robertson joined with Ehud Olmert, the mayor of Jerusalem, in announcing a new Praying for Jerusalem campaign that would include raising money from evangelical Christians for the New Jerusalem Fund, which Mayor Olmert intends to use on neighborhood cultural and urban improvement projects.[41]

Pat Robertson left no doubt in the Praying for Jerusalem campaign, which he cochairs with Mayor Olmert and evangelist Mike Evans, that prayer and politics go together. During the rally, Robertson said, "We should not ask [Israel] to withdraw [from occupied territories]—we should stand with them and fight." Strongly condemning the Palestinian *intifada,* Robertson affirmed that "Jerusalem is the eternal, indivisible capital of the state of Israel, and it must not be divided." Olmert returned the favor: "God is with us, you are with us—we will win this war against terrorists."[42]

THE COSTS OF COOPERATION

Both sides pay a price for this alliance. To build and keep their ties with Israel, some evangelicals have had to tone down their historic commitment to evangelize Jews. As already discussed, dispensationalists believe that when Jesus returns, those Jews who have not died at the Antichrist's hand will accept Christ as their Messiah. But for most of their history, dispensationalists have been unwilling to wait until the second coming to evangelize the chosen people. Instead, they have set up missions to the Jews to lead as many to Christ as possible before the end times. Until recently, then, dispensationalists believed there was no conflict between supporting the restoration of Jews to Israel and trying to convert them to Christ.

But in the world of *realpolitik,* conflicts between "comforting" Jews and converting them can be huge. Many Jews equate evangelism with anti-Semitism and reject any offers of Christian support that are accompanied by efforts at conversion. Consequently, some pro-Israel dispensationalist organizations have explicit policies *against* evangelizing Jews. For example, Christians for Israel say that their Exobus ministry has a "non-missionising policy but we do share our faith in the God of Abraham, Isaac, and Jacob. . . . We emphasize the prophetic word." Similarly, Ted Beckett's Christian Friends of Israeli Communities declares that the organization "is not evangelistic. Its projects are geared to encouragement. CFIC is demonstrating its love by being concerned with the settler's needs in a practical way."[43] More specifically, Beckett warns participating churches not to engage in any overt proselytism. He says that he will "yank the charter" of any congregation that makes a direct religious appeal to Jews in Israel. Nevertheless, Beckett says that it is permissible to share one's faith if Jews ask about it first.[44]

The International Christian Embassy in Jerusalem also makes it clear that its role is to support Israel in light of biblical prophecy, not to evangelize its citizens:

> We believe it is God's desire that Christians across the world be encouraged and inspired to arise to their prophetic role in the restoration of Israel. The Bible says that the destiny of the nations, of Christians and of the Church is linked to the way they respond to this work of restoration.

Israel is the target of hostility from many quarters. We believe that Christians must take a stand against anti-Israel and anti-Semitic prejudices, and counter lies with truth. As such, our approach may at times involve political stands, but these ultimately arise from biblical principles and convictions.

We are compelled by our faith to help protect the Lord's people and to help preserve them for that time when the Lord will fulfill all of His promises to them.[45]

The ICEJ's own description of its home-care ministry tells the story of Lena, a poor, lonely Jewish woman with no family who receives regular visits from the embassy's home nurses: "Recently they spoke to her about Biblical prophecies that speak of Israel's restoration, especially Isaiah 35. When Lena read about the desert blooming, she immediately understood that this is happening now. As she read about the ransomed of the Lord 'returning to Zion with joy, and sorrow and sighing fleeing away,' she suddenly stopped. 'This is me!' she said. 'And these are us!'"[46]

These evangelical organizations do not deny that Jews need converting. They merely assert that their organizational priorities lie elsewhere. Some fellow evangelicals find such a distinction curious, to say the least. After all, Jesus' Great Commission (Matt. 28:19–20) concerned "making disciples of all nations," not making sure that Jews are restored and preserved in Israel so that prophecy can be fulfilled. In regard to Lena, most evangelicals' first instinct would have been to tell her about Jesus and to enfold her into a new family of faith, not to read her passages about the Jews' restoration to the land of Israel. Ultimately, what good does it do to get Lena relocated in the Holy Land, then to sit back while she heads for a rendezvous with the Antichrist or an eternity without her Savior? A number of missions to the Jews have been especially critical of the ICEJ for taking such a hands-off approach.[47]

Some Jews are also critical of the political and religious motives of Christian Zionists. For example, Josh Ruebner, the cofounder of Jews for Peace in Palestine and Israel, a Washington-based group committed to establishing a Palestinian state as the means to obtain lasting peace in the region, called the alliance between Israel and the Christian Coalition "repugnant." "Most of the right-wing elements which make up the Christian Coalition are truly anti-Semitic at heart. These are people who believe that Jewish souls cannot go to heaven and that Jews will have to be converted before the end of days."[48] James Rudin, the interreligious affairs director of the American Jewish Committee, pointed out that "some of the very same people who are most supportive of the state of Israel and its security and well-being don't see Judaism as a full and valid religion. It's like 'Israel si, Jews no.'" Rudin also believes that his fellow Jews should be more selective about the kinds of support they are willing to accept. "Many American Jews will say: 'Any port in a storm. If they support Israel, . . . don't worry about the apocalypse.'"[49]

While many Jews object to the domestic policies or religious views of Christian conservatives and are opposed to any alliance with them, other Jews disagree. In 1982, in the early stages of the construction of the new Israel–conservative Christian alliance, Nathan Perlmutter, director of the Anti-Defamation League of B'nai B'rith, discounted the concerns of liberal Jews over the politics of pro-Israel Christian fundamentalists. "Jews can live with all the domestic priorities of the Christian Right on which liberal Jews differ so radically, because none of these concerns is as important as Israel." Perlmutter was also unconcerned about dispensationalists' belief that most Jews will be killed by the Antichrist with the rest converting to Jesus at his return: "We need all the friends we have to support Israel. . . . If the Messiah comes, on that day we'll consider our options. Meanwhile, let's praise the Lord and pass the ammunition."[50] In a perceptive statement regarding the Moral Majority in 1981, Rabbi Marc H. Tanenbaum observed that since most evangelicals were staunch supporters of Israel, "it is just plain self-destructive to alienate that support by engaging in theological casuistry over why evangelicals and fundamentalists really support Israel. It is wise Rabbinic teaching that 'even though the intention may not be pure (for the sake of heaven), the effects can be pure.'"[51] Likewise, in 1984, Irving Kristol advised Jewish liberals to rethink their attitudes toward Christian fundamentalists. In the past, it was easy to equate fundamentalism with anti-Semitism, but now fundamentalists are "unequivocally pro-Israel." With the enemies of Israel definitely on the rise, pro-Israel fundamentalist support might "in the near future, turn out to be decisive for the very existence of the Jewish state."[52]

Esther Levens was aware that most of her National Unity Coalition for Israel partners were conservative Christians with a particular view of Bible prophecy, but she chose not to pay much attention to the details. She was not bothered by dispensationalists' belief that Israel had a particular role to play in the end times, which included its worst holocaust ever and the mass conversion of Jewish survivors to Jesus Christ. Ultimately, what she cared about was their unbending current support for Israel's security and sovereignty. Ira Nosenchuk of Brooklyn, who attended the April 1998 NUCI conference in Washington, D.C., also approached the issue pragmatically: "When you have people supportive of your beliefs, . . . you have to go with them. . . . Sometimes I feel like there are more supporters for Israel among evangelicals than among Jews."[53]

In Levens's organization, as in the other pro-Israel, prophecy-driven groups mentioned above, Christians were careful not to offend their Jewish allies by trying to evangelize them, despite the claims often leveled against them that their alliance was only a prelude or pretext to proselytism. Levens did not see any such behavior. "If that's the reason they support Israel, that would be of great concern to me. But I find so many truly dedicated Christians who are involved because of a growing awareness of their Jewish roots, and who feel they owe a real debt of gratitude, historically to the Jews."[54]

Yechiel Eckstein obviously learned to look the other way on some of these issues too. He knew evangelicals well, so he was aware of their prophetic beliefs and understood that as evangelicals their conversionist mission extended to everyone, including Jews. In a book he wrote to explain Jews and Judaism to evangelicals, Eckstein included a chapter on how Jews regard evangelical attempts to convert them. After demonstrating a thorough understanding of the conversionist convictions of his evangelical friends, he suggested that they "leave the conversion of the Jews to God."[55] While he was not able to change his evangelical supporters' minds, he did sensitize them to the issue. But, of course, evangelicals were not directly involved in Eckstein's projects; they merely provided the money for them. Thus, they could support IFCJ and still maintain their commitments to evangelization. The irony was that it was precisely those evangelical beliefs about Jews and Israel that made them generous supporters of Eckstein's work. While evangelicals did not use the rabbi's projects as opportunities for evangelism, they still believed that they were helping Eckstein do God's work by fulfilling biblical prophecy and preserving the state of Israel until the rapture and the final prophecies concerning the Jews were fulfilled. At present, then, both sides seem to be getting more than enough out of their relationship.[56]

Are such compromises cynical? Is each side simply using the other to accomplish its own ends? One can certainly view the alliance in those terms, but there is another way to look at it. Politics have always made strange bedfellows. In the so-called culture wars that have characterized much of American life since the 1980s, many new political alliances have been established by people with little in common except their commitments to pro-life or pro-choice positions or their embrace or rejection of "traditional values." In the world of single-issue (or cluster-issues) politics, then, it is not surprising that American conservative Christians with particular prophetic views and Jews should rally together under the banner of Israel's security and survival.

Since the early 1980s, many fundamentalists have shown their willingness to cooperate with people with different religious beliefs to accomplish common political ends. Jerry Falwell, who is extremely careful about his religious connections, was nevertheless able to bring together in his Moral Majority a coalition of conservative Protestants, Catholics, Mormons, and Jews—and to justify it to his fellow fundamentalists: The Moral Majority was a *political* organization, not a religious one. Likewise, Esther Levens built her own religiously diverse pro-Israel coalition around a single issue, support for Israel.

In fact, one might even argue that the dispensationalist/Jewish pro-Israel alliance is one form of interfaith cooperation, if not interfaith dialogue: Both sides retain their own distinctive convictions while finding a common-ground basis on which to work together. In such interfaith projects, people often have to swallow hard and look the other way regarding many issues to find a mutually acceptable working relationship. If they didn't, interfaith cooperation would occur only if all sides gave up cherished beliefs and accepted an anemic lowest-common-denominator form of religious expression, which in the end would keep strongly committed people from being involved. Possibly the most important thing about such cooperative endeavors is that people on both sides understand what they are getting and what they are giving away by being involved. In this case, dispensationalists and Jews seem to be building the relationship with their eyes wide open.[57]

New and Improved Missions to the Jews

At the same time that some dispensationalists were building sturdy political bridges to Jews and the state of Israel, others were stepping up their campaign to evangelize them. Even though some premillennialists decided to downplay their evangelistic impulses to further their political agenda, as evangelicals, they never stopped believing that Jews needed converting and that their religion was profoundly defective because of its refusal to acknowledge the messiahship of Jesus. As their history abundantly shows, dispensationalists saw nothing contradictory about supporting the national aspirations of Jews and trying to convert them simultaneously. Jews were special because they were God's chosen people who had a crucial role to play in the last days, but they had rejected their Messiah and needed to be brought to faith. Dispensational theology taught both. Thus, it was not surprising that while some dispensationalist leaders were staking out strong pro-Israel positions, others were developing innovative and sometimes aggressive missionary strategies.

New Developments in Jewish Missions: Jews for Jesus

Just as dispensational missionaries in the early twentieth century had changed their approach to meet the needs of the second generation of Jewish Americans, missionaries at the end of the century made an adjustment to reach the third generation, the baby boomers who were coming of age during the 1960s and 1970s. The outlook of those Jewish young people was profoundly different from that of their parents and grandparents. They were much more open to new religious ideas than the generations before them had been.

On many levels, the 1960s were a turning point in American culture. Young people challenged the mores of their parents, thanks in large part to the breakdown of respect for authority structures throughout the culture. Young people experimented with all kinds of new ideas and behaviors, including religious ones.[58] This was particularly true of young Jews who had been raised in secular or nonobservant families whose knowledge or appreciation of Judaism was minimal. Many Jewish young people felt cut off from their own heritage and discovered a sense of belonging in Eastern, occult, or new religious movements—even evangelical Christianity.[59]

Seizing the opportunity that the 1960s provided, dispensationalists started a new brand of missions to the Jews, one far more aggressive and "Jewish" than earlier versions. According to one historian of Jewish missions:

> The more avant-garde Jews for Jesus and the movement of Messianic Judaism and later on the entire missionary movement promoted, as never before, the notion that Jews were not betraying their heritage by accepting Jesus as their Savior but rather becoming better Jews and embarking on a journey of reclaiming their Jewish roots. The missions also emphasized their hopes and support for Israel. Missions reacted favorably toward Zionism from the beginning of that movement, but during the new era, in the late 1960s through the 1970s and 1980s, they proclaimed their attachment to Israel as never before. The emphasis on Jewish roots and the attachment to Israel have become the heart of the mission's rhetoric and their appeal in approaching both potential converts and donors.[60]

Jews for Jesus began in 1970 in San Francisco as a branch ministry of the venerable American Board of Missions to the Jews. As already shown, the ABMJ was founded in 1894 by Leopold Cohn in New York and eventually became the largest and most influential of all Jewish mission organizations. Jews for Jesus was founded by Moishe Rosen, who had been a missionary with ABMJ since the late 1950s. Born in 1931 in Kansas City, Rosen grew up in Denver, where his family observed Jewish holidays and engaged in liberal Democratic politics. During high school, Rosen worked in his father's junk business and demonstrated a flair for business. At eighteen he married Ceil, who became interested in Christianity shortly after they were married. In 1953, Martin (as he was then called) and Ceil converted and affiliated with a Baptist church. After studying Bible and dispensational theology at Northeastern Bible College in New Jersey, Martin went to work for the American Board in Los Angeles. He was a skillful missionary, and in 1967, the mission moved him to its headquarters in New York City to oversee a training program for new missionary recruits. He quickly concluded that the mission needed a different way of reaching disaffected, countercultural Jewish youth. He asked for and received permission to develop a new approach on the West Coast, in San Francisco, the unofficial capital of the counterculture.

Rosen gathered around him a group of young, creative, and fearless Jewish converts who developed a new way of reaching Jews with the gospel. Since he believed that Jewish culture was inherently confrontational in style, Jews for Jesus took that approach. Rosen also correctly concluded that since most Jewish youth did not know much about Judaism, let alone the Torah, the old missionary strategy of quoting Scripture to prove Jesus' messiahship would be rather meaningless to the younger generation. Rosen's approach was considerably different: His missionaries took to the streets and confronted people with the question, "Are you Jewish?" If they answered in the affirmative, they received a clever leaflet. With titles such as "Everything you always wanted to know about Jesus but were afraid to ask your rabbi" and "Jesus made me kosher," the leaflets were intended to incite interest and provoke a conversation. Some Jews were offended by such tactics, but others were willing to consider what the Jews for Jesus had to say. What many Jews found most intriguing was the claim that one could accept Jesus and remain a Jew. According to Yaakov Ariel, Jews for Jesus aimed to show that "the Christian faith . . . was not a denial of their Jewishness but rather its true fulfillment. Jews should view the Christian faith as their own and not as an alien belief. The mission's name was intended to convey exactly that message."[61] A practical implication of this approach was that Jewish believers in Yeshua needed their own Jewish-Christian congregations.

The established missions to the Jews found much to dislike in this new approach. Many were uneasy with what they considered an embrace of certain countercultural values. It was easy to come to such a conclusion in the early days of Rosen's movement. His evangelists often looked like the countercultural people they were trying to reach and openly criticized the "establishment," which the older missions believed included them. In 1974, Rosen published *The Sayings of Chairman Moishe*,[62] a tongue-in-cheek variation on *The Sayings of Chairman Mao*. In retrospect, the establishment missions had nothing to fear. While Rosen and his missionaries concentrated their evangelistic efforts on the counterculture, their own values were very much "old school." While they knew how to talk to Jewish hippies, they did not embrace their lifestyle. Inside Jews for Jesus there was no smoking, drinking, using drugs, or having sex outside marriage. Along with pushing for accepting Jesus and retaining Jewishness, Jews for Jesus advocated a rather conservative evangelical lifestyle. If anything, accepting Jesus meant leaving hippie culture behind.[63]

Beyond the question of lifestyle, the concerns of the older missions were essentially theological. Most bothersome was the claim of Jews for Jesus that converts should continue to consider themselves Jews. The older missions had faced that issue decades before, and most had concluded that it was best for Jewish converts to join gentile evangelical congregations and leave their Jewishness behind. They feared that unless converts relinquished Jewish observances and identities, they would still be entangled in the law, which, as every reader of the New Testament knew, was the opposite of grace. As in the days of the apostle Paul, such mixing of law and grace amounted to "Judaizing," which undercut essentials of Jesus' gospel. But there was a strong drive among many people in the 1960s and 1970s to rediscover roots and affirm ethnicity. Thus, Rosen and his evangelists tapped into the longing of alienated Jews who were seeking ways to connect to their own heritage. Much to the surprise—and concern—of the older missions, Jews for Jesus was able to help such spiritually hungry young Jews reconnect to their Jewishness through faith in Jesus.

In the beginning, all of this was too much for the established Jewish missions. In 1973, the ABMJ fired Rosen and jettisoned his Jews for Jesus from its program. The break with the ABMJ had few lasting negative effects on Rosen and his evangelists. By the time they were expelled, they had already gained the confidence of a significant number of evangelical churches and parachurch ministries. If anything, the break actually benefitted Jews for Jesus, which expanded its mission and refined its methods.[64] The mission took a new name, Hineni Ministries, though most people inside and outside the mission still preferred to call it Jews for Jesus. The mission quickly became famous for hosting Passover Seders in evangelical churches to explain the nature of the Jewish holiday (but always with Christian additions) and provide a venue for curious Jews to hear the gospel. It also conducted "sorties" on college campuses, inviting both Jews and gentiles to consider the claims of Jesus. The mission further raised its visibility by taking out full-page ads in major daily newspapers and national magazines such as *Time*. The advertisements were eye-catching and provocative. One ad from the late 1980s asked, "Why Can't Christmas Be a Jewish Holiday?" It continued: "Isn't Christmas the birthday of the greatest Jew who ever lived?" "Of course, Y'shua (that's the Jewish way to say Jesus) was born in a Jewish place—Bethlehem—to a Jewish mother—Miriam—according to the Jewish prophets for a Jewish purpose, 'the salvation of the world.'" The ad offered free of charge a book titled *Jesus for Jews*,[65] which contained the stories of Jews converted through Jews for Jesus.[66]

The methods of Jews for Jesus may have seemed revolutionary, but the movement's underlying theology was not. The mission did not deviate from the theological approach embraced by other missions to the Jews. Rosen's group continued to affirm the conservative evangelical and premillennial theology of its parent organization: There was no salvation apart from Jesus, and God had a crucial role for Jews to play in the end times.[67] The combination of old-time theology, Jewish identity, and strong support for Israel proved to be much more successful than the efforts of the older missions to the Jews. According to one study from the early 1990s, tens of thousands of Jews accepted Jesus through the efforts of Rosen's evangelists.[68] But the Jewish community was slow to notice. During the 1970s and 1980s, Jewish scholars wrote optimistic books about the condition of the Jewish community, its growing recognition, achievements, and strength, without even mentioning the missionaries.[69] By the end of the 1980s, however, many Jewish leaders were getting worried about the implications of the rising intermarriage rates and the growing number of Jews who were converting to other religions.[70]

MESSIANIC JUDAISM

Jews for Jesus was not the Jews' only concern. Rosen's mission was merely the most public expression of a much broader movement, Messianic Judaism, which sought to create vibrant Jewish-Christian religious communities for Jews who accepted Jesus as Messiah. As already discussed, a few turn-of-the-twentieth-century missionaries started separate congregations for their Jewish converts, but by World War I, most of the Jewish missions had repudiated the strategy for theological and practical reasons. There were a few successful Hebrew Christian (as they were called then) congregations between the world wars, thanks especially to the efforts of the Presbyterian Church, but the vast majority of Jewish converts before the 1970s ended up joining evangelical churches.[71]

There was a revival of Jewish-Christian congregations in the 1970s, thanks in large part to the success of groups such as Jews for Jesus. The earliest Messianic congregations were founded by the converts themselves, not the Jewish missions, which remained reticent. At first the congregations remained independent from one another and other ministries. It is difficult to say where and when the first Messianic Jewish congregations began, but there were probably no more than ten such congregations in existence in 1970.[72] One of the earliest was Beth Messiah in Cincinnati, which was founded by Martin Chernoff, a missionary with the American Association of Jewish Evangelism of Chicago. Chernoff had conducted a highly successful campus ministry among Jewish students at the University of Cincinnati. When he decided to organize his converts into a new congregation in the early 1970s, he did so outside his mission's control. The members of the new congregation struggled with a number of important issues: How Jewish should they be? What kinds of practices should they embrace? How should they conduct worship? Like many other Messianic Jewish congregations, Beth Messiah adopted a charismatic style, which was rather pervasive in the Jesus Movement during the 1960s and fit well with certain aspects of Jewish life. This was especially true of the singing and dancing during the services.

Another Messianic Jewish congregation that formed in the early 1970s was Beth Yeshua in Philadelphia. It grew out of the evangelistic work of a converted Jewish chemist named Joe Finkelstein, who had a special gift for working with rebellious Jewish teenagers. When his converts balked at getting involved in the Presbyterian-sponsored Hebrew Christian center in downtown Philadelphia, Finkelstein decided to start his own Messianic congregation. The group called as its first pastor Martin Chernoff of Beth Messiah in Cincinnati, who quickly established the congregation's identity as Christian, Jewish, and charismatic. Like Chernoff's former congregation, Beth Yeshua struggled with how Jewish it should be. Eventually, the members decided to hold its weekly meeting on Friday evenings, passed out yarmulkes for all male members and visitors to wear during the service, lighted Shabbat candles before the service, and installed an ark with a Torah scroll. The liturgy included readings, prayers, and songs in both Hebrew and English. Over the years, various Jewish symbols were adopted for worship, including prayer shawls for men who participated in the service. In short, Beth Yeshua was Jewish in its style, evangelical and premillennial in its theology, and charismatic in its liturgical expression. Many subsequent Messianic congregations more or less followed the same model.[73] Beth Yeshua grew to a few hundred members and became the flagship congregation for the Messianic Jewish Alliance of America and the International Alliance of Messianic Congregations and Synagogues.[74]

As the number of Messianic congregations grew, the old missions establishment dug in its heels against the new movement. Its opposition was formally expressed by the Fellowship of Christian Testimonies to the Jews, to which most of the Jewish missions belonged in the early 1970s. After Jews for Jesus was pushed out of the American Board of Missions to the Jews, it applied for membership in the FCTJ. The fellowship rejected the application, fearing both Rosen's methods and probably Rosen himself. But the FCTJ feared Messianic Judaism even more. In October 1975, the FCTJ issued a resolution that soundly rejected it. The statement accused a segment of Messianic Jews of attempting to form a fourth "denomination" within Judaism alongside Orthodox, Conservative, and Reform. It also charged that Messianic Jews sought to form synagogues, not churches, and that they urged gentile members to undergo conversion to Judaism as part of the process of joining a Messianic fellowship. The statement also expressed deep concern about Messianic Judaism's adoption of "the practices of rabbinic Judaism," including keeping kosher laws and wearing skull caps and prayer shawls. Such practices reflected a "pseudo-cultural pride" that drove wedges between Jewish and gentile believers and misrepresented the nature of the congregations themselves. By adopting such Jewish ways, Messianic Jews were being deceptive, hiding their true identity as Christian churches. The conclusion was clear: "Be it resolved, therefore, that we of the FCTJ stand apart from and in opposition to Messianic Judaism as it is evolving today."[75]

The resolution was way off the mark, since few Messianic Jews were guilty of the charges that the FCTJ leveled against the movement. Almost as soon as the resolution was made public, many critics began backtracking. In short order, even the detractors of early Messianic Judaism had to admit that the movement was more "mainstream" than they had at first thought. A year after issuing their condemnation of Messianic Judaism, the leaders of the older Jewish missionary agencies met with the leaders of the new movement to iron out their differences.[76] According to Ariel, "Not long after the FCTJ condemnation, the missionary movement began coming to terms with Messianic Judaism and its methods, adjusting itself to the new changes and trying to make the most out of the new Messianic ideology and methods, in an attempt to advance the cause of evangelism among Jews."[77] By the 1980s, many of the older missions had adopted the strategies of Messianic Judaism and had started founding Messianic congregations of their own. The transformation of perspective is best illustrated by the American Board of Missions to the Jews: Within a decade of firing Rosen and condemning Messianic Judaism, the ABMJ changed its name to Chosen People Ministries and started establishing its own noncharismatic Messianic congregations, such as the Olive Tree congregation (and its offshoots) in the Chicago area.[78] The FCTJ, which had led the early charge against Messianic Judaism, faded away in the early 1980s and was replaced by the Lausanne Consultation on Jewish Evangelism, which was dominated by Messianic Jews and their perspective.[79]

By the late 1990s, there were approximately six thousand people connected to two hundred Messianic Jewish congregations in the United States.[80] As these numbers indicate, most of the congregations were quite small, though a few numbered in the hundreds. They differed substantially in terms of their use of Jewish symbols and Torah observances, their embrace or rejection of charismatic styles of worship, and their understanding of the relationship between Messianic congregations and other churches. What they had in common was the conviction that one did not have to give up one's Jewishness to be a follower of Jesus and that the state of Israel was a part of God's plan leading to the second coming of Christ.

The movement has struggled with the best way to provide theological training for its leaders. Moody Bible Institute, Westminster Theological Seminary, and Fuller Theological Seminary have welcomed Messianic Jews, but most Messianic leaders go without formal theological training.[81] Nevertheless, the movement has produced a few theological leaders of its own. The first was Arnold G. Fruchtenbaum, who in 1974 raised serious questions in *Hebrew Christianity* about some of Messianic Judaism's early ideas and tendencies.[82] In 1983, however, he published *Israelology: The Missing Link in Systematic Theology,* which argued for a reevaluation of the Jewish roots of Christianity and their ongoing importance in the life of the church.[83] Two other significant Messianic theology works were Daniel Juster's *Jewish Roots: A Foundation of Biblical Theology for Messianic Judaism* and David Stern's *Messianic Jewish Manifesto.* Both made their case for fashioning a Jewish-Christian theology.[84]

All of these works struggled with how far Messianic congregations should go in adopting and adapting Jewish observances. Virtually all Messianic congregations celebrated the Passover, which required a blending of traditional forms and Messianic meanings. Three examples of Messianic Passover Haggadoth were Eric Peter Lipson's *Passover Haggadah: A Messianic Celebration,* J. Ron Tavalin's *Kol Hesed Messianic Haggadah,* and Harold Sevener's *Passover Haggadah for Biblical Jews and Christians.*[85] Lipson's *Passover Haggadah,* for example, contained the traditional four questions and the four cups of wine, but the traditional readings of rabbinic commentary *(midrash)* on the meaning of the Passover story in Exodus were replaced with selections from the New Testament. Among the prescribed prayers was the following: "Blessed art Thou, O Lord our God, king of the Universe, who had sent Thy son, Thine only son, Y'shua the Messiah, to be the light of the world and our Paschal Lamb, that through him we might live. Amen."[86] Most Messianic congregations also observed the other Old Testament feast days: Shavuot (Feast of Weeks or Pentecost), Rosh Hashanah (Jewish New Year), Yom Kippur (Day of Atonement), Purim, Succoth (Feast of Tabernacles), and Hanukkah. All such observances were done with Messianic adaptations to show how such celebratory events in the history of Israel found their ultimate fulfillments in the life and ministry of Jesus the Messiah.[87]

Ironically, this attempt to adapt Messianic beliefs to Jewish practices posed the biggest barrier to the effective evangelization of observant

Jews by Messianic congregations. While virtually all leaders of Messianic Judaism claimed that their approach was needed for reaching Jews with the gospel, research has shown that few observant Jews came to faith in Christ as a result of the evangelistic efforts of Messianic congregations. According to Jeffrey Wasserman, "Traditional Protestant Evangelical churches have been far more successful in Jewish evangelism than Messianic congregations. . . . Of the estimated 50,000 to 60,000 believing Jews in North America, only 5,000 to 6,000 are involved in Messianic congregations. In my survey 98% of the Jewish members of Messianic congregations were brought to faith by Gentile Christians."[88]

Part of the reason for the poor evangelistic performance of Messianic congregations was that most of the people who attended them were not even Jews. In his study of Messianic congregations in the late 1990s, Wasserman discovered that 60 percent of the membership and 50 percent of the leadership were gentile Christians.[89] In another study, Michael Schiffman found that Jews made up only 25 to 50 percent of those attending.[90] The gentile majority was composed of the spouses of converted Jews and other gentiles who were attracted to the style of worship, the sense of community, and the emphasis on Israel's prophetic role in the last days. In practical terms, the high percentage of gentile congregants meant that most members of Messianic congregations lacked a personal understanding or experience of being Jewish, which was a detriment in a religious community that was seeking to offer an authentic form of Jewish Christianity to the world. Thus, to the average observant Jewish visitor, the typical Messianic congregation often looked like a bunch of gentiles trying to figure out what a Jewish version of the Christian faith might look like. For some Jews, then, a Messianic congregation did not look, feel, or sound Jewish. Nevertheless, for many Jews who found new faith in Christ elsewhere, Messianic congregations provided a better fit than the typical gentile evangelical congregation. Certainly for those Jews with secular or nonobservant backgrounds, the hybrid Jewishness of Messianic congregations posed no problem at all.[91] For them, attending a Messianic congregation was probably the most Jewish thing they had ever done in their lives.

JEWISH REACTIONS

It is not surprising that American Jews reacted strongly to both Jews for Jesus and the whole Messianic Jewish enterprise. Here was continuing proof that dispensationalists were really intent on proselytizing Jews, notwithstanding their support for the state of Israel. For most of the twentieth century, the Jewish community did not take the evangelical mission to the Jews seriously. Missionary results were always meager, and the converts were usually marginal in the Jewish community. In some cases, Jewish leaders developed a grudging respect for the missionaries, who worked hard at not offending the people they were trying to convert. In short, most Jews ignored the missionaries because they were seen as basically ineffective and thus posed no threat to the stability and survivability of the Jewish community. But all that changed in the 1960s and 1970s. As stated above, Jewish young people seemed especially susceptible to new, Eastern, and evangelical religious movements, all of which their elders categorized as cults that used deceptive methods to trap young people. Thus, many Jewish critics labeled Jews for Jesus and Messianic Judaism dangerous cults that used mind control, brainwashing, and deception to lead Jewish young people astray.[92]

A typical accusation came from an Orthodox rabbi: "If Rosen and his 'Jews for Jesus' seem less than kosher, it is not surprising. His Hebrew Christian gambit is a fraud. One can no sooner be a Christian and a Jew simultaneously than he can be a Christian and a Moslem. The claim that a Jew need not give up his Jewishness in order to join Christianity is a carefully constructed ruse . . . aimed at the enormous pool of young American Jews who were raised in assimilated, middle and upper class areas."[93] Nobel Prize winner Elie Wiesel singled out Jews for Jesus in an article titled "The Missionary Menace." He called them "hypocrites" who lacked "the courage to declare frankly that they have decided to repudiate their people and its memories."[94] Fundamentally, Jewish critics rejected the assertion that one could accept Jesus as the Messiah and retain one's identity as a Jew. Judaism and Christianity were two separate religions, they claimed, so a convert could never find a way to bring them together. The new missionaries were trying to sell an idea that was simply impossible.

But even Messianic Judaism's fiercest critics could not deny that many Jewish converts claimed that they felt more Jewish and lived better Jewish lives *after* accepting Jesus as their Messiah. They said that Yeshua had made them better Jews than before, not worse.[95] The growth of Messianic Judaism, therefore, forced many Jews to do some serious soul-searching: If some Jews felt more Jewish after becoming Christians, what did that say about the overall health of the Jewish community? As Ariel summarized, "Jewish anticult literature . . . criticized Jewish parents for failing to raise their children in committed Jewish homes, the Jewish community for its inadequacy in making Judaism attractive to the younger generation, and Jewish education for failing to transfer Judaism to the next generation. Many of the writers also criticized Jewish congregations for their lack of spirituality, warmth, and a sense of community."[96] Some Orthodox Jews wanted to hold Conservative and

Reform Judaism responsible for the confused and uncommitted state of Jewish youth.

Critics of the missionaries mustered a counterattack by putting on conferences, holding classes, and publishing booklets on "how to answer the missionaries." Many of these were essentially primers on basic Judaism for Jewish young people raised in secular or nonobservant homes.[97] Some of the literature showed considerable understanding of the missionaries' arguments and strategy, which they used to try to get the already converted to change their minds and return to their ancestral faith.[98]

What many Jews found baffling was that the same people who were trying to convert them were also outspoken supporters of Israel. Most Jews welcomed the friendship of such evangelical leaders, often without the slightest understanding of the prophetic views that motivated them. Sometimes Jews appealed to their new relationship with evangelicals to get them to stop targeting them for evangelism. This appeal got some early results. Not long after Jews for Jesus began making its mark, evangelicals announced Key '73, an ambitious nationwide evangelistic effort. A group of leading Jews, including Nathan Perlmutter of the Anti-Defamation League, met with Billy Graham, who was not directly involved in Key '73 planning or leadership, to share their concerns about being targeted for evangelism.[99] The overture put Graham in a difficult position. As an evangelist, he was committed to sharing the gospel with everyone, including Jews, but he was sensitive to Jewish complaints about being manipulated and deceived by missionaries such as Jews for Jesus. Graham issued a statement condemning evangelistic methods that "used gimmicks, coercion, or intimidation." While affirming that all people needed Jesus to be saved, he nonetheless expressed concern about singling out Jews for special evangelistic attention.[100] The Jews were pleased, but the Jewish missions were not. In fact, Rosen and others made their own trip to see Billy Graham to make their case and defend themselves against the charges made by their Jewish critics. Evidently, Billy Graham got the point: He never said another word of criticism against the Jewish missions.[101] Evangelizing Jews and supporting Israel continued on as before, moving toward Armageddon on parallel tracks.

DISPENSATIONALIST RELIGIOUS ALLIANCES IN ISRAEL

Dispensationalists also found ways to join hands with the Messianic Jewish mission inside Israel. While the International Christian Embassy and some of the other pro-Israel dispensationalist groups were careful to avoid any appearance of proselytism, other groups were busy evangelizing Jews in the Holy Land. In some ways, the Messianic Jewish movement was more successful in Israel than it was in the United States. Israeli converts did not have to work nearly as hard at proving their Jewishness as American converts did. As a result, Torah observance and the use of Jewish symbols were less frequent in Israel than in America.[102]

In his history of the modern Christian mission to the Jews, Yaakov Ariel concluded that Israel provided a more welcoming context for Messianic Judaism than did the United States.[103] From roughly three hundred in the mid-1960s, the number of Messianic Jews in Israel increased to approximately three thousand in the mid-1980s and six thousand in the mid-1990s.[104] By the end of the 1990s, there were roughly fifty congregations and fifty house groups or fellowships.[105] The growth came from all parts of Israeli society, including Israel-born Jews (the so-called *sabras*) and Jews from the former Soviet Union and Ethiopia, who arrived in Israel by the tens of thousands. Following the close call of the Yom Kippur War of 1973, many Israelis lost confidence in the Zionist ideology that had held Israeli culture together since the nation's founding and were willing to consider other religious and political perspectives. Messianic Jews were able to speak effectively to Israel's changing cultural context. Ariel was convinced that "some of the growth was due to the fact that Messianic congregations were effective in conveying to prospective converts a strong sense of community and a safe haven with an alternative set of morals to that of a general culture."[106]

The story of Messianic Judaism in Israel illustrates the same kinds of complexities experienced in the United States. Starting in the 1970s, Israelis welcomed and learned to rely on the friendship and support of America's Christian Zionists. The Likud Party recognized evangelical leaders such as Jerry Falwell and Pat Robertson with the Jabotinsky Order Medal for their work on behalf of Israel. At the same time, the Orthodox parties within Likud worked hard to outlaw missionary activity in Israel. In 1978, the Knesset passed a law prohibiting the offering of money or other economic advantages in exchange for conversion. The result of the law was negligible for two reasons: The missionaries did not offer monetary inducements for conversion, and the Israeli minister of justice made it clear that the law would not be enforced without the direct authorization of the attorney general, who simply refused to invoke the law against the missionaries. In practical terms, the law made no difference to missionary practices or the growth of the Messianic movement.

In 1996, Orthodox and non-Orthodox members of the Knesset joined forces to pass another anti-missionary law. The measure survived a first reading in the Knesset but fell prey to the realities of the complicated relationship between the Israeli government and its Christian Zionist supporters in the United States. The Messianic community in Israel called on its supporters in America to apply pressure on the Israeli government not to seek final approval of the law. American evangelicals inundated the Israeli embassy in Washington and its consulates in the rest of the country with mail, phone calls, and protest petitions via the Internet. The same kind of networking that gave pro-Israel American dispensationalists such a long reach into the U.S. Congress and State Department was now being used against the Israeli government. Almost immediately some of the law's most significant supporters began backing off, most notably Prime Minister Netanyahu, who had at first endorsed the bill. Finally, a compromise of sorts was struck: The Israeli government declared its opposition to the bill in exchange for a promise by certain Christian groups not to evangelize further. Once again, this agreement packed little punch. According to Ariel, "The Christian groups that promised not to evangelize Jews were not engaged in such activity anyhow, and those who made it their goal to missionize Jews made no promises to stop their activity."[107] The Jewish mission in Israel was saved.

As the above episode illustrates, American dispensationalists have close ties with the Messianic Jewish community in Israel. Most leaders of the Israeli movement are financially supported from outside Israel, either by American denominations or individual local churches. Messianic leaders from Israel and the United States know one another and communicate often. Furthermore, many members of Israeli Messianic congregations are actually transplanted Americans, both Jews and gentiles. As a result, congregations with a significant number of American Messianic believers are much more interested in Torah observances than are those whose members are primarily Israeli. Secular Jews and Russian Jewish immigrants, two groups from which most Israeli Messianic believers come, often have little experience with or affinity for the practices of rabbinic Judaism. Since they are already considered Jews and citizens of Israel, they have nothing to prove concerning their identities in Messianic congregations. Likewise, thanks to the dynamics of the American Messianic experience, Israeli Messianic congregations are divided according to charismatic and noncharismatic worship styles.[108] Probably the most glaring evidence of the close relationship between the two groups is that when Israeli Messianic Jews feel threatened, they do not hesitate to ask their American dispensational "friends of Israel" for help. As shown, their friends know how to deliver.

Probably the biggest irony concerning dispensationalists' involvement in the religious life of Israel is their lack of interest in the largest group of believers in Israel and the West Bank, the Palestinian Christians. While there are 6,000 Messianic believers in Israel, there are 145,000 Palestinian Christians who never seem to make it on the premillennial list of concerns. The history of Christianity in the Middle East is long and involved, but Palestinian Christians claim a heritage that goes back to apostolic times. They see themselves as the "living stones" that cry out a continuous Christian testimony throughout the centuries but now face near dissolution due to a massive Christian exodus from the Middle East. Accurate numbers are always difficult to come by, but there is no doubt that more Palestinian Christians now live outside the Holy Land than in it.[109] Since the Six-Day War of 1967, thousands of Palestinian Christians have fled the West Bank, Gaza, and East Jerusalem to seek homes elsewhere. For example, more Palestinian Christians from Ramallah live in Detroit, Michigan, and Jacksonville, Florida, than in Ramallah on the West Bank.[110] The reasons for the decline in the population are many, from economics to low birth rates to feelings of hopelessness that come from being caught in the middle between Muslim Arabs and Jewish Israelis.[111]

Why are American dispensationalists so neglectful of their Palestinian Christian brothers and sisters? One reason is that American evangelicals do not seem to have much in common with them. Most Palestinian Christians belong to one of the Eastern Orthodox families—Greek, Syrian, Coptic, Ethiopian, and even Russian. Roughly one-third of Palestinian Christians are Roman Catholic (called Latin Catholic in the Middle East). The uniate churches, the Maronites and the Melkites, recognize Roman primacy but retain their own distinctive Eastern rites. In the minority are Protestant Christians of various kinds, Anglicans, Lutherans, Baptists, and other independent evangelicals. Thus, American dispensationalists would find only a small number of Palestinian Christians whose style and beliefs are similar to theirs. As a general rule, American evangelicals do not engage in ecumenical enterprises. Therefore, they stay clear of the Middle East Council of Churches, which attempts to speak with a united Christian voice in a conflicted and dangerous context.

Even those Palestinians who speak fluent "evangelical" view the world differently than do American Christian Zionists. Since dispensationalism sees Arabs as God's enemies in the end times, it does not find many takers among Palestinian Christians who believe that *they* are Israel's victims, not vice versa. If American dispensationalists cannot understand why fellow Christians would align themselves against God's plan for Israel, Palestinian believers are equally confused by dispensationalists' preference for Israelis over other Christian believers. They wonder why evangelical tourists treat Palestinian Christian communities such as Bethlehem and Nazareth like museums of ancient Christianity rather than living religious communities with their own important stories to tell. Why would evangelical tour groups prefer to hear from Israeli generals than fellow Christians who are suffering? Why do the pro-Israel

Christian Zionist groups extend more comfort to Russian Jewish émigrés than to them? Even evangelical Palestinians are bitter and outspoken over the loss of ancestral homes and lands and Israeli policies they find oppressive.[112] Such sentiments are not welcome among American dispensationalists who are convinced that Palestinians—even Christian Palestinians—have no right to the land of Israel and are destined to play a negative role in events leading to the second coming. Many evangelical tourists to Israel are surprised to discover that there are Palestinian Christians, since they had assumed that all Palestinians are Muslims and the enemies of both Christians and Jews.[113] In the end, dispensational prophecy does not leave much room for Palestinian believers, which means that dispensationalists do not have to pay them any mind.

Some evangelicals have taken up the Palestinian cause. Donald Wagner is probably the most outspoken and effective spokesman for Palestinian Christians. He is the executive director of the Center for Middle Eastern Studies at North Park University in Chicago and administrative director of Evangelicals for Middle East Understanding. He has spent considerable time in the Middle East getting to know Christians, Muslims, and Jews on all sides of the Israeli-Palestinian conflict. He too knows how to take tour groups to Israel, but his itineraries include Palestinian areas as well as Israeli territory. In his own analysis of the current situation, he recognizes that views of Bible prophecy have often impeded work for peace because devotees already have the players all figured out and firmly placed in an inevitable end-times script. Despite the efforts of Wagner and others, the story of Palestinian believers is seldom heard in dispensationalist circles.[114]

Since the Six-Day War, then, American dispensationalists have taken a much more hands-on approach. Fearing for Israel's security, dispensationalists have become more than predictors of Israel's future. They have organized politically to offer various kinds of support to the Jewish state. They have forged strong and unprecedented relationships, much to the surprise and dismay of people on the left. At the same time, dispensationalists have continued to seek the conversion of Jews to Christ, though their close personal and political ties to Jews and Israel have sometimes complicated their evangelistic enterprise. By the end of the twentieth century, dispensationalists were Israel's best friends, for better and, as we will see in the next chapter, for worse.

9

How Dispensationalists May Be Helping Prophecy Happen

If dispensationalists have been Israel's best friends for the last thirty years, what has such a friendship produced? Certainly, one result has been the emergence of a strong and apparently unwavering supporter of Israel in the United States. The many pro-Israel organizations created by dispensationalists have undoubtedly made a difference. In a political world in which popular pressure counts, Israel is in a stronger position today because of the willingness of American premillennialists to throw their political clout around. The New Christian Right remains a potent force in American politics, and the willingness of Christian conservatives to stand up for Israel has helped U.S.-Israeli relations stay strong. By now it should be obvious that the pro-Israel lobby is not just Jewish; it consists of strong conservative Christian support that emanates from particular views of Bible prophecy.

But friendships often have dysfunctional sides to them. In the real world, friends sometimes unintentionally work against one another's best interests. In their attempt to help, they end up doing harm. There is a downside to the dispensationalist/Israeli friendship. In their commitment to keep Israel strong and moving in directions prophesied by the Bible, dispensationalists are currently supporting some of the most dangerous elements in Israeli society. They do so because such political and religious elements seem to conform to dispensationalist beliefs about what is coming next for Israel. By lending their support—both financial and spiritual—to such groups, dispensationalists are helping the future they envision come to pass.

Preparing for the End: Dispensationalists and the Israeli Far Right

Throughout their history, dispensationalists have predicted that before the final events of the end times can take place, the temple must be rebuilt in Jerusalem. According to their scenario, halfway through the great tribulation, the Antichrist will enter the restored temple and declare himself to be God. To outsiders, such predictions always seemed far-fetched. For hundreds of years, Islam's third holiest shrine, the Dome of the Rock, had occupied the Temple Mount—or the Noble Sanctuary, as the Arabs call it. But in the Six-Day War, Israel gained control of the entire city of Jerusalem, including the Temple Mount. Suddenly, all things seemed possible, at least to some people.

LOOKING FOR A NEW TEMPLE

Anticipating a third temple was nothing new for dispensationalists. For over a century they had been predicting that once Jews regathered in the Holy Land, they would eventually build a new temple on the site of the previous two. Actually, dispensationalists believed that there would be two new temples in Israel's future:

> It is necessary to distinguish in the context of the Old Testament whether the future Tribulation or millennial temple is in view. The Tribulation temple will be built by unbelieving Jews and desecrated by the Antichrist (Dan. 9:27; cf. 11:36–45). The millennial temple will be built by the Messiah (Zech. 6:12–13) and redeemed Jews, and as a particular sign of restoration, assisted by representatives from Gentile nations (Zech. 6:15; Hag. 2:7; cf. Isa. 60:10). It will be distinguished from the tribulation temple as the restoration temple by a return of the Shekinah Glory of God (Ezek. 43:1–7; cf. Ezek. 10:4, 18–19; 11:22–23) and by Gentile worship (Isa. 60:6; Zeph. 3:10; Zech. 2:11; 8:22; 14:16–19).[1]

Not all dispensationalists agreed on all the details, but in general they saw a rebuilt temple as indispensable to the completion of God's prophetic program. According to John F. Walvoord, not long after the Antichrist brings his false peace to the Middle East, he will assist the Jews in building the temple on the Temple Mount, as a symbol of national security and their redemption. Grateful Jews will hail him as their Messiah and commence Old Testament patterns of animal sacrifice. After three and a half years, the Antichrist will betray Israel by entering the restored temple, declaring himself to be God, and demanding worship. This is the ultimate "abomination of desolation" of biblical prophecy. Many Jews will resist such blasphemy, which will provoke the Antichrist to launch the worst holocaust in Jewish history. During this phase of the great tribulation, a missionary force of 144,000 converted Jews will spread the gospel of Jesus and the coming kingdom and will suffer martyrdom for their efforts. Though the Antichrist's power will be formidable, his days will be numbered. God will pour out divine wrath on those who follow the Antichrist, who will be finally defeated by Christ at his second coming. Surviving Jews will hail Jesus as their conquering and true Messiah. King Jesus will then set up his millennial throne in Jerusalem and construct a millennial temple, the fourth and final temple in Israel's history, where Jews and Gentiles will gather to worship in spirit and in truth.[2]

There were many practical impediments to the realization of these hopes, not the least of which was the existence of the Dome of the Rock and the Al-Aqsa Mosque on the site of these future temple projects. How could the temple be built when the Temple Mount was already occupied by Muslim sacred sites? The answer to this question varied. While dispensationalists knew that the temple had to be built, they did not agree on *how* it was going to happen. In the 1980s, John Wesley White summarized what all dispensationalists believed: A new temple "is an absolute necessity for the completion of the prophetic picture."[3] But the details were elusive.

Dispensationalists could not even agree on *where* the new temple would be built. There were three theories about place based on elaborate archaeological study and speculation.[4] According to Asher Kaufman, a professor of physics at Hebrew University, the original two temples were located on the Temple Mount to the north of the Dome of the Rock. He published his findings in the *Biblical Archaeological Review* in 1983, but his arguments convinced few other archaeologists. Kaufman did attract the attention of some leading dispensationalists, however. David Lewis, Hal Lindsey, Chuck Smith, and Chuck Missler pondered the theory with some eagerness. According to Lewis, "The importance could be—this is just a possibility—that the Dome of the Rock might not be destroyed when the Temple is built."[5] Some dispensationalists invited Kaufman to America to lecture on his findings, but Kaufman was often bewildered by some of their concerns, especially their insistence that in the new temple, priests would perform the ancient animal sacrifices. Kaufman anticipated a bloodless temple that would become "a unifying force for the Jewish people all over the world—a demonstration of the divine presence within the Jewish people. . . . It would replace the Western Wall as a central place in Judaism."[6]

A Tel Aviv architect named Tuvia Sagiv championed another theory that located past and future temples in between the Dome of the Rock and the Al-Aqsa Mosque. According to his "southern theory," when Muslims conquered Jerusalem and asked Jewish inhabitants where the temple of Solomon had stood, the Jews pointed them to the site of Hadrian's Temple of Jupiter. There the unsuspecting conquerors constructed the Dome of the Rock, thus leaving the actual site vacant. Sagiv used a variety of techniques to prove his point, including infrared photography, which he believed showed the outlines of the ancient temple stretching between the dome and the mosque. Sagiv hoped that his findings would deter radicals who believed that to rebuild the temple they would have to destroy the Dome of the Rock, which he feared would lead to World War III. He predicted that Muslims would someday allow excavations to prove the site of the temple: "We'll break through the Western Wall and be able to look at the remains of the Temple. They'll be above, and we'll be below, until the coming of the messiah. . . . I have problems with sacrifices. . . . Just looking could be more spiritual."[7] Of course, dispensationalists who accepted Sagiv's theory believed that such information would be put to a different use. Sagiv became the favorite of Chuck Missler, who arranged for Sagiv to lecture to his tour groups in Israel and for a while had him speak at his temple conferences. "The infrared information I've seen is not conclusive, but tends to support Tuvia Sagiv. . . . What interests us is not the specifics, but the fact that the . . . [research] is being pursued . . . that somewhere along the way the Temple will be rebuilt."[8]

The third theory placed the ancient and future temple site directly under the Dome of the Rock. Most Israeli archaeologists favored this view. The most advanced work in support of the theory for a "central location" was done by Leen Ritmeyer, a Dutch-born Christian archaeologist who went to Israel shortly after the Six-Day War. Behind the science of his investigations stood strong convictions about the future temple that would be built on the original site. Most dispensationalists agreed with Ritmeyer's location for the temple. Shortly after the Six-Day War, Wilbur Smith wrote that he expected the temple to be built soon—where the Dome of the Rock stood.[9]

A few Bible teachers speculated about how the problem of the dome's presence could be solved. As early as 1930, a Bible teacher suggested that a bomb might easily clear the site, an observation made by many others in the years following. In 1982, Louis Goldberg of Moody Bible Institute stated that in some future Arab-Israeli war, a surface to surface missile fired from Jordan or Syria might accidently go off course and destroy the Muslim site. Dispensationalist fiction writers also gave it a try: In Salem Kirban's novel *666*, the Antichrist vaporizes the mosque with his ruby laser ring, and in Charles Colson's *Kingdoms in Conflict,* American prophecy believers finance a plot by Israeli radicals to blow up the dome.[10]

Still, other dispensationalists wanted to avoid, if possible, the awful consequences of an Israeli attack on the dome and the mosque. In 1973, Malcom Couch speculated in an article in *Moody Monthly* that if the temple were built a little to the east of the current dome, where some recent research located the original Holy of Holies, the dome could remain untouched. Ten years later, Couch produced a film titled *The Temple,* which followed a similar argument from Thomas McCall and Zola Levitt's book *Satan in the Sanctuary.*[11] Of course, one could always wait on God to remove the dome and the mosque. In *The Late Great Planet Earth,* Hal Lindsey was willing to leave everything to divine initiative. He quoted Israeli historian Yisrael Eldad: "Who knows, maybe there will be an earthquake."[12] Clearly, most dispensationalists cared more about affirming that the temple would be rebuilt than worrying about the angst that such a move would cause Muslims. According to Arnold T. Olson, "The Temple will be rebuilt. Israel has the will, access to the means, and now the site. What remains is the problem of how to occupy that site without bringing on themselves the wrath of the Arabs stirred up to what would be to them a real holy war. But build she will."[13]

Such views were deeply embedded in the dispensationalist rank and file. On one of her Falwell-sponsored tours of Israel in the 1980s, Grace Halsell ran into these beliefs regularly. As one group neared the Temple Mount, the guide pointed to the Dome of the Rock and the Al-Aqsa Mosque and declared, "There we will build our Third Temple. We have all the plans drawn for the temple. Even the building materials are ready. They are hidden in a secret place. There are several shops where Israelis work, making the artifacts we will use in the new temple." Later on, Halsell asked a well-informed fellow tour member about the prophecies concerning a third temple. He told her that it was not going to be up to Christians to get rid of the Muslim shrines, "but I'm sure the shrines will be destroyed." What about the possibility that destroying the dome might lead to World War III? "Yes, that's right," he went on. "We are near the End Times. . . . Orthodox Jews will blow up the mosque and this will provoke the Muslim world. It will be a cataclysmic holy war with Israel. This will force the Messiah to intervene."[14]

Of course, any talk about rebuilding the temple was unacceptable to the Muslim population. They were not about to share sacred space with the Jews or give it up without a fight. In fact, in a futile attempt to turn the Jews' attention elsewhere, some Muslims argued that there never was a Jewish temple on the Temple Mount. That is the position of the director of the Al-Aqsa Mosque, Sheikh Muhammad Hussein: "This is an Islamic holy site. It never has been related to anything else."[15] In the pamphlet given to tourists by the Waqf, the keepers of the holy place, the assertion is the same: "Some believe it [the Al-Aqsa Mosque] was the site of the Temple of Solomon, peace be upon him . . . or the site of the Second Temple . . . although no documented historical or archaeological evidence exists to support this."[16] As Gershom Gorenberg points out, such statements amount to rewriting even Muslim history, but current tensions have a way of clouding memories of the past. In the Middle East, the past and the future are tightly bound, so to deny the possibility of a future temple, one must deny that a temple ever existed there.[17]

For that reason, Muslims in charge of the Noble Sanctuary have opposed Israeli archaeological explorations in the area to prove the location of the second temple or activity intended to show the placement of the future third temple. Attempts to do either have led to violent reactions. In 1989, for example, Gershon Salomon, the founder of the Temple Mount Faithful (a movement to be described in more detail below), announced his intention to lead a contingent of his followers to the Temple Mount to lay the cornerstone of the third temple. The Israeli police turned Salomon and his party away. The next year, Salomon announced a repeat performance: He and the Temple Mount Faithful planned to lay a four-and-a-half-ton cornerstone during the Feast of Tabernacles. Again the Israeli police refused to allow them access to the Temple Mount. But on October 8, three thousand Palestinians responded to the call to defend the Muslim holy places. As twenty thousand Jews gathered before the Western Wall for the beginning of the Feast of Tabernacles, the Palestinians wrongly believed that Salomon's group was approaching. From the walls of the Temple Mount they let loose a barrage of stones on the worshipers below. Eventually, the Israeli paramilitary police shot back, killing roughly twenty Palestinians. Serious rioting broke out throughout the occupied territory.[18]

In the fall of 1996, there was bloodshed over the opening of a tourist tunnel near the Temple Mount. On September 23, just before midnight, workmen began knocking a hole in a wall just north of the Temple Mount in the Muslim Quarter along the Via Dolorosa, the street Jesus had walked on the way to his crucifixion. The excavators knew what they were looking for and quickly uncovered a stairway to a two-thousand-year-old tunnel that connected to a modern tunnel dug by the Religious Affairs Ministry along the Temple Mount's west side. Thanks to the link, tourists could enter the tunnel from the Western Wall plaza, then walk north to the Muslim Quarter, passing by the huge stones of Herod's wall. The tunnel never actually went under the Temple Mount, only alongside it, but Muslims considered the excavation a violation of their sacred space. In fact, for years they had strongly resisted similar tunnel building around the Noble Sanctuary. Nevertheless, then prime minister Benjamin Netanyahu had approved the project, but he had arranged for it to take place late at night to avoid potential trouble. He had not been careful enough. Muslims reacted strongly, starting the next morning. Protests erupted in the Muslim Quarter, and the Palestinian Authority called the new tunnel opening "part of a Zionist-Israeli plot to Judaize the Holy City and damage Al-Aqsa mosque." A statement from the Arab League accused the Israeli government of advancing its plan to build a Jewish temple by undermining the mosque. The riots that followed quickly escalated from stone throwing to pitched battles between the Israeli Defense Force and Palestinian police. Israeli police clashed with Muslim worshipers on the Temple Mount. The violence spread to other places in the West Bank and Gaza, resulting in the most severe clash between Palestinians and Jews since the Six-Day War. According to Gorenberg, "The crisis showed again that the Mount is a sacred blasting cap, that even shaking the ground nearby can set it off."[19]

As it turned out, the Palestinians' strong reaction to the tunnel was in part produced by their own prophetic literature, which foresees a future Jewish Antichrist who will threaten Islam until he is vanquished by the return of Jesus, whom Muslims consider one of their own greatest prophets. Muslims expect Jews to undermine the Dome of the Rock and the Al-Aqsa Mosque as the end approaches. Their loyalty to Allah will force them to resist at all costs.[20] Thus, Muslim prophetic expectations predisposed defenders of Islam to view Israeli actions in particular ways.

FORMING ATTACHMENTS TO THE TEMPLE MOVEMENT

Muslims had a right to worry, since over the years there had been a number of attempts to destroy the dome and the mosque. Such activities were connected in one way or another to a small but growing movement on the far right of Israeli politics and religion—the Temple Movement. Though most Israelis do not believe in the necessity of a new temple to secure Israel's future, a minority is convinced that Israel's current problems are due to its failure to occupy the Temple Mount and rebuild the temple there. Some of these pro-temple Israelis are committed to doing what they can to make it happen, and some dispensationalists are supporting their efforts.

In 1969, Dennis Michael Rohan, an Australian tourist who had gone to Israel to study Hebrew and work on a *kibbutz,* entered the Al-Aqsa Mosque before normal visiting hours one day and set fire to the mosque. It took many Israeli firefighters and sixteen fire trucks hours to put out the fire. Local Muslims blamed Israelis for the arson, accusing Jews of spraying gasoline on the fire and cutting off the water supply to ensure the mosque's destruction. When Rohan was arrested and identified as a Christian foreigner, it made little difference. Muslims called for a general strike in the occupied territory, and Arab leaders from Egypt and Saudi Arabia called for a holy war against Israel. At his trial, Rohan's motives became clear: He believed that God had called him to rebuild the temple and then rule over Jerusalem. The Israeli court judged him to be insane and sent him to a mental institution. The Israelis thus claimed that they were not responsible, but most Muslims believed that any attempt to destroy the dome or the mosque served the purposes of Israel, no matter who did the actual attack.[21]

In 1979, an underground group of Israeli extremists led by Yehudah Etzion, Menachem Livni, and Yehudah Ben-Shushan began plotting to blow up the Dome of the Rock. Most of their followers were from the Gush Emunim (the Believers' Block), an organization founded in 1974 by religious Zionist settlers on the West Bank who believed that God had returned Judea and Samaria and all of Jerusalem to its rightful owners in the Six-Day War. They were followers of Rabbi Tzvi Yehudah Kook, the leader of the religious Zionists. For them, allowing Muslims to retain practical control of the Temple Mount was an abomination. Israel's ultimate redemption depended on Jews regaining absolute control over the mount on which the ancient temples of Israel had stood. The group hoped that the destruction of the dome would stop Israeli plans to evacuate the Sinai Peninsula, which was part of the Camp David Accords, and would rally the rest of Israel to what Etzion called the Redemption Movement.

For over two years they planned their attack, which included strapping twenty-eight explosive charges to the pillars of the dome. They stole the explosives from the Israeli army. But by the time they were ready to act in 1982, the Israeli withdrawal from the Sinai had already taken place and one of the plot's leaders had fallen ill. Without enough manpower to make it work, the plot dissolved. The group did not completely give up hope, however. The Gush Emunim bombed the cars of the Palestinian mayors of El Bireh, Ramallah, and Nablus. In revenge for the murder of a yeshiva student in Hebron, in 1983, two men from the group entered the Islamic college there and murdered three Muslim students. The next year the group set out to blow up five Arab buses in East Jerusalem during the evening rush hour. The Shin Bet (the Israeli FBI) got wind of the plot and made arrests before it could be carried out. At the trial, prosecutors were able to unravel the group's elaborate conspiracies. The judges who heard the case agreed that if they had succeeded in destroying the Dome of the Rock, millions of Muslims would have responded to the call for holy war, thereby increasing "the risk of world conflagration." Nevertheless, the eighteen convicted Gush Emunim spent relatively few years behind bars. Almost immediately strong voices in the Likud government began urging clemency. Three who had received life sentences were released in fewer than seven years, after their sentences were reduced three times. Etzion left prison in 1989 after serving fewer than five years. To the Muslim community, the affair proved that they and their holy places were in mortal danger.[22]

Other Israeli groups were equally intent on building the temple but chose organization over violent plots of destruction, at least in the short term. One of the most interesting was the Temple Mount and Land of Israel Faithful, founded in the late 1980s by Gershon Salomon, who had been one of the Israeli soldiers who had liberated the Temple Mount during the Six-Day War. When Israeli defense minister Moshe Dayan returned control of the Temple Mount to the Muslims, Salomon felt betrayed and vowed to return the mount to its rightful owners, the Jews. According to the Temple Mount Faithful's purpose statement, "He has dedicated himself to the vision of consecrating the Temple Mount to the Name of G-d, to removing the Muslim shrines placed there as a symbol of Muslim conquest, to the soon rebuilding of the Third Temple there, and the G-dly redemption of the people of the Land of Israel."[23] Salomon believed that Dayan had committed "a terrible, sinful mistake" when he gave up the Temple Mount to Muslim control. The task of the new generation was to get it back. For that reason, Salomon scheduled the two attempts to lay a new cornerstone for the temple in 1989 and 1990. The resulting bloodshed did not bother him in the least: The Temple Mount Faithful were doing God's work, and even his failure to set the cornerstone had raised the issue of the temple for all to see.[24]

Most Israelis looked on the Temple Mount Faithful as fanatics who were courting disaster by their threatening behavior toward Muslim holy places. Salomon, however, found a new clientele among American dispensationalists who were strongly attracted to his mission, which fit nicely with their own prophetic scenario of the last days. Dispensationalists saw Salomon as a pious Jew who taught with great conviction that God's plan for the chosen people in the last days included three things: restoration of a new Jewish state, the regathering of Jews from around the world, and the reconstruction of the temple on the Temple Mount—all in anticipation of the Messiah's coming. Of course, dispensationalists believed that such prophetic fulfillments pointed to the Messiah's *return,* but they liked Salomon's style and believed that his actions in favor of a new temple were serving God's purposes.

In the 1990s, Salomon became a favorite lecturer for evangelical tour groups to Israel. In 1999, he went to a Jerusalem hotel to lecture to an evangelical tour group led by Irvin Baxter, a Pentecostal evangelist who edited his own prophecy newsletter, *Endtimes*. Salomon and Baxter were friends, and Baxter often let Salomon teach about the coming temple on his own radio program. Salomon told the tourists exactly what they wanted to hear: "We are the blessed generation which got chosen to be the generation of redemption. . . . In our lifetime will be built the Third Temple."[25] What about the Dome of the Rock? somebody asked. Not to worry, Salomon replied, it will be moved to Mecca. After Salomon finished his talk, Baxter took a "love offering" for the work of the Temple Mount Faithful.

Some observers of Salomon's organization claimed that he had a greater following in the United States among American premillennialists than he did in Israel among Jews. Without financial support from America, the work of the Temple Mount Faithful would not have been possible. Salomon earned much of his organization's budget during his annual summer speaking tour in evangelical churches in the United States. One woman from Orlando, Florida, was clearly sold on Salomon and his message: "The Temple Mount has to be cleansed. We don't know how God is going to do it, by an earthquake or sending a group of people in, but we know it's going to be cleansed."[26]

A clear example of the Temple Mount Faithful's connection to American dispensationalists is illustrated in the work of Stanley Goldfoot, a South African immigrant to Israel in the 1930s who became a leading terrorist against the British and the U.N. during the fight for Israeli independence. Goldfoot was connected to the Stern Gang *(Lehi)* and played a major role in the 1946 bombing of the King David Hotel and the 1948 murder of U.N. Middle East emissary Count Bernadotte. Unlike Salomon, Goldfoot was a secular Jew with little interest in Bible prophecy or the coming of the Messiah, but like many others on Israel's far right, he believed that Israel needed to gain complete sovereignty over the Temple Mount, then build a temple there as a symbol of Israeli power, unity, and independence. Despite his secular stance, he became one of the early leaders in the Temple Mount Faithful movement.

Despite his brutal past, Goldfoot became popular among a number of leading American dispensationalists who found his support of a third temple compatible with their own views. In the early 1980s, he and a number of American dispensationalists, including Terry Reisenhoover, James DeLoach, Doug Kreiger, Charles Monroe, and Hilton Sutton, founded the Jerusalem Temple Foundation in Los Angeles to provide financial support for the Temple Movement in Israel. Reisenhoover, who failed in numerous attempts to find oil in Israel (whose revenues he wanted to use to finance the temple building), served as the foundation's board chair. He appointed Goldfoot as the foundation's international secretary and sponsored him on numerous speaking tours of American evangelical churches, during which he raised millions of dollars for the cause.

Goldfoot was responsible for the foundation's involvement in a rather unique archaeological project to locate the original site of the first two temples. Goldfoot learned about the new archaeological techniques of Lambert Dolphin, a physicist at the Stanford Research Institute in California. Dolphin was a committed dispensationalist believer who had developed a ground-penetrating radar system for "x-raying" underground archaeological sites. When Goldfoot learned that Dolphin had been using his new techniques on Egyptian tombs, he suggested that he try them on the Temple Mount.[27] For the needed funding, Goldfoot turned to two old friends, Chuck Smith and Chuck Missler, who liked the idea of settling the issue of the temple's location once and for all. Smith was also excited by Goldfoot's suggestion that Dolphin's investigation might find the secret room where some people believed the ancient ark of the covenant was hidden. Missler, Smith, and Smith's Calvary Chapel put up close to one hundred thousand dollars for the expedition.

Dolphin and his crew of seven arrived in Israel in the spring of 1983. After testing the equipment on other archaeological sites, the team prepared to conduct similar tests under the Temple Mount. Late one May night, Dolphin's group arrived at the Western Wall, but before they could set up their equipment, Israeli police arrived and told them to leave the site immediately and report to police headquarters the next morning. The police explained that they had been watching them and knew what they intended to do. The Muslims objected to any electronic testing of the Temple Mount, and Dolphin would not be allowed to carry out any work there. Though the expedition came to nothing, it showed how far some dispensationalists were willing to go to support groups, such as the Temple Mount Faithful, whose goals were similar to their own.[28]

Another American dispensationalist group with close ties to the Temple Mount Faithful is the Battalion of Deborah, an organization founded in Texas by dispensationalist women. According to the organization's purpose statement:

> We have dedicated our lives and hearts in service to the G-d of Israel in this most Holy cause, to the Mission of the Temple Mount and Land of Israel Faithful. In great Love and devoted Friendship, we support the Leadership of Adon Gershon Salomon in making these G-dly events, G-dwilling, a reality in the lifetime of this generation. We stand in agreement with the Temple Mount Faithful that "the Temple in Jerusalem was, and will again be, a focus for godly, spiritual, moral and cultural values, not only for Israel, but also for all the world." The

Battalion of Deborah believes that it is a privilege and our duty to support the rebuilding of G-d's House in Jerusalem in anticipation for the Arrival of the Moshiach (Messiah) and the establishment of His Peace, as a real and eternal peace in the Land of Israel, the region, and the world, forevermore.[29]

One has to look hard on the organization's website to determine that the Battalion of Deborah is a Christian organization. Its commitment to the Temple Mount Faithful is based on a dispensational reading of Bible prophecy, which members are anxious to see fulfilled to the letter.

The Temple Mount Faithful is not the only right-wing Israeli group to benefit from American dispensational support. Another is the Temple Institute, founded by Rabbi Yisrael Ariel in 1986. Its purpose is to educate Israelis about the importance of the third temple and to prepare the way for its establishment. Ariel was another veteran of the liberation of the Temple Mount during the Six-Day War who was infuriated by its return to Muslim control. Ariel believes that Israel's future depends on rebuilding the temple. Once that is accomplished, God's original promises to Abraham will be fulfilled (Gen. 15:18–21), including Israel's possession of the vast territories promised to Abraham's descendants—modern-day Egypt, Jordan, Lebanon, Syria, and parts of Iraq and Saudi Arabia. Such expanded territory will be necessary to hold all the Jews from around the world who will move back to Israel after the temple is built.[30]

Ariel undertook a number of actions to establish a Jewish presence on or under the Temple Mount. In 1983, Ariel and a number of his yeshiva students and members of the IDF devised a plan to tunnel under the Al-Aqsa Mosque to conduct Passover prayers. Some believed that Ariel's ultimate goal was to set up a small Israeli settlement there to establish a Jewish presence on the mount. Israeli authorities stopped the expedition before it got started. In 1989, Ariel and Joel Lerner of the Sanhedrin Institute did get access to the Temple Mount, where they intended to offer a Passover sacrifice, the first since the second temple's destruction in 70 A.D. Again, they were stopped before they could complete the ceremony.[31]

Ariel is a doer who is not afraid to justify violence in the achievement of his ends. During the mid- and late 1980s, he was the leader of Tzfiyah ("expectation"), a right-wing group organized to support members of the Jewish underground who had been jailed after their attempt to blow up the Dome of the Rock. Ariel was furious that some members of the Gush Emunim had condemned the actions of the underground. He argued that "thou shalt not kill" applied only to killing fellow Jews, not non-Jews. Though still a sin punishable by God, killing the enemies of Israel should not be the concern of Israeli courts. Furthermore, in the

Tzfiyah's journal, he condemned all Jews who did not support the building of the third temple and declared that since Christians and Muslims were idolaters, they should not be allowed to live in Israel.[32]

Ariel's extreme views do not keep dispensationalists from visiting his institute, however. Over one hundred thousand visitors a year tour the institute's displays on the history of the temple, its implements, and its ancient practices. Young students by the busload come, as do Orthodox yeshiva students who need educating about what may be a part of their own future. But 60 percent of the visitors are non-Jews. The institute is a regular stop on many evangelical tour itineraries. In fact, without the evangelical tourists, it is doubtful that the institute could carry on its many programs.[33]

Dispensationalists are thrilled to see what is going on there, since the plan fits well with their own expectations for the end. According to Ariel, "The Temple Institute in Jerusalem was established with the purpose of acting. Its goal is to prepare the research, planning and organizational foundation for building the Third Temple."[34] Dispensationalists are comforted by knowing that under the institute's auspices, small groups of Israelis are sewing priestly vestments, manufacturing implements for animal sacrifice, and teaching a new generation of temple priests what will be expected of them. It seems to matter little that the desire for a new temple has the potential of precipitating a holy war. Such things are clearly predicted in the Bible, so such matters cannot be deterred.

Israelis who are not committed to the idea of a third temple have noticed, often with some alarm, the close connection between American dispensationalists and the Temple Movement. As early as 1983, the *Jerusalem Post* saw such close ties developing: "There are growing numbers of Christians, many organized into small churches and larger groups, who see the construction of a Third Temple as the cornerstone of their beliefs. Though there is a clear divergence in religious belief between these Christians and Jews who work toward the rebuilding of the Temple, they willingly and enthusiastically cooperate."[35] In 1990, for example, Jan Wilem van der Hoeven, who was then director of the International Christian Embassy, announced plans to lead thousands of Christians to the Temple Mount at the conclusion of the embassy's annual Feast of Tabernacles March to pray for the rebuilding of the temple. Fearing a violent reaction from the Muslim community, Jerusalem mayor Teddy Kollek talked van der Hoeven out of it, but the latter's willingness to provoke both Jews and Arabs demonstrated the lengths to which some dispensationalist Christians were ready to go to encourage the building of the third temple. Van der Hoeven's impatience over the lack of progress concerning temple building led in part to his break from the International Christian Embassy in 1997 and the founding of his own, more militant

International Christian Zionist Center. On the organization's website, van der Hoeven made it clear that he expected Christians to be involved in the temple-building process: "It is important for believers to understand the reality of the battle for the Temple Mount. The evil one knows it is on this mountain that the Lord shall bring an end to his kingdom. The fact is that the battle over Jerusalem is shifting into full gear, and believers have a vital part to play."[36] Many in the Temple Movement understand the prophetic rationale behind dispensationalists' support but are willing to accept it to achieve their common goal.[37]

THE RED HEIFER SACRIFICE

One of the most blatant attempts by dispensationalists to help prophecy happen centered on the production of a red heifer. According to Numbers 19, to purify people who had come in contact with the dead, the priests had to sacrifice "a red heifer without spot, wherein is no blemish, and upon which never came yoke" (v. 2). The priests were to mix the heifer's ashes with water, then sprinkle the mixture on the defiled so that they could resume their normal temple activities. Consequently, Orthodox rabbis taught that prior to rebuilding the third temple, they would need to locate a red heifer for sacrifice.

The problem was that the birth of a perfect red heifer was extremely rare. In the twelfth century, Moses Maimonides declared in the *Mishneh Torah* that only nine such red heifers had been born during the entire history of Israel. Ashes from the last heifer had run out shortly after the destruction of the second temple by the Romans in 70 A.D. According to Maimonides, the tenth and final heifer would be born just in time for the coming of the Messiah and the building of the third temple. Gershom Gorenberg has clearly stated the importance of the red heifer for some modern Israelis (and their dispensationalist friends):

> From the Six-Day War on, Israel's leading rabbis have overwhelmingly ruled that Jews should not enter the gates of the Mount. One of the most commonly cited reasons—even if the sages have not always explained their decree in full—is that under religious law, every Jew is presumed to have had contact with the dead. For lack of a red heifer's ashes, there is simply nothing to be done about it: no way for Jews to purify themselves to enter the sacred square, no way for Judaism to reclaim the Mount, no way to rebuild the Temple. Government officials and military leaders could only regard the requirement for the missing heifer as a stroke of sheer good fortune preventing conflict over the Mount.[38]

Since so much was riding on the sacrifice of a perfect red heifer, it was not surprising that some American dispensationalist cattle breeders stepped forward to help produce the needed livestock. Clyde Lott was a Pentecostal cattleman from Canton, Mississippi, who was well schooled in the science of producing champions. In the late 1980s, Lott learned from prophecy teachers that before the temple could be rebuilt in Jerusalem, a perfect red heifer was needed for sacrifice. Given his expertise in cattle production, Lott decided he could help. Through a long process he finally made contact with Rabbi Chaim Richman of the Temple Institute, who was very interested in what Lott had to say.

In 1990, Lott traveled to Jerusalem to meet with Richman and the institute's founder, Rabbi Yisrael Ariel. Lott spelled out some of the financial realities of raising red heifers, and the three began searching for the right location in Israel to start a cattle business. The original plan was to transport two hundred pregnant cows to Israel via ocean liners at two thousand dollars per head. By using the methods of genetic science, they were confident that the new herd would eventually produce the perfect red heifer. While the search for land continued in Israel, Lott started his selective breeding program back home in Mississippi. In 1994, Rabbi Richman visited Lott's operation in Canton, and Lott showed him four recently born calves. To his utter amazement, Richman found among the four a red heifer that seemed to meet all the qualifications of Numbers 19, except that it had been born in the wrong place—in Mississippi, not in Israel. But Richman was convinced that Lott was capable of producing a proper sacrificial calf.

Lott's dreams kept expanding. Through his travels in Israel, he concluded that Israel's entire beef cattle industry was in need of his services. He believed that given their approach to cattle production, Israeli cattle breeders were not only incapable of producing a suitable red heifer but were also producing inferior beef cattle. He intended to greatly improve the quality of Israel's beef industry at the same time he used his skills to produce a red heifer for the new temple. To that end, he started breeding Red Angus cattle in Nebraska in hopes of shipping thousands of beef cattle to Israel. In 1998, he and Guy Garner founded the Canaan Land Restoration of Israel, Inc., as a nonprofit organization through which Lott hoped to achieve his ambitious goals. Lott proposed to provide cattle free of charge to qualified Israeli cattle breeders on the condition that after a few years they would return to Canaan Land the same number of calves they had received and that they would allow Canaan Land to take every newborn calf that was "special," that is, met the qualifications of Numbers 19. Lott set out to raise money to finance the project from fellow Christians who wanted to see the temple rebuilt too. He visited churches, went on Christian television, and developed other fund-raising strategies.[39]

Lott was not the only dispensationalist cattle breeder who wanted to help make prophecy happen. Gershon Salomon of the Temple Faithful reported that he had been in contact with another concerned Christian in Texas who had attended some of Salomon's meetings in the United States and had become convinced that God was calling him to help in the temple's rebuilding by producing the needed red heifer. In fact, the rancher eventually reported that he had successfully done so and inquired about the proper care of such a special calf. According to Salomon, the requirements were many: "A Red Heifer needs to be raised and handled in a very special way like a holy thing which is completely dedicated to G-d. It has to be raised in a very special, clean stall and to be fed with special food, and even to be spoiled. She cannot be raised with other calves and especially not with males."[40]

In the end, none of these cattle breeding attempts by prophecy-believing ranchers produced the perfect red heifer. Despite his efforts, Lott's project never quite got off the ground. Before Canaan Land could accomplish any of its goals, Lott and Richman had a falling out over finances and Richman's discovery that Lott intended to spread the gospel in Israel, which was a deal breaker as far as the Orthodox rabbi was concerned. As it turned out, even before the relationship between Lott and Richman soured, a red heifer was born in Israel without the help of American breeders.

In the summer of 1996, on the dairy farm of the Orthodox Kfar Hasidim agricultural school near Haifa, an all-red heifer was born to a black and white Holstein that had been impregnated with semen from Switzerland. News of the birth of Melody, as the school boys at Kfar Hasidim called her, spread quickly. Soon carloads of Orthodox rabbis converged on the dairy farm to see the miracle for themselves. After careful inspection, one of the visiting rabbis declared Melody kosher, which set off a firestorm of media attention. In addition to extensive coverage in the Israeli press, eventually even CNN, ABC, and CBS ran stories on Melody. Most press accounts approached the story as a curious piece of religious nostalgia among the ultra-Orthodox, whose beliefs no longer mattered in the modern world.[41]

Of course, American dispensationalists viewed things differently. Soon evangelical visitors drove their tour buses to Kfar Hasidim to see the fulfillment of prophecy for themselves. One group consisting of one hundred Texas preachers inquired as to when Melody would be ready for the sacrificial altar. When they were told that the standard biblical waiting period was three years, they did the math: the end of 1999, just in time for the beginning of the new millennium. Jack Van Impe, the Michigan prophecy pundit, expressed the hope of many believers by posing the question, "Scripture requires the red heifer be sacrificed at the age of three. . . . Could Melody's ashes be used for Temple purification ceremonies as early as 2000?"[42]

The answer was no. Halfway to her rendezvous with the priest's knife, Melody sprouted white hairs on the end of her tail, which was enough to disqualify her as *the* red heifer. The tour buses stopped coming, Temple Movement devotees stood down, and Melody was quietly returned to the herd. But the search for the perfect red heifer continued. In the spring of 2002, another red heifer was born in Israel. A press release from the Temple Institute made the announcement:

> April 8, 2002
> It can now be revealed that less than one month ago, a red heifer was born in Israel. After the heifer's owner contacted the Temple Institute, on Friday, April 5th, 2002, Rabbi Menachem Makover and Rabbi Chaim Richman traveled to the farm where the heifer is located, to inspect and validate her status. The rabbis found her to be kosher and were satisfied that this heifer could indeed be a candidate to be used in the process of purification described in the book of Numbers, chapter 19. This is an important development towards the rebuilding of the Holy Temple.

Later that year, an update appeared on the institute's website: "In November 2002, the red heifer born in Israel in April became disqualified."[43] The faithful were content to wait. They continued to be certain that the red heifer was on the way, which would make the rebuilding of the temple possible.

Do such ideas matter? The vast majority of Israelis and the world's Christians do not take these matters seriously. Therefore, many people might be tempted to disregard such notions as irrelevant. But as the long history of the Middle East shows, fervent beliefs held by a few can impact the experience of everyone else. While most of the media found the announcement of the birth of Melody curious and even amusing, a few journalists understood its potential importance. David Landau of the secular Israeli newspaper *Ha'aretz* understood the power of such ideas to shape current events. He called the heifer "a four-legged bomb" that had the potential of setting the entire region on fire. Even if only a small number of people believed that God had provided the last missing piece to the prophetic process leading to the building of a third temple, the number was sufficient to result in another attempt at clearing the Temple Mount of the Dome of the Rock and the Al-Aqsa Mosque. Such firm convictions have the power to change everything in the contested Middle East, and there can be no doubt that the Temple Movement is intensely serious about changing the status quo on the Temple Mount.[44]

Dispensationalists believe that the temple is coming too, and their convictions have led them to support the aims and actions of what most Israelis believe are the most dangerous right-wing elements in their society, people whose views make any compromise necessary for lasting peace impossible. Such sentiments do not matter to believers in Bible prophecy, for whom the outcome of the quarrelsome issue of the Temple Mount has already been determined by God. Even those who actively seek to produce the red heifer through their own scientific expertise are not to blame for any violent outcome of their actions. They are simply cooperating with God's purposes for the last days and speeding the coming of Christ.

Conclusion

Since the end of the Six-Day War, then, dispensationalists have increasingly moved from observers to participant-observers. They have acted consistently with their convictions about the coming last days in ways that make their prophecies appear to be self-fulfilling. It would be too easy—and completely unwarranted—to conclude that American prophecy believers are responsible for the mess the world is in, that their beliefs have produced the current quagmire in the Middle East. Given the history of the region, the long-standing ethnic and religious hatreds there, and the attempt of many nations, both Western and Arab, to carry out their own purposes in the Holy Land, it is easy to imagine the current impasse even if John Nelson Darby and his views had never existed.

But dispensationalist views have existed for a long time, and they have had their effects on generations of Bible believers in America and elsewhere. As Paul Boyer has pointed out, dispensationalism has effectively conditioned millions of Americans to be somewhat passive about the future and provided them with lenses through which to understand the course of world events. Thanks to the sometimes changing perspectives of their Bible teachers, dispensationalists are certain that trouble in the Middle East is inevitable, that nations will war against nations, and that the time is coming when millions of people will die as a result of nuclear war, the persecution of the Antichrist, or divine judgment. Striving for peace in the Middle East, in other words, is a hopeless pursuit with no chance of success.

At the time of this writing, President George W. Bush and allies in the international community have suggested a road map to peace in the Middle East. The plan includes what many people believe are attainable steps that will lead to the founding of a Palestinian state and new levels of security for Israel. In the early stages of the peace process, there seemed to be signs that both sides had finally had enough of the cycles of bloodletting that have characterized the region for decades. Christian, Jewish, and Muslim groups voiced support and hope that this peace process might succeed where so many previous ones failed.

Not everyone is pleased with the prospects of peace. Militants on both sides do not accept the terms of the road map. Some Israelis, especially those who have settled in occupied territory, are unwilling to turn over land they believe God gave to Abraham and his descendants. Some Palestinians are adamant that Israel must not only relinquish all the land occupied in 1967 but also return territory won in the Israeli war for independence in 1948. They do not want a Jewish state in Palestine and have sworn to keep fighting until Israel no longer exists.

For the dispensational community, the future is determined. The Bible's prophecies are being fulfilled with amazing accuracy and rapidity. They do not believe the road map will—or should—succeed. According to the prophetic texts, partitioning is not in Israel's future, even if the creation of a Palestinian state is the best chance for peace in the region. Peace is nowhere prophesied for the Middle East until Jesus comes and brings it himself. The worst thing the United States, the European Union, Russia, and the United Nations can do is force Israel to give up land for a peace that will never materialize this side of the second coming. Anyone who pushes for peace in such a manner is ignoring or defying God's plan for the end of the age.

What dispensationalists are willing to do about the current peace process remains to be seen. Will they decide to oppose George W. Bush, who is probably the most popular president among evangelicals ever, or will they use their considerable political power to stop the process before it begins, if they can? What would happen if dispensationalists decided to follow the command of Jesus to be peacemakers and left the results to God? That last alternative seems to have few advocates at the present time.

The evidence shows that in the last thirty-five years, dispensationalists have believed that faithfulness to God demands that they actively support the plan. Such support has taken many forms, from lobbying the U.S. government to guarantee that pro-Israel policies remain strong, to helping Jews in the former Soviet Union immigrate to the land of promise, to traveling to the Holy Land in large numbers and marching in the streets of Jerusalem to show solidarity, to contributing financially and in other ways to Israeli settlements in the so-called occupied territories, to promoting views considered extreme and dangerous by most Israelis, to using scientific expertise to engineer a perfect red heifer to speed the building of the temple so that Jesus can return. Much to everyone's surprise, dispensationalists have become Israel's best friends, its most fierce and unwavering supporters, at the same time that they have tried to convert as many Jews as possible to the Christian faith.

One should not expect this pattern of behavior to change anytime soon. It seems clear that dispensationalism is on a roll, that its followers feel they are riding the wave of history into the shore of God's final plan. Why should they stop or change course? Why should they climb back into the stands when being on the field of play is so much more fun and apparently so beneficial to the game's outcome? As a Bridges for Peace's advertisement read, "Don't just read about prophecy when you can be part of it."[45]

Notes

Introduction

1. Thomas Robbins and Susan J. Palmer, eds., *Millennium, Messiahs, and Mayhem: Contemporary Apocalyptic Movements* (New York: Routledge, 1997); Stephen Hunt, ed., *Christian Millenarianism: From the Early Church to Waco* (Bloomington, Ind.: Indiana University Press, 2001); and Eugen Weber, *Apocalypses: Prophecies, Cults, and Millennial Beliefs through the Ages* (Cambridge: Harvard University Press, 1999).

2. Paul Boyer, *When Time Shall Be No More: Prophecy Belief in Modern American Culture* (Cambridge: Harvard University Press, 1992).

3. Nancy Gibbs, "Apocalypse Now," *Time*, 1 July 2002, 41–48.

4. Timothy P. Weber, "Millennialism and Apocalypticism," in *The Oxford Companion to United States History*, ed. Paul Boyer (New York: Oxford University Press, 2001), 503–4.

5. Stephen Stein, *The Shaker Experience in America: A History of the United Society of Believers* (New Haven: Yale University Press, 1992).

6. Spencer Klaw, *Without Sin: The Life and Death of the Oneida Community* (New York: Penguin, 1994).

7. Grant Underwood, *The Millenarian World of Early Mormonism* (Urbana, Ill.: University of Illinois Press, 1993); and Dan Erickson, *As a Thief in the Night: The Mormon Quest for Millennial Deliverance* (Salt Lake City: Signature Books, 1998).

8. Edwin S. Gaustad, ed., *The Rise of Adventism: Religion and Society in Mid-Nineteenth Century America* (New York: Harper & Row, 1974); and Ronald L. Numbers and Jonathan M. Butler, eds., *The Disappointed: Millerism and Millenarianism in the Nineteenth Century* (Bloomington, Ind.: Indiana University Press, 1987).

9. James H. Moorhead, *World without End: Mainstream American Protestant Visions of the Last Things, 1880–1925* (Bloomington, Ind.: Indiana University Press, 1999).

10. M. James Penton, *Apocalypse Delayed: The Story of Jehovah's Witnesses* (Toronto: University of Toronto Press, 1997).

11. Stuart Wright, ed., *Armageddon in Waco: Critical Perspectives on the Branch Davidian Conflict* (Chicago: University of Chicago Press, 1995); and James D. Tabor and Eugene V. Gallagher, eds., *Why Waco? Cults and the Battle for Religious Freedom in America* (Berkeley: University of California Press, 1995).

12. Brad Steiger and Hayden Hewes, *Inside Heaven's Gate* (New York: Signet, 1997); and Rodney Perkins and Forrest Jackson, *Cosmic Suicide: The Tragedy and Transcendence of Heaven's Gate* (Dallas: Pentaradical Press, 1997).

Chapter 1

1. The origins of futurism can be traced to a Spanish Jesuit named Ribera, who argued as early as 1590 that prophecies concerning the Antichrist would not be fulfilled until just before Christ's return. In this way, he attempted to undermine the Protestant claims that the Roman papacy was the fulfillment of the biblical Antichrist. Futurism made its way into the English-speaking world in the early nineteenth century. George E. Ladd, *The Blessed Hope* (Grand Rapids: Eerdmans, 1956), 35–40; and Bernard McGinn, *Antichrist: Two Thousand Years of the Human Fascination with Evil* (San Francisco: Harper, 1994), 226–30.

2. C. I. Scofield, ed., *The Scofield Reference Bible* (New York: Oxford University Press, 1909), 5.

3. C. I. Scofield, *Rightly Dividing the Word of Truth* (Oakland, Calif.: Western Book and Tract, n.d.), 18.

4. See Arnold D. Ehlert, *A Bibliographic History of Dispensationalism* (Grand Rapids: Baker, 1965); C. Norman Kraus, *Dispensationalism in America: Its Rise and Development* (Richmond: John Knox, 1958), 23–44; and Charles C. Ryrie, *Dispensationalism Today* (Chicago: Moody, 1965), 84.

5. Ryrie, *Dispensationalism Today*, 66–78. See also Daniel P. Fuller, "The Hermeneutics of Dispensationalism" (Th.D. diss., Northern Baptist Theological Seminary, Chicago, 1957), 24–25.

6. J. N. Darby, "The Covenants," in *Collected Works*, ed. William Kelly, 34 vols. (London: G. Morrish, 1967), 3:75. See also James H. Brookes, *Israel and the Church* (St. Louis: Gospel Book and Tract Depository, n.d.), 42–43; and Scofield, *Scofield Reference Bible*, 20.

7. See Alva McClain, *Daniel's Prophecy of the Seventy Weeks* (Grand Rapids: Zondervan, 1940), 12–15.

8. Scofield, *Scofield Reference Bible*, 915.

9. James H. Brookes, *Maranatha*, 3d ed. (New York: E. Brendell, 1874), 425–26.

10. Willis Jordan, *The European War from a Bible Standpoint* (New York: Charles C. Cook, 1915), 35–36; Robert Anderson, *The Coming Prince*, 13th ed. (London: Pickering & Inglis, n.d.), 123–29; and Arno C. Gaebelein, *The Prophet Daniel* (New York: Our Hope Publishing, 1936), 135.

11. For a good discussion of the postponement theory, see Fuller, "Hermeneutics of Dispensationalism," 287–337.

12. C. H. Mackintosh, *Papers on the Lord's Coming* (Chicago: Bible Institute Colportage Association, n.d.), 101–2.

13. Ibid., 104–5.

14. For typical presentations of the pretribulation rapture, see I. M. Haldeman, *The Coming of Christ* (Los Angeles: Bible House of Los Angeles, 1906), 297–325; Leander Munhall, *The Lord's Return*, 7th ed. (New York: Eaton & Mains, 1898), 179–80; and C. H. Mackintosh, "The Double Phase of the Second Advent," *Our Hope* 11 (November 1903): 322–29.

15. Samuel P. Tregelles, *The Hope of Christ's Second Coming* (London: Samuel Bagster & Sons, 1864), 35. Ernest R. Sandeen thinks the charge is groundless (Ernest R. Sandeen, *The Roots of Fundamentalism* [Chicago: University of Chicago Press, 1970], 64).

16. David McPherson, *The Incredible Cover-Up: The True Story of the Pre-Trib Rapture* (Plainfield, N.J.: Logos International, 1975).

17. Darby, *Collected Works,* 11:156. John F. Walvoord, a leading American dispensationalist scholar, similarly states that the pretribulational rapture doctrine is derived more from one's doctrine of the church than from any specific Bible passage on eschatology (John Walvoord, *The Rapture Question* [Findlay, Ohio: Dunham Publishing, 1957], 16).

18. This view of the Antichrist is not the only one found in speculation by Christians about the end of the world. For an extensive overview of the teachings about the Antichrist within the Christian tradition, see McGinn, *Antichrist.* For an examination of views found in America, see Robert Fuller, *Naming the Antichrist: The History of an American Obsession* (New York: Oxford University Press, 1995).

19. Quotations are from James H. Brookes, *Truth* 12 (1886): 109–11. See also James H. Brookes, *Truth* 20 (1894): 518.

20. James H. Brookes, *Truth* 12 (1886): 361–62, 506. See also James H. Brookes, *Truth* 15 (1889): 203–4.

21. James H. Snowden, "Summary of Objections to Premillenarianism," *Biblical World* 53 (March 1919): 172–73. See also James H. Snowden, *The Coming of the Lord: Will It Be Premillennial?* (New York: Macmillan, 1919), 32–34.

22. J. Gresham Machen, *Christianity and Liberalism* (New York: Macmillan, 1926), 49–50.

23. Mackintosh, *Papers on the Lord's Coming,* 56.

24. James H. Brookes, "Witnesses to the Hope," *Truth* 17 (1891): 310–22.

25. *Christian Workers Magazine* 16 (December 1915): 263.

26. Sandeen, *Roots of Fundamentalism,* 231; and Cornelius Woelfkin, "The Religious Appeal of Premillennialism," *Journal of Religion* 1 (May 1921): 255–63.

27. For another example of list making, see Thomas C. Horton, *These Premillennialists: Who Are They?* (Los Angeles: Privately published, 1921).

28. Reuben A. Torrey, *The Return of the Lord Jesus Christ* (Los Angeles: Bible Institute of Los Angeles, 1913), 8.

29. William Bell Riley, *The Evolution of the Kingdom* (New York: Charles C. Cook, 1913), 5.

30. Sidney Ahlstrom, *A Religious History of the American People* (New Haven: Yale University Press, 1972), 133–220; Paul A. Carter, *The Spiritual Crisis of the Gilded Age* (De Kalb, Ill.: Northern Illinois University Press, 1971); Francis P. Weisberger, *Ordeal of Faith: The Crisis of Churchgoing America, 1864–1900* (New York: Philosophical Library, 1959); Martin E. Marty, *Protestantism in the United States: Righteous Empire,* 2d ed. (New York: Macmillan, 1986); Martin E. Marty, *Modern American Religion: The Irony of It All, 1893–1919,* vol. 1 (Chicago: University of Chicago Press, 1986); and Ferenc M. Szasz, *The Divided Mind of Protestant America, 1880–1930* (Tuscaloosa, Ala.: University of Alabama Press, 1982).

31. Henry F. May, *Protestant Churches and Industrial America* (New York: Harper Torchbooks, 1967); Aaron I. Abell, *The Urban Impact on American Protestantism, 1865–1900* (Cambridge: Harvard University Press, 1943); Robert D. Cross, ed., *The Church and the City* (New York: Bobbs-Merrill, 1967); C. Howard Hopkins, *The Rise of the Social Gospel in American Protestantism, 1865–1915* (New Haven: Yale University Press, 1940); and Robert T. Handy, *A Christian America: Protestant Hopes and Historical Realities* (New York: Oxford University Press, 1971), 117–83.

32. Richard Hofstadter, *Social Darwinism in American Thought* (Boston: Beacon Press, 1944); Bert James Lowenberg, *Darwinism Comes to America, 1859–1900* (Philadelphia: Fortress, 1969); Stephen Neill, *The Interpretation of the New Testament, 1861–1961* (London: Oxford University Press, 1964); James R. Moore, *The Post-Darwinian Controversies: A Study of the Protestant Struggle to Come to Terms with Darwin in Great Britain and America, 1870–1900* (Cambridge: Cambridge University Press, 1979); Jon H. Roberts,

Darwinism and the Divine in America: Protestant Intellectuals and Organic Evolution, 1859–1900 (Madison: University of Wisconsin Press, 1988); William R. Hutchison, *The Modernist Impulse in American Protestantism* (Cambridge: Harvard University Press, 1976); Ahlstrom, *Religious History,* 764–74; and George Marsden, *Fundamentalism and American Culture* (New York: Oxford University Press, 1980), 11–32.

33. Henry Ward Beecher, *Yale Lectures on Preaching,* quoted in Winthrop Hudson, *Religion in America* (New York: Charles Scribner's Sons, 1965), 266–67.

34. Hutchison, *Modernist Impulse;* Kenneth Cauthen, *The Impact of American Religious Liberalism* (New York: Harper & Row, 1962); and Lloyd J. Averill, *American Theology in the Liberal Tradition* (Philadelphia: Westminster, 1967).

35. David N. Livingstone, *Darwin's Forgotten Defenders: The Encounter between Evangelical Theology and Evolutionary Thought* (Grand Rapids: Eerdmans, 1987).

36. James H. Brookes, *Truth* 5 (1879): 410. For more on the origins of the Bible conference movement, see Marsden, *Fundamentalism and American Culture,* 62, 133–34; and Kraus, *Dispensationalism in America,* 71–80.

37. "Fundamentals of the Faith as Expressed in the Articles of Belief of the Niagara Bible Conference" (Chicago: Great Commission Prayer League, n.d.), quoted in Sandeen, *Roots of Fundamentalism,* 273–77.

38. William Pettingill, "The Doctrine of the Lord's Coming as a Working Force in the Church and Community," in *The Coming and Kingdom of Christ,* ed. James M. Gray (Chicago: Bible Institute Colportage Association, 1914), 134.

39. I. M. Haldeman, *Professor Shailer Mathews' Burlesque on the Second Coming* (New York: Privately published, 1918), 23.

40. Sandeen, *Roots of Fundamentalism,* 132–57. The addresses of the conference were published in Nathaniel West, ed., *Pre-Millennial Essays* (New York: Revell, 1879).

41. West, *Pre-Millennial Essays,* 11.

42. The proceedings of the conferences were published as follows: Chicago, 1886: *Prophetic Studies of the International Prophetic Conference* (New York: Revell, 1886); Allegheny, Pa., 1895: *Addresses on the Second Coming of the Lord* (Pittsburgh: W. W. Waters, 1896); Boston, 1901: *Addresses of the International Prophetic Conference* (Boston: Watchword & Truth, 1901); Chicago, 1914: Gray, *Coming and Kingdom of Christ;* Philadelphia, 1918: William L. Pettingill, ed., *Light on Prophecy* (New York: Christian Herald, 1918); and New York, 1918: Arno C. Gaebelein, ed., *Christ and Glory* (New York: Our Hope Publishing, 1919).

43. Nathan O. Hatch, *The Democratization of American Christianity* (New Haven: Yale University Press, 1989).

44. Stanley Gundry, *Love Them In: The Proclamation Theology of D. L. Moody* (Chicago: Moody, 1982).

45. Virginia Lieson Brereton, *Training God's Army: The American Bible School, 1880–1940* (Bloomington, Ind.: Indiana University Press, 1990).

46. James F. Findlay Jr., *Dwight L. Moody, American Evangelist, 1837–1899* (Chicago: University of Chicago Press, 1969), 328–29.

47. Brereton, *Training God's Army, passim.*

48. Henry Ostrom, "My Personal Experience with the Doctrine of Our Lord's Second Coming," *Christian Workers Magazine* 18 (March 1918): 561–64.

49. "How I Became a Premillennialist: A Symposium," in *Coming and Kingdom of Christ,* 64ff.; and "How I Came to Believe in Our Lord's Return" (Privately published, n.d.).

50. Quoted in Henry Drummond, *Dwight L. Moody: Impressions and Facts* (New York: McClure, Phillips, 1900), 25–30.

51. A. T. Pierson, "Antagonism to the Bible," *Our Hope* 15 (January 1909): 475.

52. For a more extensive analysis of their use of the Bible, see Timothy P. Weber, "The Two-Edged Sword: The Fundamentalist Use of the Bible," in *The Bible in American Culture: Essays in Cultural History,* ed. Nathan O. Hatch and Mark A. Noll (New York: Oxford University Press, 1982), 101–20.

53. Philip Mauro, *The Seventy Weeks and the Great Tribulation* (Boston: Hamilton Brothers, 1923), 9–12; and S. D. Gordon, *Quiet Talks on the Deeper Meaning of the War and Its Relation to Our Lord's Return* (New York: Revell, 1919), 149–50.

54. James H. Brookes, *Truth* 5 (1879): 314. See also James H. Brookes, *Truth* 23 (1897): 80–82.

55. George Needham, "Introduction," in James H. Brookes, *Bible Reading on the Second Coming of Christ* (Springfield, Ill.: Edwin A. Wilson, 1877), viii. For examples of other Bible readings, see *Truth* 2 (1876): 28–32, 53–57.

56. Joseph Parker, *None Like It* (New York: Revell, 1893), 73.

57. James M. Gray, *How to Master the English Bible* (Chicago: Bible Institute Colportage Association, 1904). See also William M. Runyan, *Dr. Gray at Moody Bible Institute* (New York: Oxford University Press, 1935), 64–79.

58. James M. Gray, *Synthetic Bible Studies,* rev. ed. (New York: Revell, 1923), 11.

59. C. I. Scofield, ed., *The Scofield Reference Bible* (New York: Oxford University Press, 1909).

60. Frank Gaebelein, *The History of the Scofield Reference Bible* (New York: Oxford University Press, 1943); John Hannah, "Cyrus Ingerson Scofield," in *Dictionary of Premillennial Theology,* ed. Mal Couch (Grand Rapids: Kregel, 1996), 389–93; and Charles G. Trumbull, *The Life Story of C. I. Scofield* (New York: Oxford University Press, 1920).

61. Henry Warner Bowden, *Church History in the Age of Science* (Chapel Hill: University of North Carolina Press, 1971).

62. George P. Eckman, *When Christ Comes Again* (New York: Abingdon, 1917), 48–49. See also Snowden, *Coming of the Lord,* 243–44.

63. Harris Franklin Rall, *New Testament History* (New York: Abingdon, 1914), 301. See also Charles A. Briggs, "Millennium, Millenarianism," in *The New Schaff-Herzog Encyclopedia of Religious Knowledge,* 13 vols., ed. Johann Herzog and Philip Schaff (New York: Funk and Wagnalls, 1908–14), 7:374–78; and Charles A. Briggs, "Origin and History of Pre-Millennialism," *Lutheran Quarterly* 9 (April 1879): 244–45.

64. Albert Erdman, "Contending for the Faith," *Prophetic Studies of the International Prophetic Conference* (New York: Revell, 1886), 90.

65. A critic recognized the strong appeal of supernaturalism in the premillennial movement. Francis J. McConnell, "The Causes of Premillennialism," *Harvard Theological Review* 12 (April 1919): 179–92.

66. Howard Pope, "How I Became a Premillennialist," in *Coming and Kingdom of Christ,* 75–77.

Chapter 2

1. Francis D. Nichol, *The Midnight Cry* (Washington, D.C.: Review & Herald, 1944), 213–15, 238–40, 251; Edwin S. Gaustad, ed., *The Rise of Adventism: Religion and Society in Mid-Nineteenth Century America* (New York: Harper & Row, 1974), 154–72; Leroy Froom, *Prophetic Faith,* 4 vols. (Washington, D.C.: Review & Herald, 1946–54), 4:429–827; and Ronald L. Numbers and Jonathan M. Butler, eds., *The Disappointed: Millerism and Millenarianism in the Nineteenth Century* (Bloomington, Ind.: Indiana University Press, 1987).

2. James H. Snowden, *The Coming of the Lord: Will It Be Premillennial?* (New York: Macmillan, 1919), 157–58. See also James H. Snowden, "Summary of Objections to Premillenarianism," *Biblical World* 53 (March 1919): 169.

3. Arno C. Gaebelein, *Meat in Due Season* (New York: Our Hope Publishing, 1933), 64.

4. Dwight L. Moody, *New Sermons* (New York: Henry S. Goodspeed, 1880), 535.

5. J. Wilbur Chapman, *A Reason for My Hope* (New York: Our Hope Publishing, 1916), 4.

6. Moody, *New Sermons,* 535.

7. Ibid., 532.

8. Arthur W. Pink, *The Redeemer's Return* (Swengel, Pa.: Bible Truth Depot, 1918), 78.

9. Reuben A. Torrey, "That Blessed Hope," in *Christ and Glory,* ed. Arno C. Gaebelein (New York: Our Hope Publishing, 1919), 33–34.

10. Adoniram Judson Gordon, quoted in A. B. Simpson, *Back to Patmos* (New York: Christian Alliance Publishing, 1914), 95–96.

11. William Evans, *The Coming King: The World's Next Crisis* (New York: Revell, 1923), 95–96.

12. John Peters, *Christian Perfection and American Methodism* (New York: Abingdon, 1956); Melvin Dieter, *The Holiness Revival of the Nineteenth Century* (Metuchen, N.J.: Scarecrow Press, 1980); and Donald W. Dayton, *Theological Roots of Pentecostalism* (Grand Rapids: Francis Asbury Press, 1987).

13. Hannah Whitall Smith, *The Christian's Secret of a Happy Life* (1875; reprint, Old Tappan, N.J.: Revell, 1942), 14.

14. Douglas W. Frank, *Less Than Conquerors: How Evangelicals Entered the Twentieth Century* (Grand Rapids: Eerdmans, 1986), 114.

15. J. C. Pollock, *The Keswick Story: The Authorized History of the Keswick Convention: Its Message, Its Method, and Its Men* (London: Marshall Bros., 1907); and A. T. Pierson, *The Story of Keswick and Its Beginnings* (London: Hodder & Stoughton, 1964).

16. For a fictional but highly accurate portrayal of how Keswick teaching functioned in one of the dispensational Bible institutes in the 1940s, see Shirley Nelson, *The Last Year of the War* (San Francisco: HarperCollins, 1979).

17. Frank, *Less Than Conquerors,* 103–66. Frank is highly critical of the "higher life," equating it with cultic "mind cure," forms of gnosticism, and the like. See also George Marsden, *Fundamentalism and American Culture* (New York: Oxford University Press, 1980), 77–85, 94–101.

18. Smith, *Christian's Secret of a Happy Life,* quoted in Ruth Tucker, "Hannah Whitall Smith," in *Dictionary of Christianity in America,* ed. D. G. Reid (Downers Grove, Ill.: InterVarsity, 1990), 1096.

19. Campus Crusade for Christ widely distributes a blue booklet that explains how to keep Jesus Christ on the "throne of one's life" through cycles of "spiritual breathing." The "Bird Book," as it is commonly called by Crusaders because it has a white dove on the cover representing the Holy Spirit, contains diagrams to show how one's life becomes well ordered when Jesus is on the throne (illustrated by a chair with a cross in the seat), and how it becomes chaotic when Christ is unseated and replaced with an "E" for ego. This is pure Keswick doctrine, though there is no mention in the booklet of the rapture as a deterrent.

20. William Longstaff and George Stebbins, "Take Time to Be Holy," *Worship and Service Hymnal* (Chicago: Hope Publishing Company, 1957), no. 325.

21. Robert Speer, *The Second Coming of Christ* (New York: Gospel Publishing House, 1903), 34–35.

22. Reuben A. Torrey, "The Second Coming: A Motive for Personal Holiness," in *The Coming and Kingdom of Christ,* ed. James M. Gray (Chicago: Bible Institute Colportage Association, 1914), 229–31.

23. Leander Munhall, *The Lord's Return,* 7th ed. (New York: Eaton & Mains, 1898), 76–77.

24. Samuel H. Kellogg, "Premillennialism: Its Relation to Doctrine and Practice," *Bibliotheca Sacra* 45 (1888): 273.

25. James M. Gray, *Prophecy and the Lord's Return* (New York: Revell, 1917), 36.

26. Shirley Jackson Case, *The Millennial Hope* (Chicago: University of Chicago Press, 1918), 235–37.

27. J. J. Robinson, "Is Social Service a Part of the Apostasy?" *Christian Workers Magazine* 14 (July 1914): 729–32. For "times of the Gentiles," see Daniel 2:31–45 in C. I. Scofield, ed., *The Scofield Reference Bible* (New York: Oxford University Press, 1909), 900–901, 1345.

28. James H. Brookes, "Gentile Domination," *Truth* 6 (1880): 536.

29. Walter Rauschenbusch, *Christianity and the Social Crisis* (New York: Macmillan, 1907), 202–3.

30. Robert T. Handy, ed., *The Social Gospel in America, 1870–1920: Gladden, Ely, and Rauschenbusch,* A Library of Protestant Thought (New York: Oxford University Press, 1966); Ronald C. White Jr. and C. Howard Hopkins, *The Social Gospel: Religion and Reform in Changing America* (Philadelphia: Temple University Press, 1976); and Paul M. Minus, *Walter Rauschenbusch: American Reformer* (New York: Macmillan, 1988).

31. Arno C. Gaebelein, *Our Hope* 15 (March 1909): 536.

32. Eli Reece, *How Far Can a Premillennialist Pastor Cooperate with Social Service Programs?* (Privately published, n.d.).

33. Robert T. Handy, *A Christian America: Protestant Hopes and Historical Realities* (New York: Oxford University Press, 1971); and Timothy Smith, *Revivalism and Social Reform* (New York: Harper Torchbooks, 1957).

34. *Christian Workers Magazine* 20 (June 1920): 829; William McLoughlin, *Modern Revivalism* (New York: Ronald Press, 1959), 282–400; and Lyle W. Dorsett, *Billy Sunday and the Redemption of Urban America* (Grand Rapids: Eerdmans, 1992).

35. Charles Reihl, "Solution to Prohibition," *Truth* 15 (1889): 370–75.

36. Gray, *Prophecy and the Lord's Return,* 109.

37. James M. Gray, "And Such Were Some of You," *Christian Workers Magazine* 14 (August 1914): 785–86.

38. William M. Runyan, *Dr. Gray at Moody Bible Institute* (New York: Oxford University Press, 1935), 38–39; and *Institute Tie* 9 (November 1908): 247.

39. *Institute Tie* 9 (September 1909): 18.

40. Norris Magnuson, *Salvation in the Slums: Evangelical Social Work, 1865–1920* (Metuchen, N.J.: Scarecrow Press, 1977); and George Dollar, *A History of Fundamentalism in America* (Greenville, S.C.: Bob Jones University Press, 1973), 367.

41. *Institute Tie* 10 (July 1910): 857; and *Christian Workers Magazine* 14 (August 1914): 800.

42. William King, quoted in Snowden, *Coming of the Lord,* 233–34.

43. W. O. Carver, *Missions and the Kingdom of Heaven* (Louisville: John P. Morton, 1898), 8; and W. O. Carver, *Missions in the Plan of the Ages* (1909; reprint, Nashville: Broadman, 1951), 254.

44. Robert Speer, *The Second Coming of Christ* (New York: Gospel Publishing Company, 1903), 14, 39. Toward the end of his life, Speer seems to have abandoned his premillennialism and moved out of the "Moody circle" of his younger days. See Bradley J. Longfield, *The Presbyterian Controversy: Fundamentalists, Modernists, and Moderates* (New York: Oxford University Press, 1991), 181–230; and James A. Patterson, "Robert E. Speer, J. Gresham Machen, and the Presbyterian Board of Foreign Missions," *American Presbyterians: Journal of Presbyterian History* 64 (spring 1986): 58–68.

45. Scofield, *Scofield Reference Bible,* 1169–70.

46. A. J. Gordon, "Premillennialism and Mission," *Watchword* 8 (April 1886): 30–32; and A. J. Gordon, *The Holy Spirit in Missions* (New York: Revell, 1893).

47. A. J. Gordon, "Education and Missions, Part 1," *Missionary Review of the World* 16 (August 1893): 585.

48. Robert Speer, *The Finality of Jesus Christ* (New York: Revell, 1933), 372.

49. William R. Hutchison, *Errand to the World: American Protestant Thought and Foreign Missions* (Chicago: University of Chicago Press, 1987), 19.

50. A. T. Pierson, "Our Lord's Second Coming as a Motive to World-Wide Evangelism," in *Prophetic Studies of the International Prophetic Conference,* ed. George C. Needham (Chicago: Revell, 1886), 41.

51. William J. Erdman, "The Main Idea of the Bible," *Institute Tie* 9 (October 1908): 94.

52. John H. Cable, *A History of the Missionary Training Institute: The Pioneer Bible Schools of America* (Harrisburg, Pa.: Christian Publications, 1933); and Virginia Brereton, *Training God's Army: The American Bible School, 1880–1940* (Bloomington, Ind.: Indiana University Press, 1990), 41–49. Simpson's Missionary Training Institute eventually became Nyack College.

53. Nathan R. Wood, *A School of Christ* (Boston: Halliday Lithograph, 1953); F. L. Chapell, "Dr. Gordon and the Training School," *Watchword* 17 (February–March 1895): 61–62; and Brereton, *Training God's Army,* 49–51. After Gordon's death in 1895, A. T. Pierson assumed leadership of the school, which eventually became Gordon College and Gordon-Conwell Theological Seminary.

54. For a partial list of Bible schools founded before 1945, see Brereton, *Training God's Army,* 71–77.

55. Quoted in Joel A. Carpenter, "Propagating the Faith Once Delivered: The Fundamentalist Missionary Enterprise, 1920–1945," in *Earthen Vessels: American Evangelicals and Foreign Missions, 1880–1980,* ed. Joel A. Carpenter (Grand Rapids: Eerdmans, 1990), 104.

56. Dana L. Robert, "'The Crisis of Missions': Premillennial Mission Theory and the Origins of Independent Evangelical Missions," in *Earthen Vessels,* 35–36. See also Dana L. Robert, "The Origin of the Student Volunteer Watchword: 'The Evangelization of the World in This Generation,'" *International Bulletin of Missionary Research* 10 (October 1986): 146–49.

57. For a history of the beginnings of the faith missions movement, see Marybeth Rupert, "The Emergence of the Independent Missionary Agency as an American Institution, 1860–1917" (Ph.D. diss., Yale University, 1974); and Robert, "'Crisis of Missions,'" 29–46.

58. Kenneth Scott Latourette, *A History of the Expansion of Christianity,* 7 vols. (New York: Harper & Brothers, 1937–45), 4:326–31; Stephen Neill, *History of Christian Missions,* Pelican History of the Church, vol. 6 (London: Penguin, 1965), 333–36; Howard Taylor, *Hudson Taylor and the China Inland Mission* (London: China Inland Mission, 1919); Geraldine Guinness, *The Story of the China Inland Mission,* 2 vols. (London: China Inland Mission, 1896); and Mrs. Howard Taylor (Geraldine Guinness), *Hudson Taylor and the China Inland Mission: The Growth of a Work of God* (Philadelphia and London: China Inland Mission, 1918).

59. Alvyn J. Austin, "Blessed Adversity: Henry W. Frost and the China Inland Mission," in *Earthen Vessels,* 47–70; and Dr. and Mrs. Howard Taylor, *"By Faith . . ." Henry W. Frost and the China Inland Mission* (Philadelphia and Toronto: CIM, 1938). The CIM is now known as the Overseas Missionary Fellowship to reflect the spread of its work outside China.

60. A. E. Thompson, *The Life of A. B. Simpson* (New York: Christian Alliance Publishing, 1920). For his premillennialism, see Simpson, *Back to Patmos;* and A. B. Simpson, *The Gospel of the Kingdom* (New York: Christian Alliance Publishing, 1890).

61. A. B. Simpson, quoted in J. H. Hunter, *Beside All Waters* (Harrisburg, Pa.: Christian Publications, 1964), 17.

62. Magnuson, *Salvation in the Slums,* 14–20.

63. J. Herbert Kane, *A Concise History of the Christian World Mission: A Panoramic View of Missions from Pentecost to the Present* (Grand Rapids: Baker, 1978); and Daniel W. Bacon, *From Faith to Faith, The Influence of Hudson Taylor on the Faith Missions Movement* (Robesonia, Pa.: OMF, 1984), which counted twenty-three organizations that grew out of Taylor's work and example.

64. Mildred W. Spain, *And in Samaria* (Dallas: Central America Mission, 1954).

65. James H. Hunter, *A Flame of Fire* (Toronto: SIM, 1941).

66. Kenneth Richardson, *Garden of Miracles: A History of the Africa Inland Mission* (London: Victory, 1968).

67. Carpenter, "Propagating the Faith Once Delivered," 100.

68. The first seven IFMA members included Africa Inland Mission, Central American Mission, China Inland Mission, Inland South America Missionary Union, South Africa General Mission, Sudan Interior Mission, and the Women's Union Missionary Society.

69. A. E. Thompson, quoted in William L. Pettingill, *Light on Prophecy* (New York: Christian Herald, 1918), 157.

Chapter 3

1. C. I. Scofield, ed., *The Scofield Reference Bible* (New York: Oxford University Press, 1909), 1345; and Kenneth Richardson, *Garden of Miracles: A History of the Africa Inland Mission* (London: Victory, 1968).

2. Scofield, *Scofield Reference Bible,* 900–901. Arno C. Gaebelein, *The Prophet Daniel* (New York: Our Hope Publishing, 1936), 73–76. The key biblical passages are Daniel 2 and 7.

3. Scofield, *Scofield Reference Bible,* 1349.

4. Arno C. Gaebelein, *Our Hope* 21 (September 1914): 146.

5. Scofield, *Scofield Reference Bible,* 133, 1342.

6. Dispensationalists linked this passage to others: Zech. 12:1–4; 14:1–9; Matt. 24:14–30; and Rev. 14:14–20; 19:17–21.

7. Scofield, *Scofield Reference Bible,* 883. Arno C. Gaebelein, *The Prophet Ezekiel* (New York: Our Hope Publishing, 1918), 257–58.

8. Paul Boyer, *When Time Shall Be No More: Prophecy Belief in Modern American Culture* (Cambridge: Harvard University Press, 1992), 152–53. For a good overview of this complicated subject, see Dwight Wilson, *Armageddon Now! The Premillenarian Response to Russia and Israel since 1917* (Grand Rapids: Baker, 1977), 14–35.

9. The King James Version of 1611 translated *rosh* as "chief," not as a geographical location, as do most modern translations. But a number of scholars believe that *rosh* is a proper name. See Boyer, *When Time Shall Be No More,* 154.

10. Ibid., 155–56. See also John Cumming, *The Destiny of Nations* (London: Hurst & Blackette, 1864); James H. Brookes, *Truth* 2 (1876): 555; Alfred Burton, *The Future of Europe* (1890; reprint, New York: Bible Truth Press, 1915); Arno C. Gaebelein, *Our Hope* 16 (July 1909): 37–38; and *Our Hope* 17 (January 1911): 464–69.

11. Scofield, *Scofield Reference Bible,* 883. See also Arno C. Gaebelein, *Hath God Cast Away His People?* (New York: Gospel Publishing House, 1905), 231–32, 240.

12. Premillennialists differed in details, but the main outline of events was clearly discerned. See *Institute Tie* 10 (April 1910): 609; James M. Gray, *Prophecy and the Lord's Return* (New York: Revell, 1917), 26–27;Willis Jordan, *The European War from a Bible Standpoint* (New York: Charles C. Cook, 1915); *Christian Workers Magazine* 16 (May 1916): 686–87; *Our Hope* 21 (December 1914): 360–62; *Our Hope* 13 (March 1917): 559; F. C. Jennings, *The End of the European War in the Light of Scripture* (New York: Charles C. Cook, 1917), 11–27; *Christian Workers Magazine* 15 (November 1914): 158–60; Philip Mauro, *The World War: How It Is Fulfilling Prophecy* (Boston: Hamilton Brothers, 1918); and Charles C. Cook, *End of the Age Themes* (New York: Charles C. Cook, 1917).

13. James M. Gray, *A Text-Book on Prophecy* (New York: Revell, 1918), chap. 19 title. See Boyer, *When Time Shall Be No More,* 101.

14. Arno C. Gaebelein, "The Prophet Ezekiel," *Our Hope* 24 (November 1917): 281.

15. Wilson, *Armageddon Now!* 49–50.

16. Jennings, *End of the European War,* 35–40; and F. C. Jennings, *The World Conflict in the Light of the Prophetic Word* (New York: Our Hope Publishing), 164–65.

17. *Weekly Evangel,* 10 April 1917, 3, quoted in Wilson, *Armageddon Now!* 37–38.

18. William E. Blackstone, "The Times of the Gentiles and the War in the Light of Prophecy," *Christian Workers Magazine* 16 (May 1916): 686–87; and William J. Erdman, "An Important Query," *Christian Workers Magazine* 17 (November 1917): 194.

19. S. D. Gordon, *Quiet Talks on the Deeper Meaning of the War and Its Relation to Our Lord's Return* (New York: Revell, 1919), 69.

20. Reuben A. Torrey, *King's Business* 5 (December 1914): 685–86.

21. James M. Gray, *Christian Workers Magazine* 18 (February 1918): 447.

22. *Christian Workers Magazine* 15 (October 1914): 81–82; and *Our Hope* 21 (January 1915): 424–27.

23. Arno C. Gaebelein, *Our Hope* 20 (September 1913): 176; and Arno C. Gaebelein, *Our Hope* 18 (October 1911): 262.

24. *Christian Workers Magazine* 16 (January 1916): 374.

25. Arno C. Gaebelein, *Our Hope* 22 (April 1916): 635. See also Walter Scott, "Europe in a Blaze," *Our Hope* 21 (November 1914): 279–83.

26. James H. Snowden, *The Coming of the Lord: Will It Be Premillennial?* (New York: Macmillan, 1919), 269–72.

27. *Biblical World* 46 (July 1915): 1.

28. Shailer Mathews, *New Faith for Old* (New York: Macmillan, 1936), 196–97.

29. T. Valentine Parker, "Premillennialism: An Interpretation and Evaluation," *Biblical World* 52 (1919): 37.

30. Harris Franklin Rall, "Premillennialism and the Bible," *Biblical World* 52 (1919): 339.

31. Arno C. Gaebelein, *Our Hope* 24 (1917–18): 267, quoted in Wilson, *Armageddon Now!* 57.

32. George P. Eckman, *When Christ Comes Again* (New York: Abingdon, 1917), 9–10.

33. Shailer Mathews, *Will Christ Come Again?* (Chicago: American Institute of Sacred Literature, 1917), 280.

34. Quoted in Arno C. Gaebelein, *Our Hope* 24 (January 1918): 407–14. For another premillennialist reaction to Mathews's book, see I. M. Haldeman, *Professor Shailer Mathews' Burlesque on the Second Coming* (New York: Privately published, 1918).

35. Shirley Jackson Case, *The Millennial Hope* (Chicago: University of Chicago Press, 1918); and idem, *The Revelation of John* (Chicago: University of Chicago Press, 1919).

36. James H. Snowden, *Is the World Growing Better?* (New York: Macmillan, 1919); and idem, *Coming of the Lord.*

37. George Preston Mains, *Premillennialism: Non-Scriptural, Non-Historic, Non-Scientific, Non-Philosophical* (New York: Abingdon, 1920).

38. Harris Franklin Rall, *Modern Premillennialism and the Christian Hope* (New York: Abingdon, 1920).

39. Case, *Millennial Hope,* 226.

40. Harry A. Ironside, *Our Hope* 31 (April 1925): 628.

41. Shirley Jackson Case, "The Premillennial Menace," *Biblical World* 52 (July 1918): 16–23.

42. Shirley Jackson Case, *Chicago Daily News,* 21 January 1918.

43. Parker, "Premillennialism," 37–40.

44. William E. Leuchtenberg, *The Perils of Prosperity, 1914–1932* (Chicago: University of Chicago Press, 1993), 44.

45. James M. Gray, *Christian Workers Magazine* 18 (March 1918): 548–51.

46. Reuben A. Torrey, "Unprincipled Methods of Post-Millennialists," *Our Hope* 14 (May 1918): 679–81.

47. *Christian Workers Magazine* 19 (February 1919): 375.

48. D. M. Panton, "The Present Rise and Ultimate End of Democracy," *Christian Workers Magazine* 19 (May 1919): 637–39; and Samuel H. Kellogg, "Premillennialism: Its Relation to Doctrine and Practice," *Bibliotheca Sacra* 45 (1888): 273–74.

49. James M. Gray, "Practical and Perplexing Questions," *Christian Workers Magazine* 16 (October 1916): 97–98.

50. C. I. Scofield, *The World's Approaching Crisis* (Privately published, n.d.), 22–23.

51. Gray, "Practical and Perplexing Questions," 98.

52. Reuben A. Torrey, *King's Business* 5 (December 1914): 684.

53. Reuben A. Torrey, *King's Business* 7 (March 1916): 195; *King's Business* 7 (June 1916): 487–88; and *King's Business* 8 (April 1917): 293.

54. Reuben A. Torrey, *King's Business* 8 (October 1917): 867–68.

55. James M. Gray, "Safe for Democracy," *Christian Workers Magazine* 17 (July 1917): 853.

56. George Marsden, *Fundamentalism and American Culture* (New York: Oxford University Press, 1980), 144–45.

57. S. Ridout, "Should a Christian Go to War?" *Our Hope* 24 (September 1917): 165–69.

58. *Christian Workers Magazine* 17 (July 1917): 862–63.

59. P. A. Klein, "Compulsory Military Service," *Christian Workers Magazine* 16 (July 1916): 835–36.

60. H. F. Toews, "The Doctrine of Non-Resistance," *Christian Workers Magazine* 17 (July 1917): 862–63; and James M. Gray, "What the Bible Teaches about War," *Christian Workers Magazine* 17 (July 1917): 860–61.

61. James M. Gray, "What the Bible Teaches about War and the Christian's Attitude in the Present Crisis," *Christian Workers Magazine* 18 (November 1918): 179–80. The quote is from *Christian Workers Magazine* 18 (February 1918): 448.

62. James M. Gray, *Christian Workers Magazine* 18 (June 1918): 775.

63. Arno C. Gaebelein, *Our Hope* 24 (April 1918): 629; and idem, *Christian Workers Magazine* 25 (July 1918): 48.

64. William L. Pettingill, ed., *Light on Prophecy* (New York: Christian Herald), 10, 111.

65. The call for the conference was quoted in Arno C. Gaebelein, *Half a Century: The Autobiography of a Servant* (New York: Our Hope Publishing, 1930), 112.

66. *King's Business* 9 (May 1918): 365–66. The original *Courier-Journal* editorial was written by Henry Watterson. See Marsden, *Fundamentalism and American Culture,* 150–51.

67. Marsden, *Fundamentalism and American Culture,* 142.

68. Reuben A. Torrey, "That Blessed Hope," in *Christ and Glory,* ed. Arno C. Gaebelein (New York: Our Hope Publishing, 1934), 21–22.

69. Arno C. Gaebelein, *The League of Nations in the Light of Prophecy* (New York: Our Hope Publishing, 1920); and I. M. Haldeman, *Why I Preach the Second Coming* (New York: Revell, 1919), 121–22.

70. "The League of Nations," *Christian Workers Magazine* 19 (April 1919): 526; "The League of Nations and the Danger of Federation," *Moody Bible Institute Monthly* 21 (September 1920): 7; Joseph T. Britain, "Why Our Nation Should Not Disarm," *Moody Bible Institute Monthly* 21 (August 1921): 510–12; and D. Gretter, "Disarmament and the Signs of the Times," *Moody Bible Institute Monthly* 21 (September 1920): 806.

71. I. R. Dean, *The Coming Kingdom* (Philadelphia: Approved Book Store, 1928), 216.

72. Torrey, "That Blessed Hope," 22.

73. W. B. Riley, "The Last Days, the Last War, and the Last King," in *Christ and Glory,* 161–76.

74. *Weekly Evangel,* 7 February 1925, 6; W. Percy Hicks, "Proposed Revival of the Old Roman Empire," *Weekly Evangel,* 20 March 1926, 4; Oswald J. Smith, *Is the Antichrist at Hand? What of Mussolini?* (New York: Christian Alliance Publishing, 1927); Gerald B. Winrod, *Mussolini's Place in Prophecy* (Wichita: Defender Publishers, 1933); J. M. Ritchie, *Prophetic Highlights* (New York: Revell, 1935), 17; Arno C. Gaebelein, *As It Was, So Shall It Be: Sunset and Sunrise: A Study of the First Age and Our Present Age* (New York: Our Hope Publishing, 1937), 128; Arthur I. Brown, *The Eleventh "Hour"* (Findlay, Ohio: Fundamental Truth Publishers, 1940), chap. 4; and George D. Beckwith, *God's Prophetic Plan through the Ages* (Grand Rapids: Zondervan, 1942), 103.

75. *Weekly Evangel,* 10 September 1932, 10. The *Sunday School Times* and *Moody Bible Institute Monthly* also repeated the story.

76. James M. Gray, editorial, *Moody Bible Institute Monthly* 34 (November 1933): 96.

77. James M. Gray, *Moody Bible Institute Monthly* 34 (February 1934): 252.

78. Leonard Sale-Harrison, "The Resurrection of Imperial Rome," *Moody Bible Institute Monthly* 36 (June 1936): 493–94. See also his "League of Nations and the Coming Superman," *Moody Bible Institute Monthly* 36 (August 1936): 605–6.

79. See Alva J. McClain, "The Four Great Powers of the End-Time," *King's Business* 39 (February 1938): 97.

80. Louis Bauman, *Light from Bible Prophecy* (New York: Revell, 1940), 18–30. See also his "Socialism, Communism, Fascism," *King's Business* 36 (August 1935): 293.

81. Scofield, *Scofield Reference Bible,* 883. See also Alfred H. Burton, *Russia's Destiny in the Light of Prophecy* (New York: Gospel Publishing House, 1917); and Leonard Sale-Harrison, *The Coming Great Northern Confederacy: Or the Future of Russia and Germany* (London: Pickering & Inglis, 1928). For some exceptions to this interpretation of Gog and Gomer, see Wilson, *Armageddon Now!* 113.

82. Editorial, *Moody Bible Institute Monthly* 32 (March 1932): 328.

83. See Thomas Chalmers, "Russia and Armageddon," *Weekly Evangel,* 14 April 1934, 6; and Dan Gilbert, "Views and Reviews of Current News," *King's Business* 30 (January 1930): 8.

84. Louis S. Bauman, *God and Gog* (Long Beach, Calif.: Privately published, 1934), 19.

85. Louis S. Bauman, "Russia and Armageddon," *King's Business* 29 (September 1938): 287.

86. Louis S. Bauman, "Gog and Gomer, Russia and Germany, and the War," *Sunday School Times* 81 (16 December 1939): 911–12; idem, *Light from Bible Prophecy*, 24–37; and Arno C. Gaebelein, "The Great North-Eastern Confederacy," *Our Hope* 46 (1939–40): 234–35.

87. Arno C. Gaebelein, "God's Hand in Prophetic Conferences," *Our Hope* 40 (November 1939): 129, 170. For an early announcement of the conference, see *Moody Monthly* 39 (June 1939): 536. (In its March 1938 issue, *Moody Bible Institute Monthly* changed its name to *Moody Monthly*.) For a report of the conference, see C. B. Nordland, "A Report of the International Prophetic Conference," *Our Hope* 40 (January 1940): 249, 298.

88. Wilson, *Armageddon Now!* 146.

89. *Weekly Evangel*, 12 July 1941, 10.

90. William Culbertson, editorial, *Moody Monthly* 42 (July 1942): 627.

Chapter 4

1. Nathaniel West, *The Thousand Years in Both Testaments* (New York: Revell, 1889), 424–26, 632; William E. Blackstone, *Jesus Is Coming* (New York: Revell, 1908), 165, 171–72; William Bell Riley, *The Evolution of the Kingdom* (New York: Charles C. Cook, 1913), 48; I. M. Haldeman, *The Coming of Christ* (Los Angeles: Bible House of Los Angeles, 1906), 205; J. F. Silver, *The Lord's Return* (New York: Revell, 1914), 279; and James H. Brookes, *Maranatha*, 3d ed. (New York: E. Brendell, 1874), 389–445.

2. For standard texts on the history of Jews in America, see Nathan Glazer, *American Judaism* (Chicago: University of Chicago Press, 1957); Joseph Blau, *Judaism in America: From Curiosity to Third Faith* (Chicago: University of Chicago Press, 1976); Seymour Liebman, *New World Jewry, 1493–1825: Requiem for the Forgotten* (New York: Ktav, 1982); and Arnold Eisen, *The Chosen People in America: A Study in Jewish Religious Ideology* (Bloomington, Ind.: Indiana University Press, 1983).

3. Melvin I. Urofsky, *American Zionism from Herzl to the Holocaust* (Garden City, N.Y.: Anchor Books, 1976), 41–230. See also Glazer, *American Judaism*.

4. *Our Hope* 10 (July 1903): 3–4; *Our Hope* 10 (November 1903): 339; and *Our Hope* 13 (August 1906): 119–20.

5. *Institute Tie* 8 (October 1907): 128; *Our Hope* 10 (February 1904): 513–14; Blackstone, *Jesus Is Coming*, 210–11; and Arno C. Gaebelein, *Hath God Cast Away His People?* (New York: Gospel Publishing House, 1905).

6. *Our Hope* 5 (August–September 1898): 101–2.

7. Gaebelein, *Hath God Cast Away His People?* 200–201.

8. Arno C. Gaebelein, "The Present Day Restoration Movement among the Jews and Its Significance," *Our Hope* 16 (September 1909): 103–7; and *Institute Tie* 9 (September 1908): 40.

9. The best summary and analysis of Blackstone's life is Yaakov Ariel, *On Behalf of Israel: American Fundamentalist Attitudes toward Jews, Judaism, and Zionism, 1865–1945* (Brooklyn, N.Y.: Carlson Publishing, 1991), 55–96. See also Paul Charles Merkley, *The Politics of Christian Zionism, 1891–1948* (London: Frank Cass, 1998), 59–74.

10. Ariel, *On Behalf of Israel*, 58.

11. Quoted in ibid., 70.

12. Quoted in Reuben Fink, ed., *America and Palestine* (New York: American Zionist Emergency Council, 1944), 21. See also Urofsky, *American Zionism*, 43.

13. Quoted in Anita Libman-Lebeson, "Zionism Comes to Chicago," in *Early History of Zionism in America,* ed. Isidore S. Meyer (New York: American Jewish Historical Society and Theodore Herzl Foundation, 1958), 168–69.

14. Ariel, *On Behalf of Israel,* 75–79.

15. Quoted in ibid., 78.

16. Libman-Lebeson, "Zionism Comes to Chicago," 169.

17. Ariel, *On Behalf of Israel,* 87–90.

18. Daniel Fuchs, "Prophecy and the Evangelization of the Jews," in *Focus on Prophecy,* ed. Charles Feinberg (Westwood, N.J.: Revell, 1964), 252. Blackstone's marked Old Testament is on public display at Herzl's grave in Israel.

19. J. D. Douglas, ed., *The New International Dictionary of the Christian Church* (Grand Rapids: Zondervan, 1974), 135.

20. Recent studies include Lester I. Vogel, *To See a Promised Land: Americans and the Holy Land in the Nineteenth Century* (University Park, Pa.: Pennsylvania State University Press, 1993), 152–58; Ariel, *On Behalf of Israel,* 36–38; and Ruth Kark and Yaakov Ariel, "Messianism, Holiness, Charisma, and Community: A Protestant American-Swedish Sect in Jerusalem, 1881–1933" (unpublished paper, Hebrew University of Jerusalem, 1994). What follows is based on these sources.

21. As he sailed across the Atlantic to meet her, Horatio wrote the beloved evangelical hymn "It Is Well with My Soul" (Alfred B. Smith, compiler, *Inspiring Hymns* [Grand Rapids: Singspiration, 1951], no. 271).

22. Vogel, *To See a Promised Land,* 155. Years later, after she had abandoned her parents' belief in the second coming, Bertha Spafford Vester claimed that these were ordinary picnics. Bertha Spafford Vester, *Our Jerusalem: An American Family in the Holy City, 1881–1949* (Garden City, N.Y.: Doubleday, 1950).

23. Selma Lagerlof, *Jerusalem: A Novel,* 2 vols., trans. Velma Swanson (Garden City, N.Y.: Doubleday, 1915).

24. Quoted in a news account in *Chicago Daily News,* 14–15 May 1895.

25. See chap. 32 of Vester, *Our Jerusalem.*

26. Dwight Wilson, *Armageddon Now! The Premillenarian Response to Russia and Israel since 1917* (Grand Rapids: Baker, 1977), 14–35.

27. Ibid., 39–40.

28. *Weekly Evangel,* 26 February 1916, 6.

29. Quoted in Urofsky, *American Zionism,* 199.

30. For typical reactions by American dispensationalists to the capture of Jerusalem, see *Christian Workers Magazine* 18 (January 1918): 396; *Christian Workers Magazine* 18 (February 1918): 447; *Our Hope* 24 (February 1918): 486–90; and E. Newman, "Jerusalem and the Jews in View of Scripture Prophecy," in *The Jew in History and Prophecy* (Chicago: Chicago Hebrew Mission, 1918), 25.

31. Wilson, *Armageddon Now!* 67.

32. A. E. Thompson, *The Life of A. B. Simpson* (Brooklyn, N.Y.: Christian and Missionary Alliance Publishing Company, 1920), 276; Paul Boyer, *When Time Shall Be No More: Prophecy Belief in Modern American Culture* (Cambridge: Harvard University Press, 1992), 102; and Vogel, *To See a Promised Land,* 235.

33. Arno C. Gaebelein, *Our Hope* 24 (1917–18): 438.

34. Quoted in William L. Pettingill, ed., *Light on Prophecy* (New York: Christian Herald, 1918), 144; and Ernest R. Sandeen, *The Roots of Fundamentalism* (Chicago: University of Chicago Press, 1970), 233–35.

35. Sandeen, *Roots of Fundamentalism,* 20–22, 67, 234–35.

36. Arno C. Gaebelein, "The Capture of Jerusalem and the Great Future of That City," in *Christ and Glory,* ed. Arno C. Gaebelein (New York: Our Hope Publishing, 1919), 157.

37. W. Fuller Gooch, "The Termination of This Age," *Weekly Evangel,* 23 March 1918, 12.

38. W. W. Fereday, "After the Great War," *Our Hope* 26 (1919–20): 34.

39. William R. Nicholson, "The Gathering of Israel," in *The Second Coming of Christ: Premillennial Essays of the Prophetic Conference Held in the Church of the Holy Trinity, New York City,* ed. Nathaniel West (Chicago: Revell, 1879), 231.

40. Quoted in Beth M. Lindberg, *A God-Filled Life: The Story of William E. Blackstone* (Chicago: American Messianic Fellowship, n.d.).

41. For example, Zion's Society for Israel of the Norwegian Lutherans in America, 1878; Jewish Mission of the Evangelical Synod of Missouri, Ohio, and Other States (Lutheran), 1883; New York City Extension and Missionary Society (Methodist Episcopal), 1886; Jewish Mission of the Joint Synod of Ohio (Lutheran), 1892; Reformed Presbyterian Jewish Mission Board, 1894; Hebrew Mission of the Methodist Episcopal Church, South, 1904; plus numerous other interdenominational or nondenominational missions agencies.

42. Yaakov Ariel, *Evangelizing the Chosen People: Missions to the Jews in America, 1880–2000* (Chapel Hill: University of North Carolina Press, 2000), 3.

43. James H. Brookes, "How to Reach the Jews," *Truth* 19 (1893): 135–36.

44. Arno C. Gaebelein, *Our Hope* 20 (January 1914): 442–45.

45. *Fifty Years of Blessing: Historical Sketch of Chicago Hebrew Mission, 1887–1937* (Chicago: Chicago Hebrew Mission, 1937), published in *Jewish Era* 47 (December 1937): 3–56.

46. J. H. Ralston, "The Conference on Behalf of Israel," *Christian Workers Magazine* 16 (January 1916): 359–60.

47. Arno C. Gaebelein, "How the Hope of Israel Became Undenominational," *Our Hope* 4 (1897): 3–5.

48. There has been only one book-length biography of Gaebelein: David A. Rausch, *Arno C. Gaebelein, 1861–1945: Irenic Fundamentalist and Scholar* (New York: Edwin Mellen Press, 1982). A less hagiographic approach can be found in Ariel, *On Behalf of Israel,* 97–117. Gaebelein's autobiography is Arno C. Gaebelein, *Half a Century: The Autobiography of a Servant* (New York: Our Hope Publishing, 1930).

49. James H. Brookes, "Work among the Jews," *Truth* 20 (1894): 14–16; Sandeen, *Roots of Fundamentalism,* 214–15; and Ariel, *On Behalf of Israel,* 106.

50. Ariel, *Evangelizing the Chosen People.*

51. Charles Meeker, "Evangelization of the American Jew," *Christian Workers Magazine* 19 (August 1919): 868.

52. S. B. Rohold, "Missionary Work among the Jews in the Holy Land," *Christian Workers Magazine* 20 (May 1920): 711–14.

53. F. C. Gilbert, *From Judaism to Christianity and Gospel Work among the Hebrews* (So. Lancaster, Mass.: Good Tidings, 1920), 251–56.

54. William W. Ketchum, "Some Interesting Things about Jews," *Christian Workers Magazine* 20 (April 1920): 630–31.

55. Leopold Cohn, *A Modern Missionary to an Ancient People,* 2d ed. (New York: American Board of Missions to the Jews, 1911).

56. *Down on Throop Avenue* (New York: American Board of Missions to the Jews, 1940).

57. Joseph Hoffman Cohn, *I Have Fought a Good Fight* (New York: American Board of Missions to the Jews, 1953), 107. For another account, see Samuel Freuder, *A Missionary's Return to Judaism* (New York: Sinai Publishing, 1915).

58. Ariel, *Evangelizing the Chosen People,* 101–22.

59. Cohn, *I Have Fought a Good Fight,* 204–25; and Freuder, *Missionary's Return to Judaism,* 164–66.

60. Cohn, *I Have Fought a Good Fight,* 225.

61. "Williamsburg Mission to the Jews: Abstract of the Report of the Committee of Investigation," *Christian Workers Magazine* 17 (November 1916): 191–92.

62. Freuder, *Missionary's Return to Judaism,* 36–59.

63. Ibid., 17.

64. For another example of this genre, see Lewis A. Hart, *A Jewish Reply to Christian Evangelists* (New York: Block Publishing, 1907).

65. Arno C. Gaebelein, "Herman Warszawiak's Method of Getting Crowds to Hear the Gospel," *Our Hope* 2 (1895): 2–5; Gaebelein, *Half a Century,* 29; and Ariel, *On Behalf of Israel,* 102.

66. David Eichhorn, *Evangelizing the American Jew* (Middle Village, N.Y.: Jonathan David Publishers, 1978).

67. Ariel, *Evangelizing the Chosen People,* 70–71.

68. Freuder, *Missionary's Return to Judaism,* 86–94, 137–49.

69. Arno C. Gaebelein, *Our Hope* 10 (August 1903): 104.

70. Ariel, *Evangelizing the Chosen People,* 93–100.

71. Ibid., 88–92.

72. Ibid., 83–87.

73. Albert Huisjen, *The Home Front of Jewish Missions* (Grand Rapids: Baker, 1962); idem, *Talking about Jesus to a Jewish Neighbor* (Grand Rapids: Baker, 1964); Henry J. Heydt, *Studies in Jewish Evangelism* (New York: American Board of Missions to the Jews, 1951); idem, *The Chosen People Question Box II* (Englewood Cliffs, N.J.: American Board of Missions to the Jews, 1976); Daniel Fuchs, *How to Reach the Jew for Christ* (Grand Rapids: Zondervan, 1943); Jacob Gartenhaus, *How to Win the Jews* (Atlanta: Baptist Home Mission Board, n.d.); and idem, *Winning Jews to Christ* (Grand Rapids: Zondervan, 1963).

74. For one convert's story, see Lydia Buksbazen, *They Looked for a City* (West Collingswood, N.J.: Spearhead Press, 1955). For another's, see Lauren F. Winner, *Girl Meets God: On the Path to a Spiritual Life* (Chapel Hill: Algonquin Books, 2002).

75. Arno C. Gaebelein, "Professor Heman on the Jews and the Churches," *Our Hope* 5 (August–September 1898): 56–58.

76. Arno C. Gaebelein, "The Hope of Israel Mission," *Our Hope* 5 (July 1898): 40.

77. Ernest F. Stroeter, "The Second Coming of Christ in Relation to Israel," in *Addresses on the Second Coming of the Lord Delivered at the Prophetic Conference, Allegheny, Pa., December 3–6, 1895,* ed. Joseph Kyle and William S. Miller (Pittsburgh: W. W. Waters, n.d.), 136–56. For an intriguing study of Stroeter's views and their influence on others, including Karl Barth, see Charles Cosgrove, "The Church *with* and *for* Israel: History of a Theological Novum before and after Barth," *Perspectives in Religious Studies* 22 (fall 1995): 259–78.

78. Esther Bronstein, *Esther,* ed. Janet Thoma (Elgin, Ill.: David C. Cook, 1982).

79. Cohn, *I Have Fought a Good Fight,* 91–94.

80. Jonathan D. Sarna, "From Necessity to Virtue: The Hebrew-Christianity of Gideon R. Lederer," *Iliff Review* 37 (winter 1980): 27–33.

81. Ernest F. Stroeter, "A Misapprehension Corrected," *Our Hope* 2 (1895): 55–58.

82. Arno C. Gaebelein, "A Short Review of Our Mission and the Principles of the Hope of Israel Mission," *Our Hope* 6 (1899): 68–71; and Ariel, *On Behalf of Israel,* 108.

83. Maurice Ruben, "The Hebrew Christian Alliance Conference," *Christian Workers Magazine* 18 (September 1917): 37.

84. Ariel, *Evangelizing the Chosen People,* 123–34.

85. John S. Conning, *Our Jewish Neighbors: An Essay in Understanding* (New York: Revell, 1927). He published a periodical with the same title from the late 1920s through the mid-1930s. See Ariel, *Evangelizing the Chosen People,* 124.

86. Ariel, *Evangelizing the Chosen People,* 134.

87. Ibid., 185–91.

88. Ariel, *On Behalf of Israel,* 99–103.

89. Ibid., 101.

90. Sarna, "From Necessity to Virtue," 31.

Chapter 5

1. Yaakov Ariel, *On Behalf of Israel: American Fundamentalist Attitudes toward Jews, Judaism, and Zionism, 1865–1945* (Brooklyn, N.Y.: Carlson Publishing, 1991), 40.

2. David A. Rausch, *Zionism within Early American Fundamentalism, 1878–1918* (New York: Edwin Mellen, 1978). Rausch is correct as far as he goes, but he underplays or ignores the kinds of evidence presented here.

3. Isaac M. Haldeman, *Signs of the Times,* 5th ed. (New York: Charles C. Cook, 1914), 436–37, quoted in Paul Boyer, *When Time Shall Be No More: Prophecy Belief in Modern American Culture* (Cambridge: Harvard University Press, 1992), 217–18.

4. *The Protocols of the Meeting of the Learned Elders of Zion,* trans. Victor E. Marsden (London: Britons Publishing, 1922); and Norman Cohn, *Warrant for Genocide: The Myth of the Jewish World Conspiracy and the "Protocols of the Elders of Zion"* (New York: Harper Torchbooks, 1969).

5. Quoted in Dwight Wilson, *Armageddon Now! The Premillenarian Response to Russia and Israel since 1917* (Grand Rapids: Baker, 1977), 75.

6. Neil Baldwin, *Henry Ford and the Jews: The Mass Production of Hate* (New York: Public Affairs, 2001).

7. Joseph Hoffman Cohn, "The Devil Revives Balakism," *Chosen People* 26 (December 1920): 5–7; and idem, "Henry Ford Again," *Chosen People* 26 (April 1921): 5–7.

8. Cohn, "Devil Revives Balakism," 7.

9. Charles C. Cook, "The International Jew," *King's Business* 12 (November 1921): 1087; and Wilson, *Armageddon Now!* 76.

10. James M. Gray, "The Jewish Protocols," *Moody Bible Institute Monthly* 22 (October 1921): 598.

11. Arno C. Gaebelein, *Our Hope* 27 (November 1920): 265–66; idem, "Isaiah Chapter 19: The Conversion of Egypt," *Our Hope* 27 (April 1921): 600–606; idem, "Jewish Leadership in Russia," *Our Hope* 27 (June 1921): 734–35; and idem, "Aspects of Jewish Power in the United States," *Our Hope* 29 (August 1922): 103.

12. Much of what follows was adapted from my article on dispensationalists and Jewish conspiracy theories: Timothy P. Weber, "Finding Someone to Blame: Fundamentalism and Anti-Semitic Conspiracy Theories in the 1930s," *Fides et Historia* 24 (summer 1992): 40–55.

13. Leo P. Ribuffo, *The Old Christian Right: The Protestant Far Right from the Great Depression to the Cold War* (Philadelphia: Temple University Press, 1983), 87.

14. Gerald B. Winrod, "Unmasking the 'Hidden Hand'—A World Conspiracy," *Defender* 7 (February 1933): 3.

15. See also Gerald B. Winrod, "Facing Ten Deadly Enemies at the Beginning of 1933," *Defender* 7 (January 1933): 3, 5, 18; idem, *The Hidden Hand—The Protocols and the Coming Superman* (Wichita: Defender Publishers, 1933); idem, *The Jewish Assault on Christianity* (Wichita: Defender Publishers, 1935); and idem, *The Truth about the Protocols* (Wichita: Defender Publishers, 1935).

16. Arno C. Gaebelein, *The Conflict of the Ages: The Mystery of Lawlessness, Its Origin, Historic Development, and Coming Defeat* (New York: Our Hope Publishing, 1933).

17. Ibid., 99.

18. *Jewish Chronicles,* 14 April 1919, quoted in ibid., 98.

19. Gaebelein, *Conflict of the Ages,* 99.

20. Ibid., 147–48.

21. Ibid., 168.

22. Ibid., 157–58.

23. See Ariel, *On Behalf of Israel,* 111–17 for an overview of Gaebelein's views.

24. William Bell Riley, *Wanted—A World Leader!* (Minneapolis: Privately published, 1939), 42–43.

25. William Bell Riley, *The Protocols and Communism* (Minneapolis: L. W. Camp, 1934), 5–14.

26. William Vance Trollinger Jr., *God's Empire: William Bell Riley and Midwestern Fundamentalism* (Madison: University of Wisconsin Press, 1990), 62–82.

27. Ribuffo, *Old Christian Right,* 5–7, 181, 244–47.

28. David Rausch, *Arno C. Gaebelein, 1861–1945: Irenic Fundamentalist and Scholar* (New York: Edwin Mellen, 1983), 147–48.

29. Gerald B. Winrod, "What Is Behind Communism," *Defender* 8 (January 1934): 7–8.

30. Ribuffo, *Old Christian Right,* 3–24; and Douglas S. Strong, *Organized Anti-Semitism in America: The Rise of Group Prejudice during the Decade 1930–1940* (Westport, Conn.: Greenwood Press, 1979), 15.

31. Winrod, "Unmasking the 'Hidden Hand,'" 3.

32. Ralph Lord Roy, *Apostles of Discord: A Study of Organized Bigotry and Disruption on the Fringes of Protestantism* (Boston: Beacon Press, 1935), 40–41. See Trollinger, *God's Empire,* 62–82 for an excellent study of Riley's right-wing connections.

33. Elizabeth Knauss, "Communism and the Protocols," *Pilot* 13 (November 1932): 40–41. See also idem, "Communism and the Jewish Question," *Pilot* 13 (June 1933): 271–72.

34. Arno C. Gaebelein, "Misrepresenting 'Our Hope,'" *Our Hope* 46 (December 1939): 379–82.

35. For a discussion of the *Hebrew Christian Alliance Quarterly*'s charges, see *Moody Bible Institute Monthly* 34 (January 1934): 209.

36. Joseph Hoffman Cohn, editorial, *Chosen People* 38 (April 1933): 4.

37. Joseph Hoffman Cohn, "The Conflict of the Ages," *Chosen People* 39 (February 1934): 7–9. Newman's book review is extensively quoted in Cohn's editorial.

38. Harry A. Ironside, "Are the Jews as a People Responsible for the So-Called Protocols of the Elders of Zion?" *Chosen People* 39 (March 1934): 5–7.

39. Gray, "Jewish Protocols," 598.

40. James M. Gray, *Moody Bible Institute Monthly* 27 (September 1927): 3.

41. James M. Gray, *Moody Bible Institute Monthly* 34 (January 1934): 209.

42. *Time,* 12 November 1934.

43. James M. Gray, "The Jewish Protocols," *Moody Bible Institute Monthly* 35 (January 1935): 230.

44. Louis S. Bauman, *Shirts and Sheets: Or Anti-Semitism, a Present-Day Sign of the First Magnitude* (Long Beach, Calif.: Privately published, 1934), 18.

45. Louis S. Bauman, *The Time of Jacob's Trouble* (Long Beach, Calif.: Privately published, 1938).

46. For example, see Elias Newman, *The Jewish Peril and the Hidden Hand* (Minneapolis: Privately published, 1934); and *Weekly Evangel,* 18 May 1935, 1.

47. Gerald B. Winrod, "Editor Winrod Answers Editor Cohn," *Defender* 8 (June 1933): 6; idem, "Protocols Confirmed," *Defender* 8 (November 1933): 15; idem, "Our Answer to Dr. J. Hoffman Cohn," *Defender* 8 (December 1933): 6–7; and idem, "Stigmatize Winrod," *Defender* 8 (December 1933): 13.

48. William Bell Riley, "Cohn vs. Riley," *Pilot* 15 (May 1935): 218; idem, "Joseph Cohn Again," *Pilot* 15 (June 1935): 249–50; and idem, "Joseph Cohn's New Money-Getting Scheme," *Northwestern Pilot* 26 (December 1945): 75.

49. William Bell Riley, "The 'Protocols and Communism' No Longer on Sale," *Pilot* 16 (July 1936): 302. Riley became the WCFA's executive secretary in 1929, after resigning as president.

50. J. Frank Norris, "Protocols of the Wise Men of Zion," *Fundamentalist,* 22 October 1937, 5–7, quoted in Barry Hankins, *God's Rascal: J. Frank Norris and the Beginnings of Southern Fundamentalism* (Lexington: University Press of Kentucky, 1996), 81.

51. Norris, "Protocols of the Wise Men of Zion," 1.

52. J. Frank Norris, "Did the Jews Write the Protocols? The Upheaval in Palestine and What It Means," *Fundamentalist,* 18 February 1938, 1; idem, "Dr. W. B. Riley Goes Back to Texas Baptist Machine and Apologizes to the Machine for the Many Years He Was with Norris," *Fundamentalist,* 4 March 1938, 1–3; and idem, "The Norris-Riley Discussion of the Jews, One Hundred Thousand Copies Published," *Fundamentalist,* 1 April 1938, 1.

53. Riley, *Wanted—A World Leader!*

54. Gaebelein's reply appeared in the April 1934 issue of *Our Hope* and was reproduced in a pamphlet published by Elias Newman that contained his original book review of *Conflict of the Ages,* his rebuttal to Gaebelein's reply, and some other anti-Gaebelein materials. Elias Newman, "The Conflict or Falsehood of the Ages, Which?" (Minneapolis: Privately published, 1934).

55. Arno C. Gaebelein, *World Prospects, How Is It All Going to End?* (New York: Our Hope Publishing, 1934); and idem, *Hopeless—Yet There Is Hope* (New York: Our Hope Publishing, 1935).

56. Keith Brooks, "Manifesto to the Jews," *Prophecy Monthly* (October 1939): 18–19.

57. Keith Brooks, "Come Clean," American Prophetic League, Inc., release no. 38 (January 1942): 1.

58. Arno C. Gaebelein, quoted in Keith Brooks, "Our Manifesto," *Prophecy Monthly* (January 1940): 35.

59. Arno C. Gaebelein, *The Conflict of the Ages,* rev. ed., ed. David Rausch (Neptune, N.J.: Loiseaux Brothers, 1982).

60. *Moody Bible Institute Monthly* 35 (March 1935): 314.

61. Oswald J. Smith, "My Visit to Germany," *Defender* 11 (September 1936): 15–18.

62. Quoted in William Bell Riley, "Germany," *Pilot* 18 (November 1937): 46.

63. Letter to the editor, *Moody Bible Institute Monthly* 34 (July 1934): 506.

64. James M. Gray, "The New Germany and the Evangelical Church," *Moody Bible Institute Monthly* 34 (August 1934): 553–54.

65. Ibid.

66. James M. Gray, *Moody Bible Institute Monthly* 35 (December 1934): 152.

67. Letter to the editor, *Moody Bible Institute Monthly* 36 (October 1935): 69.

68. James M. Gray, *Moody Bible Institute Monthly* 33 (May 1933): 392.

69. Robert W. Ross, *So It Was True: The American Protestant Press and the Nazi Persecution of the Jews* (Minneapolis: University of Minnesota Press, 1980). On Buchenwald, see Bauman, *Time of Jacob's Trouble,* 17.

70. Arno C. Gaebelein, "Adolf Hitler—Will He Be Germany's Dictator?" *Our Hope* 37 (1930): 363–64. See also idem, "The Shadows of Jacob's Trouble," *Our Hope* 38 (1932): 102.

71. David Rausch, "Our Hope: An American Fundamentalist Journal and the Holocaust, 1937–1945," *Fides et Historia* 12 (spring 1980): 89–103.

72. William Bell Riley, "Why Recognize Russia and Rag Germany," *Pilot* 14 (January 1934): 109–10, 126.

73. William Bell Riley, "Facts for Fundamentalists," *Pilot* 13 (July 1933): 298–99, quoted in Trollinger, *God's Empire,* 74.

74. William Bell Riley, *Shivering at the Sight of a Shirt* (Minneapolis: Privately published, 1936); and Trollinger, *God's Empire,* 75–76.

75. Riley, *Wanted—A World Leader!*

76. William Bell Riley, *Hitlerism: Or the Philosophy of Evolution in Action* (Minneapolis: Privately published, 1941).

77. Ribuffo, *Old Christian Right,* 125–27, 187–88, 196–97, 202–3, 205, 208, 211.

78. Arthur W. Pink, *The Antichrist* (Grand Rapids: Kregel, 1923), 106, 293; E. M. Milligan, *Is the Kingdom Age at Hand?* (New York: George H. Doran, 1924), 209; and Charles G. Trumbull, *Prophecy's Light on Today* (New York: Revell, 1937), 71. All are quoted in Boyer, *When Time Shall Be No More,* 209.

79. Bauman, *Time of Jacob's Trouble.*

80. Keith Brooks, *Jews and the Passion for Israel in Light of Prophecy* (Grand Rapids: Zondervan, 1937), 42, quoted in Boyer, *When Time Shall Be No More,* 214.

81. Lewis Sperry Chafer, *Systematic Theology,* vol. 4 (Dallas: Dallas Theological Seminary, 1948), 313, quoted in Boyer, *When Time Shall Be No More,* 216.

82. *Moody Monthly* 34 (February 1934): 262–63, 294. See also "The Indestructible Jews," *Sunday School Times* 84 (3 October 1942): 381.

83. Henry E. Anderson, "Are God's Covenants about to Be Fulfilled?" *Moody Monthly* 40 (November 1940): 128–29.

84. *Moody Monthly* 40 (December 1939): 175–76. Sponsors included Harry A. Ironside, Charles E. Fuller, Louis Talbot, Will Houghton, Donald G. Barnhouse, Charles G. Trumbull, Leonard Sale-Harrison, Max Reich, Coulson Shepherd, and George T. B. Davis.

85. *Moody Monthly* 43 (April 1943): 472. The mission was the New York Jewish Evangelization Society.

86. Harry Rimmer, *Palestine: The Coming Storm Center* (Grand Rapids: Eerdmans, 1940), quoted in *Moody Monthly* 41 (October 1941): 113.

87. Will Houghton, *Moody Monthly* 40 (July 1940): 592.

88. "Appeal for Persecuted Israel," *Moody Monthly* 40 (December 1939): inside front cover.

89. *Moody Monthly* 40 (March 1940): 381.

90. Arno C. Gaebelein, *As It Was, so Shall It Be: Sunset and Sunrise: A Study of the First Age and Our Present Age* (New York: Our Hope Publishing, 1937), 162.

91. The best analysis of the complexities and variations of dispensationalist interpretations is Boyer, *When Time Shall Be No More,* 115–290.

92. John Walvoord, *Israel in Prophecy* (Grand Rapids: Zondervan, 1968), 107, 113–14.

93. John F. Walvoord and John E. Walvoord, *Armageddon: Oil and the Middle East Crisis* (Grand Rapids: Zondervan, 1974), 113–14.

94. Milton Lindberg, *The Jews and Armageddon* (Chicago: American Messianic Fellowship, 1940), 26.

95. Hal Lindsey, *The Late Great Planet Earth* (Grand Rapids: Zondervan, 1970), 111; and Boyer, *When Time Shall Be No More,* 216.

96. Arthur Bloomfield, quoted in Boyer, *When Time Shall Be No More,* 216.

97. Ibid., 213.

98. References that present this scenario are too numerous to mention, but typical of the genre are Bauman, *Time of Jacob's Trouble;* S. Maxwell Coder, *The Final Chapter: Understanding What the Bible Says about the Last Days of Human History* (Wheaton: Tyndale, 1984); Richard DeHaan, *Israel and the Nations in Prophecy* (Grand Rapids: Zondervan, 1968); Tim LaHaye, *The Coming Peace in the Middle East* (Grand Rapids:

Zondervan, 1984); Thomas McCall and Zola Levitt, *The Coming Russian Invasion of Israel* (Chicago: Moody, 1974); Alva McClain, *Daniel's Prophecy of the Seventy Weeks* (Grand Rapids: Zondervan, 1940); J. Dwight Pentecost, *Prophecy for Today* (Grand Rapids: Zondervan, 1961); Arthur W. Pink, *The Antichrist* (Swengel, Pa.: Bible Truth Depot, 1923); Charles C. Ryrie, *The Final Countdown* (Wheaton: Victor Books, 1982); Wilbur M. Smith, *The Israeli-Arab Conflict and the Bible* (Van Nuys, Calif.: Regal, 1967); Jack Van Impe and Roger F. Campbell, *Israel's Final Holocaust* (Troy, Mich.: Jack Van Impe Ministries, 1979); and John Wesley White, *WW III* (Grand Rapids: Zondervan, 1977).

99. Ribuffo believes that personal misfortunes and failures were behind the easy acceptance of anti-Semitic conspiracy theories, and Trollinger argued the same in his study of William Bell Riley. See Ribuffo, *Old Christian Right,* 25–79, 110, 128–77; and Trollinger, *God's Empire,* 69.

100. George Marsden, *Fundamentalism and American Culture* (New York: Oxford University Press, 1980), 287–88.

Chapter 6

1. David Fromkin, *A Peace to End All Peace: The Fall of the Ottoman Empire and the Creation of the Modern Middle East* (New York: Avon Books, 1989); and Bernard Lewis, *The Middle East: A Brief History of the Last 2000 Years* (New York: Scribners, 1995).

2. Barbara W. Tuchman, *Bible and Sword: England and Palestine from the Bronze Age to Balfour* (New York: Ballantine Books, 1956).

3. Ibid., 176–207, 249–51.

4. Blanche E. C. Dugdale, *Arthur James Balfour, First Earl Balfour,* 2 vols. (New York, 1937), 1:324, quoted in ibid., 311; and Donald E. Wagner, *Anxious for Armageddon: A Call to Partnership for Middle Eastern and Western Christians* (Scottdale, Pa.: Herald Press, 1995), 85–95. See also Kenneth Young, *Arthur James Balfour* (London: G. Bell & Sons, 1963).

5. Tuchman, *Bible and Sword,* 335–36.

6. Ibid., 306.

7. Fromkin, *Peace to End All Peace,* 173–99; Sami Hadawi, *Bitter Harvest: A Modern History of Palestine* (New York: Olive Branch Press, 1989), 7–18; and Conor Cruise O'Brien, *The Siege: The Saga of Israel and Zionism* (New York: Simon & Schuster, 1986), 81–195.

8. Fromkin, *Peace to End All Peace,* 558–67.

9. Ibid., 263–75.

10. All quotes are from Tuchman, *Bible and Sword,* 345–47.

11. Ibid.

12. Bruce Feiler, *Abraham: A Journey to the Heart of Three Faiths* (New York: William Morrow, 2002).

13. Karen Armstrong, *Jerusalem: One City, Three Faiths* (New York: Knopf, 1996).

14. Yohannan Aharoni and Michael Avi-Yonah, *The Macmillan Bible Atlas* (New York: Macmillan, 1968), 164–65; J. D. Douglas, ed., *The New Bible Dictionary* (Grand Rapids: Eerdmans, 1962), 618–19; and Gershom Gorenberg, *The End of Days: Fundamentalism and the Struggle for the Temple Mount* (New York: Free Press, 2000), 63.

15. In the mid-nineteenth century, Mark Twain was part of what many consider to be the first American tour of Israel. His account of visiting Jerusalem and the Temple Mount is intriguing, if not irreverent. Mark Twain, *The Innocents Abroad* (1869; reprint, New York: Signet Classic, 1966), 428–34.

16. Gorenberg, *End of Days,* 72.

17. Armstrong, *Jerusalem,* 376–82; and O'Brien, *Siege,* 178–88.

18. Gorenberg, *End of Days,* 63.

19. Wagner, *Anxious for Armageddon,* 141–42; and Armstrong, *Jerusalem,* 383.

20. Quoted in O'Brien, *Siege,* 226.

21. Ibid.

22. Ibid., 252.

23. Ibid., 268–69; and Armstrong, *Jerusalem,* 385.

24. Dwight Wilson, *Armageddon Now! The Premillenarian Response to Russia and Israel since 1917* (Grand Rapids: Baker, 1977), 86–106.

25. See Keith Brooks, *Prophecy* 3 (October 1931): 7.

26. Agnes Scott Kent, "Palestine Is for the Jew," *King's Business* 22 (November 1931): 494.

27. Aaron Judah Kligerman, "Israel and Palestine," *Moody Bible Institute Monthly* 30 (August 1930): 587–88.

28. J. A. Huffman, "The Jew and Arab Controversy over Palestine," *King's Business* 21 (September 1930): 417–18.

29. William Pettingill, "Signs of the End of the Age," *Sunday School Times* 89 (12 April 1947): 360.

30. Wilson, *Armageddon Now!* 128.

31. *Weekly Evangel,* 5 April 1947, 10.

32. *Our Hope* 53 (1946–47): 424.

33. T. DeCourcy Rayner, "Hidden Hands in Palestine," *Moody Bible Institute Monthly* 48 (December 1947): 264.

34. *Weekly Evangel,* 17 February 1940, 11.

35. *Weekly Evangel,* 22 November 1941, 4.

36. *Weekly Evangel,* 20 March 1948, 10.

37. *Sunday School Times* 82 (20 April 1940): 319.

38. Arno C. Gaebelein, *Our Hope* 57 (1940–41): 341.

39. James M. Gray, *Moody Bible Institute Monthly* 31 (January 1931): 346.

40. Wilson, *Armageddon Now!* 100–102.

41. Frederick Childe, "Christ's Answer to the Challenge of Communism and Fascism," *Weekly Evangel,* 31 October 1935, 1.

42. Keith Brooks, *Prophecy,* quoted in *Weekly Evangel,* 4 July 1936, 4.

43. W. F. Smalley, "Another View of the Palestine Situation," *King's Business* 21 (June 1930): 290–92.

44. T. A. Lambie, "Palestine Focus of World Attention," *Sunday School Times* 87 (4 May 1946): 401.

45. O'Brien, *Siege,* 277–86; Hadawi, *Bitter Harvest,* 82–96; and Armstrong, *Jerusalem,* 385–89.

46. Louis T. Talbot, *King's Business* 39 (June 1948): 4. See also Louis T. Talbot and William W. Orr, *The New Nation of Israel and the Word of God!* (Los Angeles: Bible Institute of Los Angeles, 1948).

47. *Weekly Evangel,* 18 June 1948, 8.

48. The two quotations are from Wilson, *Armageddon Now!* 132.

49. George T. B. Davis, *Rebuilding Palestine according to Prophecy* (Philadelphia: Million Testaments Campaigns, 1935), 112.

50. *Weekly Evangel,* 8 March 1936, 6.

51. U. S. Grant, "Things to Come," *Weekly Evangel,* 21 May 1949, 2.

52. Wilson, *Armageddon Now!* 142.

53. *King's Business* 43 (March 1952): 7.

54. *Weekly Evangel,* 30 April 1949, 9.

55. Michael B. Oren, *Six Days of War: June 1967 and the Making of Modern Israel* (New York: Oxford University Press, 2002), 6–7.

56. Ibid., 9.

57. Ibid., 11. See also O'Brien, *Siege,* 387.

58. Oren, *Six Days of War,* 11–12; O'Brien, *Siege,* 391–97; and A. J. Barker, *Arab-Israeli Wars* (New York: Hippocrene Books, 1980), 27–40.

59. George T. B. Davis, "A Divine Promise That Changed History," *Sunday School Times* 99 (16 March 1957): 205–6.

60. Wilson, *Armageddon Now!* 168.

61. William L. Hull, *Israel—Key to Prophecy* (Grand Rapids: Zondervan, 1964), 35.

62. Oswald T. Allis, "Israel's Transgression in Palestine," *Christianity Today* 1 (24 December 1956): 9.

63. Wilbur M. Smith, "Israel in Her Promised Land," *Christianity Today* 1 (24 December 1956): 7–9.

64. Paul S. Allen, "Arab or Israeli," *Alliance Witness* 92 (8 May 1957): 2.

65. Oren, *Six Days of War;* O'Brien, *Siege,* 404–16; J. N. Westwood, *The History of the Middle East Wars* (Westwood, N.J.: Exeter Books, 1984); Trevor N. Dupuy, *Elusive Victory: The Arab-Israeli Wars, 1947–1974* (New York: Harper & Row, 1978); S. L. A. Marshall, *Swift Sword: The Historical Record of Israel's Victory, June 1967* (New York: American Heritage Publishing, 1967); Richard B. Parker, *The Politics of Miscalculation in the Middle East* (Bloomington, Ind.: Indiana University Press, 1993); and Richard B. Parker, *The Six-Day War* (Jacksonville, Fla.: University of Florida Press, 1997).

66. Barker, *Arab-Israeli Wars,* 41–96.

67. Gorenberg, *End of Days,* 99–102.

68. Armstrong, *Jerusalem,* 398–404; Gorenberg, *End of Days,* 97–104; and Oren, *Six Days of War,* 240–56.

69. Oren, *Six Days of War,* 305–9.

70. Ibid., 321–22.

71. Kenneth W. Stein, *Heroic Diplomacy: Sadat, Kissinger, Carter, Begin, and the Quest for Arab-Israeli Peace* (New York: Routledge, 1999), 55.

72. Ibid., 312–27.

73. L. Nelson Bell, "Unfolding Destiny," *Christianity Today* 11 (21 July 1967): 1044–45.

74. John F. Walvoord, "The Amazing Rise of Israel," *Moody Monthly* 68 (October 1967): 22.

75. *Moody Monthly* 67 (October 1967).

76. See S. Maxwell Coder, "Jerusalem: Key to the Future," *Moody Monthly* 74 (October 1973): 32–33.

77. Alan Johnson's comments were later published in *Moody Monthly* 67 (July–August, 1967): 22–24.

78. Harold Sevener, "Israel: The World's Timetable," *Christian Life* 35 (August 1973): 28.

79. "A Proclamation Concerning Israel and the Nations" (1967), quoted in Wilson, *Armageddon Now!* 194.

80. Charles C. Ryrie, "Perspective on Palestine," *Christianity Today* 13 (23 May 1969): 8.

81. Wilbur M. Smith, *Israeli/Arab Conflict and the Bible* (Glendale, Calif.: Regal, 1967), 80.

82. Charles L. Feinberg, "Isaac and Ishmael," *King's Business* 58 (July 1968): 23.

83. William Ward Ayer, "The Arab and the Jew," *Weekly Evangel,* 30 July 1967, 6.

84. Francis Fukuyama, *The Great Disruption: Human Nature and the Reconstruction of the Social Order* (New York: Touchstone Books, 1999).

Chapter 7

1. Hal Lindsey, *The Late Great Planet Earth* (Grand Rapids: Zondervan, 1970).

2. Hilton Sutton, *World War III: God's Conquest of Russia* (Tulsa: Harrison House, 1982), front matter, quoted in Paul Boyer, *When Time Shall Be No More: Prophecy Belief in Modern American Culture* (Cambridge: Harvard University Press, 1992), 188.

3. Thomas D. Ice, "Lindsey, Harold L.," in *Dictionary of Premillennial Theology*, ed. Mal Couch (Grand Rapids: Kregel, 1996), 242–43; and Robert G. Clouse, Robert N. Hosack, and Richard V. Pierard, *The New Millennium Manual: A Once and Future Guide* (Grand Rapids: Baker, 1999), 124–25. I was an eyewitness to the events at U.C.L.A.

4. Lindsey, *Late Great Planet Earth*, 53–58.

5. Ibid., 168.

6. Ibid., 186.

7. Ibid., 186–88.

8. Robert M. Price, "The Paper Back Apocalypse," *Wittenburg Door* (October/November 1981): 3–5. See also Timothy P. Weber, "Happily at the Edge of the Abyss: Popular Premillennialism in America," *Ex Auditu* 6 (1990): 91–92.

9. Boyer, *When Time Shall Be No More*, 7.

10. Clouse, Hosack, and Pierard, *New Millennium Manual*, 126.

11. The list is long: *Satan Is Alive and Well on Planet Earth* (1972); *There's a New World Coming* (1973); *Guilt Trip: How to Realize God's Forgiving Love* (1973); *The Liberation of Planet Earth* (1974); *When Is Jesus Coming Again?* (1975); *The Terminal Generation* (1976); *The World's Final Hour: Evacuation or Extinction* (1976); *The 1980s: Countdown to Armageddon* (1980); *The Rapture: Truth or Consequences* (1983); *Prophetic Walk through the Holy Land* (1983); *The Promise* (1984); *Combat Faith* (1986); *The Road to Holocaust* (1989); *Israel and the Last Days* (1991); *The Final Battle* (1995); *The Messiah* (1996); *Planet Earth Two Thousand A.D.: Will Mankind Survive?* (1996); *Blood Moon* (1996); *Apocalypse Code* (1997); *Planet Earth: The Final Chapter* (1997); *Vanished into Thin Air: The Hope of Every Believer* (1999); *Facing Millennial Midnight* (1999); *The Greatest Gift: God's Amazing Grace* (1999); *Why Do We Have Trials?* (2001); *The Everlasting Hatred: The Roots of Jihad* (2002); and *Last Days Chronicle* (2002).

12. Clouse, Hosack, and Pierard, *New Millennium Manual*, 126.

13. Ibid., 131–37; and Weber, "Happily at the Edge of the Abyss," 92.

14. Tim and Beverly LaHaye, *The Act of Marriage: The Beauty of Sexual Love* (Grand Rapids: Zondervan, 1976).

15. Tim LaHaye, *The Battle for the Mind* (New York: Revell, 1980).

16. John Cloud, "Meet the Prophet," *Time*, 1 July 2002, 50–53.

17. For example, Tim LaHaye, *The Beginning of the End* (Wheaton: Tyndale, 1972); *Revelation: Illustrated and Made Plain* (Grand Rapids: Zondervan, 1974); *The Coming Peace in the Middle East* (Grand Rapids: Zondervan, 1984); *How to Study the Bible Prophecy for Yourself* (Eugene, Ore.: Harvest House, 1990); and *No Fear of the Storm* (Sisters, Ore.: Multnomah, 1992). The last book was reissued in 1998 under a new title, *Rapture under Attack: Can We Still Trust the Pre-Trib Rapture?*

18. Tim LaHaye cofounded the Center with Tommy Ice in 1994. See www.tim lahaye.com.

19. Nancy Gibbs, "Apocalypse Now," *Time*, 1 July 2002, 40–48.

20. The website is found at www.leftbehind.com.

21. Steve Rabey, "Left Behind No More," *Christianity Today* 46 (22 April 2002): 26.

22. Michael R. Smith, "Author LaHaye Sues *Left Behind* Film Producers," *Christianity Today* 45 (23 April 2001): 20; Steve Rabey, "Left Behind: Success of Novels Spins Disputes," *Religion News Service,* 26 October 2000; and Ted Olsen, "At the Box Office, Left Behind Gets . . . Well, You Know," *Christianity Today* 44 (5 February 2001).

23. "Judge Dismisses All Claims Brought by Tim LaHaye against Cloud Ten," *CWS News Service,* 27 March 2003.

24. Mel Odom, *Apocalypse Dawn* (Wheaton: Tyndale, 2003); and Neesa Hart, *End of State* (Wheaton: Tyndale, 2004).

25. Announcement of the new series can be found on www.leftbehind.com.

26. David D. Kirkpatrick, "Best-Selling Minister Branches Out," *New York Times,* 11 February 2002.

27. Gibbs, "Apocalypse Now," 43.

28. Hal Lindsey, *The 1980s: Countdown to Armageddon* (King of Prussia, Pa.: Westgate Press, 1980), 4.

29. Ibid., *passim.*

30. Conor Cruise O'Brien, *The Siege: The Saga of Israel and Zionism* (New York: Simon & Schuster, 1986), 561–619.

31. Lindsey, *1980s,* 47, 61–62.

32. In this section, I am following my arguments in *Living in the Shadow of the Second Coming: American Premillennialism, 1875–1982* (Chicago: University of Chicago Press, 1987), 219; and "Happily at the Edge of the Abyss," 93.

33. Lindsey, *1980s,* 89–91, 101.

34. Ibid., 171, 154, 129.

35. Ibid., 157.

36. Ibid., 146.

37. Ibid.

38. Ibid., 165.

39. Ibid., 176.

40. Erling Jorstad, *The Politics of Doomsday: Fundamentalists of the Far Right* (Nashville: Abingdon, 1970); Flo Conway and Jim Siegelman, *Holy Terror: The Fundamentalist War on America's Freedoms in Religion, Politics, and Our Private Lives* (Garden City, N.Y.: Doubleday, 1982); Carol Flake, *Redemptorama: Culture, Politics, and the New Evangelicalism* (Garden City, N.Y.: Anchor Press, 1984); A. G. Mojtabai, *Blessed Assurance: At Home with the Bomb in Amarillo, Texas* (Boston: Houghton Mifflin, 1986); Grace Halsell, *Prophecy and Politics: Militant Evangelists on the Road to Nuclear War* (Westport, Conn.: Lawrence Hill, 1986); Michael D'Antonio, *Fall from Grace: The Failed Crusade of the Christian Right* (New York: Farrar, Straus, Giroux, 1989); and James Davison Hunter, *Culture Wars: The Struggle to Define America* (New York: Basic Books, 1991).

41. Weber, *Living in the Shadow of the Second Coming,* 99.

42. Francis Fukuyama, *The Great Disruption: Human Nature and the Reconstitution of Social Order* (New York: Touchstone Books, 2000).

43. Clyde Wilcox, Sharon Linzey, and Ted G. Jelen, "Reluctant Warriors: Premillennialism and Politics in the Moral Majority," *Journal for the Scientific Study of Religion* 30 (1991): 245–58.

44. David Douglas, "God, the World, and James Watt," *Christianity and Crisis* 41 (5 October 1981): 258, 269–70.

45. Gibbs, "Apocalypse Now," 47.

46. For a good summary of the sources and extent of Reagan's prophetic views, see Grace Halsell, *Prophecy and Politics: The Secret Alliance between Israel and the U.S. Christian Right* (Chicago: Lawrence Hill Books, 1986), 40–50.

47. Ronnie Dugger, "Does Reagan Expect a Nuclear Armageddon?" *Washington Post,* 8 April 1984, C1, C4.

48. Joe Cuomo, "Ronald Reagan and the Politics of Armageddon," produced at WBAI Radio, New York City, 1984.

49. The press conference received extensive coverage by the media. For example, John Herbers, "Armageddon View Prompts a Debate," *New York Times,* 24 October 1984, A1, A25; and Miles Harvey, "Religious Authorities Ask Reagan, Mondale to Repudiate 'Armageddon Ideology' on Nuclear War," *Los Angeles Times,* 24 October 1984, part 1.

50. "Washington Diarist: The End Is Nigh," *New Republic,* 12 November 1984, 50; and Andrew Lang, "The Politics of Armageddon," *Convergence: Report from the Christic Institute* (fall 1984): 3, 12, 16.

51. Richard Ostling, "Armageddon and the End Times," *Time,* 5 November 1984, 73; Kenneth L. Woodward, "Arguing Armageddon," *Newsweek,* 5 November 1984, 91; Walter Goodman, "Religious Debate Fueled by Politics," *New York Times,* 28 October 1984; and "The End Is Near," *Tribune* (Oakland, Calif.), 23 October 1984, B8.

52. Gibbs, "Apocalypse Now," 47.

53. Michael Barkun, "Nuclear War and Millenarian Symbols: Premillennialists Confront the Bomb" (paper delivered at the annual meeting of the Society for the Scientific Study of Religion, Savannah, Ga., October 1985).

54. Boyer, *When Time Shall Be No More,* 115–51.

55. Hal Lindsey, *There's a New World Coming: A Prophetic Odyssey* (Santa Ana, Calif.: Vision House, 1973).

56. Boyer, *When Time Shall Be No More,* 127.

57. Ibid., 133–35. The quotation is from David Wilkerson, *Set the Trumpet to Thy Mouth* (Lindale, Tex.: World Challenge, 1985), 1.

58. Boyer, *When Time Shall Be No More,* 150.

59. Leo P. Ribuffo, "Reagan, Ronald," in *The Oxford Companion to United States History,* ed. Paul Boyer (New York: Oxford University Press, 2001), 652–53.

60. Boyer, *When Time Shall Be No More,* 325–26.

61. For example, "Jack Van Impe Presents," Trinity Broadcasting Network, 5 September 1990; and Hal Lindsey, "Praise the Lord," Trinity Broadcasting Network, 5 September 1990.

62. Boyer, *When Time Shall Be No More,* 326.

63. David Hunt, *Global Peace and the Rise of Antichrist* (Eugene, Ore.: Harvest House, 1990).

64. Clouse, Hosack, and Pierard, *New Millennium Manual,* 130–32; David E. Harrell Jr., *Pat Robertson: A Personal, Religious, and Political Portrait* (San Francisco: HarperCollins, 1988); John Donovan, *Pat Robertson: The Authorized Biography* (New York: Macmillan, 1988); and Alec Foege, *The Empire God Built: Inside Pat Robertson's Media Machine* (Hoboken, N.J.: John Wiley & Sons, 1996).

65. Mark G. Toulouse, "Pat Robertson: Apocalyptic Theology and American Foreign Policy," *Journal of Church and State* 31 (winter 1989): 73–99.

66. Pat Robertson, *The New World Order* (Dallas: Word, 1991).

67. Ibid., 251–52.

68. Ibid., 252.

69. Ibid., 253.

70. Ibid., 256–57.

71. Ibid., 256.

72. Ibid., 258–68.

73. Eric Anderson, "The Millerite Use of Prophecy: A Case Study of a 'Striking Fulfillment,'" in *The Disappointed: Millerism and Millenarianism in the Nineteenth*

Century, ed. Ronald L. Numbers and Jonathan M. Butler (Bloomington, Ind.: Indiana University Press, 1987), 78–91.

74. John F. Walvoord, *Armageddon, Oil, and the Middle East* (Grand Rapids: Zondervan, 1973).

75. Lester Sumrall, *The Holy War Jihad: The Destiny of Iran and the Moslem World* (Tulsa: Harrison House, 1980).

76. Jim McKeever, quoted in Boyer, *When Time Shall Be No More,* 327.

77. Michael Hirsley and Jorge Casuso, "Mideast Crisis Sparks Talk of Armageddon," *Chicago Tribune,* 14 October 1990, sec. 1, pp. 1, 14.

78. Boyer, *When Time Shall Be No More,* 327–30.

79. Lindsey, *1980s,* 68, 74.

80. C. I. Scofield, ed., *The New Scofield Reference Bible* (New York: Oxford University Press, 1967), 1369–70.

81. Mal Couch and Joseph Chambers, "Babylon," in *Dictionary of Premillennial Theology,* 61–62.

82. Lindsey, *Late Great Planet Earth,* 114–34.

83. Lindsey, *There's a New World Coming,* 242; and "Iraq—Rebuilding Babylon," *Christianity Today* 32 (18 November 1988): 71.

84. Charles Taylor, quoted in Boyer, *When Time Shall Be No More,* 330.

85. Ibid.; and Charles Dyer, *The Rise of Babylon* (Wheaton: Tyndale, 1991).

86. *Jack Van Impe Presents,* Trinity Broadcasting Network, 8 October 1990. Van Impe had always seen the connection between Iran and Iraq. See Jack Van Impe, *Israel's Final Holocaust* (Troy, Mich.: Jack Van Impe Ministries, 1979), 134.

87. Tim LaHaye and Jerry B. Jenkins, *Tribulation Force* (Wheaton: Tyndale, 1996), 278.

88. Ibid.

89. Charles Taylor, quoted in ibid., 328.

90. Don Lattin, "War in Babylon Has Evangelicals Seeing Earth's Final Days," *San Francisco Chronicle,* 22 March 2003. Lattin evidently did not find a single person willing to draw a strong connection between the war with Iraq and the end times.

91. Bill Broadway, "Direst of Predictions for War in Iraq: End-Time Interpreters See Biblical Prophecies Being Fulfilled," *Washington Post,* 8 March 2003, B09.

92. Michael Clancy, "For Faithful, Prayer Is Key to Facing War," *Arizona Republic,* 22 March 2003.

93. Bob Briggs, "Area Pastors and Church Members Share Opinions, Feelings about War," *Kennebec Online Journal,* www.centralmaine.com/news/stories/030322briggs_s.shtml (accessed 22 March 2003).

94. "The End Is Not Yet: An Interview with Mark Bailey," *Christianity Today,* www.christianitytoday.com/ct/2003/112/44.0.html (accessed 27 March 2003).

95. "The Iraq War Has Little Effect on the Rapture Index: An Interview with Todd Strandberg," *Christianity Today,* www.christianitytoday.com/ct/2003/112/43.0.html (accessed 27 March 2003).

96. Ibid. The Rapture Index may be viewed at RaptureReady.com.

Chapter 8

1. Carl F. H. Henry, *Confessions of a Theologian: An Autobiography* (Waco: Word, 1986), 334–36.

2. Mark O'Keefe, "Israel's Evangelical Approach: U.S. Christian Zionists Nurtured as Political, Tourism Force," *Washington Post,* 26 January 2002, B11. See also Grace Halsell,

Prophecy and Politics: The Secret Alliance between Israel and the U.S. Christian Right (Chicago: Lawrence Hill Books, 1986), 123.

3. See www.gospelcom.net/shofar/joshuatravel/index.php.

4. See www.sorisrael.com/sori.

5. See Yaakov Ariel, *Evangelizing the Chosen People: Missions to the Jews in America, 1880–2000* (Chapel Hill: University of North Carolina Press, 2000), 276; and www.levitt.com.

6. Halsell, *Prophecy and Politics*, 120–24.

7. See the ICEJ's website, www.icej.org, for these statements.

8. William A. Orme Jr., "Succoth in Israel, and Here Come the Evangelicals," *New York Times*, 29 September 1999, A4.

9. Ibid.

10. "Address by Prime Minister Benjamin Netanyahu, the Feast of Tabernacles Conference," 5 October 1999, National Christian Leadership Conference for Israel website, www.nclci.org/NETANYAHU-Tabernacles.htm (accessed 15 April 2003).

11. "Address by Israeli Prime Minister Ariel Sharon," 22 September 2002, www.internationalwallofprayer.org/A-087-Address-by-Israeli-Prime-Minister-Ariel-Sharon-Feast-of-Tabernacles-Jerusalem.html (accessed 25 September 2002).

12. For an extensive analysis of the ICEJ, see Donald E. Wagner, *Anxious for Armageddon: A Call to Partnership for Middle Eastern and Western Christians* (Scottdale, Pa.: Herald Press, 1995), 96–113.

13. Ibid., 12, 71–77.

14. "Falwell's Liberty University Plans Huge Class Trip to Israel," *Western Recorder*, 13 October 1998, 8.

15. Halsell, *Prophecy and Politics*.

16. Ibid., 51–67.

17. Ibid., 58.

18. Ibid., 12.

19. Gayle White, "Israel Finds Strong Support among Conservative American Christians," *Albuquerque Tribune*, www.abqtrib.com/arc/news010599_america.htm (accessed 29 December 2002).

20. Donna DeMarco, "Israel Tourism Suffers," *Washington Times*, 5 April 2002, www.washtimes.com/business/20020405-27345031.htm (accessed 9 March 2003).

21. Halsell, *Prophecy and Politics*, 147–54.

22. Paul Boyer, *When Time Shall Be No More: Prophecy Belief in Modern American Culture* (Cambridge: Harvard University Press, 1992), 204. Yona Malachy visited Biola College (formerly the Bible Institute of Los Angeles) and encouraged its leaders to issue a strong pro-Israel statement. See also Yona Malachy, *American Fundamentalism and Israel: The Relation of Fundamentalist Churches to Zionism and the State of Israel* (Jerusalem: Hebrew University, 1978).

23. Phyllis Bennis, "Praise God and Pass the Ammunition: The Changing Nature of Israel's US Backers," *Middle East Report* (fall 1998), www.tni.org (accessed 19 October 2001).

24. Boyer, *When Time Shall Be No More*, 204.

25. Ibid., 204–5.

26. "What Is the NCLCI?" www.nclci.org/whatis.htm (accessed 22 April 2003).

27. The Washington Rally description, www.nclci.org/washrally-SrRose.htm (accessed 22 April 2003).

28. For the Christians for Israel website, see www.c4israel.org.

29. Debra Cohen, "Premier Meets with Evangelicals," *Jewish News of Greater Phoenix*, 11 April 1997.

30. Most of the information on the National Unity Coalition for Israel comes from its website, www.israelunitycoalition.com. See also Rod Dreher, "Evangelicals and Jews Together: An Unlikely Alliance," *National Review Online,* 5 April 2002, www.nationalreview.com/script/printpage.asp?ref=dreher/dreher040502.asp (accessed 29 December 2002); and Timothy P. Weber, "How Evangelicals Became Israel's Best Friend," *Christianity Today* 42 (5 October 1998): 38–49.

31. For Bridges for Peace website, see www.bridgesforpeace.com.

32. Christian Friends of Israeli Communities, "Adopt-a-Settlement Program," www.jermall.com/cfoic (accessed 24 April 1998); and Ilene R. Prusher, "A US Christian Who's 'Doing Deals for the Lord' in Israel," *Christian Science Monitor,* 24 April 1998, 6.

33. Ibid.

34. Ilene R. Prusher, "Israel's Unlikely Ally: American Evangelicals," *Christian Science Monitor,* 24 April 1998, 1, 6. For Faith Bible Chapel's website, see www.fbci.org.

35. A partial list of his books include John Hagee, *Hagee 3-in-1: Beginning of the End, Final Dawn over Jerusalem, and Day of Deception* (Nashville: Nelson, 2000); idem, *From Daniel to Doomsday: The Countdown Has Begun* (Nashville: Nelson, 2000); idem, *Attack on America: New York, Jerusalem, and the Role of Terrorism in the Last Days* (Nashville: Nelson, 2001); and idem, *The Battle for Jerusalem* (Nashville: Nelson, 2003).

36. Cornerstone Church's website is www.sacornerstone.com; John Hagee Ministries' website is www.jhm.org.

37. Ariel, *Evangelizing the Chosen People,* 266.

38. "Endorsements," www.ifcj.org (accessed 22 April 2003).

39. "About Our Programs," the International Fellowship of Christians and Jews, www.ifcj.org (accessed 22 April 2003).

40. "Stand for Israel," the International Fellowship of Christians and Jews, www.ifcj.org.

41. "Pat Robertson Forms Alliance with Mayor of Jerusalem," *Religion News Service,* 11 November 2002, www.baptiststandard.com/2002/11_11/print/robertson.html (accessed 15 November 2002).

42. Aparna Kumar, "Christian Coalition Calls for Solidarity with Israel," *Religion News Service,* 11 November 2002, www.baptiststandard.com2002/11_11print/israel.html (accessed 15 November 2002).

43. Taken from promotional literature about "Adopt-a-Settlement."

44. Weber, "How Evangelicals Became Israel's Best Friends," 48.

45. "About Us," www.icej.org (accessed 25 September 2002).

46. "Comforting Israel: In-Home Care," www.icej.org (accessed 25 September 2002).

47. Dreher, "Evangelicals and Jews Together"; and Yaakov Ariel, "A Christian Fundamentalist Vision of the Middle East: Jan Willem van der Hoeven and the International Christian Embassy," in *Spokesmen for the Despised: Fundamentalist Leaders of the Middle East,* ed. Scott Appleby (Chicago: University of Chicago Press, 1997), 363–97.

48. "Adopt-a-Settlement," CFIC, promotional material.

49. Weber, "How Evangelicals Became Israel's Best Friends," 48.

50. Nathan Perlmutter and Ruth Ann Perlmutter, *The Real Anti-Semitism in America* (New York: Arbor House, 1982), quoted in Halsell, *Prophecy and Politics,* 155.

51. Marc H. Tanenbaum, "The Moral Majority: Threat or Challenge?" in *A Prophet for Our Time: An Anthology of the Writings of Rabbi Marc H. Tanenbaum,* ed. Judith H. Banki and Eugene J. Fisher (New York: Fordham University Press, 2002), 255.

52. Irving Kristol, "The Political Dilemma of American Jews," *Commentary* 78 (July 1984): 25.

53. Weber, "How Evangelicals Became Israel's Best Friends," 49.

54. Dreher, "Evangelicals and Jews Together."

55. Yechiel Eckstein, *What Christians Should Know about Jews and Judaism* (Waco: Word, 1984), 299.

56. For a good study of the complicated relationship between fundamentalists and Jews, see Merrill Simon, *Jerry Falwell and the Jews* (Middle Village, N.Y.: Jonathan David, 1984).

57. Ariel, *Evangelizing the Chosen People*, 287–92.

58. Todd Gitlin, *The Sixties: Years of Hope, Days of Rage* (New York: Bantam, 1987); Wade Clark Roof, *A Generation of Seekers: The Spiritual Journeys of the Baby Boom Generation* (San Francisco: HarperSanFrancisco, 1993); Robert S. Ellwood, *The Sixties Spiritual Awakening* (New Brunswick, N.J.: Rutgers University Press, 1994); Francis Fukuyama, *The Great Disruption: Human Nature and the Reconstitution of Social Order* (New York: Touchstone Books, 1999); and Steven M. Tipton, *Getting Saved from the Sixties* (Berkeley: University of California Press, 1982).

59. Judith Linzer, *Torah and Dharma: Jewish Seekers in Eastern Religions* (Northvale, N.J.: Jason Aronson, 1996); Phillip Lucas, *The Odyssey of a New Religion: The Holy Order of MANS from New Age to Orthodoxy* (Bloomington, Ind.: Indiana University Press, 1995); Roger Kamenetz, *The Jew in the Lotus: A Poet's Rediscovery of Jewish Identity in Buddhist India* (New York: HarperCollins, 1994); and David Biale, Michael Galchinsky, and Susannah Heschel, eds., *Insider / Outsider: American Jews and Multiculturalism* (Berkeley: University of California Press, 1998).

60. Ariel, *Evangelizing the Chosen People*, 198. See also Nancy Ammerman, "Fundamentalists Proselytizing Jews: Incivility in Preparation for the Rapture," in *Pushing the Faith: Proselytism and Civility in a Pluralistic World*, ed. Martin E. Marty and Frederick E. Greenspahn (New York: Crossroad, 1988), 109–22.

61. Ariel, *Evangelizing the Chosen People*, 205.

62. Moishe Rosen, *The Sayings of Chairman Moishe* (Carol Stream, Ill.: Creation House, 1974).

63. Ariel, *Evangelizing the Chosen People*, 211.

64. For the story of the early days of Jews for Jesus, see Moishe Rosen and William Proctor, *Jews for Jesus* (Old Tappan, N.J.: Revell, 1974).

65. Ruth Rosen, ed., *Jesus for Jews* (San Francisco: Messianic Jewish Perspective, 1987).

66. Ariel, *Evangelizing the Chosen People*, 217.

67. Moishe Rosen and Ceil Rosen, *Share the New Life with a Jew* (Chicago: Moody, 1976). The Jews for Jesus doctrinal statement can be found in Juliene G. Lipson, *Jews for Jesus: An Anthropological Study* (New York: AMS Press, 1990), 182–83.

68. Sidney Goldstein, "Profile of American Jewry: Insights from the 1990 National Jewish Population Survey," *American Jewish Yearbook 92* (Philadelphia: Jewish Publication Society, 1992), 77–143.

69. Calvin Goldscheider and Alan Zuckerman, *The Transformation of the Jews* (Chicago: University of Chicago Press, 1984); and Charles Silberman, *A Certain People: American Jews and Their Lives Today* (New York: Summit Books, 1985).

70. Leonard Fein, *Where Are We? The Inner Life of America's Jews* (New York: Harper & Row, 1988); Arthur Herzberg, "End of American Jewish History," *New York Review of Books* 36 (23 November 1989): 26–30; and Goldstein, "Profile of American Jewry."

71. For the history of Messianic Judaism, see B. Z. Sobel, *Hebrew Christianity: The Thirteenth Tribe* (New York: Wiley, 1974); Arnold G. Fruchtenbaum, *Hebrew Christianity: Its Theology, History, and Philosophy* (Washington, D.C.: Canon, 1974); Hugh Schonfield, *The History of Jewish Christianity: From the First to the Twentieth Century* (London: Duckworth, 1936); and David Rausch, *Messianic Judaism: Its History, Theology, and Polity* (Lewiston, N.Y.: Edwin Mellen Press, 1982). See also Benjamin Beit-Hallahmi, *Despair*

and Deliverance: Private Salvation in Contemporary Israel (Albany: State University of New York Press, 1991).

72. Jeffrey S. Wasserman, *Messianic Jewish Congregations: Who Sold This Business to the Gentiles?* (New York: University Press of America, 2000), 51.

73. Ibid., 88–91; and Ariel, *Evangelizing the Chosen People,* 225–27.

74. Wasserman, *Messianic Jewish Congregations,* 88.

75. The FCTJ's resolution is quoted in Ariel, *Evangelizing the Chosen People,* 232–33.

76. Ibid., 242.

77. Ibid., 235–36.

78. Wasserman, *Messianic Jewish Congregations,* 77–82; and Ariel, *Evangelizing the Chosen People,* 243–44. See also John Fischer, *The Olive Tree Connection: Sharing Messiah with Israel* (Downers Grove, Ill.: InterVarsity, 1983).

79. Ariel, *Evangelizing the Chosen People,* 285–86.

80. Ibid., 240.

81. Wasserman, *Messianic Jewish Congregations,* 137.

82. Arnold G. Fruchtenbaum, *Hebrew Christianity: Its Theology, History, and Philosophy* (Washington, D.C.: Canon Press, 1974).

83. Arnold G. Fruchtenbaum, *Israelology: The Missing Link in Systematic Theology* (Tustin, Calif.: Ariel Ministries, 1983).

84. Daniel Juster, *Jewish Roots: A Foundation of Biblical Theology for Messianic Judaism* (Rockville, Md.: Davar Publishing, 1986); and David Stern, *Messianic Jewish Manifesto* (Jerusalem: Jewish New Testament Publications, 1988).

85. Eric Peter Lipson, *Passover Haggadah: A Messianic Celebration* (San Francisco: JFJ Publications, 1986); J. Ron Tavalin, *Kol Hesed Messianic Haggadah* (N.p.: Dogwood Press, 1993); and Harold Sevener, ed., *Passover Haggadah for Biblical Jews and Christians* (Orangeburg, N.Y.: Chosen People Publications, n.d.).

86. Lipson, *Passover Haggadah,* 23.

87. Wasserman, *Messianic Jewish Congregations,* 94–96.

88. Ibid., 106.

89. Ibid., 160, 164 n. 15.

90. Michael Schiffman, *Return of the Remnant: The Rebirth of Messianic Judaism* (Baltimore: Lederer Publications, 1992), quoted in Ariel, *Evangelizing the Chosen People,* 247.

91. Wasserman, *Messianic Jewish Congregations,* 160–61.

92. For an analysis of Jewish reactions, see Ariel, *Evangelizing the Chosen People,* 252–69.

93. Dov Aharoni Fisch, *Jews for Nothing: On Cults, Intermarriage, and Assimilation* (New York: Feldheim Publishers, 1984), 28–29.

94. Elie Wiesel, "The Missionary Menace," in *Smashing the Idols: A Jewish Inquiry into the Cult Phenomenon,* ed. Gary Eisenberg (Northvale, N.Y.: Jason Aronson, 1988), 162.

95. See Rosen, *Jesus for Jews.*

96. Ariel, *Evangelizing the Chosen People,* 255.

97. Aryeh Kaplan, *The Real Messiah? A Jewish Response to Missionaries* (New York: National Conference of Synagogue Youth, 1976); and Gerald Sigal, *The Jew and the Christian Missionary: A Jewish Response to Missionary Christianity* (New York: Ktav Publishing House, 1981).

98. For example, see Shmuel Golding, *A Guide to the Misled* (Jerusalem: Jerusalem Institute of Biblical Polemics, 1983).

99. David Rausch, *Communities in Conflict: Evangelicals and Jews* (Philadelphia: Trinity Press International, 1991), 111–21.

100. Billy Graham, "Billy Graham on Key '73," *Christianity Today* 17 (16 March 1973): 625.

101. Ariel, *Evangelizing the Chosen People*, 214, 265–66.

102. Wasserman, *Messianic Jewish Congregations*, 132.

103. Ariel, *Evangelizing the Chosen People*, 270–86.

104. Ibid., 273.

105. Wasserman, *Messianic Jewish Congregations*, 124.

106. Ariel, *Evangelizing the Chosen People*, 275.

107. Ibid., 278.

108. Wasserman, *Messianic Jewish Congregations*, 113–51.

109. Mitri Raheb, *I Am a Palestinian Christian* (Minneapolis: Fortress, 1995), 19.

110. Wagner, *Anxious for Armageddon*, 160.

111. See Charles M. Sennott, *The Body and the Blood: The Holy Land's Christians at the Turn of a New Millennium* (New York: Public Affairs, 2001); and William Dalrymple, *From the Holy Mountain: A Journey among the Christians of the Middle East* (New York: Henry Holt, 1997).

112. Audeh G. Rantisi and Ralph K. Beebe, *Blessed Are the Peacemakers: A Palestinian Christian in the Occupied West Bank* (Grand Rapids: Zondervan, 1990).

113. Halsell, *Prophecy and Politics*, 51–67.

114. Wagner, *Anxious for Armageddon*. See also Donald E. Wagner and Dan O'Neill, *Peace or Armaggedon: The Unfolding Drama of the Middle East Peace Accord* (Grand Rapids: Zondervan, 1993); Donald E. Wagner, Don Betz, and Janice Abu-Shakrah, *Israeli Settler Violence* (Chicago and Jerusalem: Palestine Human Rights Campaign, 1985); Donald E. Wagner, "Holy Land Christians Worry about Survival," *Christian Century*, 24 April 1991, 452–54; idem, "Evangelicals and Israel: Theological Roots of a Political Alliance," *Christian Century*, 4 November 1998, 1020–26; and idem, "Marching to Zion," *Christian Century*, 11 July 2003, 20–24.

Chapter 9

1. J. Randall Price, "The Temple, Future," in *Dictionary of Premillennial Theology*, ed. Mal Couch (Grand Rapids: Kregel, 1996), 404.

2. John Walvoord, *Israel in Prophecy* (Grand Rapids: Zondervan, 1962), 97–99, 107–12. Dispensationalist literature on the expected temple is voluminous. See, for example, Arnold T. Olson, *Inside Jerusalem: City of Destiny* (Glendale, Calif.: Regal Books, 1968); Thomas McCall and Zola Levitt, *Satan in the Sanctuary* (Chicago: Moody, 1973); John Wesley White, *The Coming World Dictator* (Minneapolis: Bethany, 1981); and Doug Clark, *Shockwaves of Armageddon* (Eugene, Ore.: Harvest House, 1982).

3. White, *Coming World Dictator*, quoted in Paul Boyer, *When Time Shall Be No More: Prophecy Belief in Modern American Culture* (Cambridge: Harvard University Press, 1992), 199.

4. For good summaries of the three positions, see Gershom Gorenberg, *The End of Days: Fundamentalism and the Struggle for the Temple Mount* (New York: Free Press, 2000), 63–80; and Randall Price, *The Coming Last Days Temple* (Eugene, Ore.: Harvest House, 1999), 337–60.

5. Quoted in Gorenberg, *End of Days*, 65–66.

6. Ibid., 67.

7. Quoted in ibid., 75. For Sagiv's website, see www.templemount.org. See also Price, *Coming Last Days Temple*, 340–42.

8. Quoted in Gorenberg, *End of Days*, 76.

9. Wilbur Smith, *Israeli/Arab Conflict and the Bible* (Glendale, Calif.: Regal Books, 1967), 110.

10. Salem Kirban, *666* (Wheaton: Tyndale, 1970), 120–21; and Charles Colson, with Ellen Santilli Vaughn, *Kingdoms in Conflict* (New York: William Morrow, 1987), 12–40. See also Boyer, *When Time Shall Be No More,* 198–99.

11. Malcom Couch, "When Will the Jews Rebuild Their Temple?" *Moody Monthly* 74 (December 1973): 34–35, 86; and McCall and Levitt, *Satan in the Sanctuary.* See also Dwight Wilson, *Armageddon Now! The Premillenarian Response to Russia and Israel since 1971* (Grand Rapids: Baker, 1977), 199–201.

12. Hal Lindsey, *The Late Great Planet Earth* (Grand Rapids: Zondervan, 1970), 57.

13. Olson, *Inside Jerusalem,* 133.

14. Grace Halsell, *Forcing God's Hand: Why Millions Pray for a Quick Rapture . . . and Destruction of Planet Earth* (Beltsville, Md.: Amana Publications, 2002), 64–66.

15. Gorenberg, *End of Days,* 70.

16. Ibid.

17. Ibid., 70–72.

18. Ibid., 170–71; and Price, *Coming Last Days Temple,* 437–38.

19. Gorenberg, *End of Days,* 182–85. See also Boyer, *When Time Shall Be No More,* 199.

20. For an excellent discussion of Muslim eschatology and how it bears on the current Middle East crisis, see Gorenberg, *End of Days,* 185–202.

21. Ibid., 107–10.

22. Ibid., 132–37.

23. Price, *Coming Last Days Temple,* 434.

24. See the Temple Mount Faithful's website at www.templemount.org. The website contains information about the three theories of the first two temples' location on the Temple Mount, including numerous articles by American dispensationalists. One of the website managers is Lambert Dolphin, the American scientist who tried to "x-ray" the temple site under the Temple Mount.

25. Gorenberg, *End of Days,* 171.

26. Ibid., 171–72.

27. Ibid., 124. See also www.ldolphin.org for a discussion of Dolphin's methods and his experiences.

28. Gorenberg, *End of Days,* 124–26; and Grace Halsell, *Prophecy and Politics: The Secret Alliance between Israel and the U.S. Christian Right* (Chicago: Lawrence Hill Books, 1986), 101–3.

29. Price, *Coming Last Days Temple,* 433. See also www.battalionofdeborah.org.

30. Price, *Coming Last Days Temple,* 400–401.

31. Ibid., 401–402.

32. Gorenberg, *End of Days,* 176.

33. Ibid., 77–78.

34. Quoted in ibid., 175.

35. *Jerusalem Post,* 30 September 1983, quoted in Price, *Coming Last Days Temple,* 159.

36. Gorenberg, *End of Days,* 161–62, 230. See also the International Christian Zionist Center's website at www.israelmybeloved.com.

37. Price, *Coming Last Days Temple,* 160–62.

38. Gorenberg, *End of Days,* 13.

39. Ibid., 7–29; and Price, *Coming Last Days Temple,* 361–75.

40. Quoted in Price, *Coming Last Days Temple,* 373.

41. Gorenberg, *End of Days,* 10.

42. Ibid., 13–16.

43. See www.templeinstitute.org/current-events/RedHeifer/index.html. See also Rod Dreher, "Red Heifer Days," *National Review Online,* 11 April 2002, www.nationalreview.com/dreher/dreher041102.asp.

44. David Landau, "A Red Heifer—It's Not Funny," *Ha'aretz,* 26 March 1997, quoted in Gorenberg, *End of Days,* 10.

45. For the Bridges for Peace website, see www.bridgesforpeace.com.

Bibliography

Primary Sources

BOOKS

Addresses of the International Prophetic Conference. Boston: Watchword and Truth, 1901.

Addresses on the Second Coming of the Lord. Pittsburgh: W. W. Waters, 1896.

Anderson, Robert. *The Coming Prince.* 13th ed. London: Pickering & Inglis, n.d.

Bauman, Louis. *God and Gog.* Long Beach, Calif.: Privately published, 1934.

―――. *Light from Bible Prophecy.* New York: Revell, 1940.

―――. *Shirts and Sheets: Or Anti-Semitism, a Present-Day Sign of the First Magnitude.* Long Beach, Calif.: Privately published, 1934.

―――. *The Time of Jacob's Trouble.* Long Beach, Calif.: Privately published, 1938.

Beckwith, George D. *God's Prophetic Plan through the Ages.* Grand Rapids: Zondervan, 1942.

Blackstone, William E. *Jesus Is Coming.* New York: Revell, 1908.

Bronstein, Esther. *Esther.* Edited by Janet Thoma. Elgin, Ill.: David C. Cook, 1982.

Brookes, James H. *Bible Reading on the Second Coming of Christ.* Springfield, Ill.: Edwin A. Wilson, 1877.

―――. *Israel and the Church.* St. Louis: Gospel Book and Tract Depository, n.d.

―――. *Maranatha.* 3d ed. New York: E. Brendell, 1874.

Brooks, Keith L. *Jews and the Passion for Israel in Light of Prophecy.* Grand Rapids: Zondervan, 1937.

Brown, Arthur I. *The Eleventh "Hour."* Findlay, Ohio: Fundamental Truth Publishers, 1940.

Buksbazen, Lydia. *They Looked for a City.* West Collingswood, N.J.: Spearhead Press, 1955.

Burton, Alfred. *The Future of Europe.* New York: Bible Truth Press, 1915.

———. *Russia's Destiny in the Light of Prophecy.* New York: Gospel Publishing House, 1917.

Carver, W. O. *Missions and the Kingdom of Heaven.* Louisville: John P. Morton, 1898.

———. *Missions in the Plan of the Ages.* Nashville: Broadman, 1951.

Case, Shirley Jackson. *The Millennial Hope.* Chicago: University of Chicago Press, 1918.

———. *The Revelation of John.* Chicago: University of Chicago Press, 1919.

Chapman, J. Wilbur. *A Reason for My Hope.* New York: Our Hope Publishing, 1916.

Clark, Doug. *Shockwaves of Armageddon.* Eugene, Ore.: Harvest House, 1982.

Coder, S. Maxwell. *The Final Chapter: Understanding What the Bible Says about the Last Days of Human History.* Wheaton: Tyndale, 1984.

Cohn, Joseph Hoffman. *I Have Fought a Good Fight.* New York: American Board of Missions to the Jews, 1953.

Cohn, Leopold. *A Modern Missionary to an Ancient People.* 2d ed. New York: American Board of Missions to the Jews, 1911.

Colson, Charles, with Ellen Santilli Vaughn. *Kingdoms in Conflict.* New York: William Morrow, 1987.

Conning, John S. *Our Jewish Neighbors: An Essay in Understanding.* New York: Revell, 1927.

Cook, Charles C. *End of the Age Themes.* New York: Charles C. Cook, 1917.

Cumming, John. *The Destiny of Nations.* London: Hurst & Blackette, 1864.

Darby, John Nelson. *Collected Works.* 34 vols. Edited by William Kelly. London: G. Morrish, 1967.

Davis, George T. B. *Rebuilding Palestine according to Prophecy.* Philadelphia: Million Testaments Campaigns, 1935.

Dean, I. R. *The Coming Kingdom.* Philadelphia: Approved Book Store, 1928.

DeHaan, Richard. *Israel and the Nations in Prophecy.* Grand Rapids: Zondervan, 1968.

Down on Throop Avenue. New York: American Board of Missions to the Jews, 1940.

Drummond, Henry. *Dwight L. Moody: Impressions and Facts.* New York: McClure, Phillips, 1900.

Dyer, Charles. *The Rise of Babylon.* Wheaton: Tyndale, 1991.

Eckman, George P. *When Christ Comes Again.* New York: Abingdon, 1917.

Eckstein, Yechiel. *What Christians Should Know about Jews and Judaism.* Waco: Word, 1984.

Eichhorn, David. *Evangelizing the American Jew.* Middle Village, N.Y.: Jonathan David Publishers, 1978.

Evans, William. *The Coming King: The World's Next Crisis.* New York: Revell, 1923.

Feinberg, Charles, ed. *Focus on Prophecy.* Westwood, N.J.: Revell, 1964.

Fifty Years of Blessing: Historical Sketch of Chicago Hebrew Mission, 1887–1937. Chicago: Chicago Hebrew Mission, 1937.

Fischer, John. *The Olive Tree Connection: Sharing Messiah with Israel.* Downers Grove, Ill.: InterVarsity, 1983.

Freuder, Samuel. *A Missionary's Return to Judaism.* New York: Sinai Publishing, 1915.

Fruchtenbaum, Arnold G. *Hebrew Christianity: Its Theology, History, and Philosophy.* Washington, D.C.: Canon Press, 1974.

———. *Israelology: The Missing Link in Systematic Theology.* Tustin, Calif.: Ariel Ministries, 1983.

Fuchs, Daniel. *How to Reach the Jew for Christ.* Grand Rapids: Zondervan, 1943.

"Fundamentals of the Faith as Expressed in the Articles of Belief of the Niagara Bible Conference." Chicago: Great Commission Prayer League, n.d.

Gaebelein, Arno C. *As It Was, so Shall It Be: Sunset and Sunrise: A Study of the First Age and Our Present Age.* New York: Our Hope Publishing, 1937.

———. *The Conflict of the Ages: The Mystery of Lawlessness, Its Origin, Historic Development, and Coming Defeat.* New York: Our Hope Publishing, 1933.

———. *The Conflict of the Ages.* Rev. ed. Edited by David Rausch. Neptune, N.J.: Loiseaux Brothers, 1982.

———. *Half a Century: The Autobiography of a Servant.* New York: Our Hope Publishing, 1930.

———. *Hath God Cast Away His People?* New York: Gospel Publishing Office, 1905.

———. *Hopeless—Yet There Is Hope.* New York: Our Hope Publishing, 1935.

———. *The League of Nations in the Light of Prophecy.* New York: Our Hope Publishing, 1920.

———. *Meat in Due Season.* New York: Our Hope Publishing, 1933.

———. *The Prophet Daniel.* New York: Our Hope Publishing, 1936.

———. *The Prophet Ezekiel.* New York: Our Hope Publishing, 1918.

———. *World Prospects, How Is It All Going to End?* New York: Our Hope Publishing, 1934.

Gaebelein, Arno C., ed. *Christ and Glory.* New York: Our Hope Publishing, 1919.

Gartenhaus, Jacob. *How to Win the Jews.* Atlanta: Baptist Home Mission Board, n.d.

———. *Winning Jews to Christ.* Grand Rapids: Zondervan, 1963.

Gilbert, F. C. *From Judaism to Christianity and Gospel Work among the Hebrews.* So. Lancaster, Mass.: Good Tidings, 1920.

Golding, Shmuel. *A Guide to the Misled.* Jerusalem: Jerusalem Institute of Biblical Polemics, 1983.

Gordon, A. J. *The Holy Spirit in Missions.* New York: Revell, 1893.

Gordon, S. D. *Quiet Talks on the Deeper Meaning of the War and Its Relation to Our Lord's Return.* New York: Revell, 1919.

Gray, James M. *How to Master the English Bible.* Chicago: Bible Institute Colportage Association, 1904.

———. *Prophecy and the Lord's Return.* New York: Revell, 1917.

———. *Synthetic Bible Studies.* Rev. ed. New York: Revell, 1923.

———. *A Text-Book on Prophecy.* New York: Revell, 1918.

Gray, James M., ed. *The Coming and Kingdom of Christ.* Chicago: Bible Institute Colportage Association, 1914.

Guinness, Geraldine. *The Story of the China Inland Mission.* 2 vols. London: China Inland Mission, 1896.

Hagee, John. *Attack on America: New York, Jerusalem, and the Role of Terrorism in the Last Days.* Nashville: Nelson, 2001.

———. *The Battle for Jerusalem.* Nashville: Nelson, 2003.

———. *From Daniel to Doomsday: The Countdown Has Begun.* Nashville: Nelson, 2000.

———. *Hagee 3-in-1: Beginning of the End, Final Dawn over Jerusalem, and Day of Deception.* Nashville: Nelson, 2000.

Haldeman, I. M. *The Coming of Christ.* Los Angeles: Bible House of Los Angeles, 1906.

———. *Professor Shailer Mathews' Burlesque on the Second Coming.* New York: Privately published, 1918.

———. *Signs of the Times.* 5th ed. New York: Charles C. Cook, 1914.

———. *Why I Preach the Second Coming.* New York: Revell, 1919.

Hart, Lewis A. *A Jewish Reply to Christian Evangelists.* New York: Block Publishing, 1907.

Henry, Carl F. H. *Confessions of a Theologian: An Autobiography.* Waco: Word, 1986.

Heydt, Henry J. *The Chosen People Question Box II.* Englewood Cliffs, N.J.: American Board of Missions to the Jews, 1976.

———. *Studies in Jewish Evangelism.* New York: American Board of Missions to the Jews, 1951.

Horton, Thomas C. *These Premillennialists: Who Are They?* Los Angeles: Privately published, 1921.

Huisjen, Albert. *The Home Front of Jewish Missions.* Grand Rapids: Baker, 1962.

———. *Talking about Jesus to a Jewish Neighbor.* Grand Rapids: Baker, 1964.

Hull, William L. *Israel—Key to Prophecy.* Grand Rapids: Zondervan, 1964.

Hunt, David. *Global Peace and the Rise of Antichrist.* Eugene, Ore.: Harvest House, 1990.

Jennings, F. C. *The End of the European War in the Light of Scripture.* New York: Charles C. Cook, 1917.

———. *The Jew in History and Prophecy: Addresses Delivered at a Conference on Behalf of Israel Held at the Moody Tabernacle, North Clark Street and North Avenue, Chicago, January 22–25, 1918.* Chicago: Chicago Hebrew Mission, 1918.

———. *The World Conflict in the Light of the Prophetic Word.* New York: Our Hope Publishing, 1917.

Jordan, Willis. *The European War from a Bible Standpoint.* New York: Charles C. Cook, 1915.

Juster, Daniel. *Jewish Roots: A Foundation of Biblical Theology for Messianic Judaism.* Rockville, Md.: Davar Publishing, 1986.

Kaplan, Aryeh. *The Real Messiah? A Jewish Response to Missionaries.* New York: National Conference of Synagogue Youth, 1976.

Kirban, Salem. *666.* Wheaton: Tyndale, 1970.

Ladd, George E. *The Blessed Hope.* Grand Rapids: Eerdmans, 1956.

Lagerlof, Selma. *Jerusalem: A Novel.* 2 vols. Translated by Velma Swanson. Garden City, N.Y.: Doubleday, 1915.

LaHaye, Tim. *The Battle for the Mind.* New York: Revell, 1980.

———. *The Beginning of the End.* Wheaton: Tyndale, 1972.

———. *The Coming Peace in the Middle East.* Grand Rapids: Zondervan, 1984.

———. *How to Study the Bible Prophecy for Yourself.* Eugene, Ore.: Harvest House, 1990.

———. *No Fear of the Storm.* Sisters, Ore.: Multnomah, 1992.

————. *Revelation: Illustrated and Made Plain.* Grand Rapids: Zondervan, 1974.

LaHaye, Tim, and Beverly. *The Act of Marriage: The Beauty of Sexual Love.* Grand Rapids: Zondervan, 1976.

LaHaye, Tim, and Jerry B. Jenkins. *Left Behind.* Wheaton: Tyndale, 1996.

————. *Tribulation Force.* Wheaton: Tyndale, 1996.

Lindberg, Beth M. *A God-Filled Life: The Story of William E. Blackstone.* Chicago: American Messianic Fellowship, n.d.

Lindberg, Milton. *The Jews and Armageddon.* Chicago: American Messianic Fellowship, 1940.

Lindsey, Hal. *The Late Great Planet Earth.* Grand Rapids: Zondervan, 1970.

————. *The 1980s: Countdown to Armageddon.* King of Prussia, Pa.: Westgate Press, 1980.

————. *There's a New World Coming: A Prophetic Odyssey.* Santa Ana, Calif.: Vision House Publishers, 1973.

Lipson, Eric Peter. *Passover Haggadah: A Messianic Celebration.* San Francisco: JFJ Publications, 1986.

Machen, J. Gresham. *Christianity and Liberalism.* New York: Macmillan, 1926.

Mackintosh, C. H. *Papers on the Lord's Coming.* Chicago: Bible Institute Colportage Association, n.d.

Mains, George P. *Premillennialism: Non-Scriptural, Non-Historic, Non-Scientific, Non-Philosophical.* New York: Abingdon, 1920.

Malachy, Yona. *American Fundamentalism and Israel: The Relation of Fundamentalist Churches to Zionism and the State of Israel.* Jerusalem: Hebrew University, 1978.

Mathews, Shailer. *New Faith for Old.* New York: Macmillan, 1936.

————. *Will Christ Come Again?* Chicago: American Institute of Sacred Literature, 1917.

Mauro, Philip. *The Seventy Weeks and the Great Tribulation.* Boston: Hamilton Brothers, 1923.

————. *The World War: How It Is Fulfilling Prophecy.* Boston: Hamilton Brothers, 1918.

McCall, Thomas, and Zola Levitt. *The Coming Russian Invasion of Israel.* Chicago: Moody, 1974.

————. *Satan in the Sanctuary.* Chicago: Moody, 1973.

McClain, Alva. *Daniel's Prophecy of the Seventy Weeks.* Grand Rapids: Zondervan, 1940.

Milligan, E. M. *Is the Kingdom Age at Hand?* New York: George H. Doran, 1924.

Moody, Dwight L. *New Sermons.* New York: Henry S. Goodspeed, 1880.

Munhall, Leander. *The Lord's Return.* 7th ed. New York: Eaton & Mains, 1898.

Newman, Elias. *The Conflict or Falsehood of the Ages, Which?* Minneapolis: Privately published, 1934.

———. *The Jewish Peril and the Hidden Hand.* Minneapolis: Privately published, 1934.

Olson, Arnold T. *Inside Jerusalem: City of Destiny.* Glendale, Calif.: Regal Books, 1968.

Orr, William W. *The New Nation of Israel and the Word of God!* Los Angeles: Bible Institute of Los Angeles, 1948.

Parker, Joseph. *None Like It.* New York: Revell, 1893.

Pentecost, J. Dwight. *Prophecy for Today.* Grand Rapids: Zondervan, 1961.

Pettingill, William L., ed. *Light on Prophecy.* New York: Christian Herald, 1918.

Pierson, A. T. *The Story of Keswick and Its Beginnings.* London: Hodder & Stoughton, 1964.

Pink, Arthur W. *The Antichrist.* Swengel, Pa.: Bible Truth Depot, 1923.

———. *The Redeemer's Return.* Swengel, Pa.: Bible Truth Depot, 1918.

Price, Randall. *The Coming Last Days Temple.* Eugene, Ore.: Harvest House, 1999.

Prophetic Studies of the International Prophetic Conference. New York: Revell, 1886.

The Protocols of the Meeting of the Learned Elders of Zion. Translated by Victor E. Marsden. London: Britons Publishing, 1922.

Raheb, Mitri. *I Am a Palestinian Christian.* Minneapolis: Fortress, 1995.

Rall, Harris Franklin. *Modern Premillennialism and the Christian Hope.* New York: Abingdon, 1920.

———. *New Testament History.* New York: Abingdon, 1914.

Rantisi, Audeh G., and Ralph K. Beebe. *Blessed Are the Peacemakers: A Palestinian Christian in the Occupied West Bank.* Grand Rapids: Zondervan, 1990.

Rauschenbusch, Walter. *Christianity and the Social Crisis.* New York: Macmillan, 1907.

Reece, Eli. *How Far Can a Premillennialist Pastor Cooperate with Social Service Programs?* N.p.: Privately published, n.d.

Riley, William Bell. *The Evolution of the Kingdom.* New York: Charles C. Cook, 1913.

———. *Hitlerism: Or the Philosophy of Evolution in Action.* Minneapolis: Privately published, 1941.

———. *The Protocols and Communism.* Minneapolis: L. W. Camp, 1934.

———. *Shivering at the Sight of a Shirt.* Minneapolis: Privately published, 1936.

———. *Wanted—A World Leader!* Minneapolis: Privately published, 1939.

Rimmer, Harry. *Palestine: The Coming Storm Center.* Grand Rapids: Eerdmans, 1940.

Ritchie, J. M. *Prophetic Highlights.* New York: Revell, 1935.

Robertson, Pat. *The New World Order.* Dallas: Word, 1991.

Rosen, Moishe. *The Sayings of Chairman Moishe.* Carol Stream, Ill.: Creation House, 1974.

Rosen, Moishe, and William Proctor. *Jews for Jesus.* Old Tappan, N.J.: Revell, 1974.

Rosen, Moishe, and Ceil Rosen. *Share the New Life with a Jew.* Chicago: Moody, 1976.

Rosen, Ruth, ed. *Jesus for Jews.* San Francisco: Messianic Jewish Perspective, 1987.

Ross, Robert W. *So It Was True: The American Protestant Press and the Nazi Persecution of the Jews.* Minneapolis: University of Minnesota Press, 1980.

Runyan, William M. *Dr. Gray at Moody Bible Institute.* New York: Oxford University Press, 1935.

Ryrie, Charles C. *Dispensationalism Today.* Chicago: Moody, 1965.

———. *The Final Countdown.* Wheaton: Victor Books, 1982.

Sale-Harrison, Leonard. *The Coming Great Northern Confederacy: Or the Future of Russia and Germany.* London: Pickering & Inglis, 1928.

Scofield, C. I. *The New Scofield Reference Bible.* New York: Oxford University Press, 1967.

———. *Rightly Dividing the Word of Truth.* Oakland, Calif.: Western Book and Tract, n.d.

Scofield, C. I., ed. *The Scofield Reference Bible.* New York: Oxford University Press, 1909.

Sevener, Harold, ed. *Passover Haggadah for Biblical Jews and Christians.* Orangeburg, N.Y.: Chosen People Publications, n.d.

Sigal, Gerald. *The Jew and the Christian Missionary: A Jewish Response to Missionary Christianity.* New York: Ktav Publishing, 1981.

Silver, J. F. *The Lord's Return.* New York: Revell, 1914.

Simpson, A. B. *Back to Patmos.* New York: Christian Alliance Publishing, 1914.

———. *The Gospel of the Kingdom.* New York: Christian Alliance Publishing, 1890.

Smith, Hannah Whitall. *The Christian's Secret of a Happy Life.* Old Tappan, N.J.: Revell, 1942.

Smith, Oswald J. *Is the Antichrist at Hand?—What of Mussolini?* New York: Christian Alliance Publishing, 1927.

Smith, Wilbur M. *The Israeli-Arab Conflict and the Bible.* Glendale, Calif.: Regal Books, 1967.

Snowden, James H. *The Coming of the Lord: Will It Be Premillennial?* New York: Macmillan, 1919.

Speer, Robert. *The Finality of Jesus Christ.* New York: Revell, 1933.

———. *The Second Coming of Christ.* New York: Gospel Publishing, 1903.

Stern, David. *Messianic Jewish Manifesto.* Jerusalem: Jewish New Testament Publications, 1988.

Sumrall, Lester. *The Holy War Jihad: The Destiny of Iran and the Moslem World.* Tulsa: Harrison House, 1980.

Sutton, Hilton. *World War III: God's Conquest of Russia.* Tulsa: Harrison House, 1982.

Tavalin, J. Ron. *Kol Hesed Messianic Haggadah.* N.p.: Dogwood Press, 1993.

Taylor, Dr. and Mrs. Howard. *"By Faith . . ." Henry W. Frost and the China Inland Mission.* Philadelphia and Toronto: CIM, 1938.

Taylor, Howard. *Hudson Taylor and the China Inland Mission.* London: China Inland Mission, 1919.

Taylor, Mrs. Howard (Geraldine Guinness). *Hudson Taylor and the China Inland Mission: The Growth of a Work of God.* Philadelphia and London: China Inland Mission, 1918.

Thompson, A. E. *The Life of A. B. Simpson.* New York: Christian Alliance Publishing, 1920.

Torrey, Reuben A. *The Return of the Lord Jesus Christ.* Los Angeles: Bible Institute of Los Angeles, 1913.

Tregelles, Samuel P. *The Hope of Christ's Second Coming.* London: Samuel Bagster & Sons, 1864.

Trumbull, Charles G. *The Life Story of C. I. Scofield.* New York: Oxford University Press, 1920.

———. *Prophecy's Light on Today.* New York: Revell, 1937.

Twain, Mark. *The Innocents Abroad.* New York: Signet Classic, 1966.

Van Impe, Jack, and Roger F. Campbell. *Israel's Final Holocaust.* Troy, Mich.: Jack Van Impe Ministries, 1979.

Vester, Bertha Spafford. *Our Jerusalem: An American Family in the Holy City, 1881–1949.* Garden City, N.Y.: Doubleday, 1950.

Wagner, Donald E. *Anxious for Armageddon: A Call to Partnership for Middle Eastern and Western Christians.* Scottdale, Pa.: Herald Press, 1995.

Wagner, Donald E., Don Betz, and Janice Abu-Shakrah. *Israeli Settler Violence.* Chicago and Jerusalem: Palestine Human Rights Campaign, 1985.

Wagner, Donald E., and Dan O'Neill. *Peace or Armaggedon: The Unfolding Drama of the Middle East Peace Accord.* Grand Rapids: Zondervan, 1993.

Walvoord, John. *Israel in Prophecy.* Grand Rapids: Zondervan, 1968.

———. *The Rapture Question.* Findlay, Ohio: Dunham Publishing, 1957.

Walvoord, John F., and John E. Walvoord. *Armageddon—Oil and the Middle East Crisis.* Grand Rapids: Zondervan, 1974.

West, Nathaniel. *The Thousand Years in Both Testaments.* New York: Revell, 1889.

West, Nathaniel, ed. *Pre-Millennial Essays.* New York: Revell, 1879.

White, John Wesley. *The Coming World Dictator.* Minneapolis: Bethany, 1981.

———. *WW III.* Grand Rapids: Zondervan, 1977.

Wilkerson, David. *Set the Trumpet to Thy Mouth.* Lindale, Tex.: World Challenge, 1985.

Winner, Lauren F. *Girl Meets God: On the Path to a Spiritual Life.* Chapel Hill: Algonquin Books, 2002.

Winrod, Gerald B. *The Hidden Hand: The Protocols and the Coming Superman.* Wichita: Defender Publishers, 1933.

———. *The Jewish Assault on Christianity.* Wichita: Defender Publishers, 1935.

———. *Mussolini's Place in Prophecy.* Wichita: Defender Publishers, 1933.

———. *The Truth about the Protocols.* Wichita: Defender Publishers, 1935.

Articles

Allen, Paul S. "Arab or Israeli." *Alliance Witness* 92 (8 May 1957): 2.

Allis, Oswald T. "Israel's Transgression in Palestine." *Christianity Today* 1 (24 December 1956): 9.

Anderson, Henry E. "Are God's Covenants about to Be Fulfilled?" *Moody Monthly* 40 (November 1940): 128–29.

Ayer, William Ward. "The Arab and the Jew." *Weekly Evangel,* 30 July 1967, 6.

Bauman, Louis. "Gog and Gomer, Russia and Germany, and the War." *Sunday School Times* 81 (16 December 1939): 911–12.

———. "Russia and Armageddon." *King's Business* 29 (September 1938): 287.

———. "Socialism, Communism, Fascism." *King's Business* 36 (August 1935): 293.

Bell, L. Nelson. "Unfolding Destiny." *Christianity Today* 11 (21 July 1967): 1044–45.

Blackstone, William E. "The Times of the Gentiles and the War in the Light of Prophecy." *Christian Workers Magazine* 16 (May 1916): 686–87.

Briggs, Charles A. "Millennium, Millenarianism." *The New Schaff-Herzog Encyclopedia of Religious Knowledge*. 13 vols. Edited by Johann Herzog and Philip Schaff, 7:374–78. New York: Funk and Wagnalls, 1908–14.

———. "Origin and History of Pre-Millennialism." *Lutheran Quarterly* 9 (April 1879): 244–45.

Britain, Joseph T. "Why Our Nation Should Not Disarm." *Moody Bible Institute Monthly* 21 (August 1921): 510–12.

Brookes, James H. "Gentile Domination." *Truth* 6 (1880): 536.

———. "How to Reach the Jews." *Truth* 19 (1893): 135–36.

———. "Witnesses to the Hope." *Truth* 17 (1891): 310–22.

———. "Work among the Jews." *Truth* 20 (1894): 14–16.

Brooks, Keith. "Come Clean." *American Prophetic League, Inc.,* release no. 38 (January 1942): 1.

———. "Manifesto to the Jews." *Prophecy Monthly* (October 1939): 18–19.

———. "Our Manifesto." *Prophecy Monthly* (January 1940): 35.

Case, Shirley Jackson. "The Premillennial Menace." *Biblical World* 52 (July 1918): 16–23.

Chalmers, Thomas. "Russia and Armageddon." *Weekly Evangel,* 14 April 1934, 6.

Chapell, F. L. "Dr. Gordon and the Training School." *Watchword* 17 (February–March 1895): 61–62.

Childe, Frederick. "Christ's Answer to the Challenge of Communism and Fascism." *Weekly Evangel,* 31 October 1935, 1.

Coder, S. Maxwell. "Jerusalem: Key to the Future." *Moody Monthly* 74 (October 1973): 32–33.

Cohn, J. H. "The Conflict of the Ages." *Chosen People* 39 (February 1934): 7–9.

———. "The Devil Revives Balakism." *Chosen People* 26 (December 1920): 5–7.

———. "Henry Ford Again." *Chosen People* 26 (April 1921): 5–7.

Cook, Charles C. "The International Jew." *King's Business* 12 (November 1921): 1087.

Couch, Malcom. "When Will the Jews Rebuild Their Temple?" *Moody Monthly* 74 (December 1973): 34–35, 86.

Davis, George T. B. "A Divine Promise That Changed History." *Sunday School Times* 99 (16 March 1957): 205–6.

Erdman, William J. "An Important Query." *Christian Workers Magazine* 17 (November 1917): 194.

———. "The Main Idea of the Bible." *Institute Tie* 9 (October 1908): 94.

Feinberg, Charles L. "Isaac and Ishmael." *King's Business* 58 (July 1968): 23.

Fereday, W. W. "After the Great War." *Our Hope* 26 (1919–20): 34.

Gaebelein, Arno C. "Adolf Hitler—Will He Be Germany's Dictator?" *Our Hope* 37 (1930): 363–64.

———. "God's Hand in Prophetic Conferences." *Our Hope* 40 (November 1939): 129, 170.

———. "Herman Warszawiak's Method of Getting Crowds to Hear the Gospel." *Our Hope* 2 (1895): 2–5.

———. "The Hope of Israel Mission." *Our Hope* 5 (July 1898): 40.

———. "How the Hope of Israel Became Undenominational." *Our Hope* 4 (1897): 3–5.

———. "Misrepresenting 'Our Hope.'" *Our Hope* 46 (December 1939): 379–82.

———. "The Present Day Restoration Movement among the Jews and Its Significance." *Our Hope* 16 (September 1909): 103–7.

———. "Professor Heman on the Jews and the Churches." *Our Hope* 5 (August–September 1898): 56–58.

———. "The Prophet Ezekiel." *Our Hope* 24 (November 1917): 281.

———. "The Shadows of Jacob's Trouble." *Our Hope* 38 (1932): 102.

———. "A Short Review of Our Mission and the Principles of the Hope of Israel Mission." *Our Hope* 6 (1899): 68–71.

Gilbert, Dan. "Views and Reviews of Current News." *King's Business* 30 (January 1930): 8.

Gooch, W. Fuller. "The Termination of This Age." *Weekly Evangel,* 23 March 1918, 12.

Gordon, A. J. "Education and Missions, Part 1." *Missionary Review of the World* 16 (August 1893): 585.

———. "Premillennialism and Mission." *Watchword* 8 (April 1886): 30–32.

Graham, Billy. "Billy Graham on Key '73." *Christianity Today* 17 (16 March 1973): 625.

Grant, U. S. "Things to Come." *Weekly Evangel,* 21 May 1949, 2.

Gray, James M. "And Such Were Some of You." *Christian Workers Magazine* 14 (August 1914): 783–86.

———. "The Jewish Protocols." *Moody Bible Institute Monthly* 22 (October 1921): 598.

————. "Practical and Perplexing Questions." *Christian Workers Magazine* 16 (October 1916): 97–98.

————. "What the Bible Teaches about War." *Christian Workers Magazine* 17 (July 1917): 860–61.

————. "What the Bible Teaches about War and the Christian's Attitude in the Present Crisis." *Christian Workers Magazine* 18 (November 1918): 179–80.

"The Great North-Eastern Confederacy." *Our Hope* 46 (1939–40): 234–35.

Gretter, D. "Disarmament and the Signs of the Times." *Moody Bible Institute Monthly* 21 (September 1920): 806.

Hicks, W. Percy. "Proposed Revival of the Old Roman Empire." *Weekly Evangel,* 20 March 1926, 4.

Huffman, J. A. "The Jew and Arab Controversy over Palestine." *King's Business* 21 (September 1930): 417–18.

Ironside, Harry A. "Are the Jews as a People Responsible for the So-Called Protocols of the Elders of Zion?" *Chosen People* 39 (March 1934): 5–7.

Kent, Agnes Scott. "Palestine Is for the Jew." *King's Business* 22 (November 1931): 494.

Ketchum, William. "Some Interesting Things about Jews." *Christian Workers Magazine* 20 (April 1920): 630–31.

Klein, P. A. "Compulsory Military Service." *Christian Workers Magazine* 16 (July 1916): 835–36.

Kligerman, Aaron Judah. "Israel and Palestine." *Moody Bible Institute Monthly* 30 (August 1930): 587–88.

Knauss, Elizabeth. "Communism and the Jewish Question." *Pilot* 13 (June 1933): 271–72.

————. "Communism and the Protocols." *Pilot* 13 (November 1932): 40–41.

Lambie, T. A. "Palestine Focus of World Attention." *Sunday School Times* 87 (4 May 1946): 401.

"The League of Nations." *Christian Workers Magazine* 19 (April 1919): 526.

"The League of Nations and the Danger of Federation." *Moody Bible Institute Monthly* 21 (September 1920): 7.

Mackintosh, C. H. "The Double Phase of the Second Advent." *Our Hope* 11 (November 1903): 322–29.

McClain, Alva J. "The Four Great Powers of the End-Time." *King's Business* 39 (February 1938): 97.

McConnell, Francis J. "The Causes of Premillennialism." *Harvard Theological Review* 12 (April 1919): 179–92.

Meeker, Charles. "Evangelization of the American Jew." *Christian Workers Magazine* 19 (August 1919): 868.

"The New Germany and the Evangelical Church." *Moody Bible Institute Monthly* 34 (August 1934): 553–54.

Nordland, C. B. "A Report of the International Prophetic Conference." *Our Hope* 40 (January 1940): 249, 298.

Norris, J. Frank. "Did the Jews Write the Protocols?—The Upheaval in Palestine and What It Means." *Fundamentalist,* 18 February 1938, 1.

———. "Dr. W. B. Riley Goes Back to Texas Baptist Machine and Apologizes to the Machine for the Many Years He Was with Norris." *Fundamentalist,* 4 March 1938, 1–3.

———. "The Norris-Riley Discussion of the Jews, One Hundred Thousand Copies Published." *Fundamentalist,* 1 April 1938, 1.

———. "Protocols of the Wise Men of Zion." *Fundamentalist,* 22 October 1937, 5–7.

Ostrom, Henry. "My Personal Experience with the Doctrine of Our Lord's Second Coming." *Christian Workers Magazine* 18 (March 1918): 561–64.

Panton, D. M. "The Present Rise and Ultimate End of Democracy." *Christian Workers Magazine* 19 (May 1919): 637–39.

Parker, T. Valentine. "Premillennialism: An Interpretation and Evaluation." *Biblical World* 52 (1919): 37.

Pettingill, William. "Signs of the End of the Age." *Sunday School Times* 89 (12 April 1947): 360.

Pierson, A. T. "Antagonism to the Bible." *Our Hope* 15 (January 1909): 475.

Rall, Harris Franklin. "Premillennialism and the Bible." *Biblical World* 52 (1919): 339.

Ralston, J. H. "The Conference on Behalf of Israel." *Christian Workers Magazine* 16 (January 1916): 359–60.

Rayner, T. DeCourcy. "Hidden Hands in Palestine." *Moody Bible Institute Monthly* 48 (December 1947): 264.

Reihl, Charles. "Solution to Prohibition." *Truth* 15 (1889): 370–75.

Ridout, S. "Should a Christian Go to War?" *Our Hope* 24 (September 1917): 165–69.

Riley, William Bell. "Cohn vs. Riley." *Pilot* 15 (May 1935): 218.

———. "Facts for Fundamentalists." *Pilot* 13 (July 1933): 298–99.

———. "Germany." *Pilot* 18 (November 1937): 46.

———. "Joseph Cohn Again." *Pilot* 15 (June 1935): 249–50.

———. "Joseph Cohn's New Money-Getting Scheme." *Northwestern Pilot* 26 (December 1945): 75.

———. "The 'Protocols and Communism' No Longer on Sale." *Pilot* 16 (July 1936): 302.

———. "Why Recognize Russia and Rag Germany." *Pilot* 14 (January 1934): 109–10, 126.

Robinson, J. J. "Is Social Service a Part of the Apostasy?" *Christian Workers Magazine* 14 (July 1914): 729–32.

Rohold, S. B. "Missionary Work among the Jews in the Holy Land." *Christian Workers Magazine* 20 (May 1920): 711–14.

Ruben, Maurice. "The Hebrew Christian Alliance Conference." *Christian Workers Magazine* 18 (September 1917): 37.

Ryrie, Charles C. "Perspective on Palestine." *Christianity Today* 13 (23 May 1969): 8.

Sale-Harrison, Leonard. "League of Nations and the Coming Superman." *Moody Bible Institute Monthly* 36 (August 1936): 605–6.

———. "The Resurrection of Imperial Rome." "League of Nations and the Coming Superman." *Moody Bible Institute Monthly* 36 (June 1936): 493–94.

Scott, Walter. "Europe in a Blaze." *Our Hope* 21 (November 1914): 279–83.

Sevener, Harold. "Israel: The World's Timetable." *Christian Life* 35 (August 1973): 28.

Smalley, W. F. "Another View of the Palestine Situation." *King's Business* 21 (June 1930): 290–92.

Smith, Oswald J. "My Visit to Germany." *Defender* 11 (September 1936): 15–18.

Smith, Wilbur M. "Israel in Her Promised Land." *Christianity Today* 1 (24 December 1956): 7–9.

Snowden, James H. "Summary of Objections to Premillenarianism." *Biblical World* 53 (March 1919): 172–73.

Stroeter, Ernest F. "A Misapprehension Corrected." *Our Hope* 2 (1895): 55–58.

Toews, H. F. "The Doctrine of Non-Resistance." *Christian Workers Magazine* 17 (July 1917): 862–63.

Torrey, Reuben A. "Unprincipled Methods of Post-Millennialists." *Our Hope* 14 (May 1918): 679–81.

Walvoord, John F. "The Amazing Rise of Israel." *Moody Monthly* 68 (October 1967): 22.

"Williamsburg Mission to the Jews: Abstract of the Report of the Committee of Investigation." *Christian Workers Magazine* 17 (November 1916): 191–92.

Winrod, Gerald B. "Editor Winrod Answers Editor Cohn." *Defender* 8 (June 1933): 6.

———. "Facing Ten Deadly Enemies at the Beginning of 1933." *Defender* 7 (January 1933): 3, 5, 18.

———. "Our Answer to Dr. J. Hoffman Cohn." *Defender* 8 (December 1933): 6–7.

———. "Protocols Confirmed." *Defender* 8 (November 1933): 15.

———. "Stigmatize Winrod." *Defender* 8 (December 1933): 13.

———. "Unmasking the 'Hidden Hand'—A World Conspiracy." *Defender* 7 (February 1933): 3.

———. "What Is Behind Communism." *Defender* 8 (January 1934): 7–8.

Woelfkin, Cornelius. "The Religious Appeal of Premillennialism." *Journal of Religion* 1 (May 1921): 255–63.

Secondary Sources

Books

Abell, Aaron I. *The Urban Impact on American Protestantism, 1865–1900.* Cambridge: Harvard University Press, 1943.

Aharoni, Yohannan, and Michael Avi-Yonah. *The Macmillan Bible Atlas.* New York: Macmillan, 1968.

Ahlstrom, Sidney. *A Religious History of the American People.* New Haven: Yale University Press, 1972.

Ariel, Yaakov. *Evangelizing the Chosen People: Missions to the Jews in America, 1880–2000.* Chapel Hill: University of North Carolina Press, 2000.

———. *On Behalf of Israel: American Fundamentalist Attitudes toward Jews, Judaism, and Zionism, 1865–1945.* Brooklyn, N.Y.: Carlson Publishing, 1991.

Armstrong, Karen. *Jerusalem: One City, Three Faiths.* New York: Knopf, 1996.

Averill, Lloyd J. *American Theology in the Liberal Tradition.* Philadelphia: Westminster, 1967.

Bacon, Daniel W. *From Faith to Faith, The Influence of Hudson Taylor on the Faith Missions Movement.* Robesonia, Pa.: OMF, 1984.

Baldwin, Neil. *Henry Ford and the Jews: The Mass Production of Hate.* New York: Public Affairs, 2001.

Banki, Judith H., and Eugene J. Fisher, eds. *A Prophet for Our Time: An Anthology of the Writings of Rabbi Marc H. Tanenbaum.* New York: Fordham University Press, 2002.

Barker, A. J. *Arab-Israeli Wars.* New York: Hippocrene Books, 1980.

Beit-Hallahmi, Benjamin. *Despair and Deliverance: Private Salvation in Contemporary Israel.* Albany: State University of New York Press, 1991.

Biale, David, Michael Galchinsky, and Susannah Heschel, eds. *Insider/Outsider: American Jews and Multiculturalism.* Berkeley: University of California Press, 1998.

Blau, Joseph. *Judaism in America: From Curiosity to Third Faith*. Chicago: University of Chicago Press, 1976.

Bowden, Henry Warner. *Church History in the Age of Science*. Chapel Hill: University of North Carolina Press, 1971.

Boyer, Paul. *When Time Shall Be No More: Prophecy Belief in Modern American Culture*. Cambridge: Harvard University Press, 1992.

Brereton, Virginia Lieson. *Training God's Army: The American Bible School, 1880–1940*. Bloomington, Ind.: Indiana University Press, 1990.

Cable, John H. *A History of the Missionary Training Institute: The Pioneer Bible Schools of America*. Harrisburg, Pa.: Christian Publications, 1933.

Carpenter, Joel A., ed. *Earthen Vessels: American Evangelicals and Foreign Missions, 1880–1980*. Grand Rapids: Eerdmans, 1990.

Carter, Paul A. *The Spiritual Crisis of the Gilded Age*. De Kalb, Ill.: Northern Illinois University Press, 1971.

Cauthen, Kenneth. *The Impact of American Religious Liberalism*. New York: Harper & Row, 1962.

Clouse, Robert G., Robert N. Hosack, and Richard V. Pierard. *The New Millennium Manual: A Once and Future Guide*. Grand Rapids: Baker, 1999.

Cohn, Norman. *Warrant for Genocide: The Myth of the Jewish World Conspiracy and the "Protocols of the Elders of Zion."* New York: Harper Torchbooks, 1969.

Conway, Flo, and Jim Siegelman. *Holy Terror: The Fundamentalist War on America's Freedoms in Religion, Politics, and Our Private Lives*. Garden City, N.Y.: Doubleday, 1982.

Couch, Mal, ed. *Dictionary of Premillennial Theology*. Grand Rapids: Kregel, 1996.

Cross, Robert D., ed. *The Church and the City*. New York: Bobbs-Merrill, 1967.

Dalrymple, William. *From the Holy Mountain: A Journey among the Christians of the Middle East*. New York: Henry Holt, 1997.

D'Antonio, Michael. *Fall from Grace: The Failed Crusade of the Christian Right*. New York: Farrar, Straus, Giroux, 1989.

Dayton, Donald W. *Theological Roots of Pentecostalism*. Grand Rapids: Francis Asbury Press, 1987.

Dieter, Melvin. *The Holiness Revival of the Nineteenth Century*. Methuen, N.J.: Scarecrow Press, 1980.

Dollar, George. *A History of Fundamentalism in America*. Greenville, S.C.: Bob Jones University Press, 1973.

Donovan, John. *Pat Robertson: The Authorized Biography*. New York: Macmillan, 1988.

Dorsett, Lyle W. *Billy Sunday and the Redemption of Urban America.* Grand Rapids: Eerdmans, 1992.

Douglas, J. D., ed. *The New International Dictionary of the Christian Church.* Grand Rapids: Zondervan, 1974.

Dugdale, Blanche E. C. *Arthur James Balfour, First Earl Balfour.* 2 vols. New York: Putnam's Sons, 1937.

Dupuy, Trevor N. *Elusive Victory: The Arab-Israeli Wars, 1947–1974.* New York: Harper & Row, 1978.

Ehlert, Arnold D. *A Bibliographic History of Dispensationalism.* Grand Rapids: Baker, 1965.

Eisen, Arnold. *The Chosen People in America: A Study in Jewish Religious Ideology.* Bloomington, Ind.: Indiana University Press, 1983.

Eisenberg, Gary, ed. *Smashing the Idols: A Jewish Inquiry into the Cult Phenomenon.* Northvale, N.Y.: Jason Aronson, 1988.

Ellwood, Robert S. *The Sixties Spiritual Awakening.* New Brunswick, N.J.: Rutgers University Press, 1994.

Erickson, Dan. *As a Thief in the Night: The Mormon Quest for Millennial Deliverance.* Salt Lake City: Signature Books, 1998.

Feiler, Bruce. *Abraham: A Journey to the Heart of Three Faiths.* New York: William Morrow, 2002.

Fein, Leonard. *Where Are We? The Inner Life of America's Jews.* New York: Harper & Row, 1988.

Findlay, James F., Jr. *Dwight L. Moody, American Evangelist, 1837–1899.* Chicago: University of Chicago Press, 1969.

Fink, Reuben, ed. *America and Palestine.* New York: American Zionist Emergency Council, 1944.

Fisch, Dov Aharoni. *Jews for Nothing: On Cults, Intermarriage, and Assimilation.* New York: Feldheim Publishers, 1984.

Flake, Carol. *Redemptorama: Culture, Politics, and the New Evangelicalism.* Garden City, N.Y.: Anchor Press, 1984.

Foege, Alec. *The Empire God Built: Inside Pat Robertson's Media Machine.* Hoboken, N.J.: John Wiley & Sons, 1996.

Frank, Douglas W. *Less Than Conquerors: How Evangelicals Entered the Twentieth Century.* Grand Rapids: Eerdmans, 1986.

Fromkin, David. *A Peace to End All Peace: The Fall of the Ottoman Empire and the Creation of the Modern Middle East.* New York: Avon Books, 1989.

Fuller, Daniel P. "The Hermeneutics of Dispensationalism." Th.D. diss., Northern Baptist Theological Seminary, Chicago, 1957.

Fuller, Robert. *Naming the Antichrist: The History of an American Obsession.* New York: Oxford University Press, 1995.

Fukuyama, Francis. *The Great Disruption: Human Nature and the Reconstruction of the Social Order.* New York: Touchstone Books, 1999.

Gaebelein, Frank. *The History of the Scofield Reference Bible.* New York: Oxford University Press, 1943.

Gaustad, Edwin S., ed. *The Rise of Adventism: Religion and Society in Mid-Nineteenth Century America.* New York: Harper & Row, 1974.

Gitlin, Todd. *The Sixties: Years of Hope, Days of Rage.* New York: Bantam, 1987.

Glazer, Nathan. *American Judaism.* Chicago: University of Chicago Press, 1957.

Goldscheider, Calvin, and Alan Zuckerman. *The Transformation of the Jews.* Chicago: University of Chicago Press, 1984.

Gundry, Stanley. *Love Them In: The Proclamation Theology of D. L. Moody.* Chicago: Moody, 1982.

Hadawi, Sami. *Bitter Harvest: A Modern History of Palestine.* New York: Olive Branch Press, 1989.

Halsell, Grace. *Forcing God's Hand: Why Millions Pray for a Quick Rapture . . . and Destruction of Planet Earth.* Beltsville, Md.: Amana Publications, 2002.

————. *Prophecy and Politics: Militant Evangelists on the Road to Nuclear War.* Westport, Conn.: Lawrence Hill Books, 1986.

Handy, Robert T. *A Christian America: Protestant Hopes and Historical Realities.* New York: Oxford University Press, 1971.

Handy, Robert T., ed. *The Social Gospel in America, 1870–1920: Gladden, Ely, and Rauschenbusch.* A Library of Protestant Thought. New York: Oxford University Press, 1966.

Hankins, Barry. *God's Rascal: J. Frank Norris and the Beginnings of Southern Fundamentalism.* Lexington: University Press of Kentucky, 1996.

Harrell, David E., Jr. *Pat Robertson: A Personal, Religious, and Political Portrait.* San Francisco: HarperCollins, 1988.

Hatch, Nathan O. *The Democratization of American Christianity.* New Haven: Yale University Press, 1989.

Hofstadter, Richard. *Social Darwinism in American Thought.* Boston: Beacon Press, 1944.

Hopkins, C. Howard. *The Rise of the Social Gospel in American Protestantism, 1865–1915.* New Haven: Yale University Press, 1940.

Hunt, Stephen, ed. *Christian Millenarianism: From the Early Church to Waco.* Bloomington, Ind.: Indiana University Press, 2001.

Hunter, J. H. *Beside All Waters.* Harrisburg, Pa.: Christian Publications, 1964.

Hunter, James Davison. *Culture Wars: The Struggle to Define America.* New York: Basic Books, 1991.

Hunter, James H. *A Flame of Fire.* Toronto: SIM, 1941.

Hutchison, William R. *Errand to the World: American Protestant Thought and Foreign Missions.* Chicago: University of Chicago Press, 1987.

———. *The Modernist Impulse in American Protestantism.* Cambridge: Harvard University Press, 1976.

Jorstad, Erling. *The Politics of Doomsday: Fundamentalists of the Far Right.* Nashville: Abingdon, 1970.

Kamenetz, Roger. *The Jew in the Lotus: A Poet's Rediscovery of Jewish Identity in Buddhist India.* New York: HarperCollins, 1994.

Kane, J. Herbert. *A Concise History of the Christian World Mission: A Panoramic View of Missions from Pentecost to the Present.* Grand Rapids: Baker, 1978.

Klaw, Spencer. *Without Sin: The Life and Death of the Oneida Community.* New York: Penguin, 1994.

Kraus, C. Norman. *Dispensationalism in America: Its Rise and Development.* Richmond: John Knox, 1958.

Leuchtenberg, William E. *The Perils of Prosperity, 1914–1932.* Chicago: University of Chicago Press, 1993.

Lewis, Bernard. *The Middle East: A Brief History of the Last 2000 Years.* New York: Scribners, 1995.

Liebman, Seymour. *New World Jewry, 1493–1825: Requiem for the Forgotten.* New York: Ktav, 1982.

Linzer, Judith. *Torah and Dharma: Jewish Seekers in Eastern Religions.* Northvale, N.J.: Jason Aronson, 1996.

Lipson, Juliene G. *Jews for Jesus: An Anthropological Study.* New York: AMS Press, 1990.

Livingstone, David N. *Darwin's Forgotten Defenders: The Encounter between Evangelical Theology and Evolutionary Thought.* Grand Rapids: Eerdmans, 1987.

Longfield, Bradley J. *The Presbyterian Controversy: Fundamentalists, Modernists, and Moderates.* New York: Oxford University Press, 1991.

Lowenberg, Bert James. *Darwinism Comes to America, 1859–1900.* Philadelphia: Fortress, 1969.

Lucas, Phillip. *The Odyssey of a New Religion: The Holy Order of MANS from New Age to Orthodoxy.* Bloomington, Ind.: Indiana University Press, 1995.

Magnuson, Norris. *Salvation in the Slums: Evangelical Social Work, 1865–1920.* Metuchen, N.J.: Scarecrow Press, 1977.

Marsden, George. *Fundamentalism and American Culture.* New York: Oxford University Press, 1980.

Marshall, S. L. A. *Swift Sword: The Historical Record of Israel's Victory, June 1967.* New York: American Heritage Publishing, 1967.

Marty, Martin E. *Modern American Religion: The Irony of It All, 1893–1919.* Vol. 1. Chicago: University of Chicago Press, 1986.

———. *Protestantism in the United States: Righteous Empire.* 2d ed. New York: Macmillan, 1986.

May, Henry F. *Protestant Churches and Industrial America.* New York: Harper Torchbooks, 1967.

McGinn, Bernard. *Antichrist: Two Thousand Years of the Human Fascination with Evil.* San Francisco: Harper, 1994.

McLoughlin, William. *Modern Revivalism.* New York: Ronald Press, 1959.

McPherson, David. *The Incredible Cover-Up: The True Story of the Pre-Trib Rapture.* Plainfield, N.J.: Logos International, 1975.

Merkley, Paul Charles. *The Politics of Christian Zionism, 1891–1948.* London: Frank Cass, 1998.

Meyer, Isidore S., ed. *Early History of Zionism in America.* New York: American Jewish Historical Society and Theodore Herzl Foundation, 1958.

Minus, Paul M. *Walter Rauschenbusch: American Reformer.* New York: Macmillan, 1988.

Mojtabai, A. G. *Blessed Assurance: At Home with the Bomb in Amarillo, Texas.* Boston: Houghton Mifflin, 1986.

Moore, James. *The Post-Darwinian Controversies: A Study of the Protestant Struggle to Come to Terms with Darwin in Great Britain and America, 1870–1900.* Cambridge: Cambridge University Press, 1979.

Moorhead, James H. *World without End: Mainstream American Protestant Visions of the Last Things, 1880–1925.* Bloomington, Ind.: Indiana University Press, 1999.

Neill, Stephen. *A History of Christian Missions.* Pelican History of the Church, vol. 6. London: Penguin, 1965.

———. *The Interpretation of the New Testament, 1861–1961.* London: Oxford University Press, 1964.

Nelson, Shirley. *The Last Year of the War.* San Francisco: HarperCollins, 1979.

Numbers, Ronald L., and Jonathan M. Butler, eds. *The Disappointed: Millerism and Millenarianism in the Nineteenth Century.* Bloomington, Ind.: Indiana University Press, 1987.

O'Brien, Conor Cruise. *The Siege: The Saga of Israel and Zionism.* New York: Simon & Schuster, 1986.

Oren, Michael B. *Six Days of War: June 1967 and the Making of Modern Israel.* New York: Oxford University Press, 2002.

Parker, Richard B. *The Politics of Miscalculation in the Middle East.* Bloomington, Ind.: Indiana University Press, 1993.

————. *The Six-Day War.* Jacksonville, Fla.: University of Florida Press, 1997.

Penton, M. James. *Apocalypse Delayed: The Story of Jehovah's Witnesses.* Toronto: University of Toronto Press, 1997.

Perkins, Rodney, and Forrest Jackson. *Cosmic Suicide: The Tragedy and Transcendence of Heaven's Gate.* Dallas: Pentaradical Press, 1997.

Peters, John. *Christian Perfection and American Methodism.* New York: Abingdon, 1956.

Pollock, J. C. *The Keswick Story: The Authorized History of the Keswick Convention: Its Message, Its Method, and Its Men.* London: Marshall Bros., 1907.

Rausch, David A. *Arno C. Gaebelein, 1861–1945: Irenic Fundamentalist and Scholar.* New York: Edwin Mellen Press, 1982.

————. *Communities in Conflict: Evangelicals and Jews.* Philadelphia: Trinity Press International, 1991.

————. *Messianic Judaism: Its History, Theology, and Polity.* Lewiston, N.Y.: Edwin Mellen Press, 1982.

————. *Zionism within Early American Fundamentalism, 1878–1918.* New York: Edwin Mellen Press, 1978.

Ribuffo, Leo P. *The Old Christian Right: The Protestant Far Right from the Great Depression to the Cold War.* Philadelphia: Temple University Press, 1983.

Richardson, Kenneth. *Garden of Miracles: A History of the Africa Inland Mission.* London: Victory, 1968.

Robbins, Thomas, and Susan J. Palmer, eds. *Millennium, Messiahs, and Mayhem: Contemporary Apocalyptic Movements.* New York: Routledge, 1997.

Roberts, Jon H. *Darwinism and the Divine in America: Protestant Intellectuals and Organic Evolution, 1859–1900.* Madison: University of Wisconsin Press, 1988.

Roof, Wade Clark. *A Generation of Seekers: The Spiritual Journeys of the Baby Boom Generation.* San Francisco: HarperSanFrancisco, 1993.

Roy, Ralph Lord. *Apostles of Discord: A Study of Organized Bigotry and Disruption on the Fringes of Protestantism.* Boston: Beacon Press, 1935.

Rupert, Marybeth. "The Emergence of the Independent Missionary Agency as an American Institution, 1860–1917." Ph.D. diss., Yale University, 1974.

Sandeen, Ernest R. *The Roots of Fundamentalism.* Chicago: University of Chicago Press, 1970.

Schiffman, Michael. *Return of the Remnant: The Rebirth of Messianic Judaism*. Baltimore: Lederer Publications, 1992.

Schonfield, Hugh. *The History of Jewish Christianity: From the First to the Twentieth Century*. London: Duckworth, 1936.

Sennott, Charles M. *The Body and the Blood: The Holy Land's Christians at the Turn of a New Millennium*. New York: Public Affairs, 2001.

Silberman, Charles. *A Certain People: American Jews and Their Lives Today*. New York: Summit Books, 1985.

Simon, Merrill. *Jerry Falwell and the Jews*. Middle Village, N.Y.: Jonathan David, 1984.

Smith, Timothy. *Revivalism and Social Reform*. New York: Harper Torchbooks, 1957.

Sobel, B. Z. *Hebrew Christianity: The Thirteenth Tribe*. New York: Wiley, 1974.

Spain, Mildred W. *And in Samaria*. Dallas: Central America Mission, 1954.

Steiger, Brad, and Hayden Hewes. *Inside Heaven's Gate*. New York: Signet, 1997.

Stein, Kenneth W. *Heroic Diplomacy: Sadat, Kissinger, Carter, Begin, and the Quest for Arab-Israeli Peace*. New York: Routledge, 1999.

Stein, Stephen. *The Shaker Experience in America: A History of the United Society of Believers*. New Haven: Yale University Press, 1992.

Strong, Douglas S. *Organized Anti-Semitism in America: The Rise of Group Prejudice during the Decade 1930–1940*. Westport, Conn.: Greenwood Press, 1979.

Szasz, Ferenc. *The Divided Mind of Protestant America, 1880–1930*. Tuscaloosa: University of Alabama Press, 1982.

Tabor, James D., and Eugene V. Gallagher, eds. *Why Waco? Cults and the Battle for Religious Freedom in America*. Berkeley: University of California Press, 1995.

Tipton, Steven M. *Getting Saved from the Sixties*. Berkeley: University of California Press, 1982.

Trollinger, William Vance, Jr. *God's Empire: William Bell Riley and Midwestern Fundamentalism*. Madison: University of Wisconsin Press, 1990.

Tuchman, Barbara W. *Bible and Sword: England and Palestine from the Bronze Age to Balfour*. New York: Ballantine Books, 1956.

Underwood, Grant. *The Millenarian World of Early Mormonism*. Urbana, Ill.: University of Illinois Press, 1993.

Urofsky, Melvin I. *American Zionism from Herzl to the Holocaust*. Garden City, N.Y.: Anchor Books, 1976.

Vogel, Lester I. *To See a Promised Land: Americans and the Holy Land in the Nineteenth Century.* University Park, Pa.: Pennsylvania State University Press, 1993.

Wasserman, Jeffrey S. *Messianic Jewish Congregations: Who Sold This Business to the Gentiles?* New York: University Press of America, 2000.

Weber, Eugen. *Apocalypses: Prophecies, Cults, and Millennial Beliefs through the Ages.* Cambridge: Harvard University Press, 1999.

Weber, Timothy P. *Living in the Shadow of the Second Coming: American Premillennialism, 1875–1982.* Chicago: University of Chicago Press, 1987.

Weisberger, Francis P. *Ordeal of Faith: The Crisis of Churchgoing America, 1864–1900.* New York: Philosophical Library, 1959.

Westwood, J. N. *The History of the Middle East Wars.* Westwood, N.J.: Exeter Books, 1984.

White, Ronald C., Jr., and C. Howard Hopkins. *The Social Gospel: Religion and Reform in Changing America.* Philadelphia: Temple University Press, 1976.

Wilson, Dwight. *Armageddon Now! The Premillenarian Response to Russia and Israel since 1917.* Grand Rapids: Baker, 1977.

Wood, Nathan R. *A School of Christ.* Boston: Halliday Lithograph Corp., 1953.

Wright, Stuart, ed. *Armageddon in Waco: Critical Perspectives on the Branch Davidian Conflict.* Chicago: University of Chicago Press, 1995.

Young, Kenneth. *Arthur James Balfour.* London: G. Bell & Sons, 1963.

ARTICLES

Ammerman, Nancy. "Fundamentalists Proselytizing Jews: Incivility in Preparation for the Rapture." In *Pushing the Faith: Proselytism and Civility in a Pluralistic World,* edited by Martin E. Marty and Frederick E. Greenspahn, 109–22. New York: Crossroad, 1988.

Anderson, Eric. "The Millerite Use of Prophecy: A Case Study of a 'Striking Fulfillment.'" In *The Disappointed: Millerism and Millenarianism in the Nineteenth Century,* edited by Ronald L. Numbers and Jonathan M. Butler, 78–91. Bloomington, Ind.: Indiana University Press, 1987.

Ariel, Yaakov. "A Christian Fundamentalist Vision of the Middle East: Jan Willem van der Hoeven and the International Christian Embassy." In *Spokesmen for the Despised: Fundamentalist Leaders of the Middle East,* edited by Scott Appleby, 363–97. Chicago: University of Chicago Press, 1997.

Barkun, Michael. "Nuclear War and Millenarian Symbols: Premillennialists Confront the Bomb." Paper delivered at the annual meeting of the Society for the Scientific Study of Religion, Savannah, Ga., October 1985.

Briggs, Bob. "Area Pastors and Church Members Share Opinions, Feelings about War." *Kennebec Online Journal,* www.centralmaine.com/news/stories/030322briggs_s.shtml (accessed 22 March 2003).

Cloud, John. "Meet the Prophet." *Time,* 1 July 2002, 50–53.

Cosgrove, Charles. "The Church *with* and *for* Israel: History of a Theological Novum before and after Barth." *Perspectives in Religious Studies* 22 (fall 1995): 259–78.

Douglas, David. "God, the World, and James Watt." *Christianity and Crisis* 41 (5 October 1981): 258, 269–70.

"The End Is Not Yet: An Interview with Mark Bailey." *Christianity Today,* www.christianitytoday.com/ct/2003/112/44.0.html (accessed 27 March 2003).

Gibbs, Nancy. "Apocalypse Now." *Time,* 1 July 2002, 40–48.

Goldstein, Sidney. "Profile of American Jewry: Insights from the 1990 National Jewish Population Survey." *American Jewish Yearbook 92,* 77–143. Philadelphia: Jewish Publication Society, 1992.

Herzberg, Arthur. "End of American Jewish History." *New York Review of Books* 36 (23 November 1989): 26–30.

"Iraq—Rebuilding Babylon." *Christianity Today* 32 (18 November 1988): 71.

"The Iraq War Has Little Effect on the Rapture Index: An Interview with Todd Strandberg." *Christianity Today,* www.christianitytoday.com/ct/2003/112/43.0.html (accessed 27 March 2003).

Kark, Ruth, and Yaakov Ariel. "Messianism, Holiness, Charisma, and Community: A Protestant American-Swedish Sect in Jerusalem, 1881–1933." Paper presented at Hebrew University of Jerusalem, 1994.

Kristol, Irving. "The Political Dilemma of American Jews." *Commentary* 78 (July 1984): 25.

Landau, David. "A Red Heifer—It's Not Funny," *Ha'aretz* (26 March 1997).

Lang, Andrew. "The Politics of Armageddon." *Convergence: Report from the Christic Institute* (fall 1984): 3, 12, 16.

Olsen, Ted. "At the Box Office, Left Behind Gets . . . Well, You Know." *Christianity Today* 44 (5 February 2001).

Ostling, Richard. "Armageddon and the End Times." *Time,* 5 November 1984, 73.

Patterson, James A. "Robert E. Speer, J. Gresham Machen, and the Presbyterian Board of Foreign Missions." *American Presbyterians: Journal of Presbyterian History* 64 (spring 1986): 58–68.

Price, J. Randall. "The Temple, Future." In *Dictionary of Premillennial Theology,* edited by Mal Couch. Grand Rapids: Kregel, 1996.

Price, Robert M. "The Paper Back Apocalypse." *Wittenburg Door* (October–November 1981): 3–5.

Prusher, Ilene R. "Israel's Unlikely Ally: American Evangelicals." *Christian Science Monitor* (24 April 1998): 1, 6.

———. "A US Christian Who's 'Doing Deals for the Lord' in Israel." *Christian Science Monitor* (24 April 1998): 6.

Rabey, Steve. "Left Behind No More." *Christianity Today* 46 (22 April 2002): 26.

Rausch, David. "Our Hope: An American Fundamentalist Journal and the Holocaust, 1937–1945." *Fides et Historia* 12 (spring 1980): 89–103.

Ribuffo, Leo P. "Reagan, Ronald." In *The Oxford Companion to United States History,* edited by Paul S. Boyer. New York: Oxford University Press, 2001.

Robert, Dana L. "The Origin of the Student Volunteer Watchword: 'The Evangelization of the World in This Generation.'" *International Bulletin of Missionary Research* 10 (October 1986): 146–49.

Sarna, Jonathan D. "From Necessity to Virtue: The Hebrew-Christianity of Gideon R. Lederer." *Iliff Review* 37 (winter 1980): 27–33.

Smith, Michael R. "Author LaHaye Sues *Left Behind* Film Producers." *Christianity Today* 45 (23 April 2001): 20.

Toulouse, Mark G. "Pat Robertson: Apocalyptic Theology and American Foreign Policy." *Journal of Church and State* 31 (winter 1989): 73–99.

Wagner, Donald E. "Evangelicals and Israel: Theological Roots of a Political Alliance." *Christian Century* 115 (4 November 1998): 1020–26.

———. "Holy Land Christians Worry about Survival." *Christian Century* 108 (24 April 1991): 452–54.

———. "Marching to Zion." *Christian Century* 120 (28 June 2003): 20–24.

"Washington Diarist: The End Is Nigh." *New Republic,* 12 November 1984, 50.

Weber, Timothy P. "Finding Someone to Blame: Fundamentalism and Anti-Semitic Conspiracy Theories in the 1930s." *Fides et Historia* 24 (summer 1992): 40–55.

———. "Happily at the Edge of the Abyss: Popular Premillennialism in America." *Ex Auditu* 6 (1990): 87–101.

———. "How Evangelicals Became Israel's Best Friends." *Christianity Today* 42 (5 October 1998): 38–49.

———. "Millennialism and Apocalypticism." In *The Oxford Companion to United States History,* edited by Paul S. Boyer. New York: Oxford University Press, 2001.

———. "The Two-Edged Sword: The Fundamentalist Use of the Bible." In *The Bible in American Culture: Essays in Cultural History,* edited by Nathan O. Hatch and Mark A. Noll, 101–20. New York: Oxford University Press, 1982.

Wilcox, Clyde, Sharon Linzey, and Ted G. Jelen. "Reluctant Warriors: Premillennialism and Politics in the Moral Majority." *Journal for the Scientific Study of Religion* 30 (1991): 245–58.

Woodward, Kenneth L. "Arguing Armageddon." *Newsweek,* 5 November 1984, 91.

Electronic Sources

Albuquerque Tribune, www.abqtrib.com.

Baptist Standard, www.baptiststandard.com.

Bridges for Peace, www.bridgesforpeace.com.

Christian Friends of Israeli Communities, www.jermall.com.

Christians for Israel, www.c4israel.org.

Cornerstone Church, www.sacornerstone.com.

Faith Bible Chapel, www.fbci.org.

International Christian Embassy in Jerusalem, www.icej.org.

International Christian Zionist Center, www.israelmybeloved.com.

International Fellowship of Christians and Jews, www.ifcj.org.

John Hagee Ministries, www.jhm.org.

Joshua Travel Agency, www.gospelcom.net/shofar/joshuatravel/index.php.

Lambert Dolphin, www.ldolphin.org.

Left Behind, www.leftbehind.com.

National Christian Leadership Conference for Israel, www.nclci.org.

National Review Online, www.nationalreview.com.

National Unity Coalition for Israel, www.israelunitycoalition.com.

Rapture Index, www.RaptureReady.com.

Temple Institute, www.templeinstitute.org.

Temple Mount Faithful, www.templemount.org.

Tim LaHaye, www.timlahaye.com.

Transnational Institute, www.tni.org.

Washington Times, www.washtimes.com.

Index